Health Networks

Health Networks
Can They Be the Solution?

Thomas P. Weil, Ph.D.

Ann Arbor

THE UNIVERSITY OF MICHIGAN PRESS

2004   2003   2002   2001   4   3   2   1

A CIP catalog record for this book is available from the British Library.

Library of Congress Cataloging-in-Publication Data

Weil, Thomas P.
    Health networks : can they be the solution? / Thomas P. Weil.
      p.   cm.
    Includes index.
    ISBN 0-472-11193-0
    1. Community health services. 2. Integrated delivery of health
care.
    I. Title.
    RA394 .W455   2000
    362.1—dc21   00-11174

Publication of this book has been cosponsored
by the American College of Physician Executives,
Tampa, Florida.

DEDICATED

TO MY FATHER, H. M. WEIL, M.D.,
who as a pediatrician believed so strongly
in the importance of universal access to health services,

AND

TO MY WIFE, JANET WHALEN WEIL, R.N., M.S.,
whose interest in the health and welfare
of children has been a lifetime pursuit

Acknowledgments

The author is indebted to a number of publishers / healthcare journals for granting permission to use and to update in this book portions of materials he published earlier as author or coauthor:

American College of Healthcare Executives for "The German Health Care System: A Model for U.S. Hospital Reform?" *Hospital and Health Services Management* 37, no. 4 (1992): 533–47; "Comparison of Medical Technology in Canadian, German, and U.S. Hospitals," *Hospital and Health Services Management* 40, no. 4 (1995): 524–34; "Attracting Physicians to Underserved Communities: The Role of Health Networks," *Frontiers of Health Services Management* 15, no. 2 (1998): 3–26; and "How Health Networks and HMOs Could Result in Public Utility Regulation," *Hospital and Health Services Administration* 41, no. 2 (1996): 273–87.

American College of Physician Executives for "How to Determine the Need for MDs by Specialty," *Physician Executive* 23, no. 5 (1997): 42–49; and "Attracting Qualified Physicians to Underserved Areas," *Physician Executive,* pt. 1, 24, no. 6 (1998): 42–47; and pt. 2, 25, no. 1 (1999): 53–63.

Aspen Publications for "Competition versus Regulation: Constraining Hospital Discharge Costs," *Journal of Health Care Finance* 22, no. 3 (1996): 62–74; "Managed Care and Cost Reductions for Entitlements," *Managed Care Quarterly* 4, no. 4 (1996): 58–67; "The Blending of Competitive and Regulatory Strategies: A Second Opinion," *Journal of Health Care Finance* 23, no. 2 (1996): 46–56; "A Blended Strategy Using Competitive and Regulatory Models," *Health Care Management Review* 23, no. 1 (1997): 37–45 (with Roger M. Battistella); "Regulating Managed Care Plans: Is the Telecommunications Industry a Possible Model?" *Managed Care Quarterly* 6, no. 3 (1998): 7–16 (with Norman E. Jorgensen); "Management of Integrated Delivery Systems in the Next Decade," *Health Care Management Review* 25, no. 3 (2000): 9–23.

Catholic Health Association for "Hub and Spokes Regionalization," *Health Progress* 72, no. 8 (1991): 24–31; "Lessons from Abroad on Healthcare Reform," *Health Progress* 74, no. 6 (1993): 74–78; "Canadians Write a New Rx for Health Care Reform," *Health Progress* 75, no. 1 (1994):

32–40 (with Roger S. Hunt); "Evaluating a System CEO: Eight Questions Trustees Should Ask Themselves about CEOs and CEO Candidates," *Health Progress* 81, no. 1 (2000): 24–25, 32.

Church Livingstone for "Horizontal Mergers in the United States Health Field: Some Practical Realities," *Health Services Management Research* 13, no. 3 (2000): 137–51.

Heldref Publications for "How Do Canadian Hospitals Do It? A Comparison of Utilization and Costs in the United States and Canada," *Hospital Topics* 73, no. 1 (1995): 10–22.

Medicon International Publications for "Is Vertical Integration Adding Value to Health Systems?" *Managed Care Interface* 13, no. 4 (2000): 57–62.

Medical Society of State of New York for "Comprehensive Health Planning: New Effort or Redirected Energy," *New York State Journal of Medicine* 69, no. 17 (1969): 2350–70 (with Roger M. Battistella).

Wurzweiler School of Social Work, Yeshiva University, for "American Jewish Hospitals: Being Assimilated Too?" *Social Work Forum* 34, no. 1 (2000): 15–32.

John Wiley and Sons for "How to Enhance the Efficacy of Health Network Growth," *International Journal of Health Planning and Management* 15, no. 1 (2000): 17–38.

As the material from the author's previous publications are used through this book, appropriate citations are provided.

Contents

Tables

Preface

Almost three decades ago, in 1971, I made a major career change when I resigned a tenured professorship and the directorship of an accreditated graduate program in health services management to become a full-time hospital and health services consultant. The primary motivating force for making this significant shift in lifestyle was to gain some hands-on, practical experience of what was actually occurring in the field. I had planned to return to an academic setting a decade or so later, after I had spent considerable time "in the trenches."

Early on I realized that consulting was professionally more challenging to me than teaching and research. As a way to continue pursuing my academic interests, I decided to publish an article each year that tied the more didactic aspects of the health field to the day-to-day practice of hospital management. Over the next quarter-century the topics selected for these publications varied widely; there was always, however, the same overriding theme: enhance access, improve quality of care, and reduce health costs.

Only in more recent years did my schedule allow me to consider the possibility of preparing a book. Then it was difficult to decide on an appropriate subject that would combine my academic and consulting interests. Since I had written rather extensively on the theoretical advantages and some of the practical realities of comprehensive health planning, the multihospital systems, and the politics of mergers, the theme of the efficacy of health networks became a logical choice. It was only after publishing portions of several of the proposed chapters in various health-related journals that I perceived this venture as a practical reality.

Although assuming sole responsibility for what is contained in this book, I am deeply indebted to a large number of mentors, faculty members, classmates, colleagues, and students, first at Yale University and the University of Michigan as a graduate student in hospital administration and medical care organization, respectively; also at New York City's Mount Sinai Medical Center as the S. S. Goldwater Fellow in Hospital Administration; and, finally, at the University of California–Los Angeles and the University of Missouri–Columbia as a full-time faculty member.

Most of all, I should acknowledge my debt to my clients with whom, in some cases, I worked with on a continuing basis for almost two decades. These organizations offered me an incredibly useful and practical laboratory to experiment with what I thought then might work "best." When presented in the form of a consultant's recommendations, some of my ideas were at the time and even today not always consistent with conventional wisdom.

Finally, I am indebted to my wife and best friend, Jan, who encouraged me for several decades to complete a book that might consolidate between two covers my ideas on some aspect of how the organization, management, and financing of health services in the United States might be enhanced. I hope I have not failed her and so many others who have played such a major role in what has been both personally and professionally an exceedingly rewarding career.

March 16, 2000
Asheville, N.C.

Introduction

Most American hospitals already have joined an organized alliance by consummating a merger with a previous competitor or a nearby teaching facility or are in some other way "partnered" in a horizontally and vertically diversified health network. In early 1999 over half of the nation's community hospitals, with 60 percent of all beds, admissions, and surgeries, were involved in fostering an integrated health system.[1] A few physician practices were still being acquired by health networks in an attempt to improve their market penetration, to enhance their revenues, and to position themselves better in negotiating reimbursement rates with managed care plans. During the 1990s certainly one of the most significant trends in America's market-driven, managed care healthcare environment was the growth of these multihospital, or integrated delivery systems, alliances, and networks.

These corporate amalgamations of health resources are frequently announced to the public as a vehicle for providers and insurers to enhance access, social equity, and quality of care and to reduce cost. This theme of coordination, integration, and even consolidation in the health field has a long historical precedence in the United States. As early as 1931, the Committee on the Cost of Medical Care (CCMC) recommended that health services be organized on a regional basis with appropriately coordinated and integrated primary, secondary, and tertiary centers.[2] Over the last half-century this notion has been significantly expanded with the passage of such legislation as the Hill-Burton Act, comprehensive health planning, the regional medical program, certificate of need, the National Health Planning and Resource Development Act, and other similar endeavors. In the mid-1990s this earlier concept of coordinating health resources was clearly advanced with a merger mania among various providers and was accelerated by changes in the fiscal incentives in delivering health services that were caused by the growth in the number of managed care subscribers. At the end of 1999 the United States, as a result, was evidencing lower rates of health cost escalation, although these expenditures were still rising at a rate of roughly 50 percent more than the consumer price index (CPI).[3]

Unfortunately, most studies of America's politically and fiscally powerful health networks, which were being formed throughout the country without significant regulatory review, are not yet evidencing the operational savings that were so often forecast earlier for such corporate consolidations.[4-6] The reasons often relate to the difficulties of achieving a strategic fit, finding a middle ground when differences in culture and value surface, and implementing operating efficiencies. Still requiring further research is the question of whether these alliances, after experiencing several additional years of integration and coordination, can eventually demonstrate their earlier projected effectiveness and efficiency.

Some consumers are expressing concern that these health networks are primarily being formed by providers to reduce their current excess supply of facilities, services, and subspecialty manpower, to enhance market penetration, to better position themselves when negotiating with managed care plans, and to control prices. If the public senses that these alliances are actually becoming significantly less consumer friendly, they could exert more pressure on their elected officials so that the health field eventually would shift back to the more regulatory environment of the 1970s. There are already some early signs of this occurring as numerous state legislatures consider or enact various forms of a patients' bill of rights to curb what are considered by the public as managed care plan abuses.

What is somewhat worrisome is that any significant regulatory control over the health field, such as the formation of state health services commissions functioning as public utilities, could result in the industry becoming further politicized.[7] Possibly discouraging such a pro-government option would be consumer wariness about whether public officials can be more effective and efficient than the current competitive health networking and managed care approaches in reducing healthcare costs or improving access for all Americans, including the 44.6 million uninsured.[8]

Other unknowns in the health field that have long-term implications are such issues as: the public's acceptance and later on the consequences of capitated payment to significantly curtail health expenditures; the lump-sum payments by the federal government to the states to provide Medicaid and eventually other health benefits; and the impact of an almost inevitable major economic downturn in the United States during the next decade on the organization, management, and financing of America's health services. Interestingly, these elements, tied together, could some time in the future provide the major ingredients of a "back door" approach to something like global budgetary targets as used by almost all other industrialized nations to provide universal access and to constrain health costs.[9]

It may well be prudent for health networking or networks to be viewed in the short term simply as a logical reaction to the incentives inherent in managed care, to eliminate some of the excesses in the supply of health resources and to maintain the United States' pluralistic health-care system. Then, later on, these alliances could serve as a major vehicle to reduce health expenditures further in the United States as major corporate interests and government officials use capitated payment to force providers to share fiscal risk and to ratchet down reimbursement payments to hospitals, physicians, and other providers. With that scenario the health networks could position themselves as politically and fiscally powerful alliances to implement in each region a mandated global budgetary target process or similar approach and yet allow local leadership to set priorities on how available monies would be spent in the delivery of specific health programs and services.

How This Book Evolved

When the initial planning for this book started in the fall of 1997, its major purposes were to analyze and discuss the current trend of forming health networks (i.e., merger mania), and whether these amalgamations would result in enhanced access and social equity, reduced costs, and improved quality of care; and to study the incentives that encourage these alliances, which were being formed in almost every metropolitan area, to evolve into oligopolies that then could readily control the access and the price to be charged for a significant percentage of the region's health services. The book's chapters and some of the major findings to be included were carefully outlined. Over the next several years portions of these chapters were prepared for possible publication in various health-related journals.

The process of publishing a number of articles on the efficacy of health networks and related topics has resulted in this book having a more topically oriented focus than earlier envisioned, as I started to come to several conclusions. First, the formation of health networks and the related merger mania throughout the United States are primarily a reaction to increased pressures from major employers and public officials to reduce costs (the managed care plans playing a major role in reducing inpatient admissions and length of stay) and the surplus supply of available health resources. In addition, this corporate amalgamation of various providers into these huge alliances is simply an extension or an enhancement of the much earlier CCMC concept of regionalization[2] and the need to rationalize available health resources.

Second, as a result of its cultural heritage and values, the United States is wedded to a multipayer, pluralistic system of organizing, managing, and financing its health services. The economy-of-scale concept (as envisioned by consolidating resources) that potentially could generate significant cost savings, by integrating services and by amalgamating various provider organizations, becomes exceedingly difficult to implement. This is because such decisions almost always require eliminating some vestiges of the private sector and, therefore, are contingent on effectively overruling the likely political and economic fallout of shuttering services and facilities.

Third, health networking is being used by providers primarily as a means to increase market penetration, to reduce the excess supply of available health resources, to enhance their bargaining ability when negotiating with managed care plans, and to improve their organization's bottom-line performance. These alliances are thereby also able to position themselves as oligopolies. If any significant governmental restraints were to be utilized, one option would be for these networks to be controlled as a regulated monopoly by the states with a health services commission or similar statutory authority.

Fourth, major employers and elected officials, after experiencing an almost inevitable significant economic downturn in the United States, will be more receptive to establishing a ceiling on what the public pays for health services. Major purchasers of health insurance could exert additional pressure on insurers in America's multipayer environment to offer a broader range of capitated-type payment options, and, in turn, managed care plans would force providers to share more of the fiscal risk in delivering these covered health services. Possible outcomes of such strategies are that three-quarters or more of all Americans would be insured with a voucher that pays for a relatively comprehensive range of health services and that the providers, since they would be undoubtedly sharing more of the risk with insurers, would then more directly feel the pressure of fiscal incentives that limit patient care services, raising potentially more access and quality of care issues.

Fifth, health networks might eventually receive a lump-sum payment for a majority of the services provided (the dollar value of each voucher times the number of persons covered that year) with local officials having the discretion to decide how these funds are to be expended within the region. This global budgetary process-type approach would be opposed by the insurers and almost all providers since it could eventually set dollar limits on total health expenditures for the region. It would be considered by the public and healthcare professionals, however, to be a far more attractive option than, say, the Canadian single-payer system, the reason being that the basic elements of a pluralistic, competitive, quasi-private, and quasi-public health system would thereby be preserved in the United States.

Major Themes

From the mid-1990s through 1999 I wrote various articles related to integrated health networks, continuing to examine whether these alliances were truly sought after as an appropriate solution to reorganize the American health system. As a result, this book has become a synthesis (without an analytical framework for assessing market structures and behaviors) of some of my earlier thinking on multihospital systems, mergers, and health networks. The findings and conclusions contained herein have been influenced by a relatively short tenure as an academic teaching health services management and far more extensively by a full-time health services consulting career spanning more than a quarter-century.

On this basis the major themes of *Health Networks: Can They Be the Solution?* came together. First among them is that the formation of health networks is simply a more sophisticated attempt than those previously proposed to restructure America's health system by applying well-established business principles to the delivery of medical care services. The current pressure to curtail costs, being far more intense than ever before, is mainly responsible for this development. In addition, organizing an integrated health system, or network, in a market-driven environment that is meanwhile experiencing increasing enrollment in managed care plans is a far more involved process than is usually envisioned by the "deal makers." This is because of underlying economic, social, political, and technological complexities that almost always present themselves when one attempts to modify existing patterns in the delivery of health services.

Second, horizontal and vertical mergers will continue to be consummated in the health field (at a slower pace than in the past) as providers are concerned about being "freestanding"—in spite of the fact that there is limited operational and fiscal evidence supporting the efficacy of such amalgamations.[4-6] For these mergers eventually to achieve their earlier projected savings, the health field's leadership will be forced to implement a number of cost-cutting measures that for political and other reasons are difficult to effect. Health networks for primarily cost-containment purposes will need to integrate and consolidate the network's key clinical services more vigorously to reduce competition for revenues among partners within an alliance; shutter superfluous hospitals and centralize expensive tertiary services; and encourage surplus physicians to relocate to underserved areas.

Third, in spite of a surplus of medical manpower in the United States, health networks, when they attempt to enhance their market penetration, are encountering obstacles in attracting primary care physicians into poor rural and inner-city communities. In part this is due to the aversion of doctors to practicing there for social and economic reasons, and in part it is due to the reluctance of elected officials representing middle- and upper-income taxpayers to support spending additional resources or even redirecting existing public funds to meet the health needs of those now medically underserved.

Fourth, Americans prefer a pluralistic, quasi-public, quasi-private health system. Whether health networks should experience more market-driven competition or more government regulation is now at the center stage of America's health policy debate. In such discussions it is relevant to evaluate the more entrepreneurial paradigms utilized in the United States such as the investor-owned hospital chains, the for-profit HMOs, and the physician practice management corporations as well as the more regulated approaches that are used by Canada and Germany to enhance access and social equity and to reduce total national health expenditures. On this basis of evaluating various competitive and regulatory prototypes, a blended approach is proposed, in which the best of each option is chosen and the emphasis is on practicality rather than ideological exactness.

Fifth, as cost-containment issues become paramount, health networks are experiencing increasing difficulty in recruiting qualified leaders who are able to balance the health field's core mission of getting everyone well with the pressures being exerted by a broad range of community leaders, major employers, and insurers to reduce their operating expenses. How well these alliances will be organized, managed, and financed and how effectively they can deliver healthcare relates directly to the capabilities, the specific training, and the experience of their chief executive officers and their most senior managers.

Sixth, American health networks could potentially play a far more major role in enhancing access, social equity, and quality and reducing costs if they would demonstrate reasonable interest in the community's overall well-being and be exceedingly judicious in balancing the public's need for health services with the availability of private and public funds. If the alliances stray too far from such a path, consumers will demand more government intervention into America's health system, perhaps in the form of more stringent regulatory measures, such as setting ceilings on health expenditures on a state-by-state, sector-by-sector basis. Any additional governmental constraints would be expected to be designed in such a manner that the United States would continue to maintain its primarily competitive and pluralistic system of organizing, managing, and financing its health services.

This book is not intended to be all-inclusive in evaluating all the options or all the solutions that health networks could offer in restructuring America's health system. Nor is it being assumed that the nation's health networks are solely responsible for reorganizing America's health system. Instead, it considers a limited number of specific topics that I selected based on having actively worked in the field for over four decades; serving as a hospital and health services consultant on over one hundred potential healthcare mergers; and carefully reviewing a number of recent consulting studies and analyzing the most critical elements that typically play a major role in assessing the likelihood that an integrated health system endeavor will, in fact, significantly enhance the delivery of America's health services.

Target Audience

This book was written primarily for practitioners who are interested in a historical overview of the major factors that led to the current trend of forming health networks and who wonder whether and in what ways health networks and America's current merger mania have any efficacy in enhancing the delivery of health services and where all these horizontal and vertical amalgamations in the health field might be heading in the future. This book has also been designed as a primer of potential strategies to consider in enhancing the effectiveness and efficiency of a health network and in furthering the reader's professional career. Finally, it describes for the practitioner a number of coordinating and integrating approaches that have been used with relative success in the health field.

Academics and graduate students in health services management programs might find this book useful in first examining and then comparing the vast conceptual advantages of forming health networks with some of the economic, social, and political realities. Part-time students, who are frequently continuing to work in the field, may find this book of particular value in that it describes the various dynamics of health networking—particularly as these alliances downsize by eliminating employees and achieve significant market concentration in almost every metropolitan area.

Most simply stated, health networks are expected to serve as a major political and fiscal force throughout the United States as they attain almost monopolistic powers over the health marketplace and each amasses annual revenues of one billion dollars or more. This book should assist those in the health field to assess their personal or organizational fit in such a rapidly emerging environment of corporate consolidations.

Definitional Concerns

One of the most obvious issues in preparing this book is the lack of agreement on the appropriate definition of such terms as *health networks, health alliances, integrated delivery systems, health systems, multihospital systems, corporate consolidations, mergers,* and *affiliations.* Only recently were all hospital networks and systems defined into tidy groups based both on how much they differentiate and how much they centralize their hospital services, physician arrangements, and insurance products.[10] In this book I am not overly concerned with such definitional preciseness. I consider the experiences of these various types of corporate amalgamations, once they are applied in the "real world," to be far more important than any definitional preciseness in meeting this book's goals and objectives.

For the purposes of this book *health networks* are defined as two or more hospitals (although they usually consist of a more complex horizontal and vertical array of health resources) that have merged in increasingly competitive marketplaces in order to engage in such strategic efforts as are necessary to enhance their collective survival. Horizontal diversification occurs when two similar organizations (e.g., two hospitals) merge into one corporate entity. This differs from vertical diversification, in which a health network, made up primarily of hospitals, acquires somewhat dissimilar health entities such as a primary care physician practice, a home health agency, an HMO, and a long-term care facility.

It also should be noted that, technically, *merger* and *corporate consolidation* are discrete types of corporate reorganization that potentially cover a wide spectrum of changes in ownership or governance. Mergers generally refer to the dissolution of one or more entities and their assimilation by another, whereas consolidation usually involves the dissolution of two or more entities and the formation of a new one. These two terms are used herein interchangeably, since the book's focus is on the efficacy of any type of corporate amalgamation.

The phrases *managed care plans* and *health maintenance organizations (HMOs)* are used interchangeably in this book. Points-of-service continue to gain popularity among the managed care plans since they provide patients greater flexibility in selecting a provider. Concurrently, the capitated payment reimbursement methodology is losing enrollment as providers express disfavor in assuming additional fiscal risk. It is predicted, however, that in a more economically constrained environment capitated payment would well gain greater favor, since its strengths focus on providers assuming more risk and controlling total health expenditures on a per capita basis.

Organization by Chapter

The first chapter of the book, "Forming Health Networks Is Simply Repackaging an Old Concept," provides a historical prospective of health networking as a concept dating back to the early 1930s, when a three-tier regional approach (primary, secondary, and tertiary) was proposed. Since then, I argue, the concept has simply been "rebottled." Those involved in the current trend toward health networking face many of the same issues that were noted earlier[11–12] when striving to enhance access, social equity, and quality and to reduce cost; when attempting to utilize available health resources more effectively and efficiently; and when implementing comprehensive health planning concepts.

Chapter 2, "How to Enhance the Efficacy of Health Network Growth," describes the data and other information needed and what steps an organization might use in evaluating its strengths and weaknesses during a decision-making process that leads to the possible consummation of a merger.[13] The strategies that such an organization might employ to gain the most beneficial outcomes from such a potential alliance are outlined, if such an analysis results in a provider or insurer deciding to seek some form of corporate amalgamation.

Chapter 3, "Horizontal Mergers in the Health Field: Some Practical Realities," provides an overview of the theoretical advantages and the performance of horizontal mergers in the health and nonhealth fields.[4–6, 14–17] Unfortunately, these consolidations for the most part are still experiencing disappointing fiscal outcomes. This chapter also discusses the implications to the community of forming these fiscally and politically powerful health networks, which often function as oligopolies, and then proceeds with an analysis of the impact that these alliances have on their major players (e.g., physicians, insurers, government).

Chapter 4, "Is Vertical Diversification Adding Value to Health Networks?" offers the potential advantages of consolidating almost all health resources within a region under one corporate umbrella. The chapter then evaluates the experiences to date of consummating such a strategy[18] and particularly why networks experience poor fiscal results when they acquire physician practices or when they start their own HMO plans.

Chapter 5, "Can Health Networks Attract Physicians in Underserved Communities?" first describes approaches that were frequently used in the past to attract doctors to practice in poor rural and urban areas.[19–20] It summarizes the difficulties that health networks experience in recruiting physicians to these areas and evaluates the potential solution of having doctors receive "premium" income and fringe benefits when practicing in poor rural and inner-city settings. A major barrier to implementing such a concept turns out to be middle- and upper-income taxpayers, and therefore elected officials, not willing to support increased spending or the redirection of existing funds to invest additional resources in poor inner-city and rural environments.

Chapter 6, "Health Networks Battling in the Marketplace," discusses several competitive and regulatory strategies that health networks might encounter in the next several decades while enhancing the delivery of medical care services: more managed competition and managed care; the further privatization of America's health services; and replicating either the Canadian or the German universal national health insurance program.[21-34] The major findings here are that all healthcare systems have compromises and most Americans would prefer the continuation of the current quasi-private, quasi-public approach to delivering health services.

Chapter 7, "Blending Competitive and Regulatory Approaches," explores a critical topic. The Americans demand a pluralistic health system, since they have limited trust in either a solely private or a totally public approach to the delivery of health services. To evaluate such an option the models selected for analysis include establishing in each state a health services commission that functions as a public utility; replicating the Telecommunications Act of 1996 and thereby allowing for both "regulated" competition and consolidation to occur; and having the general media disclose publicly each provider's clinical and fiscal performance within the region or state.[7, 35-40]

Chapter 8, "Leadership for Health Networks: What's Needed?" focuses on the attributes, knowledge, and competencies required to provide leadership for America's health networks. Furthermore, it discusses the critical intangibles required by these CEOs; some of the impediments experienced when mounting sound educational programs to train these leaders; the criteria that governing boards might utilize when selecting and evaluating a health network CEO; and the advisability of appointing outside directors to broaden a governing board's policy decision-making capabilities.[41]

Chapter 9, "Can Health Networks Be the Solution?" summarizes the earlier chapters and outlines what needs to be achieved to insure these alliances' maximum effectiveness and efficiency in enhancing access, social equity, and quality and reducing cost. Since in most metropolitan areas these huge and powerful health networks are well on their way to controlling how health services are delivered, the discussion then considers a number of external and internal factors that are critical when piecing together an overall design whereby these alliances could potentially serve as major players in the restructuring of America's health system. This means that their leaders must modify some earlier miscalculations, such as too often overpaying when acquiring physician practices, hospitals, and other healthcare resources and overestimating the projected savings to be expected from these amalgamations; and they must understand that it is exceedingly complex to consolidate clinical services.[42]

The chapter concludes with a discussion that argues that, by drastically cutting costs as a result of reduced Medicare, Medicaid, and managed care reimbursement, health networks will need to accelerate the divestiture of unprofitable physician practices; shutter more unproductive programs, services, and facilities; eventually eliminate a significant number of administrative, business office, and related positions; and exert pressure to form a federal medicine patent commission to control pharmaceutical costs. Although an inevitable economic downturn in the United States would hasten the implementation of such cost-cutting strategies, no meaningful universal national health insurance initiative is foreseen in this scenario. Instead, the leadership of health networks can expect to continue offering roughly the same three tiers of care as exist today: fee-for-service or point-of-service for the wealthy; HMOs that more often limit the choice of providers for the middle class; and continued access problems for the uninsured, except in cases of an emergency.

Immigration, "taking care of one's own," discrimination, and the special place that the medical profession occupies in Jewish culture were major factors by 1975 in encouraging the establishment of thirty-three Jewish-sponsored, acute-care general hospitals in the United States. The case study "America's Jewish-Sponsored Hospitals: An Endangered Species?" examines why eight of the original thirty-three Jewish-sponsored hospitals already have been shuttered as inpatient facilities and only twelve remain as freestanding institutions. The Jewish-sponsored hospitals are not unique in portraying how health networks have evolved and why some facilities within the alliance have later closed. The major purpose of including this study is to add real-life material to the earlier theoretical discussion concerning the efficacy of health networks and networking.

"Epilogue" was prepared early in 2000, when the United States was experiencing almost a decade-long economic boom yet there were more uninsured Americans, President Clinton was proposing further cutbacks in Medicare among hospitals to pay for pharmaceutical benefits for the poor aged, and an increasing number of health providers and insurers were filing for bankruptcy protection. Health was no longer appearing to be a major growth industry, so the question arose as to which sectors or subsectors of the health delivery system that are currently demonstrating weak operational and fiscal performance will in the new millennium most seriously imperil the way health networks are organized, managed, and financed. In fact, this epilogue clearly illustrates in fiscal terms why as of early 2000 the networks are experiencing such difficulty in meeting their goals of improving access, social equity, and quality, and reducing health costs.

REFERENCES

1. American Hospital Association (AHA). "Statistics for Multihospital Health Care Systems and Their Hospitals." In *AHA Guide 1999–2000 Edition,* B58. Chicago: AHA.

2. Perkins, B. B. "Economic Organization of Medicine and the Committee on the Costs of Medical Care." *American Journal of Public Health* 88, no. 11 (1998): 1721–26.

3. American Hospital Association. "Consumer Price Index." *AHA News* 35, no. 46 (1999): 3.

4. Clement, J. P., McCue, M. J., Luke, R. D., Bramble, J. D., Rossiter, L. F., Ozcan, Y. A., and Pai, C.-W. "Strategic Hospital Alliances: Impact on Financial Performance." *Health Affairs* 16, no. 6 (1997): 193–203.

5. Connor, R. A., Feldman, R., Dowd, B. E., and Radcliff, T. A. "Which Types of Hospital Mergers Save Consumers Money?" *Health Affairs* 16, no. 6 (1997): 62–74.

6. Melnick, G., Keeler, E., and Zwanziger, J. "Market Power and Hospital Pricing: Are NonProfits Different?" *Health Affairs* 18, no. 3 (1999): 167–173.

7. Weil, T. P. "How Health Networks and HMOs Could Result in Public Utility Regulation." *Hospital and Health Services Administration* 41, no. 2 (1996): 273–287.

8. Vistnes, J. P., and Zuvekas, S. H. "Health Insurance Status of the Civilian Noninstitutional Population: 1997." Rockville, Md.: Agency for Health Care Policy and Research, 1999.

9. Pfaff, M. "Differences in Health Care Spending Across Countries: Statistical Evidence." *Journal of Health Politics, Policy and Law* 15, no. 1 (1990): 1–68.

10. Bazzoli, G., Shortell, S. M., Dubbs, N., Chan, C., and Kralovec, P. "A Taxonomy of Health Networks and System: Bringing Order Out of Chaos." *Health Services Research* 33, no. 6 (1999): 1683–1717.

11. Battistella, R. M., and Weil, T. P. "Comprehensive Health Planning: New Effort or Redirected Energy." *New York State Journal of Medicine* 69, no. 17 (1969): 2350–70.

12. Weil, T. P. "Reaching Toward Unity. Catholic Facilities Can Triumph with Geographically Linked Regional Systems." *Health Progress* 70, no. 3 (1989): 24–31.

13. Weil, T. P. "How to Enhance the Efficacy of Health Network Growth." *International Journal of Health Planning and Management* 50, no. 1 (2000): 17–38.

14. Pearl, G. M., and Weil, T. P. "Final Say—Integrated Delivery Systems: Six Tough Questions." *Health Progress* 79, no. 3 (1998): 78–80.

15. Weil, T. P. "Horizontal Mergers in the United States Health Field: Some Practical Realities." *Health Services Management Research* 13, no. 3 (2000): 137–51.

16. Weil, T. P., and Pearl, G. M. "Merger Mania: Physicians Beware." *Physician Executive* 24, no. 2 (1998): 6–11.

17. Dolan, R., and Weil, T. P. "Mergers in the Health Field: Enhancing Human Resources Management." *Physician Executive* 24, no. 2 (1998): 12–18.

18. Weil, T. P. "Is Vertical Integration Adding Value to Health Systems?" *Managed Care Interface* 13, no. 2 (2000): 57–62.

19. Weil, T. P. "Attracting Qualified Physicians to Underserved Communities." *Physician Executive,* Part I, 24, no. 6 (1998): 42–47; and Part II, 25, no. 1 (1999): 53–63.

20. Weil, T. P. "Attracting Physicians to Underserved Communities: The Role of Health Networks." *Frontiers of Health Services Management* 15, no. 2 (1998): 3–26, 40–44.

21. Weil, T. P. "Managed Care Plans: Their Future Under National Health Insurance." *The Western Journal of Medicine* 115, no. 5 (1991): 533–37.

22. Weil, T. P. "Managed Competition for the Poor: More Promise than Value? *Journal of the Health Care for the Poor and Underserved* 5, no. 3 (1994): 158–168.

23. Weil, T. P. "The American Health System: A Contentious Environment in the 21st Century." *Physician Executive* 22, no. 1 (1996): 16–21.

24. Weil, T. P. "Managed Care and Cost Reductions for Entitlements." *Managed Care Quarterly* 4, no. 4 (1996): 58–67.

25. Weil, T. P. "A Universal Access Plan: A Step Toward National Health Insurance?" *Hospital and Health Services Administration* 37, no. 1 (1992): 37–53.

26. Weil, T. P. "Preparing for Increased Hospital Use in a Reformed System." *Health Affairs* 11, no. 4 (1992): 258–60.

27. Weil, T. P. "The German Health Care System: A Model for U.S. Hospital Reform?" *Hospital and Health Services Administration* 37, no. 4 (1992): 533–47.

28. Weil, T. P. "Lessons from Abroad on Healthcare Reform," *Health Progress* 74, no. 6 (1993): 74–78.

29. Weil, T. P., and Hunt, R. S. "Canadians Write a New Rx for Health Care Reform." *Health Progress* 75, no. 1 (1994): 32–40.

30. Weil, T. P. "Health Reform in Germany: An American Assesses the New Operating Efficiencies." *Health Progress* 75, no. 7 (1994): 24–29.

31. Weil, T. P. "How Do Canadian Hospitals Do It? A Comparison of Utilization and Costs in the United States and Canada." *Hospital Topics* 73, no. 1 (1995): 10–22.

32. Weil, T. P. "Slow Down in the Acquisition of Medical Technology." *Health Affairs* 14, no. 1 (1995): 319–20.

33. Weil, T. P. "Comparisons of Medical Technology in Canadian, German, and U.S. Hospitals." *Hospital and Health Services Administration* 40, no. 4 (1995): 524–34.

34. Weil, T. P. "Managed Care Merged with the German Model." *American Journal of Medical Quality* 12, no. 1 (1997): 19–24.

35. Weil, T. P., and Jorgensen, N. E. "A Tripartite Regulation of Health Networks: A Commentary." *Journal of Public Health Management and Practice* 2, no. 3 (1996): 46–53.

36. Jorgensen, N. E., and Weil, T. P. "Regulating Managed Care Plans: Is the Telecommunications Industry a Possible Model?" *Managed Care Quarterly* 6, no. 3 (1998): 7–16.

37. Weil, T. P. "The Blending of Competitive and Regulatory Strategies: A Second Opinion." *Journal of Health Care Finance* 23, no. 2 (1996): 46–56.

38. Weil, T. P., and Battistella, R. M. "A Blended Strategy Using Competitive and Regulatory Models." *Health Care Management Review* 23, no. 1 (1997): 37–45.

39. Weil, T. P. "Let's Merge Competitive and Regulatory Strategies to Achieve Cost Containment." *Journal of Health Care Finance* 25, no. 3 (1999): 65–73.

40. Weil, T. P. "Public Disclosure in the Health Field: Why Not a SEC-Type Commission?" *American Journal of Medical Quality* 16, no. 1 (2001): 23–33.

41. Weil, T. P. "Evaluating a System CEO: Eight Questions Trustees Should Ask Themselves about CEOs and CEO Candidates." *Health Progress* 81, no. 1 (2000): 24–25, 32.

42. Weil, T. P. "Management of Integrated Delivery Systems in the Next Decade." *Health Care Management Review* 23, no. 3 (2000): 9–23.

1

Forming Health Networks Is Simply Repackaging an Old Concept

ABSTRACT.   Health planning has been an increasingly important endeavor in the United States since the early 1930s, when the Commission on the Cost of Medical Care (CCMC) recommended a three-tier regional approach to organizing health facilities and services. The CCMC proposed that healthcare be arranged with primary care centers referring more complex cases to secondary-type providers and tertiary services being offered at major medical centers with teaching and research capabilities. Over the next six and a half decades this concept was embellished with the advent of the Hill-Burton program, comprehensive health planning, health system agencies, multihospital systems, health alliances, integrated delivery systems, and health networks. This chapter's major theses are that these latter health planning approaches were modeled along the same conceptual framework suggested earlier in the CCMC's final report, and, therefore, health networks or networking could well be considered "old wine simply being rebottled or repackaged" to meet an increasingly complex and far more competitive environment.

Objectives for health planning such as enhancing access, social equity, and quality and reducing costs are easy to explain, yet for the past sixty-five years health networking has been difficult to implement because the United States has a highly politicized, pluralistic approach to delivering healthcare; self-interest among consumers and providers is pervasive; most communities are reluctant to expend significant resources for general planning purposes or for consumer-oriented studies that might determine local healthcare priorities; there is lack of agreement among professionals on what critical quantitative measures to use when evaluating healthcare needs; and among most Americans there is an intense fear that health planning can result in restricting one's ability to obtain quality healthcare as well as infringing on one's political freedom.

The Planning Process

The formation of a health network or an alliance is now a familiar and acceptable phrase, but several decades ago the mere mention of this approach conjured up visions of infringement on institutional and personal freedom and more governmental regulation.[1] In the 1930s and 1940s health and hospital leaders such as Bachmeyer,[2] Davis,[3] Falk,[4] Goldwater,[5] MacEachern,[6] Mountain,[7] Ring,[4, 8] and Rorem[4, 8, 9] wrote frequently on the need to develop regional health systems. This concept received minimal heed among practitioners in the field until the late 1970s, when the multihospital system model became conventional wisdom.[10] A decade later health networking gained momentum as a result of increased enrollment in managed care plans and a growing surplus of inpatient facilities, tertiary services, and physician manpower among the superspecialties. As a fallout of rightsizing or downsizing in almost every metropolitan area, there has been a mammoth surge of mergers of various types throughout the United States, creating numerous huge and powerful health networks.

Opposition to planning has faded with the course of contemporary social, economic, and political events. Although resistance to regional planning exists among those with vested interests or with strong ties to the status quo, the process is generally becoming recognized in almost all circles as a legitimate activity. Citizen and consumer groups, industrial leaders, public officials, and the media are now among its strongest advocates. Even special interest groups, who were originally most hostile to the concept, have reluctantly come to the conclusion that planning health services, often previously left to the discretion of the market or to the ingenuity of its participants, must now be subjected to more responsible scrutiny.

Planning in the United States is primarily a long-range endeavor, looking backward to be sure about historical trends, looking around at current developments, and primarily searching for options and recommendations that steer the public to the most positive outcomes in the future. Myrdal[11] attributes America's historical resistance to its planning efforts to fears surrounding governmental intervention and "a general tendency to nearsightedness among both politicians and experts." Many have feared that broad and comprehensive planning would yield intolerable tyranny and control and would thereby become a frightful influence over one's livelihood as well as one's political freedom.

The rapid pace of industrialization and urbanization and their resultant problems have encouraged, in spite of fears about more centralized control, a more favorable attitude nationally toward planning. Local leaders and citizens alike have become increasingly aware of the foolhardiness of their regional health delivery systems making significant changes in their governance or how they deliver health services without some prior long-range strategic planning efforts.

Today the need to plan is no longer seriously debated, yet with this often arduous process a number of questions arise. What conceptual framework should be utilized in a regional planning endeavor? What specific criteria should be used? What data and other information should be collected to plan most effectively for a region's delivery of health services? Who is responsible for bringing about wise regional health planning decisions? Should major regional health policy changes undergo any external public review and, if so, by whom?

Although responding to these questions could be intellectually stimulating, the purposes of this chapter are more limited: (1) to demonstrate that health planning concepts as they are currently being pursued by America's health networks are consistent with earlier regional approaches (i.e., these new alliances should not be considered as a new or a novel approach); and (2) to propose that America's health networks face many of the same issues in achieving improved access, social equity, and quality and reducing costs as earlier attempts to regionalize health resources or to implement comprehensive health planning concepts. This chapter argues that the regionalization of health services is an old concept that has been supported by private and public sponsors for decades and that the issues and problems in currently applying this concept are the same as those experienced over the past sixty-five years.

Planning Is an Old Concept

Many cities, towns, and corporations throughout the world have produced some form of blueprint that delineates their aims, objectives, and physical development. Evidence for the design and use of such plans to build their central cities can be found in ancient Greece and Rome, in the villages of medieval Europe, and in many New England towns.[12] Major L'Enfant's design for the physical layout and development of our nation's capital is one of the more outstanding instances of American city planning.[13]

Social, economic, and health planning, as a distinctive organizational process, became a basic discipline of study roughly seventy years ago. The pioneering work of Stein,[14] the New York Commission of Housing and Regional Planning,[15] Mumford,[16] and MacKay[17] are examples of the concern of social scientists and others in the 1920s with city and regional planning and the development of conservation programs and recreational resources. Their major objective was to improve the ills of the cities caused by the industrial revolution. Although these early studies appear simplistic in the light of today's needs and conditions, their continued use and enhancement might have given us today cities of greater beauty and livability. The tragedy is that urban planning has been largely ignored until relatively recently because of what Woodbury[18] refers to as the "intellectual blight of laissez faire."

Although there was some economic planning prior to World War I, it was the depression of the 1930s that first demonstrated the overriding need for attention to private and public expenditures, interest rates, and levels of employment.[19] With the formation of such groups as the Council of Economic Advisors, the Congressional Joint Economic Committee, and the Committee for Economic Development, economic planning had become an essential and legitimate function in American society. Healthcare planning as we recognize it today formally started during the same period.

Commission on the Cost of Medical Care

Regional and comprehensive healthcare planning in the United States can be traced back to the establishment in 1929 of the Committee on the Costs of Medical Care (CCMC).[20] This committee was formed in response to the desire of leading physicians, experts in public health, and social scientists for sound studies on the economic and social aspects of delivering health services. Supported by one million dollars from six foundations, the committee and its staff studied the incidence of disease and disability in the United States, how to improve the integration of healthcare facilities and services, the relationships of family income and the receipt of health services, and the income earned by health providers.

Citing the rising costs for the diagnosis and treatment of illness and disability and the inequitable distribution of health services across the nation, the committee's final report (i.e., the majority of the committee, since there were several important dissenting opinions) recommended the regionalization of health resources by coordinating primary and specialty services within a defined geographic area, the establishment of medical group practices, and the formation of not-for-profit group prepayment plans.

In the CCMC context regionalization denoted integrated networks, with primary care being delivered through rural or outlying hospitals and ambulatory care centers; secondary (more specialized, consultant care) services located at district, or "intermediate," hospitals; and tertiary (highly specialized, technologically based care) provided at major teaching centers. In other words, a conceptual framework similar to that being proposed by most health networks today.

Following the CCMC recommendations, the Bingham Associates

Fund in rural New England worked to coordinate medical services for its residents by developing linkages to the New England Medical Center and the Tufts University School of Medicine.[21] Later, in Michigan, the Hospital Survey Commission explored the state's bed needs in the context of a carefully designed regional plan.[22]

The most controversial CCMC recommendation called for an integration of medical group practice and group (voluntary) prepayment for the enhanced provision and financing of health services. Even though the majority report endorsed group health insurance coverage, it opposed compulsory national health insurance. A voluntary plan was considered by the majority as a desirable first step. It was argued that it would be better to develop strong group practice arrangements before insurance became compulsory, since a prepaid approach would tend to freeze individual medical practice in place.

The sharpest dissent in the CCMC report to the majority's recommendations concerned group practice and came from eight of the committee's private practitioners, who viewed the proposal as a "technique of big business . . . and that of mass production." They also opposed the majority's recommendation that these medical group practices be located in or adjacent to hospitals. The eight physicians proposed that "general practitioners should be restored to their central place in medical practice" and that prepaid health insurance should only be available when such plans "can be kept under professional control and destructive competition is eliminated."[20]

Although there was a lack of consensus on several major recommendations, over succeeding decades the CCMC report stimulated a number of significant changes in the delivery of healthcare services (e.g., Blue Cross / Blue Shield and the early prepaid group practice plans). Also, it is rather significant that some of the arguments expressed in the CCMC report about how healthcare services should be organized and financed—and therefore affect the viability of various health planning options—for the next six and a half decades emerged from similar interest groups. Most of the CCMC proposals are still currently applicable, with a number of the recommendations being as contentious today as they were in the early 1930s.

The Hill-Burton Act

The first major attempt by the federal government to translate the CCMC planning concepts into action came in 1946 with the passage of the Hospital Survey and Construction Act, better known as the Hill-Burton program. The purposes of the act were to enhance acute care services on the basis of hospital bed-to-population ratios and to build newer facilities. Because of the Depression and later World War II, only modest hospital renovation or expansion had occurred during the prior 15 years.

The Hill-Burton program provided federal grant assistance to the states for surveying their health needs, and, based on these findings, they were able to develop priorities for hospital facility construction. With well-documented plans for expanding facilities, and with minimum standards for hospitals incorporated into state licensing laws, federal funds were made available on a priority basis, and the monies were matched up to one-third of the total project cost to construct and equip public and voluntary nonprofit general, mental, tuberculosis, and chronic disease hospitals and public health centers.

The program's mandate for issuing a state health facilities plan, and the requirement that a single state agency would assume responsibility for its development and program implementation, were significant. For the first time, a determination of need for construction and renovation was available to form the basis of priorities for action, and such rankings were to be explicitly stated. Rather than first insisting on the coordination and integration of health resources and on that basis proceeding with the construction of needed facilities and services, the law emphasized building or renovating acute care beds. The Hill-Burton program is thus typically viewed as a single state agency primarily responsible for the orderly management of federal funds and not as a means to regionalize health services. Forcing hospitals and other providers to undertake joint planning as a condition for future federal funding would simply have been politically unacceptable.

The legislation that continued the Hill-Burton program into the 1970s not only maintained the grant program but also provided both guaranteed and direct loans for construction, modernization, or replacement purposes. With regard to area-wide planning, the continuing legislation stipulated that, in order to be approved, projects must comply with plans established by state or area-wide planning agencies, this provision serving as a major foundation for the passage of the Comprehensive Health Planning (CHP) Act of 1966.

The Hill-Burton program was not an unqualified success. It focused on institutional rather than comprehensive, regional approaches to remedy health delivery system inadequacies. Its overwhelming emphasis on reducing acute care bed scarcity indicated the absence of a broader goal-setting process rooted in identified community needs. Unfortunately, the Hill-Burton planning efforts involved minimal interaction between providers and consumers and between Hill-Burton officials and other voluntary health planning agencies.[23]

The Comprehensive Health Planning Act of 1966

During the tenure of the 89th Congress, in 1966, more health legislation affecting the organization, financing, and delivery of health services was enacted than in any prior period. Medicare; Medicaid; the heart disease, cancer, and stroke centers (i.e., the regional medical program); and the comprehensive health planning initiative, with their respective issues relating to appropriate implementation, placed on the nation's threshold a major shift in health policy. These federal provisions went a long way in affirming, conceptually and pragmatically, a number of important dimensions of the principle that all Americans are entitled to comprehensive health services of high quality, regardless of income, ability to pay, or age.

Referred to colloquially as the "partnership for health bill," the Comprehensive Health Planning and Public Health Service Amendments Act of 1966 (P.L. 89-649) was drafted by a team of representatives from the Association of State and Territorial Health Officers, the Association of State and Territorial Mental Health Officers, and the United States Public Health Service. The act, signed into law by President Lyndon Johnson, incorporated a two-pronged strategy for beefing up and expanding state influence and responsibility in health planning matters.

The law's first objective was to encourage the states to develop and carry out comprehensive health planning, both for the state as a whole and within regional and local areas. Its purpose was to promote a unification of all of the vital threads—hospitals and related facilities, manpower and population health needs—to permit more rational decision making and enable the states to provide more meaningful direction of the total health effort.

The second objective was to give state health agencies greater administrative freedom and flexibility in setting priorities. Toward this end former categorical federal grant programs were replaced by a system of noncategorical, or block, grants. This change occurred as a result of significant criticism about the inefficiencies of various categorical grants. A noncategorical approach, it was proposed, would have the effect of focusing programs on people instead of specific diseases. Depending on its population and level of financial need, each state was now given a lump-sum allotment.

The first approach, outlined in section 314a, encouraged the states to establish and maintain a comprehensive plan for tying together the total health effort and to establish priorities. To qualify for planning and noncategorical grant support, each state was required to establish or designate a single state agency—not necessarily the health department—to carry out the prescribed planning. Furthermore, for purposes of policy formulation and the establishment of general targets and goals, each state was required to establish a broadly representative planning council to advise the agency in its planning activities. A majority of the council members were required to be consumer representatives.

The second approach, outlined in section 314b, concerns the granting of federal assistance, commonly 50 percent but up to 75 percent of the total cost for limited periods in special hardship cases, for the development and operation of comprehensive local, metropolitan area, and regional planning for the coordination of health services. This aspect of the act was specifically designed to encourage more local planning and to expand the efforts of already existing local planning agencies.

The final planning provision of the bill, section 314c, extended federal support to public and nonprofit agencies and universities for research, demonstrations, and training to improve comprehensive health planning efforts.

The opportunity and inducement given to states to assume a greater leadership responsibility for health affairs within their borders constituted the major thrust of the comprehensive health planning act. The assertion of the doctrine of "state primacy" in health affairs concerned many consumers and providers, since it potentially led to a shrinking of the role of local leadership in the health arena. The regionalization of health services, although advanced to achieve various economies, was found for a number of reasons to be politically infeasible. In most states the force of tradition and the strong urge for self-determination by local residents and providers required that the regional and state health planning agencies compromise.

Promise and potential aside, the comprehensive health planning program needed to overcome a number of additional problems. A particularly thorny issue involved how other types of health planning endeavors such as the regional medical program, Hill-Burton, model cities, and mental health would relate to and be coordinated with comprehensive health planning at the national, state, and local levels. With each of these programs going their separate way, it was hard to conceive of comprehensive health planning as a real force. The problem was especially severe in the case of the regional medical programs, which were frequently steering the medical schools and major medical centers on a course separate from state health planning efforts and outside the scope of normal public accountability controls. With the academic health centers dominating the regional medical programs, it is easy to see why comprehensive health planning had difficulty in engaging in true regional planning, let alone restructuring health services more efficiently or effectively.

Another problem involved the wisdom of working through the states. Because of variations in resources and differences in attitudes toward planning and social change among various states, a consequence of this policy was unevenness in implementing and attaining comprehensive health planning goals as outlined in the 1966 initial legislation. In the main the history of previous federal-state ventures in the health field suggests that regulatory approaches often raise as many issues as they are able to solve.

It might be argued, nevertheless, that the introduction of the comprehensive health planning act came at a time when the states were becoming increasingly aware of the need to modernize their operational capabilities. They were recognizing more than ever before that the continued inability or unwillingness on their part to meet population needs and demands would lead only to a further erosion of their powers and prerogatives. Whether in the field of education, corrections, public safety, transportation, housing, or health, the message was clear: if the states are not up to doing the job that needs to be done, the federal government will either do it alone or work through new organizational and administrative mechanisms.

Possibly the most serious problem faced by comprehensive health planning involved the congressional prohibition against action detrimental to the status quo of medical practice. Public Law 89-649 called on the program "to assure comprehensive health services of high quality for every person but without interference with existing patterns of the private professional practice of medicine, dentistry, and related health arts." Since the 1966 health planning legislation prohibited interference with the existing patterns of private professional practice, it is somewhat ironic that the health networks and the investor-owned physician management corporations of the 1990s were aggressively acquiring physician practices. Even today what taxes the imagination is trying to provide comprehensive healthcare of high quality within a health services structure that is characterized by grossly fragmented patient care services, numerous competing institutions, and general social and administrative disorganization. In this regard the comprehensive health planning program, like the regional medical program, which had a similar prohibition against taking any action that was detrimental to the status quo of medical practice, faced a difficult challenge.

Certificate of Need

During the same period that the comprehensive health planning effort was being established at the federal level, the states began initiating laws requiring hospitals to demonstrate community need before they could start constructing new facilities or undertaking the major renovation or expansion of existing services. Essentially, certificate of need (CON) programs established criteria to determine public need for health care facilities and programs against which requests for changes in a physical plant and, in certain states, program offerings of individual healthcare institutions were reviewed and then approved or disapproved. By mid-1975, 23 states had certificate of need legislation covering at least some types of health facilities.

The certificate of need process was akin to the federal capital expenditures review program carried out by the comprehensive health planning agencies and later by the health systems agencies under section 1122 of the 1972 Social Security Act amendments. What gave section 1122 importance was an amendment that tied reimbursement (by Medicare, Medicaid, and the maternal and child health programs for depreciation, interest, or return on equity for a capital expenditure) to obtaining prior approval from an area-wide and state planning agency for the requested project.

Like all regulatory mechanisms, certificate of need had its limitations. One was the impossibility of establishing any quantitative criteria of need acceptable to a diverse group of technical experts. Without those specific guidelines it was difficult for the area-wide and state agencies to disapprove a project. Another criticism was that the process was too slow, too political, too ineffective, and too costly. In 1977 Salkever and Bice[24] concluded that CON legislation in a number of cases had encouraged local physicians to join together to acquire sophisticated technology rather than the intended objective of restraining hospital capital investments. Therefore, this regulatory approach had a negligible impact on reducing healthcare costs. What was even more unfortunate was that the CON process was primarily negative in terms of approving or rejecting a project, rather than emphasizing community health planning strategies.

The National Health Planning and Resources Development Act of 1975

Wholly state-defined and -initiated CON programs came to an end in 1974, when President Nixon signed P.L. 93-641, the National Health Planning and Resources Development Act of 1975. This new law required all states to institute CON programs in accord with federal regulations or lose federal dollar support for their state health planning efforts; more critical was their potential loss of grant dollars made available under the Public Health Service Act and the alcohol and drug addiction entitlements.

Sufficient dollars were at stake to cause a doubling of the number of state CON programs that became operational. By the fall of 1978, 41 states had passed certificate of need legislation. When all states had done so, Section 1122 reviews were phased out of existence. By ending what was perceived as a fragmented approach to health planning, Congress apparently had hoped to realize more than the minimal results recorded until that time to improve the delivery and to control the utilization and the expenditures for health services. Certainly, the lawmakers wished to increase the external pressures directed at containing the persistent rise in health care expenditures that had been evident since the end of World War II.

The new planning act required that the Secretary of the Department of Health, Education and Welfare (HEW) issue national health planning goals based on the health priorities made explicit in the law. This approach was perceived as a major policy shift, since previously health planning had been characterized by relatively loosely framed mandates for rational planning without reference to any specific objectives.

At the core of the whole program were the health systems agencies (HSAs). State governors designated health planning areas within their states. Designated areas, each with a federally funded HSA, were formed based on population size, the availability of such health resources as a major medical center, and the possible coordination with a standard metropolitan statistical area(s). It was permissible for an HSA to be either a public or private nonprofit entity but not an educational institution, thus excluding the medical schools that had so dominated the regional medical program.

Each HSA, under section 1513 of P.L. 93-641, was charged with a number of functions: gathering and analyzing suitable data; establishing health systems plans (HSPs) and annual implementation plans (AIPs); coordinating activities with the Professional Standards Review Organizations (PSROs); reviewing and approving or disapproving applications for projects that resulted in federal funding within the area; and assisting the states in CON-type reviews and in evaluating institutional health services with respect to the appropriateness of such services.

A major incongruity quickly came to the forefront in P.L. 93-641 between its broad goals at the area-wide planning level and the HSAs' limited ability to control the regions' healthcare expenditures. In fact, this gap had been for decades characteristic of health planning legislation in the United States. What was obviously missing was the HSAs' ability to merge traditional planning data and information with financial data on revenues, costs, and sources of payment.

P.L. 93-641 also created two planning bodies at the state level. The first, called the State Health Planning and Development Agency (SHPDA), used input from the area-wide HSAs to create a statewide health plan. The second, called the Statewide Health Coordinating Council (SHCC), reviewed the HSA plans and budgets and state applications for federal funds. Each HSA was represented on the SHPDA and SHCC, and at least 50 percent of the council's members had to be consumers. Under P.L. 93-641 perhaps the most noteworthy departure from prior health planning legislation was perceived to be a closer relationship between the federal government and the HSAs within the states.

Late in 1978 the General Accounting Office (GAO) completed a study of the first few years of activity under the HSA system.[25] Noting that it was too early to tell whether the goals of the National Health Planning and Resources Development Act of 1975 were being achieved, the GAO leveled its major criticisms at details of the program's administration and implementation and not at matters of principle. Thus, concerns were raised over the slowness of federal officials in publishing regulations and guidelines, problems in collecting and coordinating data, the inability to recruit appropriate staff, confusion over the roles of the HSA and the SHPDA in states having only one HSA area, problems with the technical assistance program established under the act, and difficulties in creating knowledgeable and effective HSA and state boards. The Department of Health, Education and Welfare concurred with most of the recommendations and outlined actions to be taken or planned to meet the deficiencies cited.

The Nixon and Carter Administrations

Restraining health costs by almost any means possible became a central concern of the Nixon and Carter administrations. Aside from signing, in 1975, the National Health Resources Planning Act and Resources Act of 1975 (P.L. 93-641), President Nixon's staff also proceeded early on with three additional strategies to implement cost constraint: (1) the Economic Stabilization Program (ESP), a short-term effort (August 1971 to April 1974) to control prices; (2) legislation mandating the surveillance of physicians' decisions regarding the length of their patients' stay in hospitals (i.e., the Professional Standards Review Organizations [PSROs]); and (3) an act encouraging the establishment and growth of health maintenance organizations (HMOs). While for the most part ESP and state rate setting for hospitals[26-27] was ill conceived, highly politicized, and technically flawed, the latter approach, the creation of HMOs, obviously had a far more significant long-term impact on America's health delivery system, in general, and on health providers, in particular.

HMOs were first visualized as essentially group practices with salaried physicians, who provided prepaid (capitated payment) coverage for a specific insured population. This concept had been proposed earlier by the CCMC's majority report and was considered radical by mainstream providers, even though in the 1970s single- and multispecialty group practices were becoming an increasingly common method of delivering physicians' services. It was only when HMOs were packaged by Enthoven[28] as part of a competitive, market-driven strategy to reduce cost that there was broad support from the health establishment to use this reimbursement methodology that focused on reducing unnecessary utilization of services, particularly hospital admissions and inpatient days.

The Carter administration inherited healthcare cost containment issues that actually had been gathering momentum since the passage of President Johnson's Great Society programs of the 1960s. Since healthcare historically has been so deeply rooted in a community's economic, political, and social fabric, slowing down the increase in health expenditures seemed to be beyond the capacity of any administration. Commonly perceived by the public was the view that money should not be allowed to interfere with a provider's mission to heal the body regardless of cost. During his campaign President Carter had promised some kind of national health insurance program and was even pressed to do so by labor union leaders and many liberal members of Congress, but he found it impossible to deliver. The country was simply not ready for such a major shift in health policy.

Carter's administration also inherited an obligation to provide the planning guidelines for the National Health Planning and Resources Development Act. On September 23, 1977, HEW Secretary Califano issued more definitive regulations,[29] several of which are summarized here:

1. Maternity units in service areas of more than 100,000 persons should each handle annually at least 2,000 deliveries and maintain an average annual occupancy of 75 percent.
2. At least 200 open-heart procedures should be performed annually in any hospital providing open-heart surgery, and no additional open-heart unit should be approved unless existing or previously approved units in the area are operating at a minimum of 350 cases per year.
3. Each CAT scanner for head and body should perform annually at least 2,500 procedures, and no new scanner should be approved for the service area unless the existing scanner(s) performs more than 4,000 patient procedures a year.

The intent of these national planning guidelines was clear: Medicare and Medicaid benefits were consuming 10 percent of the federal budget and almost 40 percent of U.S. health expenditures. Using restrictive planning guidelines was thought to be the route to save healthcare dollars, but these efforts were of little avail.

Movement toward Resource Consolidation

The process of "building more and better" facilities and services, tougher planning and reimbursement regulations (including Medicare's diagnostic-related groups), and corporate and public officials becoming more concerned with the increasing cost of healthcare started to force providers to initiate more ways to economize and to gain market share often at the expense of their competitors. The movement during the 1980s and early 1990s was toward resource consolidation through management contracts, affiliations, joint ventures, consortia, and multihospital or multihealth systems. These types of amalgamations and the growth of enrollment in managed care plans were at least in part a reaction to a half-century of health planning with an increasingly regulatory emphasis. In fact, by the start of President Reagan's administration most Americans were anxious to move in the opposite direction—one based far more on market-driven, competitive forces.

A planning strategy in either a regulatory or a competitive environment that links one organization to another creates new mutual dependency patterns and often ends up in dividing the winners from the losers. In the 1980s management contracts, affiliations, consortia, and similar loosely tied organizational relationships were popular in the health field. Health executives acknowledged the need for such linkages, but generally none of the parties to these agreements were particularly interested in making notable changes in their organizations' governance. Since these arrangements usually specify some form of joint control, the significant economies of shuttering or curtailing a major service did not often become an option from such arrangements. Although such linkages are helpful to start dialogue and to bring the interested parties to the table, there is usually at the outset implicit or explicit agreement that central governance is necessary to enhance greater effectiveness and efficiencies. It was recognized even then, however, that total consolidation presents the political barrier of someone possibly losing control of all or part of their organization's resources.

Health Planning and Mergers

Starkweather[30] suggested that there are three major types of hospital mergers: The first is the "specialty referral" merger best illustrated by a community hospital being anxious to obtain highly specialized capabilities for its service area residents, whereby the major teaching hospital anticipates attracting an additional number of tertiary-type referrals. The second type is a "closure/survival" or "whale-guppy" type merger, in which the prime motivation is the operational and financial support of at least parts of one or more hospitals that face serious fiscal difficulties. The third type of integration, "utility status merger," is where a hospital that is the area's dominant provider acquires (without expending significant capital) other nearby facilities in order to eliminate duplication or to enhance its market share. These models that are being implemented now help explain why a previously highly decentralized, locally dominated hospital industry shifted in the 1990s from primarily competition among individual hospitals to competition among hospital systems and later among health networks.

What the CCMC report recommended and what occurred nationwide during the early 1990s, when diligent strategic health planning efforts began to be undertaken routinely, was the start throughout the United States of the formation of geographically linked regional systems by horizontal and vertical mergers that embodied at least some of the following characteristics:

1. Credible values and culture, high name recognition, and a focus on high-quality patient care regardless of the person's race, creed, or ability to pay, the latter becoming increasingly difficult to provide given fiscal shortfalls surrounding Medicare, Medicaid, and managed care reimbursement.
2. A large, high-quality tertiary facility that is the region's dominant healthcare provider and is surrounded by horizontally integrated acute care hospitals so most physician referrals and patient choices are kept within the system. The combined average daily census of this geographically linked system should be at least 700 acute care inpatients to insure maximum efficiencies of less frequently utilized tertiary services.
3. Several effective and efficient vertically integrated healthcare facilities, services, and programs such as a managed care plan, home health services, ambulatory care satellites focusing on diagnostic services, an ambulatory surgery center, durable medical equipment companies, and a number of other similar resources that might be solely or jointly owned by the system.
4. Annual revenues of at least $0.5 billion with a likely increase to $1.5 billion by 2005 and the financial strength that assumes favorable operating results, the ability to borrow additional capital for worthwhile projects, and a cost and service structure of value to consumers of health services.

5. Coordinated and possibly centralized financial and information systems that serve attending physicians, various care givers, and management so that comprehensive, high-quality, cost-effective patient care can be delivered anywhere within the system.
6. A base of power to contract effectively with any purchaser of care directly, including major industry corporations within the area, managed care plans, government agencies, and others.
7. Extraordinary leadership and management competence throughout, in which overall corporate policy is set centrally and sufficient autonomy is given to each operating subsidiary.

Although a number of factors affect the successful integration of a health system or network, several critical variables follow: whether the member facilities are the dominant providers in their primary and secondary service areas; and whether these facilities are close enough in travel time to facilitate clinical coordination, administrative-type economies of scale, and ease of referrals. It is difficult to develop a health network with facilities that do not maintain a high market penetration within their primary and secondary areas and are not somewhat geographically contiguous.

Among the reasons that Catholic hospitals, for example, often experience more difficulties in developing geographically linked health systems is the infrequency of their being the dominant or the "best" facility in a major metropolitan area (in 1989 Denver and Des Moines were the exceptions) and the geographical dispersion of their facilities. What is sometimes forgotten is that, in the long run, far greater economies and improved patient care will be forthcoming by hospitals being able to coordinate and integrate clinical services than by merging administrative and related services. Because religious institutes historically were organized to meet specific community needs, some of the nation's largest Catholic health systems have hospitals in 4 to 12 states, which explains why they have particular difficulties in developing networks that are clinically closely knit together.[31]

Health Planning Issues during the 1990s

Health planning efforts were often stifled during the 1990s since there is the inherent struggle to balance the authority, responsibility, and powers of the subsidiary facilities with those of the parent corporation. On the one hand, local governing boards, medical staffs, and health executives want to act in what they consider to be a prudent manner to meet their facility's mission. Yet, on the other hand, with the fiscal condition of many healthcare systems deteriorating, a trend toward centralized policy formation and fiscal control continues. Third- and fourth-level governing board members within these large systems increasingly question whether they are trustees or simply local advisors to the health network.

Theoretically, systems or networks provide competent executives with significant vertical mobility within one holding company. Some healthcare managers want their own governing boards that are able to exercise the final authority and responsibility in making policy decisions. Communities with facilities experiencing weaker governance and management might be well served by members of a system reviewing each major policy decision. Talented and aggressive governing boards and health services administrators, however, can have trouble working in a highly hierarchical environment, particularly if the system's central office is more than two hours away and communication is impaired because of geographic distance or possible differences in culture, values, and perceived priorities.

As systems continue to centralize policy formation and develop more elaborate corporate staffs in planning and marketing, finance, managed care, operations, and joint purchasing, more dotted lines of accountability arise at the subsidiary level. Is a facility's chief fiscal officer primarily responsible to the hospital's chief executive officer or to the system's chief financial officer?

The realities are that health networks now face an increasingly difficult environment with reimbursement constraints, physicians becoming more disenchanted with the professional and fiscal controls promulgated by many of the managed care plans, employees being required to work harder with less than commensurate increases in wages and fringe benefits, and a public that is often concerned about access to their providers of personal choice, any out-of-pocket cost, and the quality of care provided. Although there may be overall public dissatisfaction with the U.S. health system, consumers respond with positive ratings when asked about their personal physicians and local hospitals.

CCMC Regional Concept Is Health Networking

The CCMC three-tier (primary, secondary, and tertiary) regional model for health facilities, services, and programs recommended in the early 1930s is currently being aggressively implemented as health networks are being formed in almost every U.S. metropolitan area. Health alliances until recently were anxious to acquire primary physician practices and smaller hospitals, the latter in recent years focusing on ambulatory care services to insure their fiscal survival. Such strategies are followed primarily to increase the network's market penetration, to insure more referrals and inpatient admissions at the system's clinical hub, to be better positioned in negotiating with managed care plans, and to reassure the general public that as many communities as possible are provided with at least basic health services.

With managed care and when forming these three-tier regional systems, the consumer is most concerned about access to a physician of choice and an acute facility that is located within reasonable travel time. A frequent issue in implementing this three-tier type approach is deciding what range and complexity of services should be available at primary versus secondary facilities. There is an inherent conflict because the consumer desires easy access to a maximum range of services and the network's leadership is more intent on consolidating services at fewer sites to save dollars and improve quality.

Specialty-type services that cannot be effectively or efficiently provided at the primary care level but are not considered to be tertiary programs should be made available at intermediate or secondary centers. Basic cardiology, gastroenterology, oncology, pulmonary medicine, neurology, neurosurgery, and otolaryngology are examples of services that should be available on a full-time basis at these secondary facilities. What has complicated defining the discrete functions at these "middle-range" centers is that an increasing number of specialists and subspecialists are locating full-time or with satellite offices in what might be considered primary care areas, and, therefore, these acute care facilities have acquired clinical expertise that is far more sophisticated than that envisioned by the CCMC concept. For some of the same reasons a significant number of these secondary centers now provide what have been generally considered tertiary services such as cardiac catheterization, open-heart surgery, and lithotripsy.

Often the most distinctive characteristic of a tertiary versus a secondary center is that the former is actively engaged in a broad range of teaching and research activities tied to a medical school. But we know that many primary and secondary types of illness are diagnosed and treated at these major medical centers, although their fiscal viability and educational programs are dependent on experiencing a steady flow of referrals from physicians practicing within the health network. The tertiary facilities are the "hub," while the primary and secondary centers provide those spokes to allow the health network to function and be fiscally viable.

Cost containment strongly encouraged by managed care, rather than a regulatory approach, interestingly became the leading edge to implement finally the CCMC report's regionalization approach, or what in reality are the concepts that are being utilized in the formation of health networks throughout the United States. In addition, the CCMC majority report proposed group practice and prepaid health insurance, so it would have also endorsed the modern-day multispecialty group practices and HMOs being closely tied to the nation's health alliances. Not only are there significant similarities between the CCMC and the current trend of health networking, but the minority reports written in the early 1930s forewarned us about some of the more serious issues that would emerge (e.g., control, sharing of monies) in implementing the concept of either regionalization or health networking, particularly if they are tied to medical group practice and managed care plans.

Sixty-five Years of Health Planning

In some ways it is difficult to assess how far the United States has progressed by using health planning approaches in enhancing the delivery of healthcare in the sixty-five years between the CCMC recommendations and the implementation of health networks today. No one knows what would have occurred if the federal government, for example, had not provided various forms of subsidy for health facility construction and renovation, and a framework and funding for comprehensive health planning to more effectively and efficiently regionalize health services. Yet over the past six and a half decades there are a number of common threads with respect to health planning that allow us to conclude that health networking is basically repacking some old CCMC concepts and yet experiencing some of the same barriers when actively pursuing a more effective and efficient health delivery system:[32]

"Optimal" health services. Even today there is really no well-accepted definition of the terms *optimal delivery of health services* and *effective delivery of health services.* In fact, we do not have any reliable data on the absolute need or on the reservoir of untreated conditions that could be successfully managed or controlled if brought under proper medical scrutiny.

The detectable demand for such health services as hospital care, physician visits, and dental services is not known. This is one of the reasons why it has been so difficult to implement meaningful incentives that could create strong pressures for innovation, improved quality, and an efficient scale and management of operations and provide an economically sound range of services among hospitals and other health providers. There is undoubtedly a difference between what people want and desire and the services utilized in the health marketplace. The lack of adequate quantification of medical needs constitutes an important stumbling block in the development of any highly productive national health planning effort.

It is noteworthy that the 1933 Lee and Jones data,[33] part of the CCMC report, in many states was the basis of developing the Hill-Burton priorities three decades later and the allocation of funds. Today we know that there are significant differences in the utilization of health services among various regions in the United States.[34] The northeast region, for example, has experienced twice as many hospital days per 1,000 residents as the far west. Does this mean that the northeast provides a higher quality of services, or can such differences be explained by disparities in physician practice patterns?

What is so obvious, yet difficult to effect, is that more intense study and research needs to be given to define in quantitative and qualitative terms what are "optimal health services" and an "effective delivery of health services." Otherwise, planners are not quite sure what services are needed and to be planned for whom.

Goals and objectives. Without having the most accurate measures of regional healthcare needs, it is difficult for an individual or a group of providers accurately to plan their programmatic and service goals and objectives five or ten years hence. Although the methodology and tools for such an analysis are far from being refined (yet they are, on a specific clinical basis, more reliable now than in the past), there are some less formal approaches that could be used in the meantime on individual projects that would help provide us with answers. A few more obvious ones are spending more resources on community household surveys that focus on asking the area's residents concerning their unmet healthcare needs and several providers coordinating their efforts to meet a shared community-oriented objective rather than competing for revenues.

Frequently, a serious problem arises in defining a provider's service area or selecting the appropriate variable and related parameters for analysis. There are vital distinctions between (1) the medically self-contained area in terms of the relationship between the people to be served and the major health technology required, which has historically dominated most health planning efforts; and (2) the simplistic unquestioning attitude that the boundaries of a single region will properly serve, in terms of clinical, administrative, and economic efficiency, more than one function or specialized health service. For instance, the hospital's service area for open-heart surgery and complicated neurosurgical procedures is usually quite different than for obstetrics and general medical and surgical care.

If rigorous regional planning is undertaken by the area's major provider, concern is usually expressed among the smaller facilities and their medical staffs that the major medical center is developing strategies to squeeze out its nearby competitors. Yet how do health facilities and services coordinate and eliminate duplication of effort unless they assume a more regional approach in their planning efforts? This lack of agreement within a region among consumers and particularly among providers (as they compete among themselves for revenues) on health goals and objectives has been a major factor in explaining why comprehensive health planning concepts during the 1930–2000 period generally failed and why the CCMC regionalization concept continues to be "rebottled" in the United States.

Composition of a policy-setting board. Although there are some exceptions, generally the leadership of most governing boards of health planning groups historically has been made up of hospital trustees, hospital administrators, physicians, and prepayment executives, serving primarily for purposes of institutional, organizational, or personal self-interest. Most frequently, a less politically influential minority of the board has represented the region's consumers, labor unions, and other citizens. The composition of the current leadership of most health networks is much the same. The health alliance's board members generally are officers of the region's major corporations, community leaders frequently with significant personal resources, key physicians, the network's chief executive officer, and others, who represent the area's economic and political power. This is in contrast to the argument that in the planning process more emphasis needs to be given to consumer-type representatives in view of the stronger social, economic, and political forces that are demanding a more dominant voice in health and hospital policy formation; this notion, however, frequently falls on deaf ears.

In reality, most health planning groups, either public or private, consumer or provider dominated, have had only the most nominal control over the expansion of the area's health facilities and services.[32] The same issue can be raised with respect to the fiscally and politically powerful networks that are being formed throughout the United States. Questions frequently asked in this regard are whether the providers of healthcare can also be its major planners and whether the public is knowledgeable enough to be the policy makers for these planning endeavors. In addition, one of the other major variables related to these various planning efforts is how to establish and operationalize the controls or sanctions that should be placed against providers that do not comply with the priorities set out as representing unmet community healthcare needs. Until we have some agreement on these issues, the CCMC concept of regionalization will continue to be simply "rebottled," although with the health networks acquiring some weaker providers many of these planning efforts have been concentrated within fewer organizations.

Shortage of experienced planners. During the 1930–80 period there was a significant shortage of component professional planners available to manage the increasing number of health planning groups that were then being formed throughout the nation. In some ways this has been corrected in the last decade or so. The health services administration programs have been the major source of such talent, but most of their young graduates in the earlier years were not sufficiently experienced to handle the complex political, social, and economic factors involved in health and hospital planning.

With mostly self-interested board members and less than seasoned health planning executives, it is not difficult to predict that most communities obtained results from these planning efforts of less value than they really deserved. Even today the planning office in most health networks is viewed as primarily the source of intelligence information to enhance the network's market penetration and revenues. A far lower priority is to implement the regionalization concept, which means to enhance access, social equity, and quality and to reduce cost, as outlined in the CCMC report.

Shortage of funds for community health planning efforts. The majority of voluntary health planning groups in the 1950s and 1960s received their initial financial support on the basis of "pilot" grants from the Hill-Burton program. Under P.L. 89-649 the federal government paid up to a ceiling of 75 percent of the planning agency's total operational cost.

Although the federal government through the 1980s continued to be the major financial resource for funding health planning endeavors, the trend had been for hospitals in most areas to contribute an increasing dollar amount to support these agencies' operating expenditures. The planning efforts might have been more effective if the planning group had obtained broad-based community resources (although sometimes difficult to acquire) instead of using federal or hospital monies as the major revenue source. This proposed change in funding might have resulted in greater community participation, and, therefore, the planning groups and their executives would have been more readily accountable to the citizens of the area rather than to government agencies or to the health providers. In fact, the CCMC concept of regionalization continues to be rebottled, because how the delivery of healthcare is organized has to date not been a sufficiently high enough priority so that broad-based community planning funds are expended for such purposes as surveying local health priorities.

Maldistribution of health personnel. After their formal training young physicians, dentists, nurses, technologists, and therapists want to settle in relatively prosperous communities, where a high percentage of patients have health insurance and where the technology exists to support their newly acquired skills. One of the most pressing issues, because of an inadequate geographic distribution of personnel, has been how to provide comprehensive health services in poor rural and inner-city areas.

Without the appropriate distribution of health personnel, it is difficult to develop an effective system of regionalized medical care. Historically, major health planning efforts have been directed toward enhancing access to health services to those less fortunate, but to date the results of such projects cannot be considered overly encouraging.

Federal and state funding legislation. Medicare, Medicaid, the regional medical program, comprehensive health planning, mental health legislation, model and experimental cities, and Office of Equal Opportunity (OEO) neighborhood health centers, if they had all been tied together, could have been critical factors in achieving more comprehensive and integrated health systems in the United States. With an increasing percentage of a provider's income stream coming from these federal and state programs, it is unfortunate that health planners were unable to become more familiar, more attuned, and more involved in tying together the planning and financing of health services.

In the 1946–80 period there was certainly a sufficient volume of health planning legislation, but it contained limited emphasis on finding ways to integrate the region's health services and to contain costs. This external direction was not easily achievable, since providers strongly resisted public agencies taking an aggressive role in limiting their acquisition of sophisticated technology or forcing some hospitals to shutter various clinical services (e.g., obstetrics and pediatrics) to achieve larger and more effective units at fewer hospitals.

Power politics. Health planning was almost doomed to fail in the past because middle-class Americans in the labor force received most of their health insurance coverage as a fringe benefit (not an out-of-pocket expense) and desired access to the broadest range of services within their local community. Hospital board members and their administrative and medical staffs have various incentives to adhere to their local residents' expectations. Until relatively recently, added clinical sophistication did not cost the community much out of pocket, gave each party greater status, and even provided the community with an increasing number of well-paying jobs.

Aside from the fiscal concerns expressed by a few board members about the ability of their organization to repay the capital required, providers expanded almost as they wished during this sixty-five-year period as they recognized that not-for-profit and public planning agencies had insufficient clout to disapprove more than a minimal number of projects. In addition, the providers in the earlier years gained the upper hand in the health planning process because most of these agencies' governing boards were plagued with self-interest, there were too many inexperienced health planners, most of the funding to operate the planning agencies came from the federal government or hospitals in the region, and most state health planning councils lacked stature. It was a highly politicized process in which for the most part the health establishment pushed around public and not-for-profit health planning organizations to maximize the level of patient services available within their respective communities.

In more recent years the CCMC regionalization concept has been rebottled in terms of the region's major providers acquiring weaker facilities and services and thereby organizing a three-tier system of care—primary, secondary, and tertiary. As long as the politics "works out" and the money "holds up," the networks' deal makers will continue to develop huge and powerful alliances advising the public that these mergers will enhance access, social equity, and quality of care, and reduce costs.

Interestingly, the regionalization concept outlined in the CCMC report more than six and a half decades ago is now being slowly implemented by America's health networks. Moreover, the CCMC's minority report expressing concern over this type of amalgamation of facilities, medical group practices, and health insurance plans has become a major issue in the delivery of health services at the expense of the solo practicing physician. It is rather significant that many of the same arguments were being expressed decade after decade, whether the theme at that point in time was regionalization, comprehensive health planning, or the formation of integrated health delivery systems. The major change is that these issues now seem to be more visible in the public media.

For reasons outlined earlier, the health network concept for the most part has to be considered simply a rebottled version of the regionalization concept outlined in the 1929–32 CCMC reports—perhaps the major reason being that the American public demands a pluralistic system, since it has limited trust in either a totally private or a totally public approach to the delivery of health services.

REFERENCES

1. Friedman, M. *Capitalism and Freedom.* Chicago: University of Chicago Press, 1962.

2. Bachmeyer, A. C. "Problems Confronting American Hospitals." *Hospital Review* (1945): 13.

3. Davis, M. M. *Medical Care for Tomorrow.* New York: Harper Bros., 1955.

4. Falk, I. S., Rorem, C. R., and Ring, M. D. *The Costs of Medical Care: A Summary of Investigations on the Economic Aspects of the Prevention and Care of Illness.* Chicago: University of Chicago, 1933.

5. Goldwater, S. S. "The Preservation of a Free Hospital System." *Hospitals* 16 (1942): 13.

6. MacEachern, M. T. *Hospital Organization and Management,* 29. 2d ed. Chicago: Physicians Record Co., 1951.

7. Mountain, J. W. *Selected Papers.* Washington, D.C.: Joseph W. Mountain Memorial Committee, 1956.

8. Rorem, C. R., and Ring, M. D. *The Cost of Medical Care.* Chicago: American Legislators' Association, 1933.

9. Rorem, C. R. *Capital Investment in Hospitals: The Place of "Fixed Charges" in Hospital Financing and Costs.* Washington, D.C.: Committee on the Costs of Medical Care, 1930.

10. Zuckerman, H. S. "Multi-Institutional Systems: Promise and Performance." *Inquiry* 16, no. 4 (1979): 291–314.

11. Myrdal, G. *Challenge to Affluence.* London: V. Gollancz, 1963.

12. Lewis, N. P. *The Planning of the Modern City: A Review of the Principles Governing City Planning.* New York: John Wiley and Sons, 1916.

13. De Vore, H. L. *City on the Potomac: Washington in Pen and Ink.* New York: Beechhurst Press, 1946.

14. Stein, C. *Toward New Towns for America.* Liverpool: University Press of Liverpool, 1951.

15. Ford, J. *Slums and Housing, with Special Reference to New York City: History, Conditions, and Policy.* Cambridge: Harvard University Press, 1936.

16. Mumford, L. *The Culture of Cities.* New York: Harcourt, Brace, and Co., 1938.

17. MacKay, B. *The New Exploration: A Philosophy of Regional Planning.* New York: Harcourt, Brace and Co., 1928.

18. Woodbury, C. *The Future of Cities and Urban Redevelopment,* 637. Chicago: University of Chicago Press, 1953.

19. Keynes, J. *The General Theory of Employment, Interest, and Money.* New York: Harcourt, Brace, and Co., 1936.

20. Committee on the Cost of Medical Care. *Medical Care for the American Public: The Final Report of the Committee.* 152–92. Chicago: University of Chicago Press, 1932.

21. Garland, J. E. *An Experiment in Medicine: The First Twenty Years of the Pratt Clinic and the New England Center Hospital of Boston.* Cambridge: Riverside Press, 1960.

22. Commission on Hospital Care. *Hospital Resources and Needs: The Report of the Michigan Hospital Survey.* Battle Creek, Mich.: W. K. Kellogg Foundation, 1939.

23. Gottlieb, S. "A Brief History of Health Planning in the United States." In Havighurst, C. C., ed. *Regulating Health Facilities Construction,* chap. 1. Washington, D.C.: American Institute for Public Policy Research, 1974.

24. Salkever, D. S., and Bice, T. W. *The Hospital Certificate-of-Need Controls: Impact on Investment, Costs, and Use.* Washington, D.C.: American Enterprise Institute, 1979.

25. Comptroller General. "Status of the Implementation of the National Health Planning and Resources Development Act of 1974." Washington, D.C.: U.S. Government Printing Office, 1978.

26. Ashby, J. L., Jr. "The Impact of Hospital Regulatory Programs on Per Capita Costs, Utilization, and Capital Investment." *Inquiry* 21, no. 1 (1984): 45–59.

27. Eby, C. L., and Cohodes, D. R. "What Do We Know about Rate-Setting?" *Journal of Health Politics, Policy and Law* 10, no. 2 (1985): 299–326.

28. Enthoven, A., and Kronick, R. "A Consumer-Choice Health Plan for the 1990s," pts. 1–2. *New England Journal of Medicine* 320, no. 1 (1989): 29–37; and 320, no. 2 (1989): 94–101.

29. Anderson, O. W. *Health Services in the United States: A Growth Enterprise since 1875.* 230. Ann Arbor, Mich.: Health Administration Press, 1985.

30. Starkweather, D. B. *Hospital Mergers in the Making.* Ann Arbor, Mich.: Health Administration Press, 1981.

31. Weil, T. P. "Reaching toward Unity: Catholic Facilities Can Triumph with Geographically Linked, Regional Systems." *Health Progress* 70, no. 3 (1989): 24–31.

32. Battistella, R. M., and Weil, T. P. "Comprehensive Health Planning: New Effect or Redirected Energy." *New York State Journal of Medicine* 69, no. 17 (1969): 2350–70.

33. Lee, R. I., and Jones, L. W. *The Fundamentals of Good Medical Care: An Outline of the Fundamentals of Good Medical Care and an Estimate of the Service Required to Supply the Medical Needs of the United States.* Chicago: University of Chicago Press, 1933.

34. American Hospital Association. *The Dartmouth Atlas of Health Care, 1998.* Chicago: American Hospital Publishing, 1998.

2

How to Enhance the Efficacy of
Health Network Growth

ABSTRACT. In almost every American metropolitan area health executives are busily enhancing the efficacy of their health networks by corporate restructuring so that their organization can evolve into a fiscally and politically powerful integrated health delivery system. When these alliances are initially announced by the local media, they are reported to be vehicles to enhance access, social equity, and quality of care and to reduce costs. Since an increasing number of these health networks are currently experiencing fiscal, operational, cultural, and other difficulties, it is critical to study: (1) what factors should be considered when developing an effective and efficient health network; (2) what the practical issues in their strategic formation and management are so they can eventually achieve their full potential; and (3) why some divestitures among these health networks will occur and how these corporate "spin-offs" impact consumers, providers, insurers, and governmental agencies. Within the next decade the United States will face some inevitable economic difficulties, and networks will need to divest themselves of some of their "losers." Enhancing access and reducing costs at that time will become even more critical for health networks. As a result, these alliances may then need to be more responsive to consumer pressures as the United States shifts its political proclivities from its current quasi-competitive to a more quasi-regulatory position.

The American public with increasing frequency either reads about or personally experiences circumstances evidencing that the health field can be expected to encounter more turbulent conditions in the next decade. Meanwhile, in many rural and inner-city areas major health insurers, because of financial shortfalls, have decided to forgo renewing their Medicare and Medicaid HMO contracts.[1] The Allegheny Health, Education, and Research Foundation, a major health network with a medical school and 15 hospitals located primarily in the Pittsburgh and Philadelphia metropolitan areas, filed for bankruptcy protection in the summer of 1998, with $1.2 billion in debt.[2] (Subsequently, existing providers purchased various of its facilities, and a few subsidiaries were shuttered.)

Powerful health networks still consummate additional acquisitions, but for public relations and political reasons these amalgamations are referred to in the public media simply as mergers. These corporate restructuring efforts are often announced as a means to react positively to projected Medicare, Medicaid, and managed care shortfalls and to enhance access, social equity and quality of care and to reduce costs among local health providers. Yet the number of uninsured Americans until recently increased annually by almost a million persons,[3] and U.S. health expenditures grow at a rate of 50 percent more than the rise in the nation's consumer price index (CPI). Although the managed care plans have enhanced cost-containment efforts, America's gross domestic product expenditure for health was projected earlier to increase to 17.9 percent by 2005.[4] As a result, the public is looking to the leaders of these networks to improve the health field's effectiveness and efficiency.

Within a few years almost every physician and hospital in the United States will likely be affiliated, with roughly 850 regional networks.[5] This finding should be of considerable concern since an increasing number of studies suggest that hospital mergers and the acquisition of physician practices now being consummated by these alliances are primarily being sought not as a means of curtailing costs but to maintain or even enhance market penetration and to control pricing. Unfortunately, only a few of these amalgamations to date have achieved significant economies, despite the time and dollar resources devoted by various health providers to restructure their organizations.[6]

The general management literature also contains a significant number of citations that analyze the efficacy of corporate restructuring. The published findings of these mergers generally report disappointing outcomes, if the results are to be evaluated on the basis of improved efficiency or profitability,[7-10] the major exception being those amalgamations of similar-size organizations in which the leadership of the existing management orchestrates its own acquisition (i.e., a management buyout).

While cost cutting has always been a key implied objective in any corporate restructuring, the actual driving forces behind these physician and hospital mergers have been the increased enrollment and the fiscal incentives inherent in the managed care concept. Interestingly, subscribers' growth has not been matched by a comparable rise in the number of HMOs. The total number of third-party payers peaked in the 1980s, and, despite the entry of additional insurers, there has been a trend toward more concentration of subscribers among fewer managed care plans.[11] This decline of managed care plans has occurred because 149 HMOs have folded between 1986 and 1993, and another 80 HMOs have vanished primarily through acquisitions.

A decreasing number of available HMOs in the marketplace should also be of considerable concern to consumers and elected officials, since managed care plans that experience the most competition offer the lowest premiums.[11] In fact, in another study that estimated the effect of managed care plan mergers on HMO premiums it was reported that these corporate amalgamations have not benefited the public by the expected result of reducing the cost of health insurance coverage.[12]

The overriding conclusion, therefore, is that the economies of scale that are supposedly to result from hospital, HMO, and similar mergers to date have not generally been passed on to American consumers in the form of decreased costs or enhanced access to quality patient care.

Purposes of This Chapter

Although a significant number of publications describe in primarily conceptual terms the virtues of forming, and the early experiences of, integrated health delivery systems or health networks or health alliances (here used as synonymous terms),[13–14] only a few articles have discussed the practical aspects and critical political ramifications encompassing such corporate consolidations.[15–16] This chapter's first and major purpose, therefore, is to outline the critical elements that should be carefully evaluated by governing boards and health executives in hospital, medical group practice, or HMO merger discussions. These topics are pivotal in enhancing the likelihood of the various parties reaching an agreement that results in forming an effective and efficient health network.

A health provider's major objective in consummating a merger should be to meet patient or community healthcare needs. The most frequent reason to initiate discussions concerning the possibility of becoming a partner of an existing health network, however, is based on the realization that sometime in the near future one's organization could experience significant negative fiscal outcomes. Once merger negotiations are under way between the various parties and even after the agreement is signed, questions of governance, money, and politics often come to the forefront. The second purpose of this chapter, therefore, is to discuss some of the practical issues surrounding the strategic formation and management of these health networks so that they actually achieve their full potential.

Major medical centers everywhere are anxious to improve their current market penetration and must continuously worry about pricing and costs. Most health networks spend significant resources to acquire within the region inpatient facilities, ambulatory care satellites, and physician groups with the expectation of increasing the number of referrals to their specialists and, in turn, generating additional admissions to their highly sophisticated patient care services. Over the next decade some of these arrangements are destined to result in highly contentious disputes because of mismatched goals and fiscal incentives among health networks and physician groups, particularly when the magnitude of superfluous tertiary facilities, services, and medical manpower becomes more apparent. This chapter's third purpose, therefore, is to discuss why divestitures will occur among these health networks and how these corporate spin-offs will impact consumers, providers, insurers, and government officials.

Critical Elements in Health Network Formation

Theoretically, at the outset, the specific goals and objectives an organization wants to achieve by a merger will establish the overall scope of the study. This conceptual framework, in turn, should delineate the outline of the data and other information to be collected in preparation for negotiations that might potentially modify an organization's governance, financing, style of management, and scope of programs and services. The objectives and the analysis needed are quite different for a fiscally sound, medium-sized, not-for-profit health network located in a major metropolitan area that is seeking more acquisitions to become an oligopolist, compared to a small, underfinanced, county-owned rural facility interested in merging with a well-respected partner that has "deep pockets" and thereby can insure its existence for the next five years as a full-service facility.

The elements outlined here in forming or expanding an existing health network constitute a far more comprehensive inventory than is needed in most merger discussions but can serve as a checklist in evaluating whether an organization is adequately prepared to discuss potential modifications in its current corporate structure.

Where are we now, and where should our organization be heading in the future? Before starting any serious negotiations concerning possibly joining any health network, every provider should undertake a detailed assessment of its current and future goals and objectives. Some critical questions include: What would be achieved by becoming a partner of an established health network? What terms and conditions is our organization willing to compromise on to consummate a potentially successful merger? Is it possible, without consummating a merger, for our organization to enhance its resources so it can better meet additional community needs? Are we looking for a 50/50-type "marriage"? Is a potential merger contingent on our agreeing to be actually "acquired" by a regional network? What do we require "in trade" to agree to being acquired by a larger, well-financed health network?

This strategic planning process must focus on an evaluation of the organization's current and projected mission statements, a vision of the present and the future locally, regionally, and nationally, and then a comparison of these findings and conclusions with its recent operating and fiscal performance. Such a candid self-assessment process can assist in determining the hospital, medical group practice, or HMO's strengths and weaknesses, and opportunities and threats, an analysis that should serve as important background information of where a health network merger study and possible negotiations should be heading in the future.

Population and demographic information is important when evaluating the future volume of specific programs and services and the need for physicians and other health manpower. Projected population increases or decreases, vital health statistics, and the age distribution of service area residents are critical variables when estimating the future demand for health services and for physician manpower by specialty. Also, often overlooked in this inquiry is the importance of the area's major roadway system, since health networks can be far more effective if their various satellites are located so they are convenient to usual travel or trade patterns.

Although frequently more difficult to obtain, the service area's third-party payer mix is critical to the analysis. What percentage of the population is fee-for-service, managed care, Medicare, Medicaid, uninsured, or a combination is a major factor in what types of services should be offered, how they should be provided, and whether they are fiscally viable. A provider's bottom line could well be more favorably or adversely affected by its patients' payer mix than by its management's effectiveness and efficiency.

Patient origin and market penetration data are critical in determining the total number and type of patients within the region who are served by the various providers. This analysis should definitely include the market penetration of the organization's major competitors. Potentially, such an evaluation can answer the question of whether a specific provider can realistically change its population-service mix to attract more patients and, therefore, more revenues.

Historical and comparative utilization data should provide the information necessary for an analysis that focuses on the trends in usage during the past three years for the region's major providers and whether they have similar or different utilization patterns than state and national averages. Although there are significant regional differences in hospital use rates (e.g., the rate in the eastern United States is far greater than in the west), comparing admissions, surgical procedures, emergency department visits, and other ambulatory care visits per 1,000 service area residents can be beneficial in evaluating possible over- or underutilization of specific services. Table 1 illustrates a hospital experiencing utilization data that is less than the state average (Commonwealth of Pennsylvania) but greater than the national average.

Of considerable concern, and a factor that could encourage a facility to merge into a health network, is when a hospital experiences high admission and inpatient day utilization rates per 1,000 residents compared with "norms" and, within the same area, the providers perceive that a managed care plan using a capitated-type payment reimbursement methodology is expected to gain considerable market penetration within the foreseeable future. In addition, the number of emergency department and other outpatient visits per 1,000 service area residents compared to state and national averages can provide insight into the efficacy of the facility's

TABLE 1. Comparative Hospital Utilization Data, Orange Memorial Hospital, Pennsylvania, and the United States, 1996

Variable	Orange Memorial Hospital	Pennsylvania	United States
Service area population	65,000	12,000,000	265,000,000
Acute care beds (in use)	250	48,534	872,736
Beds per 1,000 service area population	3.85	4.04	3.29
Total hospital inpatient admissions	9,100	1,810,118	30,945,367
Admissions per 1,000 service area population	140.2	150.8	116.8
Total inpatient days	55,250	12,346,057	199,876,367
Days per 1,000 service area population	850	1,028.84	754.25
Average length of hospital stay	6.06	6.82	6.46
Average percentage of occupancy	60.5	69.7	62.7
Average daily inpatient census (days)	151.4	33,825	547,602
Number of births	845	150,575	3,764,763
Births per 1,000 service area population	13	12.5	14.2
Number of surgical procedures	7,150	1,446,029	23,162,917
Surgical procedures per 1,000 service area population	110	120.5	87.4
Number of emergency department visits	24,713	4,934,863	94,745,938
Emergency department visits per 1,000 service area residents	380.2	411.2	357.5
Number of outpatient visits	90,610	21,927,320	319,598,902
Outpatient visits per 1,000 service area residents	1,394	1,827.3	1,206

Source: Orange Memorial Hospital, 1998; and American Hospital Association (AHA), Hospital Statistics, 1996–97 (Chicago: AHA, 1997).

ambulatory care volumes. Often this information can suggest whether the organization's outpatient services can be expanded by merging with a health network that is the region's dominant provider—or, irrespective of a merger, because the organization is in such a favorable position, whether in the future a new competitor might establish an ambulatory care center within the service area, thus creating potential fiscal concerns.

The composition and utilization patterns of a hospital's medical staff have a direct impact on where patients seek care, what specific programs and services are provided at a facility, whether becoming a partner within a health network might enhance the facility's clinical acumen, and whether the primary care or other physician practices should be acquired by the health network. The composition of a hospital's medical staff is usually studied in terms of office location, age, specialty, and board certification, and the physician's utilization patterns are often evaluated in terms of revenue dollars provided (by treating patients and those generated by the hospital), inpatient admissions, patient days, operative procedures, and deliveries. A few physicians producing a significant percentage of any provider's total income suggests a precarious position for a hospital or for a large multispecialty group practice.

Whether the addition of a few key physicians (usually specific specialists) will significantly improve an organization's total revenue stream is a critical analysis that should be undertaken prior to the start of any serious merger negotiations. There are a number of remedies to the possible shortcomings in medical manpower: the freestanding hospital and a medical group might jointly attempt to recruit their own physicians rather than merge into a health network; they might consummate an affiliation agreement with an academic health center to encourage specialists completing their residency training to practice there; or they might decide that a more appropriate solution would be to include a provision within the merger agreement stating that specific specialists will be provided by the network's major medical center(s).

A *physician manpower needs analysis* by clinical specialty or subspecialty offers a rough estimate of any major gaps for additional physicians and can demonstrate whether there is already a surplus of doctors in specific disciplines within the service area. The underlying assumptions, the quantitative steps required to undertake this analysis, and how to interpret these findings are relatively complex issues.[17] Health executives who believe that the number and type of physicians available within a service area closely approximates the hospital or a multispecialty group's demand function will consider these findings of the need for physicians to be critical in possible merger discussions or in pursuing other options.

Consumer, major employer, and physician surveys are useful in presenting a perception of how a provider is viewed by its "community." Once having collected such information, how you utilize such findings will depend on a number of factors (e.g., the number and type of positive and negative conclusions).

Whether, and if so, how you integrate the community's various publics into the merger negotiations can often become a contentious issue because: (1) the public and medical staff believe that an acute care hospital, for example, is a community resource and its future destiny should be shaped by representatives of its many interested parties; and (2) a not-for-profit governing board (most often made up of community leaders and a few key physicians) usually suggests that the topic of a merger is too complicated for public discussion; the negotiations "in obtaining the best deal" from competing health networks are more effectively handled behind closed doors; and the decision of whether to merge and, if so, with whom should be left to the "experts," since a public referendum on who should be "the partner" usually results in a "political" decision rather than one focusing on the best way to achieve effective and efficient healthcare for the area's residents. This "closed" approach might be perceived as, or in fact be, most beneficial to the professional and personal interests of those "in power."

A detailed *financial ratio analysis* that compares the hospital's fiscal performance with national and regional "norms" provides insight into the fiscal strengths and weaknesses of the organization. These data should be compared, if possible, to providers of similar size and geographic location, such as those illustrated in table 2. This example portrays an institution that is plagued with serious financial difficulties primarily because of its long-term debt-to-equity ratio in spite of its low ratio of employees per occupied bed (adjusted for ambulatory volumes). Most merger negotiations will require developing *pro forma balance sheet and revenue and expense statements,* based on a number of assumptions relating to changes in volume and revenues, to illustrate what might occur operationally and fiscally if a specific merger agreement were consummated.

Honoring *existing contracts,* including those with various physicians and members of the management team, can be a sensitive issue if any of these individuals are concerned about their future employment tenure. Hospital-based physicians and senior executives can play a major role in either supporting a worthy merger or discouraging others who are involved in the negotiations, if they believe they might be adversely effected by such an amalgamation.

Similarities and differences in *corporate culture and how human resources are to be managed* need to be evaluated. Most deal makers usually underestimate the significant roles that corporate culture and employee morale play in insuring that the restructured corporation can successfully meet its intended goals and objectives.[18]

How to Start the Process

A smaller organization seeking a merger with a major health network might send out to prospective partners a request for proposal (RFP) providing a summary of its current operations, its most recent audited (financial) statement, what it expects to achieve by the merger, and an outline suggesting the major areas that health network officials might address in their responses. Later on, each of the respondents can be interviewed to answer questions or to clarify any ambiguous statements requiring further amplification within their proposal.

If a health network is seeking acquisitions in the area, it should obtain as much of the information as possible along the lines above concerning

TABLE 2. Providence Hospital's Financial and Other Ratios in Comparison to National and Regional Averages, 1996

Variable	National	Regional (100–199 beds)	Providence Hospital
Number of observations	4,705	112	—
Number of FTEs[a]	365.4	499.7	421.8
Current ratio	2.1	1.5	1.0
Days of operating expense in current assets	112.4	104.8	78.9
Months of operating expense in fund balance	6.9	5.9	1.1
Total asset turnover	0.97	0.97	1.37
Equity financing	0.57	0.50	0.13
Long-term debt to equity	0.34	0.48	4.33
Write-off percentage	36.7	42.4	37.6
Investment income percentage	0.55	0.76	0.44
Inpatient revenue per discharge (dollars)	7,963	8,576	7,753
Patient revenue per FTE case mix, adjusted (dollars)	99,528	100,544	101,679
Operating expense / discharge adjusted (dollars)	4,910	4,756	5,040
FTEs per occupied bed, adjusted	4.7	4.2	3.2
Occupancy rate (percentage)	40.7	52.3	69.3
Total discharges	3,358	4,460	4,674
Average length of stay	4.6	5.6	7.8
Number of Medicare discharges	1,341	2,038	2,518
Outpatient revenue / total patient revenue (percentage)	40.3	39.2	22.4

Source: "Viability Indicators for Hospitals, 1999 ed.," ed. G. M. Pearl, MS, Rate Control Publications, Phoenix, April 1999.

[a]FTEs = full-time equivalent employees.

each "potential" or "targeted" partner and then should prioritize these findings on the basis of: (1) what acquisition(s) would do the health network "the most good"; and (2) what acquisitions would be "the easiest" to consummate. Then the alliance's leadership needs to evaluate which provider(s) to pursue for a possible merger.

Practical Issues in Forming and Managing Health Networks

There are a significant number of practical issues involved in forming and managing health networks, perhaps the most important being about governance, capital and operating funds, a centralized or decentralized style of management, corporate politics, and whether the merger has a reasonable chance to enhance the region's delivery of health services.

Governance

The dilemma usually surrounding governance can be illustrated by the organization being acquired not wanting to lose any control over its future destiny but obtaining significant resources from the health network; conversely, usually an alliance hesitates to lend its good name and to provide substantial money and manpower resources without having some recourse to dominate the governing board's policy-making powers if the "the deal starts to turn sour." Also, the satellite facility should negotiate for some representation on the health network's corporate board not only to keep involved in the network's overall policy formation but also on occasion to seize the opportunity to pursue local interests at the alliance's highest level of decision making.

Working out an agreeable governance arrangement is usually the least difficult among similar types of organizations: Having two not-for-profits, nonsectarians, or Catholics, or two investor-owned facilities should present fewer barriers. More difficult to merge because of cultural and philosophical disparities are Catholic and non-Catholic or city- or county-sponsored and any other type of ownership.

What governance provision the smaller of the two organizations is willing to give up or the larger corporate body requires to consummate a merger is dependent on a number of variables. Often a critical element in this equation is how fiscally "healthy" is the acquired provider versus how many additional referrals as a result of the amalgamation can be anticipated at the health network's major medical center. In the final analysis the degree of similarity of the corporate culture between two organizations will play a major role in how the governance structure is finally arranged.

In general, more local control will be agreed to for the first several years after the merger is consummated, and this pattern can be expected to continue as long as the initial arrangement is effective and efficient for both parties. The top leadership group of most health networks is not anxious to micromanage local policy decisions of successful satellites, primarily because that time and effort could be more effectively used elsewhere, and there is always the possibility of causing unnecessary ill will at the local level.

Capital and Operational Financing

Most health networks when consummating a merger are anxious to gain considerable net worth (fiscal) in terms of sizable current assets, a physical plant with an average age of less than seven years, and the possibility of obtaining additional referrals from the acquired facility for its medical center's specialists. As incentives to join a health network, the prospective new partner often seeks such conditions as all of its existing debt being retired; a major commitment of new capital funds for renovation projects and the replacement of existing outdated equipment; and the provision of other resources such as information systems, assistance in negotiating managed care contracts, and the recruitment of physicians with specific clinical skills.

Style of Management

Whether the new partner of a health network will sense significant changes in how "local" management functions depends on a large number of factors, including the travel time between the alliance's central office and the hospital or medical group; the personal interrelationships and the level of trust between the central office executive staff and the senior managers at the satellite; the fiscal importance and profitability of the new partner for the health network; whether the acquired organization has an improving or deteriorating bottom line; and whether the central staff is driven by either power or greed.

A 1998 survey of hospital chief executive officers indicated that more that 50 percent of all hospitals that are part of a larger organization have not eliminated or reduced any patient services, where most of the major economies as a result of corporate restructuring should be forthcoming.[19] Half of the responding facilities had not consolidated any services, and, among those that have, most have focused more on combining financial or administrative rather than clinical or ancillary services. This finding suggests that some health networks' senior executives may be more anxious to secure additional acquisitions than to centralize critical patient care functions with the aim of reducing costs.

Corporate Politics

The "politics" of a freestanding multispecialty group practice or a community hospital is far simpler than becoming a "junior" partner within a large and complex health network that has several more layers of decision making and policy formation. A provider with a forceful governing body and an aggressive management staff that historically was able to make all policy decisions locally now having to obtain approval from a central office can be expected to provoke potential complications such as illustrated by just simple miscommunications between the two parties.

A specific partner's political power will often be dependent on that unit's importance to the health network's overall success today and in the future. Local physicians sending an increasing number of referrals to the alliance's major medical center, and a thoughtful and articulate representative of the "local" partner at the corporate board level, can also influence the political power of a provider that has recently joined a major health alliance.

Evaluating Outcomes

The formation throughout the United States of powerful health networks made up of hospitals, physician groups, and HMOs, some with annual revenues exceeding one billion dollars, clearly depicts a propensity by the health industry to consummate corporate consolidations. This is in spite of the fact that limited operational and fiscal evidence has been published to date that supports the efficacy of such amalgamations.[6, 12, 20–25]

Over the next decade a likely scenario is for the nation's politically and fiscally powerful networks to continue acquiring additional providers and insurers. Then, after gaining significant market penetration, these alliances will behave as oligopolists or regulated monopolists. For these networks eventually to achieve their earlier projected outcomes, it may well be necessary for their leaders to implement such measures as:

1. more vigorously coordinating their key clinical services to reduce competition for revenues among the various partners within an alliance;

2. shuttering superfluous hospitals and centralizing tertiary services;
3. divesting providers that are either a "mismatch" programmatically or organizationally or are not particularly profitable; the most frequent examples to be expected are physician practices and small, underutilized acute care facilities;
4. encouraging surplus physicians to relocate to underserved areas; and
5. carefully integrating the best elements of what the competitive and regulatory strategies can offer to improve access, social equity, and quality of care and to reduce total health expenditures.

Based on these above projections, some criteria that might be used in evaluating the potential outcome or efficacy of joining a specific health network might be summarized as follows:

1. Will the proposed corporate restructuring enhance the delivery of health services within the region?
2. Will it lead to improved access to services and to better insure social equity?
3. Will it contribute to a positive enhancement in the quality of patient care provided locally?
4. Will capital and operational expenditures be reduced and, in turn, decrease regional healthcare costs?
5. Will there be, as a result of such a proposed merger, an increase in regulatory constraints?

In the final analysis most of today's corporate restructuring in the health field results in some compromises—in the delivery of health care, fiscally, politically, and in other ways. What always needs to be considered in the formation or the expansion of a health network is whether the proposed solution can realistically improve the delivery of health services to the area's residents.[26]

Divestitures within Health Networks

When undertaking long-range planning endeavors such as whether to join a network or whether to expand an existing alliance, it is worthwhile to consider what might happen if the United States experienced almost inevitable economic difficulties. An anticipated outcome of a recession in the United States would be networks divesting themselves quickly of their "losers." What happens if you become part of a health network, economic hard times set in, and the alliance's leadership decides to "spin you off"?

Factors Leading to Divestitures

Facing an increasing supply of available doctors (particularly specialists), a decrease in reimbursement per unit of service, and a rise in the percentage of gross revenues expended for office overhead, an attractive option for an increasing number of physicians and medical group practices has been being "bought out" by a nearby health network or a physician management corporation. This alternative can be particularly advantageous, if the alliance is also willing to assist with the day-to-day management of these practices.

Hospitals have been anxious to bond with their primary care physicians and particularly with their major admitters, and, until relatively recently, they were willing to offer attractive cash terms and performance agreements. Some of these arrangements between health networks and physician groups, however, are destined over the next decade to result in highly contentious disputes, since physicians once having been bought out expect to work less and earn more, and hospitals, having made sizable expenditures when acquiring these practices, anticipate additional inpatient admissions from these doctors and obtaining a reasonable return on their capital investment.

While the growth in managed care enrollment has encouraged physician groups "to sell their practices" to health networks, the fiscal incentives among managed care plans (i.e., reducing utilization and cost) and how the available premium dollars are to be divided between doctors and hospitals are among the major constraints that complicate reaching any long-term operational and fiscal concurrence between a health network or an acute care facility and its medical staff.

With a decline in the available dollars for direct medical care services adjusted for healthcare inflation, physicians and hospitals, particularly when one or both are highly leveraged, will become involved in disputes that are primarily related to a significant growth sector of the market— whether specific ambulatory care services should be provided in doctors' offices or under the hospital's aegis or as a joint venture. As a result of either financial distress or a "misfit of objectives," a large number of divestitures of physician practices or of medical groups from health networks will likely occur. Simply put, physicians will become disenchanted with working for health networks, and health alliances, in turn, will find out how difficult it is for the individual doctor and the network to manage physician practices successfully at a reasonably profitable level.

Divestitures of Hospital Services

Another somewhat related occurrence is a health network shuttering a specific acute care facility and converting that physical plant to long-term care or using it as an ambulatory care satellite. Since hospitals play such a critical role in a community's overall social and economic fabric and particularly in providing a significant number of well-paying jobs, there is a reluctance everywhere for an institution or a clinical service "to be downgraded" or to be eliminated.

What could well become a more frequent occurrence in the future is a health network deciding to consolidate its tertiary services at one or at least at a smaller number of facilities to reduce cost and to improve quality. The United States, compared to Canada and Germany, per 100,000 persons has many more cardiac catheterization, open-heart surgery, lithotripsy, MRI, and other similar modalities available, but our outcomes are not significantly better.[27] Although an inconvenience to patients and physicians, the centralization of sophisticated services results in a more appropriate allocation of resources and significant cost savings.

Impact of Divestitures on Consumers

These divestitures by health networks would have a mixed impact on consumers. What should be of considerable concern to the public is that health networks will rid themselves of their fiscal losers—programs and services that are sometimes critical to the community, but adversely affect the alliance's bottom line (e.g., substance abuse services). What should also be particularly worrisome to consumers is that health networks will acquire competing programs, services, and facilities, later shutter them, and then position the alliance as an oligopoly or as a regulated monopoly.

Whether the current merger mania in the health field is to reduce cost, which would have a favorable impact on consumers, or to control prices will continue to be a contentious question. Once there are no qualified competitors in an area, insurers such as managed care plans have virtually no alternative other than to negotiate prices with the remaining provider. After a health network is positioned in the marketplace as a virtual monopoly, the incentive to cut costs to gain increased market share is substantially reduced.

The optimistic view of these divestitures would suggest that health networks will shutter only redundant services; enhance access, social equity, and quality of care; and will meanwhile reduce costs. The current health services research literature on the efficacy of health networks would suggest, however, that this scenario is unlikely to occur in the foreseeable future.[6, 12, 20–25]

Divestitures of Physician Practices

After years of rapid expansion and soaring stock prices, the physician practice management industry, overlapping in some cases with medical practices that have been acquired by health networks, is in turmoil. This $10 billion industry has been battered by bankruptcies, litigation, and physician discontent.

Physicians are becoming restless with health networks because of less than expected earnings and less autonomy to make business and clinical decisions. Only a few years ago physicians were accustomed to fee-for-service reimbursement and running their own offices. Then, soon after becoming a health network "partner," physicians realize they are faced with a significantly increasing number of patients with restrictive managed care contracts and a "bureaucratic organization" providing them with space, personnel, information systems, and other support services of varying quality and price.

As health networks shutter programs, services, and even total hospitals, physicians will be forced to obtain admitting privileges at other facilities. When a hospital is closed, its pathologists, radiologists, anesthesiologists, and other hospital-based physicians are put at an obvious and significant risk. If a health network shuts down one of its two open-heart surgery programs, does that cardiovascular surgery staff automatically obtain privileges to operate at the remaining facility providing such a service? Something that the alliance's management team likes to avoid is the shuttering of a facility or a major service, since there is a strong possibility that ill will between physicians and the health network's leadership will result.

With the United States experiencing an excess supply of physician specialists and a surplus of hospital facilities, health networks can anticipate proceeding with a significant number of divestitures of physician groups and of acute hospital services. In fact, some might suggest that such trends are difficult to avoid in an environment of excess supply of almost all health resources, an overutilization of many services, and increasing pressures to cut costs.

Divestitures among Insurers

As managed care enrollment continues to grow, the U.S. health insurance industry is experiencing further consolidation by acquisition; increasing difficulty in improving its bottom lines; more barriers, when applicable, to converting from a not-for-profit to investor-owned status; and a more hostile consumer and provider environment. Fiscally and politically powerful health networks, however, could well decide to acquire a relatively small number of existing insurance carriers or to form their own insurance component to eliminate the "middleman" costs and to gain greater control over their revenue stream. Yet are most health networks organized to establish and manage a health insurance function?

The significant losses that most integrated delivery systems are experiencing with their HMOs would suggest that networks will either decide to divest themselves from being an insurer or develop more meaningful joint ventures with established third-party payers. Of usual concern in such transactions is that the insurers will gain fiscal control over the providers. What is so often forgotten by health network executives is that the health insurance industry has been one of the nation's most powerful and well-financed lobbies, so clearly evidenced by their almost single-handed and successful efforts to defeat the Clinton administration's health reform plan.

Inability to Regulate Divestitures

Historically, federal, state, and city officials and American health policy leaders have supported the concepts of regionalization, comprehensive health planning, the regional medical program, and other similar attempts to implement the concept of tertiary services being centralized in a teaching environment at the "hub" with "spokes" around the major medical center providing secondary and primary care, as needed.[16] Government regulators, therefore, have difficulty with health networks that use the same hub-spoke approach to become oligopolists and thereby are able to control prices.

For the foreseeable future the government's role in these health network divestitures is expected for several reasons to have a minimal effect in protecting the public interest: (1) health networks are being formed as oligopolies, and they are divesting their losers without meaningful public scrutiny; and (2) the Department of Justice, the Federal Trade Commission, and similar state agencies have experienced limited success in the courts when they cite that these proposed or operational alliances conflict, or will in the future, with well-tested antitrust statutes and rulings.

As increases in health insurance premiums have been lessened as a result of managed care and lower inflation, the state departments of insurance have become more concerned about the solvency of some HMOs (e.g., Oxford Health Plans). They have been reluctant to proceed with cease-and-desist orders against insurers that continue to be highly selective in accepting new enrollees so as to avoid any potential adverse selection of risk. The inability of the Clinton health reform package to gain any support and the HMO patient bill of rights being stalled in the U.S. Congress suggest more talk than action by most of the nation's elected and appointed officials in enhancing access, social equity, and quality of care or reducing costs.

More Government Constraints Are Forthcoming

During the 1990s various public agencies such as the federal and state attorney generals' antitrust divisions and the state departments of insurance and public health generally have taken a relatively passive role in analyzing the efficacy of these huge and powerful health networks as they are initially formed or expanded. And this weak regulatory "mode" can only be expected to change when the United States experiences a serious economic turndown. Employers will then more acutely feel the squeeze in paying for health insurance benefits for their employees and dependents; public officials will find that Medicare and Medicaid benefits are far too onerous in an environment in which healthcare is already consuming 17.9 percent of the nation's GDP (so projected for 2005);[4] and there will be increasing pressure for health services from an expanding number of uninsured or underinsured Americans, who eventually might total close to 100 million persons, as there are already over 44 million without any coverage. For these reasons a shift from a quasi-competitive to a more quasi-regulatory healthcare environment is predicted within the next decade. This anticipated change in underlying economic conditions and public policy will have an impact on how health networks are organized, managed, and financed.

Public officials, aside from the enormous political, social, and economic issues that surround a recession, will experience increasing difficulty in improving access, social equity, and quality of care and providing services at an affordable cost for most Americans. Complicating the chances to reduce health expenditures is that federal and state government in the past experienced significant stumbling blocks in reining in outlays for health services irrespective of utilizing price controls,[28] hospital rate setting,[29] the certificate of need (CON) process,[30] or Medicare diagnostic related groups (DRGs).[31] These shortcomings result from a number of developments.

1. Elected officials are unwilling to make the necessary and tough policy decisions in the passage of the initial legislation, fearing possible repercussions later when seeking an additional term or higher public office. This lack of definitive legislative direction provides the executive branch with more latitude and results in more private-public disputes being contested and subjected to judicial review.
2. Providers can expend significant resources to find ways to maximize their revenues within the rules and regulations promulgated

by public agencies. They just hire outside experts to find ways, if possible, of circumventing the legislation to the providers' benefit.

3. Public officials often have insufficient resources to regulate a far larger, more powerful, and better financed private sector.

4. Price controls and regulations placed by government on programs and services that providers desire to offer in their communities are counter to the spirit of the American free enterprise system.

With the public sector being responsible for almost half of the health expenditures in the United States, the continuation of a healthcare environment that is quasi-government and quasi-private is predictable. In this context borrowing the principles contained in the Telecommunications Act of 1996[32] for the health industry or forming state health services commissions (as a public utility)[33] as possible options to maintain a competitive environment within a broader regulatory framework have been proposed.

Whether the United States can achieve an equitable quasi-private, quasi-government health delivery system will, it is hoped, be given more heed early in this new millennium. How these regulatory and market-driven elements of health networks are pieced together will have a significant impact on how they evolve in the next decade. Irrespective of the nation's political, social, and economic position, the breadth and depth of the analysis to develop health networks proposed earlier should have a positive impact on the delivery of more effective and efficient medical care by the nation's health networks.

REFERENCES

1. Kilborn, P. T. "Largest HMOs Cutting the Poor and the Elderly." *New York Times,* July 6, 1998, 1.

2. Burns, L. R., Cacciamani, J., Clement, J., and Aquino, W. "The Fall of the House of AHERF: The Allegheny Bankruptcy." *Health Affairs* 19, no. 1 (2000): 7–41.

3. Rice, D. P. "The Cost of Instant Access to Health Care." *Journal of the American Medical Association* 279, no. 13 (1998): 1030.

4. Burner, S. T., and Waldo, D. R. "National Health Expenditure Projections, 1994–2005." *Health Care Financing Review* 16, no. 4 (1995): 221–42.

5. Weil, T. P., and Jorgensen, N. E. "A Tripartite Regulation of Health Networks." *Journal of Public Health Management and Practice* 2, no. 3 (1996): 46–53.

6. Clement, J. P., McCue, M. J., Luke, R. D., Bramble, J. D., Rossiter, L. F., Ozcan, Y. A., and Pai, C.-W. "Strategic Hospital Alliances: Impact on Financial Performance." *Health Affairs* 16, no. 6 (1997): 193–203.

7. Bishop, M., and Kay, J. A. *European Mergers and Merger Policy.* New York City: Oxford University Press, 1993.

8. Litchenberg, F. R. *Corporate Takeover and Productivity.* Cambridge, Mass.: MIT Press, 1992.

9. Ravenscraft, D. J., and Scherer, F. M. *Mergers, Sell-Offs, and Economic Efficiency.* Washington, D.C.: Brookings Institution, 1987.

10. Scherer, F. M., and Ross, D. *Industrial Market Structure and Economic Performance.* Boston: Houghton Mifflin, 1990.

11. Feldman, R., Wholey, D. R., and Christianson, J. B. "A Descriptive Economic Analysis of HMO Mergers and Failures, 1985–1992." *Medical Care Research and Review* 52, no. 2 (1995): 279–304.

12. Feldman, R., Wholey, D. R., and Christianson, J. B. "Effect of Mergers on the Health Maintenance Organization Premiums." *Health Care Financing Review* 17, no. 3 (1996): 171–89.

13. Shortell, S. M., Giles, R. R., Anderson, D. A., Erickson, K. M., and Mitchell, J. B. *Remaking Healthcare in America: Building Organized Delivery Systems.* San Francisco: Jossey Bass, 1996.

14. Zuckerman, H. S., and Kaluzny, A. D. "The Management of Strategic Alliances in Health Services." *Frontiers of Health Services Management* 17, no. 3 (1991): 3–23.

15. Zuckerman, A. M. *Healthcare Strategic Planning: Approaches for the 21st Century.* Chicago: Health Administration Press, 1997.

16. Weil, T. P. "Hub-and-Spokes Regionalization." *Health Progress* 72, no. 8 (1991): 24–31.

17. Weil, T. P. "How to Determine the Need for MDs by Specialty." *Physician Executive* 23, no. 8 (1997): 19–24.

18. Dolan, R., and Weil, T. P. "Mergers in the Health Field: Enhancing Human Resources Management." *Physician Executive* 24, no. 2 (1998): 12–18.

19. Deloitte and Touche. "US Hospitals and the Future of Health Care," 4. 7th ed. Philadelphia: Deloitte and Touche, 1998.

20. Dranove, D., Shanley, M., and White, W. D. "Price and Concentration in Health Markets: The Switch from Patient-Driven to Payer-Driven Competition." *Journal of Law and Economics* 36, no. 1 (1993): 179–204.

21. Lynk, W. J. "The Creation of Economic Efficiencies in Hospital Mergers." *Journal of Health Economics* 14, no. 5 (1995): 507–30.

22. Mobley, L. R. "Tacit Collusion among Hospitals in Price Competitive Markets." *Health Economics* 5, no. 3 (1996): 183–93.

23. Bogue, R. J., Shortell, S. M., Sohn, M.-W., Manheim, L., Bazzoli, G., and Chan, C. "Hospital Reorganization after Merger." *Medical Care* 33, no. 7 (1995): 676–86.

24. Connor, R. A., Feldman, R., Dowd, B. E., and Radcliff, T. A. "Which Types of Hospital Mergers Save Consumers Money?" *Health Affairs* 16, no. 6 (1997): 62–74.

25. Alexander, J. A., Halpern, M. T., and Lee, S.-T.-D. "The Short-term Effects of Merger on Hospital Operations." *Health Services Research* 30, no. 6 (1996): 827–47.

26. Weil, T. P. "How to Enhance the Efficacy of Health Network Growth." *International Journal of Health Planning and Management* 51, no. 1 (2000): 17–38.

27. Weil, T. P. "Comparisons of Medical Technology in Canadian, German, and U.S. Hospitals." *Hospital and Health Services Administration* 40, no. 4 (1995): 525–34.

28. Feldstein, P. J. *Health Care Economics,* 174–76. 2d ed. New York: John Wiley, 1983.

29. Eby, C. L., and Cohodes, D. R. "What Do We Know about Rate-Setting?" *Journal of Health Politics, Policy and Law* 10, no. 2 (1985): 299–327.

30. Salkever, D. S., and Bice, T. W. *Hospital Certificate of Need Controls: Impact on Investment, Costs, and Use.* Washington, D.C.: American Enterprise Institute for Public Policy Research, 1979.

31. "Medicare and Medicaid Statistical Supplement, 1997." *Health Care Financing Review* (1997): 20.

32. Jorgensen, N. E., and Weil, T. P. "Regulating Managed Care Plans: Is the Telecommunications Industry a Possible Model?" *Managed Care Quarterly* 6, no. 3 (Summer 1998): 7–16.

33. Weil, T. P. "How Health Networks and HMOs Could Result in Public Utility Regulation." *Hospital and Health Services Administration* 41, no. 2 (1996): 273–87.

3

Horizontal Mergers in the Health Field: Some Practical Realities

ABSTRACT. During the last decade merger mania has been a striking trend in the health field as a strategy to improve the integration of services, to reduce expenses, and to increase the ability of providers to manage risk-based payment. During the past quarter-century, however, limited operational and fiscal evidence has been published in either the health or the general management literature that strongly supports the efficacy of horizontal mergers. This chapter further argues that a likely scenario over the next decade, in spite of disappointments among these mergers in effecting significant cost reductions, is for the nation's health networks to continue acquiring additional providers. After these alliances gain significant market penetration, they are expected to behave as oligopolists. For these mergers eventually to achieve their earlier projected savings, the health field's leadership will be forced to implement such cost-cutting measures as more vigorously coordinating the network's key clinical services to reduce competition for revenues among the partners within an alliance; shuttering superfluous hospitals and centralizing expensive tertiary services; encouraging surplus physicians to relocate to underserved areas; and providing direction to integrate carefully the best elements of what the competitive and regulatory strategies are able to offer to improve access, social equity, and quality of care and to reduce total health expenditures.

The health field for the last-quarter century has emulated the President's Council of Economic Advisors' view that "mergers and acquisitions . . . improve efficiency, transfer scarce resources to higher valued uses, and stimulate effective management."[1] The formation throughout the United States of huge health networks (frequently referred to as integrated delivery systems, or alliances) that are made up of hospitals, medical group practices, and HMOs, some with annual revenues exceeding one billion dollars, clearly illustrates a propensity by the United States' health industry to consummate corporate consolidations. In fact, as a result of these multiple mergers that are currently being consummated, by the year 2005 a vast majority of the nation's health resources could well be organized and managed by less than 850 networks (table 3).[2]

These alliances are already changing the landscape of the American health system. In fact, no health delivery system anywhere in the world has experienced so much organizational change among its hospitals as those in the United States.[3] This trend toward consolidation is evidenced by the growing number of hospital mergers and acquisitions, which increased from 100 in 1994 to 184 in 1997. The 184 transactions in 1997 involved 290 hospitals and more than 47,500 beds.[4] As a result of all these amalgamations, there is significant interest in whether all this merger mania is resulting in improved access, social equity, and quality and, particularly, a reduction in the nation's healthcare expenditures.

After first considering some conceptual and practical reasons for the formation throughout the United States of these politically influential and fiscally powerful networks, this chapter addresses questions that are often debated in the health field and among its executives, public officials, and academics: How well do horizontal mergers actually perform in reducing health expenditures? Do similar amalgamations achieve better outcomes in other U.S. industries or in corporations elsewhere throughout the world? And what might be the future impact of the United States' current merger mania on hospitals, medical group practices, insurers, and, most decisively, the public?

Horizontal rather than vertical diversification is this chapters's focus, and such amalgamations are defined here as linking under one corporate umbrella several organizations whose outputs, from the prospective of consumer demand, are substitutes. Two hospitals, two medical group practices, or two HMOs merging are obvious examples of horizontal integration. These amalgamations can be achieved either *within* a specific market (e.g., two previously competing acute care facilities) or *across* markets (e.g., the multistate investor-owned hospital chains). The fiscal and operational outcomes of these horizontal mergers among health networks, health alliances, integrated delivery systems, and multi–health systems are

TABLE 3. Projected Number of Health Networks in the United States by 2005

Standard Metropolitan Area (SMA)	No. SMAs in United States	Average No. of Networks per SMA	Projected No. of Health Networks
Under 450,000 residents	221	2	442
450,000 to 1.5 million residents	72	3.5	252
Over 1.5 million residents	28	5	140
Total	321	—	834

Source: T. P. Weil and N. E. Jorgensen, "A Tripartite Regulation of Health Networks," *Journal of Public Health Management Practice,* 2, no. 2 (1996): 46–53.

more pivotal here than a great concern over any definitional preciseness of an organization's corporate structure.

Conceptual Reasons for Mergers

When studying these corporate amalgamations in the health field, one of the key questions is: What are the major factors leading to the nation's current merger mania that is resulting in such huge and politically power-ful oligopolies, and why is this trend expected to continue? The simplest explanation could be that the parties to these potential amalgamations consider themselves to be better off by consummating a merger agreement than being without it.[5] For larger institutions it protects their existing number of referrals to their specialty programs or potentially increases the number of referrals to their specialty programs, and for the smaller facility the most frequent justification is to insure its long-term fiscal survival as a full-service, acute care hospital.

At the more conceptual level, however, there are several, sometimes interrelated motives to explain the industry's current and expected future trend toward corporate consolidation:

1. To improve efficiency and effectiveness because by combining available resources and operations it is possible to exploit cost-reducing synergies and to take fuller advantage of risk-spreading, managed care opportunities.[6-8]
2. To enhance monopolistic-type powers by consummating horizon-tal and vertical acquisitions. Such mergers usually increase market share and total revenues that eventually flow from being the sole or one of the dominant providers in the region's health delivery system. The motivation of the network and the outcome for ser-vice area residents can be quite different in the case of a merger that results in an alliance attaining a 30 percent versus, say, an 80 percent market penetration.[9]
3. To avoid the possibility of being "left out" as other competing providers join powerful alliances. Often there is an underlying con-cern about whether freestanding hospitals or solo practitioners are able to survive in an increasingly aggressive, market-driven envi-ronment.
4. To attain that some health executives will seek acquisitions to attain the power, prestige, and additional perquisites of managing a larger organization, even though some mergers are considered from the outset to be ill advised and offer no appreciable enhance-ment in the delivery of the region's health services or in the reduc-tion of its health expenditures.[10]

Practicality Surrounding Mergers

Putting aside all these conceptual arguments for advocating mergers in the health field, the most frequently cited and practical reason for their increasing number is that many hospitals and physicians sense that in the future they will face lower levels of efficiency, most often illustrated in terms of significant operating and fiscal shortfalls. An organization's leaders might agree that they will perhaps become somewhat less competitive, yet that the problems will be "easily reparable" with some corporate restructuring, as providers expend significantly greater resources to evaluate how to "best survive" in the twenty-first century.

Smaller facilities with limited local competition, but experiencing increasing managed care penetration and a decreasing number of inpatient admissions, often select as their favored option being acquired by one of the region's major integrated health delivery systems. Once arriving at such a decision, they attempt to negotiate the most favorable merger conditions with the health network of their preference. Most frequent areas of discussion are governance, capital enhancement, and a guarantee for a specified period of time to remain unimpeded as a full-service, acute inpatient facility. A health alliance anxious to protect its existing market or envisioning the opportunity to capture additional tertiary referrals will expend significant fiscal resources to further its oligopolistic ambitions.

What may temporarily derail such merger discussions that are under way between "natural partners" is a competing alliance willing to offer even more attractive terms to consummate a specific amalgamation. In this process of forming these powerful networks, and particularly where the transactions are undertaken in environments in which HMOs are experiencing sizable increases in enrollment, these organizations' senior executives are often evaluated by their trustees, physicians, and peers on their ability to "put deals together," rather than on their skills at managing these increasingly diversified enterprises that are being merged into rapidly expanding health networks. Therefore, "by competitive bidding," some small hospitals may obtain resources from a network that far exceed the potential satellite's true worth to the alliance.

Because of possibly creating a monopoly, always somewhat worrisome is when two geographically contiguous hospitals, highly competitive for decades, decide to merge so that the new consolidated organization has 75 percent or more market penetration within their service area. Some of these mergers have occurred because one of the facilities fears that its historical competitor will be acquired by an out-of-town health network. Others are consummated because the two institutions have implicitly decided that, by merging into a new consolidated organization, the new entity will be far better positioned to control competitive forces (e.g., managed care plans needing a local provider, doctors demanding new technology at both facilities).

Encouraging these consolidations were freestanding hospitals as well as health networks being tested by their primary care physicians and even by specialty medical group practices concerning their continuing loyalty. Frequently, the alliances were being pressured to pay a premium price when acquiring these professional practices. Almost all of these hospital-physician transactions are being driven as a strategy for the integrated delivery systems to enhance their position in an increasingly competitive managed care marketplace and to react to an excess supply of inpatient facilities and of specialty physicians.

As a network's leadership becomes increasingly concerned by future Medicare and Medicaid shortfalls and by the fiscal incentives that are inherent in managed care (e.g., lower inpatient utilization and decreasing volume of specialist referrals), they will be pressured to implement an overall strategy of acquiring additional facilities and physician practices. This approach, in turn, will further their objective of at least sustaining their current market share and eventually achieving the position of being the region's predominant provider. In day-to-day merger negotiations a network's eminent clinical image and impressive fiscal reserves gained over the last decade or so, which allows its leadership to make deals more favorable to these acquired hospitals and physicians than is justified based on a realistic fiscal analysis, are critical.

Hospital and HMO mergers will continue to be presented in the public media as a means to improve access, reduce cost, and improve quality of care, but are they, in reality, achieving these objectives?

The Performance of Horizontal Mergers—Health Field

A serious study of the efficacy of horizontal mergers was begun in the early 1970s, and the evidence of achieving economic benefits from such amalgamations was judged at that time to be mixed at best. The major fiscal gains reported were in the administrative departments, in which labor-saving technology could be applied and in which turf battles with physicians could be avoided. While some cost reductions were demonstrable in the nonclinical areas, there was agreement early on that far greater savings are potentially possible "through the integration of patient care and medical service areas."[11]

In a somewhat later review article summarizing the empirical findings of multihospital systems, the weight of evidence indicated that horizontal mergers tended to increase the cost of healthcare.[12] This somewhat surprising finding occurred whether costs were measured as hospital expenses, charges, or revenues, on a per diem or per discharge basis. Stronger support for this conclusion was evident among the investor-owned than the not-for-profit systems.

An increasing number of health networks being formed during the past decade has heightened the interest in studying the efficacy of horizontal mergers. In a few specific cases (e.g., Hospital Research and Education Trust; Health Care Investment Analysts)[13–14] positive results were forthcoming. Probably the most successful amalgamations reported to date[15–19] are most easily identified as the consolidation of two medium-sized, high case-mix, not-for-profit hospitals located in the same community. Additional characteristics concerning such successful mergers include cases in which:

1. the market share of the two, similar-sized merged organizations is far greater than they had previously experienced separately. Thereby the new entity is potentially able to implement economies of scale and in its local marketplace can certainly better control prices charged for its health services.
2. there is significant opportunity for operational savings because of some agreements up front to consolidate at one facility several high fixed-cost services such as obstetrics and open-heart surgery; and,
3. there is significant pressure to reduce operating costs because an increased percentage of service area residents have enrolled in managed care plans, and, simultaneously, there are significant cutbacks in Medicare and Medicaid reimbursement.

Specific Hospital Merger Studies

When Alexander and his colleagues studied the short-term effects of hospital mergers occurring in the 1982–89 period, they uncovered improved operating efficiencies as measured by a higher percentage of occupancy (this could have resulted by simply reducing the available bed complement) and by a decreasing rise over a seven-year period in the percentage of total expenses per adjusted admission.[18] Unfortunately, the same merged facilities were relatively unsuccessful in generating more admissions when offering a broader range of clinical services and reducing their total personnel complement or nursing staffing patterns. The 92 mergers resulted in an overall slowing down of cost increases rather than demonstrating any dramatic improvement in these institutions' operating performance.

The short-term fiscal savings reported as a result of these amalgamations were generally modest and differed considerably in terms of the conditions under which and when the corporate amalgamation actually occurred. Mergers that were consummated after the Medicare prospective payment system (PPS) was introduced and those between similar-sized hospitals displayed greater positive improvements in operating patterns compared to those mergers occurring earlier or those between facilities of a dissimilar bed complement. These findings were explained by the increased cost pressures experienced after PPS was enacted (as now with the increased enrollment in managed care plans) and by the greater opportunities for potential operating efficiencies in mergers that involved facilities of similar sizes and services.

Somewhat similar findings were reported based on the responses received in 1991 from the leadership of 60 of the 74 mergers that were consummated between 1983 and 1988.[16] As somewhat anticipated, 42 percent of the hospitals that were acquired (i.e., the smaller of the two institutions) remained open as an acute care facility; 41 percent of the remaining facilities were converted to other services such as long-term care and substance abuse; and 17 percent were completely shuttered.

This study of 1983 through 1988 hospital mergers suggests two interrelated strategies, both of them much in vogue today: eliminating a number of direct competitors (i.e., two hospitals in the same primary care area consolidating their resources); and building the infrastructure for a larger integrated delivery system (e.g., a large teaching hospital acquiring a rural facility to protect its referral patterns). In both cases, however, the respondents emphasized as among the key factors in consummating the merger the strengthening of their financial positions and the consolidation of their administrative and clinical services.

Where one of the two hospitals' acute inpatient services was shuttered, the respondents indicated that prior to the merger these facilities had been highly competitive with each other for both inpatient and ambulatory care services. Yet when both institutions, after they were corporately amalgamated, continued to offer acute inpatient care, significantly fewer respondents reported that the pre-merger competition between the two facilities had been intense—probably because each hospital served a geographically different patient population.

Fortunately, more recently published studies give some indication where cost savings are possible through corporate consolidation. Connor and his colleagues analyzed changes in costs in 122 horizontal mergers and reported some modest savings (7.1 percent) among these facilities.[17] The most significant cost reductions from 1986 to 1994 were associated with those hospitals with low percentages of occupancy and with those that were identified as nonteaching, nonsystem, and not-for-profit institutions. Yet, when considering the potential impact of these networks being managed as oligopolies and, therefore, the possibility of needing to tighten up because of future antitrust policy, of significant concern should be this study's conclusion that hospital mergers occurring in the more concentrated market areas had a slight cost increase (+1.4 percent) rather than an anticipated decrease.

Merger-related cost savings in areas with a high group model HMO penetration were reported to be almost twice those with lower managed care market share. Since currently hospital amalgamations tend to occur in less concentrated environments and in areas with higher HMO penetration, the merger mania occurring in the last five years might well represent a direct response to providers sensing increasing future difficulties in "cutting deals" with price-sensitive managed care plans and, at the same time, attempting to position their alliances as quickly as is expedient to behave as oligopolies.

The study by Clement and her colleagues focusing on the financial performance of strategic hospital alliances nationwide (many of which included one or more mergers) concluded that these "networks" averaged $191 more in operating expenses per adjusted (for case-mix and outpatient services) discharge than comparable freestanding facilities.[20] Although hospitals with six or more years of experience with a strategic alliance (defined as two or more hospitals joining forces to compete with other institutions) generated in fiscal 1995 higher cash flows ($921 per bed), net revenues ($96 per adjusted discharge), and lower operating expenses ($26 per adjusted discharge), these differences were not statistically significant.

These findings are consistent with an earlier study that reported fiscal savings in hospital service areas with a more concentrated managed care penetration and with a large number of employees of a nationally recognized corporation.[21] After controlling for market, environmental, and hospital operational variables, however, this research endeavor also found that differences in cash flow and expenses between network and non-aligned facilities were not statistically significant.

Specific HMO Merger Studies

A driving force in these hospital mergers has been an increased enrollment in managed care plans from less than 2 million in 1970 to almost 67.6 million in 1995. This growth in the number of subscribers has not been matched by a comparable rise in the number of HMOs.[22] The total number of plans peaked in the 1980s, and, despite the entry of additional insurers, there has been a trend toward a greater concentration of enrollees among fewer managed care plans. The decline in the number of managed care plans has occurred because 149 HMOs folded between 1986 and 1993, and another 80 HMOs have vanished primarily through acquisition.[23]

A reduced number of HMOs in the marketplace should be of concern, since managed care plans that were experiencing more competition are reported to offer lower premiums.[24] These findings are consistent with an earlier study of a 1992 merger of two large HMOs located in the Twin Cities area that predicted that such an amalgamation would increase premiums,[25] the rationale being that, since a merger reduces the number of competitors in a specific marketplace, HMO mergers tend to raise premiums.

More recently, Feldman and his colleagues estimated the effect of managed care plan mergers on HMO premiums by using 1985–93 data of all operational non-Medicaid HMOs.[26] They focused on two questions: whether HMO mergers increase or decrease premiums; and whether the effects of mergers differ according to the degree of competition among HMOs in local markets. The most critical finding of this research was that HMOs in more competitive markets had lower premiums. Another major conclusion was that HMO mergers have not benefited consumers by providing the expected result of reducing premiums. Economies of scale, which supposedly result from HMO mergers, are thus not passed on to the public through decreased fringe benefit costs.

These findings of hospital and HMO mergers suggest that amalgamations may maintain or even enhance market share but "have not yet achieved significant economies despite the time and dollar resources that have been devoted to organizational restructuring."[20] The projected benefits to consumers of these amalgamations that were alluded to earlier in conceptual terms unfortunately have not been clearly demonstrated to date, even though healthcare markets have changed dramatically and the merger mania in the field still continues in a somewhat more restrained manner.

After the nation's alliances have matured, after their respective partners have centralized their clinical services rather than competing among themselves for revenues, and after implementing other cost-saving measures, the rightful potential benefits of mergers in the health field should finally be realized. Therefore, it is worth asking if the experience with mergers in other industries in the United States and elsewhere illustrates that what has been promised has been delivered by these amalgamations for the health field—eventually improving access, reducing cost, and enhancing the quality of patient care.

The Performance of Mergers in General

Since hospital and HMO amalgamations to date have been less than impressive in their fiscal and operational outcomes, the question arises whether the nonhealth field experiences dissimilar outcomes with horizontal integration. Most early mergers in the United States were evaluated as merely a "civilized alternative" to bankruptcy or to voluntary liquidation that would transfer assets from failing to rising firms.[27] Manne reported that voluntary mergers were often a means of "lessening wasteful bankruptcy proceedings" and served as a strategy for employing more effective management for companies that had previously operated poorly.[28]

Mergers in U.S. Publicly Traded Companies

There are a significant number of citations in the general management literature that evaluate the overall success and failure of mergers by using a company's pre-merger profitability or other, similar criteria.[29-35] This provides the opportunity to analyze whether the efficacy of mergers in U.S. publicly traded companies is consistent with that experienced to date in the health field.

First, publicly held corporations most successful in diversifying through acquisitions have tended to gravitate toward higher-growth sectors of the market and to products or services in which the acquirer can realize either selling or distributional economies of scale.[36-37] These findings help explain why the nation's health networks are often anxious to acquire competing acute facilities that are relatively profitable and that at the same time will enhance their ability to serve as the region's dominant provider.

Second, conclusions drawn concerning the efficacy of corporate amalgamations that are based on the pre-merger profitability of companies they have acquired depend upon how the initial sample is drawn and the timing and the criteria selected for the specific analysis.[38] Early studies in the United States focusing on large publicly traded companies determined that the acquired enterprises' profitability was slightly below their peers' and then in later studies was about the same or slightly above them.[39-40]

The more positive outcomes were frequently explained by acquirers seeking smaller related enterprises with superior profits or consummating an acquisition during a period in which they were improving their operating performance. Anecdotal evidence from the health field suggests that similar strategies are used by providers sensing serious future fiscal distress and, therefore, most anxious to be acquired by a network. Before and during the negotiation process they attempt to embellish their financial statements and other related documents to become as attractive as possible to their potential suitors.

Third, several studies reported that, as a result of a merger, an acquired company on the average demonstrates limited improvement over time in its operational and fiscal performance.[41-42] In fact, as an organization diversifies further from its major revenue stream, its productivity tends to decline.[43] Profitability is most often barely above the control group's level and is frequently below the acquired unit's pre-merger standing. A major exception experienced in all U.S. industries is among mergers of equals, particularly those involving management buyouts. These organizations outperform their control group and their pre-merger performance, primarily because the existing management knows how to "make the deal work."[44]

Fourth, it would be unrealistic to expect that all mergers will be problem free and that no divestitures will be necessary because of a desire to pay down long-term debt, overall financial distress, or a "misfit of objectives."[45] An important question, therefore, is whether a merger contributes to or inhibits the emergence of problems and how an acquisition eventually affects problem-solving strategies. Not surprising, conglomerate-type control (i.e., essentially unrelated in the goods produced and distributed) could make matters worse by:

a. further delay in resolving problems that continue to surface in a new and more complex organizational structure;
b. slowly draining from the business those resources that are actually required to undertake the problem-solving processes; and,
c. later on, often sapping managerial morale such as with an organizational mismatch between a parent and a subsidiary attempting to find appropriate solutions but each working from a different set of underlying assumptions.[46]

It could be argued whether the example of a major medical center acquiring several mid-size and small rural hospitals fits the definition of conglomerate control. In any case, the traditional, more institutionally oriented leadership, when responsible for an integrated delivery system, has shown evidence of experiencing more difficulty in managing more complicated organizational structures.[47] Furthermore, as physicians and hospitals argue privately or in the public media about who is ultimately responsible for setting quality standards and controlling the region's delivery of health services, the divestiture of the more clinical-medical aspects of these networks is expected to become a more common occurrence.

These "sell-offs" could be most simply explained by the parent's managerial experience being less well suited for this type of complex, clinical problem-solving environment.

Finally, consummating horizontal mergers should offer more attractive cost reduction opportunities than vertical integration because of the former's ability to implement enhanced managerial expertise across more closely allied operations and the possibilities for the post-merger integration of complementary or competing operations. Yet the differences in profitability among most horizontal and vertical mergers in the United States appear to be insignificant.[48]

Mergers Elsewhere—Europe and Canada

For additional evidence on the outcome of large horizontal mergers, the European and Canadian experiences could be directly relevant.[49-50] With weaker antitrust laws and governmental policies that often actively encourage large mergers, countries across the Atlantic Ocean provide a fertile environment for such comparative analysis. The weight of findings there is that predominantly horizontal, often large, European mergers on the average have exhibited little or no tendency to raise profitability or efficiency.[51] In fact, those companies that have been bought out, on the average, were appreciably less profitable than their acquirers or control groups.[31]

The Canadians have reported that there is little evidence that by their multihospital arrangements the quality of care was improved or deployment of hospital personnel was enhanced.[52] The most striking organizational benefit for these mergers in Canada has been the trustees, medical staff, and management team giving more explicit consideration to the facility's goals and objectives.

Enhanced Results in the Future?

Straddling parts of the business press and supported by a number of academics and consultants, there is an overall theme of a mixed, or at least significant, skepticism concerning the efficacy of past horizontal mergers. Except for the cases of an amalgamation of equal partners or a management buyout, corporate consolidations in the health and other industries have shown less than impressive results, particularly if they are to be gauged by the operational and fiscal objectives that are often promised early on by these corporate realignments.[53]

Possibly the main reasons why so many mergers yield disappointing results is that it takes years to visualize the positive outcomes of any corporate amalgamation; senior executives in the pre-merger period devote insufficient effort to studying critically how to make these mergers function most effectively; and the "deal makers" are overly optimistic how the potential partners' operation can be coordinated and integrated to achieve maximum efficiency. Equally important is for the various groups' leadership to identify what cultural, strategic, and administrative problems could arise that might interfere with a newly merged organization in attaining its projected goals and objectives. All too often, the principal deal makers have simply viewed the contemplated amalgamation too optimistically.[54]

The jury is still out in the United States whether by federal-state antitrust regulators approving almost all mergers (i.e., allowing providers to boost their market penetration) these amalgamations will eventually result in more effective and efficient local health delivery systems. There is certainly also the possibility of a massive number of additional horizontal mergers in the health field revealing such clear and important consequences as the networks demonstrating monopolistic behavior.[55]

Equally critical to the analysis is that corporate restructuring does exhibit the theoretical capabilities of achieving significant operating efficiencies. The research on horizontal mergers among major U.S. and European companies, however, like most of the evidence to date in the health field, provides limited support to argue that on average the efficiency gains through a hospital or HMO merger will be appreciable.[56-57] What may be necessary to make mergers actually "work" is to search for some additional reimbursement incentives (e.g., global budgetary targets as used in many Western industrialized nations) and to implement some politically more onerous internal and external managerial decisions that primarily focus on reducing costs without adversely affecting the quality of patient care.

Some Broad Implications of Merger Mania

Since the current trend toward corporate consolidations in the health field is expected to continue, it is relevant to ask how the current merger mania will specifically affect hospitals, physician practice groups, insurers, and most decisively the public in the next decade and what positive actions might be taken by those in their key public policy positions.

Hospitals

To make mergers function more effectively and efficiently during the next decade, among those measures that the leadership of health networks will need to evaluate with increasing frequency are:

1. Shuttering superfluous hospitals, because closing an entire acute care facility has the most significant positive impact on reducing costs: it eliminates almost all variable and some fixed expenditures. This option, however, is almost always fraught with opposition because of reduced access to services, loss of community pride and jobs, and the concern of medical staff members about where in the future community-based doctors will practice and where hospital-based doctors will work. Although in some cases shuttering of a facility or a major clinical service is known at the outset to be the most appropriate solution, such discussions during merger negotiations or soon thereafter can result in some nasty wrangling; therefore, their formal pursuit tends to be avoided for an extended period at almost all costs.[58]

2. Centralizing virtually all tertiary services at major medical centers, such as evidenced in Canada and Germany (table 4), so that significantly increased volumes at higher levels of quality and at a reduced cost can be provided. Where and when appropriate, the possible consolidation of such clinical departments as emergency, obstetrics, pathology, radiology, and other similar activities should be undertaken—amalgamations that also have the potential impact of improving quality of care and of cost savings. How a network's leadership can placate those physicians and employees, who are adversely affected by such consolidations of clinical services, becomes a critical issue.

3. Eliminating a layer of management in every facility, an option that could be more readily implemented by simplifying our existing complicated prepayment system. In most mergers white-collar middle managers are more adversely effected than blue-collar employees when measured by the percentage of terminated positions and by future earnings.[59]

The German multipayer, quasi-competitive and quasi-regulatory approach might eventually be sought after as the appropriate model to provide Americans with comprehensive health insurance coverage.[60] In this central European country there is universal coverage, access to services is readily available, facilities and physicians self-police their colleagues, and their reimbursement rates are set within global budgetary targets. This prepayment approach, which would be opposed by most providers and insurers here, could potentially reduce current administrative expenses in the United States health industry by half (table 4).

While some of the cost reduction and quality enhancement measures outlined earlier are under way, networks positioned with an academic health center or a large major medical center as their "central hub" will utilize significant resources to become the region's dominant provider as expeditiously as possible. This strategy is used to increase referrals to the subspecialists on their medical staffs. The Catholic and investor-owned health systems are expected to experience greater difficulty than the non-secular and other not-for-profits in organizing a network in which their hub functions as the area's dominant provider, mainly because they generally tend to sponsor satellite facilities that are more geographically dispersed and are usually not among the region's most clinically sophisticated.

A network's leaders might be reluctant to implement any of the suggested cost-saving measures with any dispatch, primarily because such strategies might discourage possible opportunities for other future mergers. The appearance of an alliance guaranteeing one hospital as a condition of joining their network to remain viable as a full-service, acute care facility for at least five more years and, concurrently, shuttering an acquisition made three years earlier (without having agreed to similar assurances) raises negative impressions concerning the organization's commitment to deliver on its promises. In many cases significant cost-cutting,

TABLE 4.   Comparison of Medical Technology Availability and Operational Data: Canada, West Germany, and the United States, 1990–93

Variable	Canada	West Germany	United States
Health expenditure as % of gross domestic product (percentage)	9.0 (1997)	10.4 (1997)*	13.5 (1997)
Cardiac catheterization services per million	2.93 (1993)	3.41 (1993)	6.24 (1990)
MRI services per million	1.3 (1995)	5.7 (1996)*	16.0 (1995)
Radiation services per million	1.35 (1993)	4.57 (1993)	3.90 (1993)
Open heart services per million	1.69 (1993)	0.75 (1993)	3.52 (1993)
Lithotripsy service per million	0.45 (1993)	1.14 (1993)	2.00 (1993)
Hospital operating expense per discharge (dollars)	3,815 (1990)	2,972 (1990)	6,535 (1990)
Paid hours per hospital discharge	285 (1990)	144.4 (1990)	321 (1990)
Total administrative and fiscal paid hours per discharge	14.84 (1990)	NA	34.23 (1990)
Total administrative and fiscal direct expense per hospital discharge (dollars)	336 (1990)	211 (1990)	496 (1990)

Sources: G. F. Anderson and J.-P. Poullier. "Health Spending, Access, and Outcomes: Trends in Industrialized Nations," *Health Affairs* 18, no. 3 (1999): 178–92; T. P. Weil, "Comparisons of Medical Technology in Canadian, German, and U.S. Hospitals," *Hospital and Health Services Administration* 40, no. 4 (1995): 524–34; T. P. Weil, "How Do Canadian Hospitals Do It? A Comparison of Utilization and Costs in the United States and Canada," *Hospital Topics* 73, no. 1 (1995): 10–22; and T. P. Weil, "Health Reform in Germany: An American Assesses the New Operating Efficiencies," *Health Progress* 75, no. 7 (1994): 24–29.

Note: * Includes the former East Germany.

operational decisions will be required in the future by an all too often reluctant health leadership as the field becomes more quarrelsome with networks attempting to reduce expenses, improve their bottom lines, and enhance their quality of patient care.

Physicians and Medical Group Practices

Facing an increasing supply of available doctors (particularly specialists), a decrease in reimbursement per unit of service, and a rise in the percentage of gross revenues expended for office overhead, an attractive option for a number of physicians and medical groups is to be "bought out" by a nearby health network. This alternative is particularly advantageous if the alliance is willing to assist with the day-to-day management of these practices.

Hospitals are anxious to bond with their primary care physicians and particularly their major admitters and until relatively recently were willing to offer attractive cash terms and performance agreements. These arrangements between acute care facilities and physician groups, however, are destined over the next decade to result in highly contentious disputes because (1) physicians, once having been bought out, expect to work less and earn more; and (2) hospitals, having made sizable investments in acquiring these practices, anticipate additional inpatient admissions from these doctors and expect to secure a reasonable return on their capital expenditures.

While the growth in HMO enrollment has encouraged physician groups to "sell their practices," the fiscal incentives in managed care (i.e., reduced utilization and cost), and how the available premium dollars are divided between doctors and hospitals, are among the major constraints that complicate reaching any potential operational and fiscal agreements between an acute care facility and its medical staff.

With a decline in the dollars available for direct medical care services adjusted for healthcare inflation, physicians and hospitals, particularly when one or both are highly leveraged, will become involved in disputes that are primarily related to a significant growth sector of the market—whether specific ambulatory care services should be provided in doctors' offices or under the hospital's aegis. As a result of either financial distress or a "misfit of objectives," a large number of divestitures of physician practices or of medical group practices from health networks is likely. Whether U.S. medical schools, in view of current healthcare and particularly physician manpower trends, will significantly curtail their enrollments is questionable. Therefore, in almost every upper- and middle-income community there is or will be a surplus of specialty physicians and a restricted number eligible (because of being excluded from specific panels) to receive payment from some HMOs.

Although the issue is intertwined with some controversial constitutional issues, Medicare physician provider numbers could potentially be allocated by health service area and by specialty, as is now partially implemented in Germany,[61–62] in order to improve America's current poor geographic distribution of doctors. As a result of potentially tying physician office locations to the ability to bill Medicare and the major HMOs, those living in less desirable areas might as a result benefit from an improved access to a broader spectrum of medical services—an unexpected outcome of managed care and mergers in the health field.

Insurers

What is evident during the past several years among the nation's health insurers is their propensity toward corporate consolidations and, whenever possible, conversions from a not-for-profit to a for-profit ownership structure. In the most competitive markets, implementing premium increases is reported as the only significant effect of consummating HMO mergers.[26] What is so often overlooked is that these third-party payers are both the financiers and bankers of the United States' healthcare system and generally have significantly greater fiscal reserves to provide direct health services than those they reimburse.

The proposed thrust of the integrated delivery systems establishing provider-sponsored organizations (PSOs) so as to serve their communities as third-party carriers and at the same time to compete against the nation's major insurers has a number of potential pitfalls:

1. the health networks will be moving farther way from their prime business of delivering hands-on patient care;
2. the networks will need to recruit the management and technical expertise required to establish a sound health insurance endeavor, viewed as an onerous task;
3. only a few of the nation's health networks will be able to compete successfully with the fiscal resources of the United States' leading third-party payers; and,
4. network trustees will be hesitant to authorize high-risk, highly leveraged long-term borrowing to establish a PSO that is secured by the network's facilities. The position of an alliance's board simply could be: Why form a new HMO, when nationally managed care is such a highly competitive business and is experiencing declining profit margins and philosophically is not overly well received by the American public?

While the network's trustees review the advisability of funding PSOs, the leadership in academic health and major medical centers, in particular, will be encouraged by their clinical faculty and by the tertiary physicians in affiliated teaching environments to form their own HMOs to compete with Blue Cross / Blue Shield and other major insurers. There are serious competitive concerns among these major teaching centers because of their greater hospital and physician costs and because most managed care plans will contract with other providers, leaving them with a far more limited patient base for teaching purposes and with sharp decreases in their physicians' private practice plan revenues.

Although the outcomes of these mergers will be dependent on a number of variables specific to that metropolitan area, conflicts will become more contentious than is currently anticipated among the powerful networks and the insurers, each with a large percentage of market penetration in the same region. In some ways these turf battles will be between those with the highest level of clinical acumen versus those who maintain control over the region's healthcare dollars. More networks made up primarily of providers in increasing numbers will merge with the area's major third-party payer, suggesting even greater concentration of resources. Although some HMOs are currently experiencing fiscal difficulties because of declining operating margins, it is predicted that the United States' major insurers could well be the eventual winners, since they more directly control the flow of vast amounts of premium dollars.

The Public

Some hospital and HMO mergers in more concentrated market areas are reporting cost savings that are either marginal or even negative.[17, 26] As a result, the current competitive environment, as it is now being pursued, must be accompanied by more carefully considered regulations and be implemented by capable regulators who are able to protect the public interest without crippling innovation and efficiency. Of particular concern to consumers are the providers that engage in antisocial behavior to the disadvantage of patients, their community, third-party payers, and various lenders.[63]

It is often judged to take a minimum of several years for a new parent company to effect significant improvements in a subsidiary's productivity. This impression for the past two decades has provided a valid argument for antitrust prohibitions in the health industry that for the most part now remain in a state of flux, with governmental leniency continuing to be the overriding policy. In this environment the Department of Justice and the Federal Trade Commission have significant difficulty in walking the thin line that allows for the concepts of consolidation and competition, which are usually in opposition, to flourish.[64–67]

Eventually, what could provide the impetus for state officials to introduce legislation to establish health services commissions[68] are the monopolistic-type practices of health networks that enjoy a high percentage of market share in their service areas, and Medicare, Medicaid, and other third-party payers ratcheting down their reimbursements to hospitals, physicians, home care agencies, nursing homes, and other providers, resulting in further restricting access and even less social equity among the underserved. Such public utilities, in conjunction with the state departments of insurance and public health, could result in new and more complex regulatory layers, a concept that would be strongly opposed by major employers, providers, and insurers.

Aside from the valid argument that the regulatory process has not worked well to date in the U.S. health field,[69] the practical outcome is that, because of their vested interests and using their political muscle, the providers would rather quickly dominate the statutory authorities. This battle between government and the marketplace is already remaking the health field.

Making Horizontal Mergers Work

Fortunately, pluralism is one of the United States' defining cultural characteristics, and, therefore, in developing public policies for antitrust, anti-fraud, anti-abuse, health planning, and reimbursement rate-setting rules and regulations, a balanced approach of combining the best of what the competitive and regulatory concepts have to offer provides a practical compromise. Within this framework of multiple competing values and beliefs, a mixture of these two concepts, as implemented in Arizona, California, and Oregon, in setting Medicaid HMO and hospital reimbursement rates appears to provide some practical gains that are consistent with price competition, protecting the public interest, and decreasing healthcare expenditures.[70-71] These approaches should force many health networks to pursue the public interest continually within the context of what might simply be called a regulated monopoly.

It is unfortunate that in the United States the relationship between government and the marketplace is being driven by a very basic trend: a growing cynicism and skepticism about the role of government itself. Distrust of government is part of the American political scene, although in periods of crisis voters look to public officials to resolve their problems. The New Deal and World War II for the most part built confidence in government, and the Kennedy administration inspired a generation with idealism about the role of public service. In the mid-1960s, however, cynicism began to emerge as a powerful trend, stoked by the Vietnam War and domestic disturbances. Watergate and the economic travails of the 1970s further fueled the feeling.

President Clinton came into office in 1993 as a "New Democrat" and, after the overwhelming defeat of his national health insurance initiative, he proclaimed the end of the era of big government, signed a massive welfare reform bill, and promoted free markets as a fundamental objective of U.S. foreign policy now that the cold war was over. But such changes are relative. When a Republican Congress fervently sought to roll back a vast agenda of aid programs, it found that the public was not about to give up its social safety net (e.g., social security and Medicare benefits) or its basic commitment to education and the environment. A new middle actually may have emerged in American politics. It is characterized by an end to the growth of government in many spheres, some rolling back, some devolution, a continuing battle over government's expansion in the realm of social values, and a drive to adapt the mechanisms of the competitive approach to the activities of government.

A quick and naive reading of the arguments contained herein, therefore, is that most hospitals, physicians, and insurers would be just as well-off remaining freestanding in a blended competitive-regulatory environment in which the emphasis is on practicality rather than ideological exactness. Since the American health field struggles with improved access, social equity, cost reduction, and enhancing quality of patient care as its pivotal issues, and expense retrenchment and negative public opinion concerning the health industry are now key variables, a more accurate assessment is that far greater attention should be directed to making mergers function more effectively and efficiently. This is to occur in what already encompasses a quasi-competitive and quasi-regulatory environment (e.g., roughly half the U.S. health expenditures come from the public sector).

Public pressure to make mergers in the health industry work "better" to improve access and reduce costs can soon be expected to escalate, particularly where providers have a highly concentrated market share and manage their resources as an oligopoly. Moving toward being price and access sensitive will require that the region's health networks eventually grapple with a complex set of facts and issues concerning the overall policy implications relating to the nation's current merger mania. Thereafter, the health field's leadership and responsible public officials will be forced to reach some workable and practical compromises that balance clinical and business concerns in a highly complex and politically charged environment. These fundamental changes will result in a milieu that transcends competitive and regulatory approaches when reducing redundancies and implementing management efficiencies. Thereby, the nation's health executives will find a pathway to achieve a more effective U.S. healthcare system—something previously promised by mergers that were formed over the last decade without much public scrutiny but which are now briskly evolving into politically and fiscally powerful health networks.

REFERENCES

1. *Economic Report of the President,* 196. Washington, D.C.: Office of the President, February 1985.
2. Weil, T. P., and Jorgensen, N. E. "A Tripartite Regulation of Health Networks." *Journal of Public Health Management* 2, no. 3 (1996): 46–53.
3. Shortell, S. M. "The Evolution of Hospital Systems: Unfulfilled Promises and Self-Fulfilling Prophesies." *Health Services Research* 45, no. 2 (1988): 177–214.
4. *Health Care Merger and Acquisition Monthly.* New Canaan, Conn.: Irving Levin and Associates, 1998.
5. Brooks, G. R., and Jones, V. G. "Hospital Mergers and Market Overlap." *Health Services Research* 31, no. 6 (1997): 701–22.
6. Lynk, W. J. "The Creation of Economic Efficiencies in Hospital Mergers." *Journal of Health Economics* 14, no. 5 (1995): 507–30.
7. Shortell, S. M., Giles, R. R., Anderson, D. A., Erickson, K. M., and Mitchell, J. B. *Remaking Healthcare in America: Building Organized Delivery Systems.* San Francisco: Jossey Bass, 1996.
8. Zuckerman, H. S., and Kaluzny, A. D. "Strategic Alliances in Health Care: The Challenges of Cooperation." *Frontiers of Health Services Management* 7, no. 3 (1991): 3–23, 35.
9. Mobley, L. R. "Tacit Collusion among Hospitals in Price Competitive Markets." *Health Economics* 5, no. 3 (1996): 183–93.
10. Snail, T. S., and Robinson, J. C. "Organizational Diversification in the American Hospital." *Annual Review of Public Health* 19 (1998): 417–53.
11. Zuckerman, H. S. "Multi-Institutional Systems: Promise and Performance." *Inquiry* 16, no. 4 (1979): 300.
12. Ermann, D., and Gabel, J. "Multihospital Systems: Issues and Empirical Findings." *Health Affairs* 3, no. 1 (1984): 50–64.
13. Burda, D. "Study on Mergers Cut Costs, Services, Increases Profits." *Modern Healthcare* 23, no. 46 (1993): 4.
14. Greene, J. "Merger Monopolies." *Modern Healthcare* 24, no. 49 (1994): 38–48.
15. Anderson, H. J. "AHA Lists Hospital Merger Activity for a 12-Year Period." *Hospitals* 66, no. 12 (1992): 62–63.
16. Bogue, R. J., Shortell, S. M., Sohn, M.-W., Manheim, L. M., Bazzoli, G.,

and Chan, C. "Hospital Reorganization after Merger." *Medical Care* 33, no. 7 (1995): 676–96.

17. Connor, R. A., Feldman, R., Dowd, B. E., and Radcliff, T. A. "Which Types of Hospital Mergers Save Consumers Money?" *Health Affairs* 16, no. 6 (1997): 62–74.

18. Alexander, J. A., Halpern, M. T., and Lee, S.-T.-D. "The Short-Term Effects of Merger on Hospital Operations." *Health Services Research* 30, no. 6 (1996): 827–47.

19. Economic and Social Research Institute (ESRI). "Assessing the Early Impact of Hospital Mergers: An Analysis of St. Louis and Philadelphia Markets." Washington, D.C.: ESRI, 1998.

20. Clement, J. P., McCue, M. J., Luke, R. D., Bramble, J. D., Rossiter, L. F., Ozcan, Y. A., and Pai, C. W. "Strategic Hospital Alliances: Impact on Financial Performance." *Health Affairs* 16, no. 6 (1997): 193–203.

21. Robinson, J. C. "HMO Market Penetration and Hospital Cost Inflation in California." *Journal of the American Medical Association* 266, no. 19 (1991): 2719–23.

22. Hoechst Marion Roussel (HMR). *HMO-PPO Digest, 1996.* Kansas City: HMR, 1997.

23. Feldman, R., Wholey, D. R., and Christianson, J. B. "A Descriptive Economic Analysis of HMO Mergers and Failures, 1985–1992." *Medical Care Research and Review* 52, no. 2 (1995): 279–304.

24. Wholey, D. R., Feldman, R., and Christianson, J. B. "The Effect of Market Structure on HMO Premiums." *Journal of Health Economics* 14, no. 1 (1995): 81–105.

25. Feldman, R. "The Welfare Economics of a Health Plan Merger." *Journal of Regulatory Economics* 6, no. 1 (1994): 67–86.

26. Feldman, R., Wholey, D. R., and Christianson, J. B. "Effect of Mergers on the Health Maintenance Organization Premiums." *Health Care Financing Review* 17, no. 3 (1996): 171–89.

27. Dewey, D. "Mergers and Cartels: Some Reservation about Policy (in Anti-Trust Problems)." *American Economic Review* 51, no. 2 (1961): 257.

28. Manne, H. G. "Mergers and the Market for Corporate Control." *Journal of Political Economy* 73, no. 2 (1965): 110–20.

29. Louis, A. M. "The Bottom Line on Ten Big Mergers." *Fortune* 105, no. 10 (1982): 84–89.

30. Ravenscraft, D. J., and Scherer, F. M. *Mergers, Sell-Offs, and Economic Efficiency.* Washington, D.C.: Brookings Institution, 1987.

31. Bishop, M., and Key, J. A. *European Mergers and Merger Policy.* London: Oxford University Press, 1993.

32. Blackstone, E. A., and Fuhr, J. P., Jr. "Hospital Mergers and Antitrust: An Economic Analysis." *Journal of Health Politics, Policy and Law* 14, no. 2 (1989): 383–403.

33. McKinsey and Company. "The Role of the Corporate Center." MS, October 1984. This study found that only six of the fifty-eight companies it studied had

achieved returns on their merger-based diversification programs that exceeded their cost of capital.

34. Blecher, M. B. "Size Does Matter." *Hospitals and Health Networks* 72, no. 12 (1998): 28–36.

35. Passell, P. "Do Mergers Really Yield Big Results?" *New York Times,* May 14, 1998, C1.

36. Drucker, P. "Why Some Mergers Work and Many More Don't." *Forbes* 129, no. 2 (1982): 34–36.

37. Schlender, B. "The Bill and Warren Story." *Fortune* 138, no. 2 (1998): 48–64.

38. Hirshman, A. O. *Exit, Voice and Loyalty: Responses to Decline in Firms, Organizations, and States.* Cambridge, Mass.: Harvard University Press, 1981.

39. Boyle, S. E. "Pre-Merger Growth and Profit Characteristics of Large Conglomerate Mergers in the United States, 1948–1968." *St. John's Law Review* 44, no. 1 (1970): 152–70.

40. Harris, R. S., Stewart, J. F., and Carleton, W. T. "Financial Characteristics of Acquired Firms." In Kennan, M., and White, L. J., eds., *Mergers and Acquisitions: Current Problems in Perspective,* 236. Lexington, Mass.: Lexington Books, 1982.

41. Scherer, F. M., and Ross, D. *Industrial Market Structure and Economic Performance.* Boston: Houghton Mifflin, 1990.

42. Gunn, E. P. "Premium Priced." *Fortune* 139, no. 2 (1999): 99–102.

43. Stewart, J. F., and Kim, S.-K. "Mergers and Social Welfare in U.S. Manufacturing, 1985–86. *Southern Economic Journal* 59, no. 4 (1993): 701–20.

44. Jansen, M. C. "The Takeover Controversy: Analysis and Evidence." In Coffee, J. C., Jr., Lowenstein, L., and Ackerman, S. R., eds., *Knights, Raiders and Targets: The Impact of the Hostile Takeover.* Cambridge: Oxford University Press, 1988.

45. Clement, J. P., and McCue, M. J. "The Performance of Hospital Corporation of America and Healthtrust Hospitals after Leveraged Buyouts." *Medical Care* 34, no. 7 (1996): 672–85.

46. Thomas, L. G. *The Economics of Strategic Planning: Essays in Honor of Joel Dean,* 143–70. Lexington, Mass.: Lexington Books, 1986.

47. Goldsmith, J. "Hospital/Physician Relationships: A Constraint to Health Reform." *Health Affairs* 12, no. 3 (1993): 160–69.

48. Mueller, D. C. "Mergers and Market Share." *Review of Economics and Statistics* 65, no. 5 (1985): 261–66.

49. Mueller, D. C. *The Determinants and Effects of Merger: An International Comparison,* 299–302. Cambridge, Mass.: Oelgeschlager, Gunn and Hain, 1980.

50. Geroski, P. A., and Jacquemin, A. "Large Firms in the European Corporate Economy and Industrial Policy in 1980s." In Jacquemin, A., ed., *European Industry: Public Policy and Corporate Strategy,* 344–49. New York: Clarendon Press, 1984.

51. Cowling, K., et al. *Mergers and Economic Performance.* Cambridge: Cambridge University Press, 1980.

52. Markham, B., and Lomas, J. 1995. "Review of the Multi-Hospital Arrangements Literature: Benefits, Disadvantages, and Lessons for Implementation." *Healthcare Management Forum* 8, no. 3 (1995): 24–35.

53. Litchenberg, F. R. *Corporate Takeovers and Productivity.* Cambridge, Mass.: MIT Press, 1992.

54. Roll, R. "The Hubris Hypothesis of Corporate Takeovers." *Journal of Business* 59, no. 2 (1986): 197–216.

55. Farrell, J., and Shapiro, C. "Horizontal Mergers: An Equilibrium Analysis." *American Economic Review* 80, no. 1 (1990): 107–27.

56. Dranove, D. "Economies of Scale in Non–Revenue Producing Cost Centers: Implications for Hospital Mergers." *Journal of Health Economics* 17, no. 1 (1998): 69–83.

57. Woolley, J. M. "The Competitive Effects of Horizontal Mergers in the Health Industry: An Even Closer Look." *Journal of Health Economics* 10, no. 3 (1991): 373–78.

58. Dolan, R., and Weil, T. P. "The Mergers in the Health Field: Enhancing Human Resources Management." *Physician Executive* 24, no. 2 (1998): 12–18.

59. Marks, M. L., and Mirves, P. H. "Track the Impact of Mergers and Acquisitions." *Personnel Journal* 71, no. 4 (1992): 70–79.

60. Henke, K. D., Murray, M. A., and Ade, C. "Global Budgeting in Germany: Lessons for the United States." *Health Affairs* 13, no. 4 (1994): 7–21.

61. Weil, T. P. "Health Reform in Germany: An American Assesses the New Operating Efficiencies." *Health Progress* 75, no. 6 (1994): 24–29.

62. Weil, T. P., and Brenner, G. "Physician and Other Ambulatory Services in Germany." *Journal of Ambulatory Care Management* 20, no. 1 (1997): 77–91.

63. Allen, R. "Policy Implications of Recent Hospital Competition Studies." *Journal of Health Economics* 11, no. 3 (1992): 347–51.

64. Zwanziger, J. "Commentary—The Need for an Antitrust Policy for a Health Care Industry in Transition." *Journal of Health Politics, Policy and Law* 20, no. 1 (1995): 171–74.

65. Bazzoli, G. J., et al. "Federal Antitrust Merger Enforcement Standards: A Good Fit for the Health Industry." *Journal of Health Politics, Policy and Law* 20, no. 1 (1995): 137–69.

66. Nguyen, N. X., and Derrick, F. W. "Hospital Markets and Competition: Implications for Antitrust Policy." *Health Care Management Review* 19, no. 1 (1994): 34–43.

67. Whitesell, S. E., and Whitesell, W. E. "Hospital Mergers and Antitrust: Some Economic and Legal Issues." *American Journal of Economics and Sociology* 54, no. 3 (1995): 305–22.

68. Weil, T. P. "How Health Networks and HMOs Could Result in Public Utility Regulation." *Hospital and Health Services Administration* 41, no. 2 (1996): 266–80.

69. Glied, S., Sparer, M., and Brown, L. D. "Comment: Containing Health Care Expenditures in the Competition vs. Regulation Debate." *American Journal of Public Health* 85, no. 10 (1995): 1347–49.

70. Weil, T. P., and Battistella, R. M. "A Blended Strategy Using Competitive and Regulatory Models." *Health Care Management Review* 23, no. 1 (1997): 37–45.

71. Dranove, D., Shanley, M., and White, W. D. "Price and Concentration in Hospital Markets: The Switch from Patient-Driven to Payer-Driven Competition." *Journal of Law and Economics* 36, no. 1 (1993): 179–204.

4

Is Vertical Diversification Adding Value to Health Networks?

ABSTRACT.   Vertical diversification is a concept that continues to be used by health networks when attempting to achieve economies of scale, greater coordination of services, and improved market penetration. This chapter focuses on the actual outcomes of utilizing vertical integration in the health field and then compares these findings to those reported in other industries. The analysis concludes that this organizational model does not work particularly well in the health industry, as most clearly illustrated by the poor fiscal performance experienced when health alliances or integrated health systems acquire physician practices or when they start their own HMO plans.

One of the most demanding decisions that a health network confronts is whether and when to diversify vertically. Success stories abound, thinking of such companies as General Electric, Disney, and Citicorp. Yet there are probably an equal, though less well-publicized, number of costly failures, such as RCA's forays into computers, carpets, and rental cars and Quaker Oats' entry and then quick exit from the fruit juice business with Snapple.

What makes vertical diversification for health networks (that consist primarily of hospitals) so unpredictable and such a high-stakes game is that their management teams often face critical decision making in an atmosphere and with a timetable that are not necessarily conducive to careful strategic analysis. The major owner of an investor-owned, long-term care facility that is two blocks away from the alliance's largest hospital suddenly decides to obtain a buyer for his long-term care facility because of an impending divorce decree. The county health department's home health care agency faces serious regulatory and fiscal problems, and local politicians pressure the network's leadership for this service to be acquired as expeditiously as possible.

When deciding whether to continue diversifying vertically, a health network's leadership usually considers these questions at the outset:

1. Will this proposed vertically diversified acquisition improve the network's quality of patient care and concurrently reduce the region's total health expenditures?

2. What does the health network achieve by consummating such a vertically diversified acquisition? Will the health network be able to enhance the value of this "new" venture and, if so, with what level of investment and within what time frame?
3. With this potential acquisition will the health network be simply just another player in this new market, or will the alliance be the dominant provider of such services?
4. What additional resources does the health network need to bring "to the table" in order to succeed with this potential new acquisition? Will this proposed vertically diversified project take away resources that would better serve other existing, worthwhile endeavors?
5. Does the network currently have the necessary management skills available to operate this new endeavor effectively and efficiently, or must it recruit additional staff?
6. Finally, will the values and culture of the health network and those of the potential acquisition, the latter often having a different patient care focus, be reasonably compatible, and will these two entities arrive at shared goals and objectives within a reasonable period of time?

What Is Vertical Diversification and What Are Its Benefits?

Unlike horizontal diversification in the health field, in which two hospitals merge, vertical integration attempts to bring under one organizational umbrella additional or, in a few cases, almost all of the various healthcare activities that are necessary for the provision of improved patient care. A simple example is a home health care agency vertically diversifying by acquiring a durable medical equipment company to provide supplies and equipment to the region's homebound sick more effectively and efficiently.

A hospital-oriented health network can vertically integrate by acquiring and then establishing under one corporate umbrella almost all the means of organizing, managing, and financing the region's health services. Such a model could include assuming a continuum of care that starts with primary care physicians' offices, extends through all acute in- and outpatient services, also provides for institutional and homebound long-term care, and even entails establishing an appropriate insurance mechanism so that residents within the region can prepay a majority of their health expenditures.

If and how vertical integration is approached is frequently contingent upon the network's leadership deciding on "to make" versus "to buy" decisions. Management has to analyze the effectiveness and efficiency of pursuing such linkages through market transactions made at arm's length, long-term contracts, unified ownership, or a combination thereof. A mini-regional, rural health center can be organized by an acute hospital selling adjacent land at just below market value to entice a not-for-profit long-term care organization, the offices of most members of its medical staff, a regionally based home health care agency, and an investor-owned durable medical equipment company all to be located on the hospital's "campus." For a rural hospital without any competitors nearby, it may not be necessary for the facility to integrate vertically under one corporate umbrella. The area's residents can obtain a broad range of vertically diversified health services on "one site." But in terms of its governance responsibilities, interestingly, the hospital itself does not meet the usual definition of being an "owned" vertically diversified network.

In the health field the presumed benefits of vertical integration relate to eliminating unneeded services, providing potential economies of scale that result in lower costs, increasing market penetration, improving negotiating power with HMOs, adding profits, generating gains in market share, improving recruitment and retention of physicians, and encouraging wider public acceptance of the network serving as the region's major health resource.[1] Theoretically, vertical diversification should enhance the health status of the population by improving clinical and administrative integration, creating marketplace efficiencies when shuttering unnecessary capacity, eliminating unnecessary care, and concentrating responsibility for providing a broad continuum of care.

How effectively a health network is vertically integrated is frequently judged not on its profitability but by the outcome of heated disputes when the alliance's political muscle is tested. This evaluation can occur when negotiating with managed care plans, medical group practices, suppliers, and public agencies. In fact, how well a health network is vertically diversified could be more important in the short term in facilitating market domination than the slightly improved profitability and quality of patient care or reduced costs provided by the alliance.

Outcomes of Vertically Diversified Strategies

Healthcare services in the United States are increasingly provided through arrangements that lead to greater coordination along the conventional continuum of patient care (primary through tertiary services), in spite of the fact that only limited empirical research is available to evaluate whether vertical diversification actually enhances revenues, access, and quality of care or reduces cost.

A study that investigated the decision among California hospitals to vertically integrate into subacute care by developing hospital-based skilled nursing facilities (SNFs) reported that those acute care facilities with a relatively high percentage of Medicare patients and those sponsored by not-for-profit groups were significantly more likely to develop a hospital-based SNF.[2] While presumed economies of scale were an important factor, experiencing a low percentage of occupancy and local competitive market conditions were not significant variables when California hospitals decided to diversify into subacute care. These determinations were primarily driven by an artifact of the state's pricing of skilled nursing home care, which put market contracting solutions such as affiliations at a disadvantage and encouraged acute facilities to provide long-term care services themselves.

Earlier, when the effects of diversifying vertically on hospital financial performance were studied, the research focused on the level of profits as measured by the return on assets (ROA).[3] Unfortunately, it was reported that increased profitability was not associated with a health network undertaking prior vertical diversification strategies. In fact, vertical diversification did not even increase the hospital's short-term profits, nor did it improve the "bottom line" of the financially weakest hospitals. Clement and her colleagues then later studied the effects of related and unrelated hospital vertical diversification during 1987 on the financial performance of 35 not-for-profit hospitals in Virginia.[4] Their analysis included 162 service-producing subsidiaries spanning 14 products. The research team concluded that related diversification (e.g., acquiring an ambulatory care center) resulted in far better short-term financial performance (e.g., operating margins) than unrelated diversification (e.g., wellness center), although these differences were lessened when measured by such long-term performance indicators as ROA.

These findings were later reaffirmed in a study that evaluated the effect on revenues from 1983 to 1990 of 7 vertically integrated strategies among 242 not-for-profit hospitals in California.[5] The strategies investigated were managed care contracts, physician affiliations, ambulatory care, ambulatory surgery, home health services, inpatient rehabilitation, and skilled nursing care. The major finding was that prehospital strategies (e.g., hospital-based ambulatory care and day surgery) increased total revenue, but posthospital strategies (e.g., hospital-based inpatient rehabilitation and skilled nursing care) decreased revenue.

From 1985 through 1987 vertical diversification was again studied in 8 large multi-unit healthcare systems, where the analysis included approximately 40 different services.[6] Not-for-profit and investor-owned hospitals were reported to experience a similar percentage of profitable diversified services. Also, the areas witnessing significant positive operating margins generally were involved to a greater degree with a higher level of acute care than the unprofitable ones (e.g., ambulatory surgery vs. long-term care). The most successful vertical diversification endeavors were among those services related to the health network's existing acute care clinical and managerial competencies. The more unrelated diversification projects required different governance structures and greater autonomy in management for the subsidiary to succeed and were usually less profitable.

Vertical diversification may continue to be a popular strategy among the health network leadership and is reasonably successful when the acquisition is closely tied programmatically to traditional hospital functions (e.g., sophisticated ambulatory care services). Otherwise, diversifying vertically adds little to the network's bottom line; in fact, the opposite might be more often the truth. This analysis suggests so far that it may be far easier to assemble the elements for a vertically integrated health network than it is to make all the pieces work smoothly together to enhance profitability, access, and quality and reduce costs.

Physician-Hospital Organizations

Some of the most dramatic differences in how health networks may now need to be structured are related to the massive changes that have occurred during the past decade in physician-hospital relationships. In fact, probably among the most critical aspects of responding to the challenge of how best to organize and manage the United States' health services is for health alliances to learn more effective ways to acquire various physician groups.

Arriving at some appropriate interrelationships between physicians and hospitals is particularly complex because of the myriad forms of physician organizations currently in existence and the varied connections each group has with other entities. A few examples include: management service organizations (MSOs) that provide management services to physicians; physician-hospital organizations (PHOs) that involve a joint venture between hospitals and physicians largely for purposes of managed care contracting; and independent practice associations (IPAs), typically sponsored by local physicians. When acquiring physician practices, most health networks, as part of their vertical diversification activities, try to offer all these various models to their medical staff members to accommodate different interests, practice styles, and market preferences. But further adding to the network's administrative complexity is that each of these forms of physician organization may have multiple arrangements with different managed care plans.

Among all the vertically diversified options available to health networks, acquiring and then managing physician practices so they are profitable probably demands the highest skill level. This activity requires that the alliance has the ability to manage clinical and financial risk, properly align financial incentives, and implement total continuous quality management practices. The struggle for power, control, and monies is often reflected in the tension observed among physicians and health network executives. This is particularly noteworthy when they are continually being tested concerning their loyalty to two masters they both must serve—patients or the community, and the organization that employs them. As Shortell and his colleagues so aptly stated: "This tension manifests itself in issues of leadership, vision, mission, culture, decision-making skills, [and] managing conflict."[7]

Health networks purchasing physician practices, with subsequent employment of doctors, in spite of creating significant physician-hospital tensions, has been for the past decade often the most significant vertical diversification strategy for the nation's alliances. A major challenge with this approach is to make this a paying proposition for both parties. The health network must not only commit substantial capital to acquire these practices, but in most instances it needs to continue to subsidize them after the purchase has been consummated.

A report encompassing 290 networks published by the Health Care Advisory Board stated that 63 percent of all physician practices studied never yielded a positive return for even one year.[8] A Hospital Financial Management Association study indicated that only 17 percent of the purchased practices are yielding a positive return on their investment.[9] A study completed by Coopers and Lybrand found that physician practices acquired by hospitals in 1997 were losing on the average $97,000 per physician per year.[10] A 1998 study conducted by Towers Perrin examined the financial performance of seven hospital-sponsored primary care networks ranging in size from 50 to 150 physicians.[11] It reported negative margins per physician ranging from $52,900 to $93,900, with an average of $83,290. In spite of these losses, health networks are continuing to acquire physician practices, although at a somewhat slower rate than before, as a vertically diversified strategy.

There may be a kind of "winners' curse"[1] associated with health networks purchasing physician practices at often inflated prices. Unless the alliance purchasing the physician practices can offer a credible alternative, the current valuations of practice assets (including their goodwill) may carry a markup that reflects the current market power of certain physician groups (in terms of hospital inpatient admissions) rather than the present value of future cash flows to be generated by acquiring the physicians' practices. The logical answer is that health networks should prefer that members of their medical staffs admit their patients to alliance-sponsored facilities rather than vertically integrating these practices through acquisition. A continuing concern is that if the network in which a physician admits most of his or her patients is unwilling or unable to purchase the practice, a competing alliance probably will do so with reasonable dispatch.

Health Networks Establishing HMO Plans

There is some additional evidence that perhaps the health networks are fighting on too many fronts, trying to compete in too many disparate businesses, and faring poorly as a result. The pressure on providers to start their own health plan ("controlling the premium dollar"), so commonly pursued several years ago, is now being placed on the back burner.

In recent years a number of national investor-owned managed care corporations and large regional health plans have acquired some of the United States' largest provider-owned HMOs. Examples include Care-America (Burbank, Calif.), Phoenix-based HealthPartners Health Plans of Arizona, and Harris Methodist Texas Health Plans (Arlington), which experienced a $99.1 million operating loss in 1998. There is a general feeling that most provider-owned HMOs are inadequately capitalized and managed to sustain their continuing decreases in market share and their significant operating shortfalls. In 1998, 7.6 percent of the HMOs nationally were owned by hospitals or hospital systems, down from 8 percent in 1998. Possibly more revealing is that America's 10 largest managed care plans, none of which is provider owned, have increased their market penetration to 67 percent of all the persons enrolled in HMO plans.[12]

Aside from a relatively few provider-owned HMOs (e.g., Henry Ford Health System's Health Alliance Plan [HAP], Partners National Health Plans of North Carolina, Sparrow [Lansing, Mich.] Health System's Physician Health Plan), health network–sponsored managed care plans have experienced fiscal difficulties due to low enrollment, lack of understanding about risk selection, inability to control costs, and the fact that they are not the region's dominant managed care plan. When comparing the average operating margin of the 10 largest provider-owned HMOs to that of the publicly owned managed care plans, the hospital-oriented systems should better focus on their traditional patient care activities. While the health network–sponsored HMOs in 1994 and 1995 were turning a profit of 2 percent and 1.5 percent, respectively, their performance was well below that of the publicly owned HMOs, with an average operating margin of 7 to 8 percent (by 1998 this margin had slipped to 1.9 percent).

HMOs that are started by health networks are usually initiated for the purposes of increasing the alliance's market share and to make the managed care plan profitable by decreasing admissions and the average length of stay at hospitals among its subscribers. But a lower average daily census is often at odds with an enhanced bottom line for the hospitals. Because of these conflicting fiscal incentives and the lack of adequate capital and technical knowledge, health network–sponsored HMOs to date generally have not achieved fiscally successful outcomes for their alliances, nor are they as profitable as the investor-owned managed care plans. More simply stated, the failure of health networks to vertically diversify into HMOs is directly related to the difficulty of gaining entry into a complex and competitive prepayment business and then trying to mesh competing interests within the same organization.

Vertical Integration in Other Industries

Whether the marginal performance of vertical diversification in the health field is generally echoed in other industries is worth investigating. Somewhat surprisingly, a review of the empirical studies outside the health field suggest that owned (i.e., managed under one corporate umbrella) vertical integration does not generally achieve enhanced operating efficiencies.

Using Federal Trade Commission data, research endeavors focusing on vertically integrated and nonintegrated corporations concluded that among highly diversified firms there were increased costs of production along with greater decreases in general and administrative expenses.[13] In industries with unstable demand, production costs increased, and there were no savings in overhead expenditures. Firms that primarily implemented backwards integration (e.g., hospitals acquiring long-term care rather than primary care services) incurred higher overall costs and lower profits. The vertically integrated organizations reported to have succeeded more effectively, however, were those in which coordination, production scheduling, and planning are relatively easy; demand is certain and growing; and the industry has a few very large plants. Obviously, this portrait does not describe today's average vertically diversified health network.

Other studies concluded that ownership and backwards integration could create exit barriers that could "trap" an organization into providing products or services that may cause destructive competition and reduce programmatic viability.[14] In fact, decreased growth and profitability among health networks, such as that experienced during a recessionary period, could eventually foster a significant trend of divesting fiscal "losers." Physician practices acquired by health networks and still generating fiscal losses could be among the most logical candidates to be spun off. Such divestitures would have significant implications not only for the doctors involved but for the entire health network.

Empirical research suggesting that vertical integration results in organizational inefficiencies, not gains in profitability, is also supported by several citations in the general management literature:

1. Koch states that all research has shown that corporations are generally less profitable following vertical merger;[15]
2. Clarkson and Miller suggest that, if vertical integration worked so well, many more corporations over time would have used this organizational approach;[16]
3. Martin was unable to point to any evidence supporting any gain in social benefits from vertical mergers;[17] and,
4. Stuckey and White have suggested that vertical diversification should be considered as a structural form "of last resort."[18]

What is surprising is not only the dearth of empirical studies on the efficacy of vertical diversification in nonhealth industries but also that the available research findings suggest negative effects of owned vertical integration on performance. If vertical diversification results in such weak outcomes in the health and other industries, should health networks continue to consummate such acquisitions?

Does Vertical Integration Add Significant Value?

Many health networks, physician groups, HMOs, and other health-related organizations are starting to back away from pursuing vertical integration for a variety of reasons.[19] First, health networks view members of their medical staffs rather than patients as their major customers, and the alliance's management team continues to focus on additional ways to insure a steady flow of admissions to its facilities. For competitive reasons this strategy requires that hospitals stay away from or only jointly venture with physicians on "high-ticket" outpatient-oriented disciplines such as radiation therapy, renal dialysis, MRI, ambulatory surgery, and other similar services. When many of these health network–physician joint ventures are struck, in the most simplistic terms the hospital historically has contributed the major portion of capital investment, and the physicians have a fiscal incentive to refer their patients there, since they share in the project's operating surplus. Whether such arrangements actually improve profitability to the health network, enhance the quality of patient care, and reduce costs to patients is now more frequently being questioned by public officials, trustees of networks, and insurers.

Second, during the past decade one of the major health trends has been the acquisition of physician practices by hospitals, integrated health systems, and other similar groups. Purchasing physician practices has proven to be a terribly rough road and fiscally unproductive, since health networks frequently overpay for the practice, physicians must give up ownership and control, new management that is usually hospital oriented is superimposed on the practice, and eventually physician productivity levels off or drops. From these transactions hospitals are seeking more admissions and a fair return on their investment, while physicians expect to work fewer hours and receive more income. Too often both parties to the agreement become disappointed, even disenchanted, and, as a result, major divestitures by health networks of physician practices can be expected in the future.

Third, vertical diversification is often used as a "come from behind strategy" among those health networks already facing significant fiscal distress. One of the problems when using a vertical diversification approach is the demand for huge capital investments, while profitability can only be expected over the long-term rather than being generated as a "quick fix." When being acquired by a fiscally weak network, physicians are anxious to obtain more monies up front and more flexible terms in case they need to exit the system at a later date. Under such circumstances it is difficult for a marginal network in a highly competitive market to use this vertical diversification option as a means to improve its fiscal position significantly in a short period of time.

Fourth, vertical diversification can require some complicated organizational structures in which from the outset the chain of command, and the sharing of risk and the operating surplus, are not clearly spelled out. The health network's governing board usually judges its CEO and his or her staff on their ability to produce a sizable bottom line, how well they get along with the medical staff, and how many "deals" the network will be able to consummate to satisfy the trustees and the physicians, who experience huge gains from these transactions, and the individual executives who played a leading role in arranging the vertically diversified acquisitions. Determining the chain of command and sharing operating surpluses are usually politically sensitive issues and therefore are often delayed. In the meantime operating losses can continue to pile up from these ventures without the trustees and others being cognizant that some vertical diversification projects just do not work out and divestiture is the most appropriate solution.

Fifth, vertical integration is an organizational model that brings various health resources closer together, but it provides no guarantees of improved fiscal or clinical outcomes. It creates an environment in which more programs, services, and other resources are under one set of controls. It results in an organizational structure in which previous activities by many groups with differing goals, objectives, values, cultures, resources, and patient populations can be more closely coordinated under a single governing board and management team. But a successful (both clinical and fiscally) solo practitioner and his or her staff may not do well in such a huge bureaucracy, in which the chain of command is often fuzzy and decision making takes months rather than just a few days. In the final analysis, whether the effects of vertical integration are positive, neutral, or negative depends greatly on who is in control—the quality of the health network's leadership.

Sixth, providing effective leadership to the United States' health networks, however, is particularly complex because the role requires not only exhibiting sound business acumen but also possessing a profound understanding of how the health field functions. In today's highly competitive, market-driven environment, in which vertical integration is implemented every day, its leaders must constantly balance their constituents' demand for more and improved health services with the increasing pressures being advanced by various powerful business coalitions and public officials, which insist on stiffer cost constraints. When deciding between what makes the most clinical sense and what might be the most fiscally prudent, leaders of the nation's health networks, in considering vertical diversification, must not only demonstrate stewardship by doing things the "right way" but must satisfy the communities that these alliances serve, which depend upon a chief executive officer's wise and forthright judgment.

In spite of what appears to be an increasing number of barriers, all vertically diversified projects are not doomed from the outset. Since there are more opportunities in the health field today than at any time in the past to enhance effectiveness and efficiency, the major finding from this analysis is that each potential vertically diversified acquisition needs to be carefully evaluated in terms of whether it will enhance access, quality of care, and profitability and reduce regional healthcare costs. The overall evidence is that health networks should slow down on the number of the

98   Health Networks

acquisitions they consummate, unless the result achieves a larger market
share in one of their existing or closely related programs or services that
historically has experienced favorable outcomes.

REFERENCES

1. Walston, S. L., Kimberly, J. R., and Burns, L. R. "Owned Vertical Integration and Health Care: Promise and Performance." *Health Care Management
Review* 21, no. 1 (1996): 82–92.
2. Robinson, J. C. "Administered Pricing and Vertical Integration in the Hospital Industry." *Journal of Law and Economics* 39, no. 1 (1996): 357–78.
3. Clement, J. P. "Does Hospital Diversification Improve Financial Outcomes?" *Medical Care* 25, no. 10 (1987): 988–1001.
4. Clement, J. P., D'Anunno, T., and Poyzer, B. L. M. "The Financial Performance of Diversified Hospital Subsidiaries." *Health Services Research* 27, no. 6
(1993): 741–63.
5. Cody, M. "Vertical Integration Strategies: Revenue Effects in Hospital and
Medical Markets." *Hospital and Health Services Administration* 41, no. 3 (1996):
343–57.
6. Shortell, S. M. "The Keys to Successful Diversification: Lessons from Leading Hospital Systems." *Hospital and Health Services Administration* 34, no. 4
(1987): 471–92.
7. Shortell, S. M., Waters, T. M., Clarke, K., and Budetti, P. P. "Physicians as
Double Agents: Maintaining Trust in an Era of Multiple Accountabilities." *Journal of the American Medical Association* 280, no. 12 (1998): 1102–8.
8. Health Care Advisory Board. "American Healthcare 1997 State of the
Union." MS, Washington, D.C., 1997, 37.
9. Hill, J., and Wild, J. "Survey Profiles Data on Practice Acquisition Activity." *Healthcare Financial Management* 49, no. 9 (September 1995): 54–60.
10. "Hospitals That Gobbled Up Physician Practices Fell Ill." *Wall Street Journal* 17 (1997): Be(W), B4(E).
11. Zismer, D. K., and Lund, D. E. "Health System–Sponsored Primary Care
Networks: Achieving Best Practice Financial Performance." Chicago: Towers Perrin, September 1998.
12. Rauber, C. "Market Deflates for Provider-Owned HMOs." *Modern Healthcare* 29, no. 24 (1999): 34–46.
13. D'Aveni, R., and Ravenscraft, D. J. "Economies of Integration versus
Bureaucracy Costs: Does Vertical Integration Improve Performance?" *Academy of
Management Journal* 35, no. 5 (1994): 1167–1206.
14. Harrigan, K. "Exit Barriers and Vertical Integration." *Academy of Management* 28, no. 3 (1984): 686–97.
15. Koch, J. *Industrial Organization and Prices.* Englewood, N.J.: Prentice-Hall,
1980.

16. Clarkson, K., and Miller, R. *Industrial Organization: Theory, Evidence, and Public Policy.* New York: McGraw-Hill, 1982.

17. Martin, S. *Advanced Industrial Economics.* Boston: Blackwell Publishers, 1993.

18. Stuckey, J., and White, D. "When and When Not to Vertically Integrate." *Sloan Management Review* 34, no. 3 (1993): 71–83.

19. Weil, T. P. "Is Vertical Integration Adding Value to Health Systems?" *Managed Care Interface* 13, no. 4 (2000): 57–62.

5

Can Health Networks Attract Physicians in Underserved Communities?

ABSTRACT.   As health networks battle for additional market share and encourage additional subscribers to use their physicians and hospitals, more health executives are analyzing proposals on how to attract qualified doctors to practice in their region's poor rural and inner-city communities. Supplying more physicians to those areas by increasing the number of medical school graduates, expanding the National Health Service Corps (NHSC) program, and allowing more international medical graduates (IMGs) to pursue residency training in the United States have been relatively unsuccessful strategies to improve America's geographic maldistribution of medical manpower. This chapter focuses on several approaches that health networks might now use to increase market penetration and at the same time deliver enhanced health services to their area's underserved: providing eminent leadership in the overall design and governance of soundly conceived Medicaid HMOs; strengthening existing, or developing, additional community health / primary care centers; interfacing more effectively with local schools to foster Medicaid HMOs for children of low-income families; and reimbursing at "premium rates" primary care physicians who practice in underserved communities. The reluctance of physicians to practice in these areas and the unwillingness of middle- and upper-income taxpayers, and therefore elected officials, to support increased spending or redirect existing public funds continue to be major barriers to the health alliances being willing to invest additional medical resources in poor inner-city and rural environments.

Irrespective of how a nation's healthcare system is organized, managed, and financed, all industrialized societies experience a geographic maldistribution of medical resources. While affluent urban and suburban communities attract a surplus of qualified physicians and other providers, poor rural and inner-city residents, although they usually encounter more illnesses and disability, most often must rely on underfunded, government-sponsored resources.[1] As the American public comes to grips with realities such as the fact that the Medicaid program currently pays for 40 percent of all births in the United States, the media will focus more aggressively on the social as well as the healthcare significance of delivering needed services to the "medically underserved."

Friedman noted that Medicaid "offers enormous opportunities for organized delivery systems to develop a full spectrum of care for the chronically ill; for managed care to provide much more accessible and rational programs and procedures; . . . and for providers of conscience to become partners with Medicaid programs in taking a stand against poverty, hopelessness, unemployment, racial prejudice, and other toxins that eat away at the heart and health of this society."[2]

Certainly a broad spectrum of opportunities still exists for America's health alliances as they attempt to improve the delivery of health services to the inner-city and rural poor. Meanwhile, during the last decade the rapid growth of politically and fiscally powerful networks has been a striking trend in the health field. This amalgamation of resources now under way has the potential to improve the integration of services, decrease excess capacity, enhance price competition, and increase the ability of providers and insurers to handle risk-based prepayment.

Although 47.8 percent of the 32.1 million Medicaid eligible are already enrolled (1997) in managed care (table 5), the opportunity for considerable improvement still remains. HMOs to date have evidenced far more success in controlling price than in managing care. While subscribers demand more choice among physicians and hospitals, the insurers are threatening to increase premiums significantly in order to improve their bottom lines. Physicians and hospitals are clamoring for higher reimbursement, major employers are holding fast to their demands for rock-bottom health insurance premiums, federal and state officials are starting to enact more restrictive legislation, and stockholders are punishing HMOs whose profit margins no longer take double-digit leaps.

This chapter explores ways of attracting physicians to underserved areas in the context of: (1) the large number of Americans (probably exceeding 73 million if the assumption is made that uninsured and seriously underinsured are included),[3] many of whom now live in poor rural and inner-city environments, who need more adequate care; and (2) the health networks' aspiration to improve market penetration and increase revenues by enticing an additional number of Medicaid subscribers to use their affiliated physicians and hospitals. It first examines the strategies that have been used extensively in the past to attract more qualified physicians to underserved communities: supplying more physicians by establishing additional medical schools, expanding the National Health Service Corps and the community health center programs, and modifying the number of international medical graduates entering residency training in the United States.

Given that these earlier pursuits have not been overly successful in improving the geographic maldistribution of the nation's physician supply, this chapter next discusses several approaches that currently are being or in the future might be undertaken by health networks to enhance the delivery of healthcare to the underserved. Possible strategies include supplying eminent leadership in the overall design and governance of soundly conceived Medicaid plans, enhancing or developing additional community health / primary care centers, interfacing more effectively with local schools to foster Medicaid HMOs for children, and reimbursing at premium rates primary care physicians who practice in the nation's poor communities.

The chapter then focuses on the option of simply improving working conditions and paying substantially more to physicians willing to deliver healthcare in "less desirable" locations. Although this option is consistent with traditional economic principles, it is concluded herein that this alternative has a number of significant drawbacks: (1) American taxpayers are reluctant to finance a more costly health system for the poor; (2) there are inherent conceptual difficulties with having a capitated Medicaid HMO serve as the linchpin for organizing, financing, and delivering care for the underserved; and (3) providers in the United States will likely react in a fairly litigious way to such an approach.

Previous Strategies Used

The fact that a large number of Americans have limited access to health services is often explained as stemming from two defining and interrelated characteristics of our nation's health system: (1) there are 44.8 million Americans who are without any health insurance coverage and almost an

TABLE 5.   Medicaid Managed Care Enrollment, 1992–97 (in millions)

Year	Total Medicaid Population	Managed Care Population	Managed Care Enrollment (in percentage)
1992	30.9	3.6	11.75
1993	33.4	4.8	14.39
1994	33.6	7.8	23.17
1995	33.4	9.8	29.37
1996	33.2	13.3	40.10
1997	32.1	15.3	47.80

Source: http:www.hcfa.gov/medicaid/trends1.htm, February 27, 1998.

equal number who are underinsured[3]; and (2) healthcare professions tend to practice in relatively affluent urban and suburban areas. The preference to locate in middle- and upper-income areas is found even in countries with a universal compulsory health insurance plan.[4] Improving access to physician services has been considered a critical element in enhancing medical care to the underserved in the United States, and a number of strategies have been tried to correct the shortage of providers in poor rural and inter-city areas.

Graduate More MDs

Over the past four decades many state university officials have encouraged their legislatures to finance their first medical schools or to establish additional ones. If this trend continues to be unchecked, the number of physicians will have almost quadrupled between the years 1950 and 2020.[5] During the same period the population in the United States will have virtually doubled.

The major expenditure of public funds to start and maintain a new academic health center is usually justified politically on the grounds that the proposed institution will: (1) produce more physicians, thus increasing their supply, which will eventually result in reducing fees and total health expenditures; (2) increase the number of available primary care practitioners; and (3) provide additional doctors and other health personnel to serve the region's rural and inner-city poor. In fact, most of the new and even some of the more established medical schools have organized innovative departments of family practice and have created mandatory and elective clerkships to encourage medical students to enter the primary care specialties.

To the public the argument to establish a new primary care–oriented medical school is credible in the sense that a state-supported medical education endeavor should graduate 75 to 100 additional doctors annually. Based on traditional supply and demand considerations, a significant number of these young physicians, after completing their residency training programs, would then be expected to practice in those areas with the greatest need for their services.

The additional medical schools have neither corrected the shortage of physicians in poor inner-city or rural areas nor reduced the United States' overall healthcare expenditures for a number of reasons: sociocultural factors, practice conditions, and income constraints have generally discouraged many primary care physicians from locating in underserved areas. Until relatively recently, a decreasing percentage of medical school graduates pursued primary care specialties, which are the most pertinent to practicing in these underserved areas.

The economic theory that producing more physicians would increase the supply and eventually result in a reduction of doctors' fees has proven to be fallacious.[6] In fact, an increased number of physicians generates more diagnostic testing, inpatient admissions, and surgical procedures, which adds to the nation's total health expenditures. In addition, most spouses would prefer not to live or raise their children in an unattractive rural area or to be worried about safety concerns that arise from working in a poor, inner-city location. The possibility exists for a physician to maintain a full-time inner-city office and for the family to live in a nearby attractive suburb; therefore, providing care to the urban underserved is probably more feasible than delivering primary care for the rural poor.

National Health Service Corps (NHSC)

Since 1970 the NHSC has placed physicians in underserved areas in exchange for scholarships or loan repayments for medical school and residency training. The NHSC program (2,300 scholarships in 1979, decreasing to 1,147 in 1994) allows young physicians to finance a portion of their medical school educations and related obligations; provides a reasonable modicum of medical care to some underserved communities in their federally supported community health centers; and encourages a few additional physicians to continue practicing in rural environments.[7]

To evaluate the effectiveness of this program, the December 1991 American Medical Association Master File was used to determine the practice location and specialty of the 2,903 NHSC scholarship recipients who graduated from U.S. medical schools from 1975 through 1983 and who were assigned to nonmetropolitan counties (this study included 2.2 percent of all the U.S. medical school graduates during this eight-year period). In 1991, 20 percent of the physicians assigned by the NHSC to rural areas were still practicing in the county of their initial assignment, and an additional 20 percent were located in other nonmetropolitan communities.

In another study a questionnaire was mailed in 1991 to all primary care physicians placed in rural communities from 1987 through 1990 while meeting their obligations to the NHSC program.[8] Minorities among the rural NHSC physicians (122, or 31 percent of the respondents) were less likely to have been raised in rural areas and, while they attended medical school, were less interested in rural practice. The relative urban preference among minority physicians explains in large part why this group was more dissatisfied than the nonminorities with their work and personal lives while practicing in rural community health centers. Similar low retention rates were reported for minority (15 percent) and nonminority (21 percent) NHSC physicians.

The NHSC program has demonstrated that, whenever possible, loan repayment should be used to entice candidates to trade professional time for debt forgiveness. Loan repayment programs should also select those medical school students with previous ties to rural areas, as illustrated by the Physician Shortage Area Program of the Jefferson Medical College[9] and other similar endeavors,[10–11] because they are more likely (an estimate of 35 percent or more) to establish their practices in such communities later. Although the NHSC program was never financed by the federal government at the level required to place physicians in many communities of need, it has been a high-priority program among medical educators.[12] The retention rate of those selected for NHSC-type programs has not been so encouraging that Congress has been willing to approve significant increases in funds in order to attract more physicians to underserved areas. Therefore, it is unlikely that this program will achieve the significant gains now needed to supply an adequate number of qualified physicians to poor rural and inner-city communities.

Community Health Centers

The federal Community and Migrant Health Center program enhances access to healthcare for 10 million persons in medically underserved areas. In fiscal year 1996 Congress authorized over a billion dollars for this program to help underwrite over 800 grantee health centers that provide not only physician services but also transportation, home health aides, dietary technicians, health educators, counselors, and others to assist in establishing appropriate links to local social service agencies.[13–14]

Federal- and state-supported community health centers face a rapidly changing healthcare environment as capitated Medicaid HMO plans are implemented to control costs and to enhance access to services. Most of these centers initially encountered serious fiscal difficulties when they entered into managed care contracts. They provided primary care services at $12 to $38 per patient per month, rates that were roughly half of actual costs. In more recent years some centers improved their overall financial position by obtaining revenues from a variety of funding sources (e.g., the Ryan White Comprehensive AIDS Resource Emergency Care Act).

The ability to assume the risk for subscribers' sophisticated tertiary services and to pay for costly procedures and extended lengths of acute inpatient stay constitutes a long-term concern for community health centers. In addition to encouraging more qualified physicians to practice in these centers (usually by an income subsidy), health networks could offer managed care expertise to negotiate more favorable reimbursement rates with insurers and to advise on how to manage provider risk more effectively.

Community health centers could often enhance services by becoming an integral part of the area's major health alliance. Until they face serious fiscal shortfalls, most consumer-dominated centers will delay becoming a partner of a major health network. The reasons for this resistance include a fear of losing their corporate autonomy, differences in culture and values, and the possible elimination of jobs.

These freestanding strategies among community health centers should be weighed against the practical reality that there could be fewer doctors in the nation's rural and inner-city areas. In the current managed care, market-driven environment, primary care physicians completing their training programs are being aggressively recruited by various single- and multispecialty group practices. These young physicians can select a middle-income city or suburban location with an attractive lifestyle, where there is a sharing of evening and weekend coverage by congenial colleagues and where superior earnings can be realized without any significant personal investment.

International Medical School Graduates

The use of IMGs to meet the healthcare needs of the underserved is a complex and frequently discussed topic. What has hindered limiting the increasing number of graduates of foreign medical schools from entering U.S. residency training programs are such questions as: Who will care for the millions of uninsured Americans or those eligible for Medicaid who live in our inner cities and who depend on large, privately or publicly sponsored teaching hospitals for their health services? And what would be the effect on the delivery of the nation's health services if rural communities were no longer able to recruit foreign medical school graduates?

With its advanced medical education system, the United States has assumed the responsibility to train the brightest young physicians from less developed countries. IMGs have been expected to take their new knowledge back to their own countries, although few in recent years have returned home permanently.[15–16] IMG training serves individual doctors, and a few teaching hospitals, far better than it does the countries from which they emigrated and where their earlier undergraduate medical education was subsidized. Should the richest country in the world drain underdeveloped countries of some of their most talented professionals?

Foreign medical school graduates in 1994 represented 23.6 percent (149,082 MDs) of the actively practicing physicians in the United States (table 6), and this number is expected to increase in the future. Since the early 1980s the number of graduates of U.S. medical schools has remained relatively stable, at about 17,000 annually, while the IMGs have filled an additional number of U.S. residency positions. The number of residents in U.S. allopathic hospitals who graduated from a foreign medical school increased from 11,556 in the 1988–89 academic year to 26,763 in 1995–96.

As this IMG debate has heated up, a wide range of medical, hospital, community, private foundation, and political groups, laden with self-interest and often with competing agendas, are represented in a controversy over whether to curtail the flow of these foreign medical school graduates. Medicare is possibly the most crucial element in the discussion of IMGs, because this program has made payments for graduate medical education (combined payments for all third-party payers of an estimated $190,000 per annum per resident are available in New York state) and until recently set no limits on the number of residents it would support at a specific institution. Enacted in 1965 with the major objective of financing health services for the aged, this federally sponsored program has generated significant additional funding to teaching hospitals by making direct medical education payments for residents' stipends, faculty salaries, related administrative expenses, institutional overhead allocated to residency programs, and indirect medical education adjustments to per-case payments.

By increasing the number of residents and therefore the Medicare payment, public institutions with vast indigent patient volumes have been

TABLE 6. Number of Graduates of U.S. and Foreign Medical Schools Practicing as Allopathic Physicians in the United States, 1985, 1989, and 1994

Category	1985	1989	1994	Percentage Change, 1985–94
All graduates	511,090	559,988	632,121	+23.7
Graduates of U.S. medical schools	398,430	437,165	483,039	+21.2
Graduates of foreign medical schools	112,660	122,823	149,082	+32.3
U.S. born	16,344	18,905	19,275	+17.9
Foreign born	98,316	103,918	129,807	+32.0

Source: American Medical Association, Physician Master File, Chicago: American Medical Association, 1996.

encouraged to expand their teaching programs. Academic health centers in New York, Illinois, Pennsylvania, and New Jersey, with their 10,482 residents during 1994–95 (45.5 percent of the total in the United States), are most sensitive to the changes now under way in Medicare reimbursement for graduate medical education (GME) endeavors.

The American Medical Association (AMA) and the Association of American Medical Colleges (AAMC) favor setting limits on the number of residency positions filled by IMGs, but their membership is divided on the issue. The AAMC's New York state constituency and the AMA membership who graduated from foreign medical schools are opposed to their organizations' official policy. Consequently, neither the AMA nor AAMC lobbies Congress aggressively on behalf of its position of reducing the flow of IMGs into the United States.

The Pew Health Profession Commission and the Institute of Medicine's Committee on the U.S. Physician Supply have recommended various remedial steps to reduce the number of physicians.[17–18] More recently, the AMA, the AAMC, and four other national professional associations proposed that more severe restrictions be imposed on the number of IMGs who can be trained in the United States.[19]

Neither Congress nor the Clinton administration were anxious to address the physician supply "adequacy" issue, especially not the number of residency positions to be available in U.S. hospitals. The Republicans have misgivings about government intervention generally and believe in relying on marketplace forces, yet an obvious option to more easily balance the federal budget relies on further reducing Medicare's GME payments to hospitals. But this is simpler said than done, since during congressional hearings it is not unusual that several influential committee members point to the contributions made by foreign medical school graduates in their own state or district.

The Democrats are concerned that Medicare cutbacks for medical education will adversely affect the delivery of health services among the inner-city poor in at least these ways: reducing the number of IMGs available, thereby further limiting some of their constituents' access to physician services; and eliminating from some large private and public institutions in their state or district sizable GME subsidies, which are currently being used by these facilities at their discretion to meet other operational commitments.

An estimated 77 hospitals in the United States are extremely dependent on IMGs to provide care to the poor.[20] These institutions also provide a highly disproportionate share of care to the uninsured. Expanding Medicaid managed care eligibility criteria would be an effective option to provide benefits to an additional number of underserved Americans. A sticky issue, however, is that Medicare is federally funded, while Medicaid requires the states to participate in paying a significant portion of "indigent care" expenditures.

After Mick and Lee merged the 1996 AMA Master File and Area Resources File data, they reported that "IMGs were frequently over-represented in counties where high infant mortality existed and where the physician-to-population ratio was well below average."[21] After completing their residency training, most IMGs establish their practices in densely populated urban areas, and, somewhat unexpectedly, they purse the subspecialties as aggressively as their U.S. education counterparts rather than serving the poor as primary care practitioners. The overwhelming evidence is that IMGs more often than U.S. medical school graduates care for the underserved—which is to their credit—but there can be miscommunication because of cultural-language problems between foreign medical school graduates and poor inner-city or rural patients.

Although the curtailment in the number of foreign medical school graduates entering the U.S. has numerous political, fiscal, and health delivery overtones, it is expected that their entry will wane to stabilize Medicare expenditures and the U.S. physician-population ratio. Few Americans realize that the IMGs entering from India each year (the largest group) is estimated to be comparable in size to the average number graduating annually at 10 or 11 medical schools. In the future IMGs can be expected to become a less available source of new physicians for underserved communities.

The Balanced Budget Act of 1997, which requires Medicare to absorb 56.5 percent of the required budget reductions ($116 billion over the first five years), allows more than 1,000 hospitals nationwide to participate in a program that provides continuing payment for medical residency positions that are to be phased out over a five-year period. The program is modeled after one developed in New York state, where the Health Care Financing Administration (HCFA) agreed to pay 41 hospitals $400 million for a 20 to 25 percent reduction over six years in the number of physicians trained. This subsidy could be particularly important for institutions that have relied heavily on IMGs and now will need to initiate alternative approaches to replace these physicians' services.[22] A number of New York state hospitals participated in this subsidy program and then found it fiscally onerous when they employed salaried physicians to replace the residents in meeting their institution's indigent patient demands.

Adding to the Supply of Physicians

Over the last quarter-century the strategies of building additional medical schools and thereby supplying more doctors, expanding the NHSC and community health center programs, and increasing the number of IMGs have not resulted in a sufficient number of physicians being available to deliver quality care to those in poor rural or inner-city environments. Ginzberg,[23] Kindig,[24] Mullan,[25] Rivo,[26] Wennberg,[27] and Whitcomb[28] share this view, though in some cases for reasons other than those outlined here. Further muddling the situation is mounting evidence of an impending surplus of physicians as a result of a continuing increase in the ratio of physicians to population and a surge in Medicaid managed care enrollment (from 2.7 million in 1991 to 15.4 million in 1997, or 47.8 percent of those eligible), which signals the need for fewer physicians per capita than was experienced previously with more fee-for-service reimbursement.[29–31]

Although there is the option of residing with their family in the suburbs, factors such as crime, drugs, HIV/AIDs, and poverty, which are often interrelated, discourage physicians from practicing in "tough" inner-city areas. The lack of suburban amenities and the sociocultural factors identified with farming communities experiencing economic decline are among the major deterrents to physicians locating their offices and living in poor rural areas.[32] In addition, the underserved generally experience more acute and chronic illnesses; obtain a significant percentage of their care episodically through hospital emergency departments;[33] rely at best on modest family support systems; possess limited funds to pay for medications and related items; find scheduling appointments during regular working hours and obtaining transportation to and from physicians' offices as possible roadblocks to secure care; often experience difficulty in communicating effectively with physicians and allied health personnel; and, finally, generally delay physician care until their illnesses become an emergency. To design a healthcare system that provides a solid relationship between "reluctant" physicians and "difficult" patients is a monumental task.

Thirty years after the passage of a federal-state program to provide indigent medical care, Fairbrother and colleagues published a study of New York City physicians with large Medicaid pediatric practices.[34] Over 90 percent of these physicians were IMGs, and fewer than half were board certified or had hospital staff appointments. Of the patients seen by these 33 physicians, 98 percent were eligible for Medicaid benefits, and 82 percent of the visits were for acute illnesses. With the rapid advent of state-mandated enrollment in Medicaid HMOs and with the current wide gaps in delivering medical care in the nation's inner cities, should those physicians whose qualifications are less than optimal be integrated into new managed care plans? If not, who will provide care to their existing patients?

Options for Supplying More Physicians

Several approaches are currently available to health networks that are consistent with the American Hospital Association's Campaign for Coverage to enhance access of services for disadvantaged people. These strategies not only attempt to enhance market penetration but are to improve the delivery of health services to an area's "medically needy."

Leadership in Forming Medicaid HMOs

A number of recent publications have offered guidelines on how a health network can provide leadership in the overall design and governance of a well-conceived managed care plan.[35-36] Of critical importance to consumers, employers, providers, insurers, and government officials, when discussing the desirability and feasibility of, for example, establishing and managing a Medicaid managed care plan (as the major future source of financing healthcare for the underserved), is giving appropriate consideration to such societal values as:

1. Access: insure reasonably easy availability of needed health services (based on clinical judgment);
2. Social equity: demonstrate equal concern for the total well-being of all residents in a health network's service area;
3. Respect: encourage individual dignity to include the needs and gifts of all with whom providers and insurers come in contact;
4. Cost: use more sophisticated clinical-fiscal performance methodologies to foster quality care with the least expenditure of resources;
5. Collaboration: work together for the common goal of delivering cost-effective, high-quality care for the total community; and
6. Quality of care: ensure that all patient care services are provided at the highest standard of quality possible within the parameters of affordability and reasonable cost.

Even after reaching general consensus with these societal values, the process of a health network establishing a new or enhancing an existing Medicaid HMO will involve conflict. Some beneficiaries believe that the comprehensive health coverage (e.g., including mental health and dental) is an inalienable right; employers are anxious to minimize their tax and health insurance expenditures; providers press for improved reimbursement; insurers strive for greater premiums to enhance their bottom line;

and government officials in Medicaid discussions squeeze out the most comprehensive coverage for those eligible at the least expense to the public sector. Gaining reasonable consensus with such opposing vested interests will never be an easy task.

Providing managed care to the underserved is further complicated by the fact that, as of July 1998, major insurers such as Aetna U.S. Healthcare, Pacificare, Oxford Health Plans, Kaiser Permanente, and some Blue Cross and Blue Shield plans were in the process of shutting down Medicaid coverage in at least 12 states, including Connecticut, Florida, Massachusetts, New Jersey, and New York.[37] Some of the largest HMOs in the United States are quitting managed care coverage for the Medicare and Medicaid eligible, citing fiscal losses and anticipating further cutbacks in government reimbursement to insurers. Public hospitals and related community clinics reacted by forming Medicaid HMOs that could result in a return to the underfinanced indigent care that the large sophisticated managed care plans intended to remedy for the United States' underserved.

Networks of hospitals and physicians that primarily serve the private sector can be expected to be reluctant to assume major fiscal risk in contractual arrangements relating to the "medically needy." These networks are usually fearful that the responsible public agency will pay "inadequately" or will eventually ratchet down reimbursement rates. Earlier Medicaid HMO experiences in Arizona[38] and California,[39] however, would strongly suggest that most of the health networks there have been interested in bidding on these contracts for fear of potentially losing market share and related revenues. For the networks to assume a more major role in designing, sharing the governance, and managing Medicaid HMOs is a "doable" objective to enhance the healthcare of the underserved; however, this process often involves some significant political and fiscal risks.

Positioning Ambulatory Care in Underserved Areas

Freestanding hospitals as well as health networks are often tested by their primary care physicians, medical group practices, and community health centers (if available) concerning their continuing loyalty and frequently are pressured to pay a premium price when they acquire or in some other way participate (e.g., assisting in providing management resources) in these physicians' professional practices. Almost all of these hospital-physician transactions are a means for health networks to enhance their position in the managed care marketplace by buying physicians' loyalty and a reaction to an excess supply of inpatient facilities and of specialty physicians.

Most often health networks will be more interested in acquiring existing community health centers located in underserved inner-city and rural areas rather than in establishing a new ambulatory care satellite. Acquiring a center usually minimizes capital costs and operating risk. As the nation's most powerful health networks continue to acquire additional providers experiencing financial difficulties and thereby gain additional market penetration, such alliances will behave more and more like oligopolies.

Health networks that are in fiscal distress (i.e., most public hospitals) are expected to find it almost impossible to assume more debt to develop ambulatory care centers as a strategy to attract additional Medicaid HMO patients and thereby better meet community healthcare obligations. Attracting health networks into geographic areas with a high percentage of uninsured persons will continue to be a serious challenge.

Focusing on Local Schools

Health systems must evaluate how to partner with local schools and appropriately interface with the existing Medicaid program to serve children of low-income families (per the new State Children's Health Insurance Program [CHIP] that was enacted as part of the Balanced Budget Act of 1997). The total federal allotment available through block grants for the CHIP program to participating states between fiscal years 1998 and 2002 amounts to $20.3 billion. The Congressional Budget Office projected that CHIP will cover 2.8 million previously uninsured children plus an additional 660,000 kids to be enrolled in Medicaid through special outreach and eligibility screening efforts.

One possible way for health networks to tap into these funds is to replicate the Florida Health Kids demonstration project started in the early 1990s, which extended Medicaid-like HMO coverage to indigent children in the public schools of Volusia County (Daytona Beach), Florida.[40] The results of this project suggest that the number of uninsured children in the area has dropped sharply; utilization and cost levels are indistinguishable from those of other children in the area; and measures of access and patient satisfaction are comparable, and in some cases superior, to the study's control group. Overall, the results of this project and the political pressures to mandate universal health insurance coverage for kids suggest that health networks might consider participating in a capitated payment methodology to provide coverage to indigent children in local public schools. This strategy not only serves to enhance health services to poor rural or inner-city kids but at the same time generates more revenues for providers in their alliance.

Providing "Premium" Reimbursement for Physicians

Another possible solution that has been alluded to earlier[41] but has not been adequately tested in recent years is to increase significantly the amount of reimbursement paid to primary care physicians who practice in poor rural and inner-city areas. A possible approach might be to increase the current 10 percent bonus (which cost $84.0 million in 1994) to the usual Medicare fee schedule now provided in a number of underserved environments but then to exclude premium payments to specialists with offices elsewhere who treat patients referred by doctors caring for the poor.[42] This proposed option calls for substantially enhancing the working conditions and paying a sizable premium to family practitioners, general internists, pediatricians, and obstetrician/gynecologists who are willing to practice in the nation's "less desirable" locations. The idea applies to an argument cited a number of years ago in the *New England Journal of Medicine:* "Money talks with a loud voice in the United States. If we wish to recruit a much larger proportion of able U.S. [medical] students into primary care, we must put our mouth where the money is."[43]

A growing surplus of doctors in the United States increases the feasibility of attracting a sufficient number of qualified physicians to provide care to the underserved by offering MDs and DOs premium working conditions and higher than customary incomes. The level of reimbursement that would be necessary to achieve these proposed results is a matter of some conjecture, but conventional wisdom suggests that payment that is roughly 30 percent higher than the area's average for that specialty might be necessary to achieve the proposed objectives.

With an increase in reimbursement mainstream providers, frequently reluctant to accept more than a few Medicaid beneficiaries as patients, would thereby receive substantial fiscal incentives to care for the "medically needy."[44] The average payment of $129 per year would no longer be considered appropriate for physician services for children of low-income families who are Medicaid beneficiaries (table 7).

What is visualized is a Medicaid HMO–type plan that is a carefully designed private-public partnership in which each party concentrates on what it has traditionally done best. Thus, the private sector would be principally responsible for reducing unnecessary utilization, improving provider efficiency in the delivery of health services, and enhancing the quality of patient care services. On the other hand, the government's emphasis would be on controlling any projected increases in capitated rates requested by the insurers and establishing regulations so there is a reasonable geographic distribution of quality physicians. The latter responsibility would work toward resolving the sometimes insurmountable issues of enhancing access and social equity.

Previous Experience with Medicaid HMOs

Although only a tiny fraction of the Medicaid's beneficiaries were enrolled in managed care plans from 1966 to the early 1980s, this experience remains important because of the scandals (e.g., Title XIX "mills") it produced, particularly those in Florida and California.[45] As late as 1995, Florida officials imposed severe fines on 12 Medicaid HMOs for fraudulent-type practices.

TABLE 7. **Average Expenditure per Capita for the United States, Medicare, and Medicaid, 1995 (in dollars)**

Type of Service	United States	Medicare	Medicaid	Medicaid, Children of Low-Income Families
Hospital care	1,282	2,995	1,436	384
Physician services	738	1,064	395	129
Other professional services	193	207	4	109
Home healthcare	105	308	113	24
Drugs and other medical nondurables	305	—	271	65
Vision products and other medical durables	51	122	—	—
Skilled nursing home care	285	194	801	3
Intermediate care / mental retardation	—	—	199	1
Dental services	168	—	4	—
Other	381	83	672	332
Total (average per capita)	3,508	4,973	3,895	1,047
Total expenditures (billions)	957.8	187.0	141.0	18.0
Number eligible (millions)	273.0	37.6	36.2	17.2

Sources: K. R. Levit, H. C. Lazenby, B. R. Braden, C. A. Cowan, P. A. McDonnell, L. Sivarajan, J. M. Stiller, D. K. Wou, C. S. Doukam, A. M. Long, and M. W. Stewart, "National Health Expenditures, 1995," *Health Care Financing Review* 18, no. 1 (1996): 212; and *Medicare and Medicaid Statistical Supplement, 1997, Health Care Financing Review* (1997), 191 and 219.

The Arizona experience with Medicaid HMOs, however, suggests that existing providers that serve patients eligible for Medicare, traditional fee-for-service, and a broad spectrum of managed care plans can also continue to be the loci for delivering primary care to the medically needy.[46] To minimize some of the mistakes made in the past, preference in contracting by the state and the insurers should be given, whenever possible, to health networks and other providers that are in the mainstream of the area's health-care delivery system. This strategy potentially enhances the coordination of patient care services among primary care physicians, specialists, outpatient diagnostic and treatment services, and hospital inpatient facilities.

Physician Staffing of a Medicaid HMO

Critical to the success of this proposal are some assurances that a sufficient number of physicians will be available to serve the enrolled Medicaid subscribers. In the contracting process with the state, the insurer should be required to verify annually that its panel of providers consists of a "sufficient" number of physicians by specialty to meet the needs of its enrollees.

The terms *reasonable, adequate,* and *sufficient number* for purposes of this discussion (table 8, model E) are defined as somewhere near the midpoint of the average number of physicians by specialty available in the United States (model A) and the physician staffing commonly used by established HMOs (model B) when serving primarily an employed patient population. Because of the age distribution and the specific clinical needs (e.g., high birth and addiction rates) of the Medicaid population, the estimates proposed emphasize the usual primary care specialties, obstetrics and gynecology, and psychiatry. These findings may need to be modified based on demographic factors, the clinical needs of the specific population to be served, and the availability of physician assistants and similar physician extenders. For comparative purposes table 8 includes model C (Wichita, which is dominated by fee-for-service care) and model D (Minnesota, where managed care is the usual reimbursement methodology).

Of particular interest to public officials and health services researchers will be whether the recommended physician staffing patterns for Medicaid HMO subscribers offer caregivers the opportunity to spend an "adequate" amount of time with each patient, something sought after for so long by both providers and consumers. Physician and patient surveys should be conducted to determine whether "more or longer" doctor-patient interactions actually result in improved levels of satisfaction.

TABLE 8. Projected Number of Physicians (FTEs) Needed by Specialty in Medicaid HMOs Based on 100,000 Persons and Using Various Models

Specialty	United States Model A	HMO Model B	Wichita Model C	MN Model D	Medicaid Model E
Primary care					
Family practice	31.9	15.6	29.0	34.2	25.8
General internal medicine	25.4	26.3	23.4	27.3	27.8
Pediatrics	14.2	11.1	13.1	14.1	15.2
Medical subspecialties					
Allergy	1.2	0.9	0.7	1.3	1.0
Cardiology	5.3	2.6	3.5	4.4	3.6
Dermatology	2.7	2.1	1.4	2.8	2.2
Endocrinology	0.9	0.8	0.8	0.8	0.8
Gastroenterology	2.6	2.8	1.3	1.9	1.6
Hematology/oncology	2.1	2.2	1.2	2.3	2.0
Infectious disease	0.7	0.8	0.8	0.8	1.3
Nephrology	1.2	1.1	1.1	1.1	1.1
Neurology	2.9	2.2	2.1	2.5	2.1
Pulmonary medicine	2.0	0.9	1.4	1.6	1.1
Rheumatology	1.0	1.2	0.4	0.8	0.4
Surgical specialties					
General surgery	11.8	5.1	9.6	9.1	6.4
Neurosurgery	1.5	0.5	0.9	1.3	0.5
Obstetrics/gynecology	12.4	11.5	8.4	9.2	12.4
Ophthalmology	6.1	5.1	3.5	5.6	4.2
Orthopedic surgery	7.1	5.1	5.9	7.7	5.6
Otolaryngology	2.9	3.4	2.0	2.4	2.2
Plastic surgery	1.7	0.7	1.1	0.7	1.1
Thoracic surgery	0.8	0.8	0.8	0.8	0.8
Urology	3.4	3.2	2.6	2.7	2.6
Hospital-based specialties					
Anesthesiology	10.0	9.0	7.0	8.0	7.0
Emergency medicine	9.4	6.2	2.7	4.4	6.6
Pathology	4.4	5.3	4.1	4.3	4.1
Psychiatry	13.1	3.3	7.2	9.9	9.2
Radiology	6.1	8.6	8.0	5.1	6.2
Total	185.0	138.4	144.0	167.1	154.9

Sources: J. P. Weiner, "Forecasting the Effects of Health Reform on U.S. Physician Workforce Requirement Evidence from HMO Staffing Patterns," *Journal of the American Medical Association* 272, no. 3 (1994): 222–30; D. C. Goodman, E. S. Fisher, T. A. Bubolz, J. E. Mohr, J. F. Poage, and J. E. Wennberg, "Benchmarking the U.S. Physician Workforce: An Alternative to Needs-Based or Demand-Based Planning," *Journal of the American Medical Association* 276, no. 11 (1996): 1811–17; and T. P. Weil, "How to Determine the Need for MDs by Specialty," *Physician Executive* 23, no. 5 (1997): 42–49.

Physicians' Income Increased

Offering premium income and fringe benefits to primary care practitioners serving Medicaid HMO beneficiaries and other medically needy patients is considered a critical element in implementing this proposal to improve the current geographic maldistribution of physicians. Among the factors that influence the decision of what specialty to pursue after graduating medical school, anticipated income and working conditions have been ranked among the most important.[47–48] There is a striking correlation between the ability of residency programs to fill positions with American medical school graduates and the average income of physicians practicing in that specialty.

To encourage more physicians to practice in underserved environments, in 1989 a 5 percent bonus payment was added when care was provided to Medicare recipients in urban and rural Health Professional Shortage Areas (HPSAs). In 1991 this amount was raised to 10 percent, where it remains. The effect this specific provision has on recruiting or encouraging physicians to continue practicing in such areas is unknown and certainly worthy of study.

There have been a number of other attempts to "tweak" Medicaid reimbursement rates to encourage more physicians to participate in providing care to the medically needy.[49] Overall, the results (based on data before the huge expansion of managed care) have been disappointing. In January 1985 New York implemented legislation intended to increase levels of participation in the state. The law allowed for a 30 percent increase in Medicaid fees for physicians providing primary care services.[50] The outcome was totally unexpected in that the state Medicaid program ended up spending more without obtaining any benefits in terms of increased physician availability. In 1986 the Maryland Medicaid program tripled reimbursement fees for deliveries to make them comparable to fees paid in the private sector, and, with some predictably, there was no significant increase in the number of obstetricians providing services to Medicaid recipients.[51]

The evidence implies that probably a substantial premium (say a 30 percent bonus) must be paid to physicians practicing in underserved areas to modify the nation's geographic maldistribution of physicians significantly. Anecdotal comments suggest, moreover, that most physicians are willing to accept considerably less income to work in an affluent community rather than practice in poor inner-city or rural areas.

Financing the Proposal of Paying More

A major source of healthcare funding for low-income Americans, most of whom are considered among the inner-city and rural poor, is the federal-state sponsored Medicaid program (table 7). Between 1985 and 1993 Medicaid costs in the United States tripled, and the number of beneficiaries increased by over 50 percent, to 32.1 million persons in 1997 (table 5). Total Medicaid costs were estimated by Health Care Financing Administration (HCFA) to increase from about $148 billion in 1996 to $337 billion in 2007.[52]

The Medicaid program already consumes 6 percent of all federal outlays (five times more than the monies devoted to Aid to Families with Dependent Children); therefore, the argument to spend even more is difficult for the public to fathom. To assess whether the Medicaid "cost problem" might be one of squandering too much for physicians' care, the 1995 average expenditure per capita by type of service was tabulated for all United States residents and those eligible for Medicare and Medicaid and specifically the children from low-income, Medicaid-eligible families (table 7). As expected, the average annual Medicare expenditure per person was the greatest ($4,973), followed by the per-person Medicaid expenditure ($3,895) and the expenditure for the average U.S. resident ($3,508); the expenditures for the 17.2 million Medicaid children from families with low incomes were considerably less ($1,047).

Roughly a quarter of the nation's Medicaid expenditure is used for senior citizens[53] who have limited remaining personal resources and are admitted to a long-term care facility. Current public policy dictates that general tax revenues rather than Medicare or the children and grandchildren of these infirm aged are responsible to pay for nursing home and related services.

An issue less frequently mentioned is that the HCFA mandates that states insure that Medicaid-eligible children, from birth through age 20, receive rather extensive health services. Included as benefits are vision, dental, and hearing screening tests; routine diagnostic services; and the medical services to correct conditions discovered as a result of these preventive care procedures. These medical services are to be rendered to Medicaid-eligible children at the average reimbursement of $238 per annum (combining physician services and other professional services in table 7), so additional monies from the public sector would need to be forthcoming.

Some Serious Barriers in Implementation

There are a number of serious barriers in implementing this proposal to "overpay" physicians to care for the underserved.

Sheer cost. The proposal's most serious barrier is related to its major theme: paying primary care doctors substantially more to practice in poor inner-city and rural environments. A similar issue now receiving considerable media attention is closing the spending gap for public education between wealthy and poor school districts and the advisability of redistributing wealth. It is politically more expedient to establish new medical schools and for general tax revenues to be used to pay for the nursing home care of parents and grandparents of upper- and middle-income Americans than to offer substantial increases in income and fringe benefits to doctors willing to provide quality care to the underserved.

If for caring for the 36.2 million Medicaid beneficiaries physicians had received the average annual healthcare expenditure for the "average American," the cost to U.S. taxpayers in 1995 would have been an additional $12.4 billion (table 7 calculated by Medicaid expenditure subtracted from U.S. expenditure multiplied by the number of people eligible for Medicaid). This estimation excludes the cost of the potential care of the 44.8 million uninsured Americans; and the significant added expenditures projected for diagnostic testing, hospital admissions, and other related services that conceivably would be generated by Medicaid beneficiaries as access to physician services improved.

The additional billions needed to offer substantial incomes to physicians practicing in underserved areas constitutes a major stumbling block; also anticipated is a reluctance on the part of American taxpayers to finance a "costly" healthcare delivery system for the poor that might work equally well or even be better than is available to the average family.[54] The question would be raised: Why should those eligible for Medicaid have access to physicians with no or modest out-of-pocket expense and be offered a comprehensive range of services that too often is unavailable to some middle-income, underinsured families?

Political considerations. Unlike most other major industrial societies, the United States has never had a one-tier healthcare system, and, based on the resounding defeat of the Clinton health reform initiative, this nation is unlikely to inaugurate one in the foreseeable future. Americans ration health services by family income and the ability to pay for care. Most elected officials view healthcare essentially as a private consumption good whereby:

1. low-income families are accorded a basic ration that is most often provided by the public sector or, in not-for-profit facilities, cross-subsidized by well-insured or private-pay patients. The poor obtain medical care when it is really needed, even if it takes longer, occurs in less than ideal surroundings, and too frequently has less than optimal outcomes.
2. middle-class families are entitled to a reasonable range of services within the not-for-profit or private (including investor-owned) sec-

tors. More employers now offer a managed care plan that often reimburses providers on a more limited basis. HMO subscribers are frequently concerned about tacit rationing and the restrictions on choice of providers, particularly relating to whether their personal physician is included in the plan's closed panel.

3. most wealthy families will continue to use the fee-for-service system with virtually no limitations on choice of providers and without being adversely affected by any possible issues relating to rationing care.

There are other reasons why attracting physicians to underserved areas has had so little political interest: (1) those who are most adversely affected are poor and have a weak political voice; (2) the fiscal responsibility and the political impact of delivering healthcare to the underserved are organizationally and fiscally diffuse; and (3) Medicaid is not a single program but consists of more than 50 programs. Medicaid programs are judged on their ability to control public sector expenditures, not on what they can accomplish in terms of improved access, quality of care, and favorable clinical outcomes.[55]

In the current American political and economic climate, in which the wealthy get wealthier and the poor are getting poorer and in which welfare reform in recent years has received such strong bipartisan support, it is difficult to imagine much willingness among upper- and middle-income Americans to increase their taxes to enhance the delivery of healthcare for the underserved. Schroeder is concerned that we "might eventually find ourselves living in a much meaner America than many of us who entered the health profession ever imagined."[56]

The principle of equal access, high quality of patient care, and social equity for all in the delivery of health services has not in the past, nor is it expected in the foreseeable future, to square up "as the American way."

Statutory concerns. In the 1985–92 period 47 states enacted 238 laws relating to the supply and distribution of generalist physicians.[57] This legislation addressed such areas as planning and oversight; financial incentives to institutions, students, and residents; and strategies that enhance the practice of medicine. Since this is such a potentially contentious undertaking, it is not surprising that only a "few states devoted resources to evaluate their efforts," although they spend $3 billion annually for medical education.

Another concern in this current quasi-market driven and quasi-regulatory environment is how Americans can achieve the passage of well-thought-out regulations that protect the public interest without crippling innovation and efficiency. Also worrisome are huge health networks with annual revenues of over $1 billion potentially engaging in antisocial behavior to the disadvantage of patients, the community, insurers, and other providers.[58-59]

What happens when there are few providers left in the region and the state, or when insurers are no longer able to negotiate one against another? In most underserved environments there are already a limited number of physicians and hospitals available. Do state officials have the responsibility to step in and enact the necessary rules and regulations to protect their consumers, providers, and the various insurers? If so, at what point?

Paying physicians at a premium rate when caring for the underserved would, it is hoped, improve the distribution of primary care doctors. On the other hand, the availability of more money per capita for caring for the poor potentially makes that environment more susceptible to fraud and abuse, and, if nothing else, insurer-provider-patient relationships could become simply more contentious and litigious.

Is capitated payment the appropriate prepayment approach? Obvious advantages and disadvantages exist for paying physicians by fee-for-service, salary, per capita income, or a combination of these options. As states encourage more capitated Medicaid HMOs, they feel increasing pressure to monitor access to and quality of services provided to beneficiaries to insure that financial incentives are not compromising the providers' clinical decisions.[60] While fee-for-service payments give physicians and hospitals fiscal inducements to render too many services, capitated payment motivates providers, who are often bearers of some fiscal risk, to render too few services.

To avoid some of the failures of the past, states will need to improve their quality assurance efforts constantly, particularly so that providers are committed to rendering preventive services to children. As more hospitals and physicians enter into Medicaid managed care underwriting, states will need to perfect their monitoring systems in order to protect the public and be able to detect when providers are accepting too much financial risk and are in potential danger of becoming insolvent (e.g., Oxford Health Plans). Whether most of the states are now up to such a broad range of responsibilities will affect the overall success of Medicaid HMOs in enhancing access, reducing cost, and improving quality of care for the medically needy.

These observations suggest that, beyond the practical problem of a high turnover among those eligible for Medicaid coverage,[61-62] there could be some inherent conceptual difficulties that hamper the monitoring of quality care, as when a capitated HMO focuses on less rather than more care, or when the managed care plan serves as the linchpin for organizing, financing, and delivering care for the medically needy. On the other hand, if federal and state officials were to increase Medicaid expenditures, an unpopular position among legislators and virtually all the public, the result might be an improved distribution of physicians for the underserved. This assumes that physicians will readily practice with a "30 percent incentive payment" in underserved communities, which is still an unanswered question according to known evidence.[63] It may be more feasible in urban areas where physicians can reside with their families in nearby upscale suburbs than in the rural areas, where the ambiance and certain social amenities are missing.

Some Concluding Thoughts

How health policy is formulated and implemented in the United States is somewhat of a paradox in the sense that the public sector unitl relatively recently has been responsible for an increasing percentage of the nation's health expenditures, yet the role of government will remain limited in any fundamental reform of the U.S. healthcare system because Americans are anxious to continue with their quasi-private, quasi-public orientation to organizing, managing, and financing health services. In the future the United States could experience a major economic shift downward. Public officials may then be faced with a serious health cost and access crisis. Elected officials could be forced to reduce public expenditures significantly and withdraw benefits from recipients whose healthcare needs justify government intervention.

The resulting outcry over such broad economic and social adversities could force a reevaluation of how tax-supported funds should be distributed. A more effective use could close the gap between the medical care provided to the middle class and that obtained by the poor. Although such equalizing would require major shifts in current health policy (e.g., more emphasis on social equity), these modifications should be shaped by our elected officials to be consistent with the nation's pluralistic values (e.g., financed from various sources and with multipayers reimbursing providers) and, therefore, could be implemented without too much additional governmental intervention.

Meanwhile, healthcare services to the rural and inner-city poor could be enhanced. The health networks could concurrently improve regional market penetration and increase their revenues by: (1) playing a more major role in the governance and management of Medicaid HMOs either by owning such a managed care plan or more likely working closely with such an endeavor; (2) strengthening existing, or developing additional, community health / primary care centers; (3) interfacing more effectively with public school systems to foster Medicaid HMO endeavors to provide benefits to traditionally uninsured children; and (4) undertaking a few well-designed demonstration projects to evaluate the results obtained when physicians practice in medically needy environments with premium working conditions and income.

Serious impediments exist for health alliances attempting to implement these proposals, because of their sheer cost; lack of political will; the inherent difficulties of government agencies working within the nation's complex and highly politicized quasi-private, quasi-public environment; and the reluctance of middle- and upper-income taxpayers to consider the geographic maldistribution of physicians as an issue of major social or economic consequence.[64] Many health networks, however, could find implementation of some of the proposals to be at least partially in their own self-interest and may decide to attract more physicians and other health services to the United States' underserved communities.

REFERENCES

1. Council on Graduate Medical Education. "Tenth Report: Physician Distribution and Healthcare Challenges in Rural and Inner-City Areas." Rockville, Md.: Department of Health and Human Services, 1998.

2. Friedman, E. "The Little Engine That Could: Medicaid at the Millennium." *Frontiers of Health Services Management* 14, no. 4 (1998): 22.

3. Rice, D. P. "The Cost of Instant Access to Health Care." *Journal of the American Medical Association* 279, no. 13 (1998): 1030.

4. Roemer, M. I. *National Health Systems of the World.* Vol. 1: *The Countries.* New York: Oxford University Press, 1991.

5. Iglehart, J. K. "Health Care Reform and Graduate Medical Education." *New England Journal of Medicine* 330, no. 16 (1994): 1167–71.

6. Grumbach, K., and Lee, P. R. "How Many Physicians Can We Afford?" *Journal of the American Medical Association* 265, no. 18 (1991): 2369–72.

7. Cullen, T. J., Hart, L. G., Whitcomb, M. E., and Rosenblatt, R. H. "The National Health Service Corps: Rural Physician Service and Retention." *Journal of the American Board of Family Practice* 10, no. 4 (1997): 272–79.

8. Pathman, D. E., and Konrad, T. R. "Minority Physicians Serving in Rural National Health Service Corps Sites." *Medical Care* 34, no. 5 (1996): 439–54.

9. Rabinowitz, H. K., Diamond, J. J., Markham, F. W., and Hazelwood, C. E. "A Program to Increase the Number of Family Practitioners in Rural and Underserved Areas: Impact after 22 Years." *Journal of the American Medical Association* 281, no. 3 (1999): 255–60.

10. Adkins, R. J., Anderson, G. R., Cullen, T. J., Myers, W. W., Newman, F. S., and Schwartz, M. R. "Geographic and Specialty Distribution of WAMI Participants and Nonparticipants." *Journal of Medical Education* 62, no. 10 (1987): 810–17.

11. Boulger, J. G. "Family Medicine Education and Rural Health: A Response to Present and Future Needs." *Journal of Rural Health* 7, no. 2 (1991): 105–15.

12. Whitcomb, M. E., and Cohen, J. J. "Obstacles to Attract Physicians to Underserved Communities." *Frontiers of Health Services Management* 15, no. 2 (1998): 36–39.

13. Nadel, M. V. "Community Health Centers. Challenges in Transitioning to Prepaid Managed Care." Report GAO/HEHS-95-138. Washington, D.C.: U.S. General Accounting Office, 1995.

14. Nadel, M. V. "Rural Health Clinics: Rising Program Expenditures Not Focused on Improving Care in Isolated Areas." Report GAO/HEHS-97-24. Washington, D.C.: U.S. General Accounting Office, 1996.

15. Iglehart, J. K. "The Quandary over Graduates of Foreign Medical Schools in the United States." *New England Journal of Medicine* 333, no. 25 (1996): 1679–83.

16. Mullan, F., Politzer, R. M., and Davis, C. H. "Medical Migration and the Physician Workforce: International Medical Graduates and American Medicine." *Journal of the American Medical Association* 273, no. 19 (1995): 1521–27.

17. Third Report of the Pew Health Professions Commission. "Critical Challenges: Revitalizing the Health Professions for the Twenty-first Century." San Francisco: Center for the Health Professions, University of California, 1995.

18. Lohr, K. N., Vanselow, N. A., and Detmer, D. E. "The Nation's Physician Workforce: Options for Balancing Supply and Requirements." Washington, D.C.: National Academy Press, 1996.

19. Association of American Medical Colleges (AAMC), American Medical Association, American Association of Colleges of Osteopathic Medicine, American Osteopathic Association, Association of Academic Health Centers, and National Medical Association. "Consensus Statement on the Physician Workforce." Washington, D.C.: AAMC, 1997.

20. Whitcomb, M. E., and Miller, R. S. "Participation of International Medical Graduates in Graduate Medical Education and Hospital Care for the Poor." *Journal of the American Medical Association* 274, no. 9 (1995): 696–99.

21. Mick, S. S., and Lee, S.-T.-D. "The Safety-Net Role of International Medical Graduates." *Health Affairs* 16, no. 4 (1997): 141–50.

22. Iglehart, J. K. "Medicare and Graduate Medical Education." *New England Journal of Medicine* 338, no. 6 (1998): 402–7.

23. Ginzberg, E. "The Future Supply of Physicians." *Academic Medicine* 71, no. 11 (1996): 1147–53.

24. Kindig, D. A. "Policy Priorities for Rural Physician Supply." *Academic Medicine* 65, no. 12, supp. (1990): S15–S17.

25. Mullan, F. "The National Health Service Corps and Inner-City Hospitals." *New England Journal of Medicine* 336, no. 22 (1997): 1601–4.

26. Rivo, M. L. "A Report Card on the Physician Work Force in the United States." *New England Journal of Medicine* 334, no. 14 (1996): 892–96.

27. Wennberg, J. E., Goodman, D. C., Nease, R. F., and Keller, R. B. "Finding Equilibrium in the U.S. Physician Supply." *Health Affairs* 12, no. 2 (1993): 89–103.

28. Whitcomb, M. E. "A Cross-National Comparison of Generalist Physician Workforce Data: Evidence for U.S. Supply Adequacy." *Journal of the American Medical Association* 274, no. 9 (1995): 692–95.

29. Miller, R. S., Jonas, H. S., and Whitcomb, M. E. "The Initial Employment Status of Physicians Completing Training in 1994." *Journal of the American Medical Association* 279, no. 9 (1996): 708–12.

30. Gamliel, S., Politzer, R. M., Rivo, M. L., and Mullan, F. "Managed Care on the March: Will Physicians Meet the Challenge?" *Health Affairs* 14, no. 2 (1995): 131–42.

31. Weiner, J. P. "Forecasting the Effects of Health Reform on U.S. Physician Workforce Requirement: Evidence from HMO Staffing Patterns." *Journal of the American Medical Association* 272, no. 3 (1994): 222–30.

32. Hassinger, E. W., Gild, L. S., Hobbs, D., Jr., and Hegeman, R. L. "Perceptions of Rural and Metropolitan Physicians about Rural Practice and the Rural Community, Missouri, 1975." *Public Health Reports* 95, no. 1 (1980): 69–79.

33. Medicaid Access Group. "Access of Medicaid Recipients to Outpatient Care." *New England Journal of Medicine* 330, no. 20 (1994): 1426–30.

34. Fairbrother, G., DuMont, K. A., Friedman, S., and Obach, K. S. "New York City Physicians Serving High Volumes of Medicaid Children: Who Are They and How Do They Practice?" *Inquiry* 32, no. 3 (1995): 345–52.

35. Kongstvedt, P. R. *The Managed Health Care Handbook.* 3d ed. Gaithersburg, Md.: Aspen Publishers, 1996.

36. Lomicka, E. W. "Building Managed Care Networks for Rural Communities." *Managed Care Quarterly* 5, no. 2 (1997): 51–65.

37. Kilborn, P. T. "Largest HMOs Cutting the Poor and the Elderly." *New York Times,* July 6, 1998, 1.

38. Scanlon, W. J. "Arizona Medicaid: Competition among Managed Care Plans Lowers Program Costs." Report GAO/HEHS-96-2. Washington, D.C.: U.S. General Accounting Office, 1996.

39. Robinson, J. C. "Decline in Hospital Utilization and Cost Inflation Under Managed Care in California." *Journal of the American Medical Association* 276, no. 13 (1996): 1060–64.

40. Coulam, R. F., Irvin, C. V., Calore, K. A., Kidder, D. E., and Rosenbach, M. L. "Managing Access: Extending Medicaid to Children through School-Based HMO Coverage." *Health Care Financing Review* 18, no. 3 (1997): 149–75.

41. Gabel, J. R., and Rice, T. "Reducing Public Expenditures for Physician Services: The Price of Paying Less." *Journal of Health Politics, Policy and Law* 9, no. 4 (1985): 595–609.

42. Nadel, M. V. "Physician Shortage Areas: Medicare Incentive Payment Not an Effective Approach to Improve Access." Report GAO-HEHS-99-36. Washington, D.C.: U.S. General Accounting Office, 1999.

43. Levinsky, N. G. "Recruiting for Primary Care." *New England Journal of Medicine* 328, no. 9 (1993): 656–60.

44. Fossett, J. W., and Peterson, J. A. "Physician Supply and Medicaid Participation. The Causes of Market Failure." *Medical Care* 24, no. 4 (1989): 386–96.

45. Iglehart, J. K. "Medicaid and Managed Care: The Evolution of Medicaid and Managed Care." *New England Journal of Medicine* 332, no. 25 (1995): 1727–31.

46. Silverstein, G., and Kirkman-Liff, B. "Physician Participation in Medicaid Managed Care." *Social Science in Medicine* 334, no. 17 (1995): 355–63.

47. Ebell, M. H. "Choice of Specialty: It's Money That Matters in the USA." *Journal of the American Medical Association* 262, no. 12 (1989): 1630.

48. McKay, N. L. "The Economic Determinants of Specialty Choice by Medical Residents." *Journal of Economics* 9, no. 3 (1990): 335–37.

49. Adams, E. K. "Effect of Increased Medicaid Fees on Physician Participation and Enrollee Service Utilization in Tennessee, 1985–1988." *Inquiry* 31, no. 2 (1994): 173–87.

50. Fanning, T., and de Alteriss, M. "The Limits of Margin Economic Incentives in the Medicaid Program: Concerns and Cautions." *Journal of Health Politics, Policy and Law* 18, no. 1 (1993): 27–42.

51. Fox, M. H., Weiner, J. P., and Phua, K. "Effect of Medicaid Payment Levels on Obstetrical Care." *Health Affairs* 11, no. 4 (1992): 150–61.

52. Smith, S., Freeland, M., Hefflec, S., McKusick, D., and the Health Expenditures Project Team. "The Next Ten Years of Health Spending: What Does the Future Hold?" *Health Affairs* 17, no. 5 (1998): 128–40.

53. *Medicare and Medicaid Statistical Supplement 1997 Health Care Financing Review,* 217.

54. Davidson, S. M. "Medicaid Taking Stock." *Journal of Health Politics, Policy and Law* 18, no. 1 (1993): 43–66.

55. Tallon, J. R., Jr. "Medicaid's Future: A Political Perspective." *Frontiers of Health Services Management* 14, no. 2 (1998): 38–40.

56. Schroeder, S. A. "The Medically Uninsured—Will They Always Be with Us?" *New England Journal of Medicine* 334, no. 17 (1996): 1130–33.

57. Rivo, M. L., Henderson, T. M., and Jackson, D. J. "State Legislature Strategies to Improve the Supply and Distribution of Generalist Physicians, 1985 to 1992." *American Journal of Public Health* 85, no. 3 (1995): 405–7.

58. Goldsmith, J. "Columbia/HCA: A Failure of Leadership." *Health Affairs* 17, no. 2 (1998): 27–29.

59. Vladeck, B. C. "Market Realities Meet Balanced Government: Another Look at Columbia/HCA." *Health Affairs* 17, no. 2 (1998): 37–39.

60. Buchanan, J. L., Lindsey, P. A., Leibowitz, A., and Davies, A. R. "HMOs for Medicaid: The Road to Financial Independence Is Often Poorly Paved." *Journal of Health Politics, Policy and Law* 17, no. 1 (1992): 71–96.

61. Ellinger, J. "The Little Engine That Could and Slowly Will: A Bureaucrat's View." *Frontiers of Health Services Management* 14, no. 4 (1998): 27–30.

62. Carrasquillo, O., Himmelstein, D. U., Woolhandler, S., and Bor, D. H. "Can Medicaid Managed Care Provide Continuity of Care to New Medicaid Enrollees? An Analysis of Tenure on Medicaid." *American Journal of Public Health* 88, no. 3 (1998): 464–66.

63. Komaromy, N., Lurie, N., and Bindman, A. B. "California Physicians'

Willingness to Care for the Poor." *Western Journal of Medicine* 162, no. 2 (1995): 127–32.

64. A concurring opinion with other reasons for this conclusion can be found in Hurley, R. "From Trickle Down to Paying Off: Making Money Talk." *Frontiers of Health Services Management* 15, no. 2 (1998): 29–32.

6

Health Networks Battling in the Marketplace

ABSTRACT.   Whether health networks should experience more market-driven competition or more government regulation is now at the center stage of the United States' health policy debate. This chapter discusses several competitive and regulatory strategies that health networks are now encountering or will face in the next several decades while enhancing the delivery of medical care: (1) managed competition or managed care; (2) the further privatization of the nation's health services; and (3) replicating either the Canadian or the German universal national health insurance program. It looks first at the more entrepreneurial models utilized in the United States. Next, it evaluates the more regulated approaches used by other industrialized nations to enhance access and social equity and to reduce total health expenditures. Finally, this chapter argues against supporting either extreme. Instead, what is favored is a blended approach, in which the best of each option is chosen and the emphasis is on practicality rather than ideological exactness. Universal compulsory health insurance is viewed as being a critical issue in promulgating universal access and social equity; managed competition or managed care is considered important to reduce utilization and cost; and global budgetary targets are perceived as being effective in maintaining increases in a nation's total health expenditures equal to the growth of its gross domestic product.

Over the last two decades the epic struggle between more market-driven competition and tougher government regulation has turned the health field upside down and has dramatically changed how health services are organized, managed, and financed. How health networks will be shaped, and any potential restructuring in the United States of the relationship between the marketplace and government, will be constantly influenced by a simple rudimentary response—the Americans experience a growing cynicism and skepticism about the ability of the public sector to function effectively and efficiently. This distrust is as old as this country and is an integral part of our nation's heritage, culture, and values.

But then one must ask the question, why have the Americans allowed government to expand to its current role and breadth of responsibility? Whenever there is a serious crisis, we look to the public sector to unravel it. For almost three decades our experiences with the New Deal and World War II built some confidence in government, which resolved the economic problems created by the 1929 depression and brought Germany, Italy, and Japan to unconditional surrender. Later on, the Kennedy administration inspired a generation with an idealism about public service and the ability of public officials to make a positive impact on the lives of its citizens.

In the mid-1960s cynicism and distrust began to emerge as a powerful trend that was stoked by the Vietnam War and domestic turbulence. Watergate and the economic travails of the 1970s further fueled misgivings. There may have been a short respite during the Reagan era, but then doubts continued to grow during the Bush and particularly the Clinton administrations. The outcome has been a lower expectation by the general public and by the nation's policy analysts that government can effectively and swiftly resolve the critical foreign and domestic issues facing our nation. This philosophical change is characterized by an end to the growth of the government's role in many spheres, some rolling back, and some devolution. This trend includes a continuing battle over the public sector expanding further into the realm of social values, and a drive to adapt to the mechanisms of the marketplace rather than adding to the activities of the existing regulatory environment. It also includes a consensus on what not so long ago in the United States seemed to be quite old-fashioned, even possibly quaint—the virtue of fiscal restraint in a period of economic prosperity of an almost unprecedented length.

Within this complicated and highly politicized framework I have authored or coauthored a number of articles during the past decade that discuss various potential market-driven and regulatory approaches to enhance the delivery of health services in the United States. The following ideas have served as the foci of my earlier publications and are recast in this and the following chapter with an emphasis on how health networks are now finding themselves battling, as they will continue to battle in the future, the competitive marketplace and more government regulation:

1. The managed competition concept, or the managed care plans (e.g., the HMOs), were touted early on as a way to enhance access, social equity, quality of care, and reduce total health expenditures. They have served as a major factor in encouraging the formation of health networks and continue to influence how health services are delivered and how these alliances are organized, managed, and financed.

2. In this current, more competitive marketplace some of the nation's "best" teaching hospitals are facing serious fiscal distress. The

question arises whether, based on the experiences of the for-profits in the health field, further privatization (i.e., converting from not-for-profit to investor-owned) of these "hub" facilities for health networks would serve the public's interest.

3. Americans could possibly replicate the Canadian single-payer healthcare system that provides universal access and relatively comprehensive benefits at a gross domestic product (GDP) expenditure for health of one-third less than the United States.

4. Americans could possibly replicate the German multipayer health system that also provides universal access and comprehensive health benefits at only one-quarter less expenditure of their GDP than the United States.

The commentary that follows in this and the next chapter, which discusses the blending of competitive and regulatory approaches to enhance future health networking, is heavily influenced by my early academic training. I came to the conclusion then that it probably was not feasible to design the "absolutely perfect" healthcare system, since even a carefully contrived plan ends up with some compromises. For example, enhancing the ease of access to services generally results in some patient abuse of benefits, higher utilization of services, and therefore "excessive" costs.

What then becomes increasingly critical in analyzing any proposed plan's outcome is to recognize and understand the significance of each option's strengths and weaknesses. In addition, once having decided how the healthcare system is to be financed and then having established the various fiscal incentives inherent in the proposed plan for consumers and providers, it becomes relatively straightforward to predict which services or providers will gain and lose utilization and revenues. Possibly this is oversimplified: advise me how the money flows, and then I can predict for the most part how the healthcare system will function and how providers will react to the specific plan's fiscal incentives.

Managed Competition / Managed Care

Access to needed services, high-quality patient care, value for the dollars expended, and patient satisfaction are considered major hallmarks of an effective and efficient managed care plan. As of July 1999, 71.9 million Americans were eligible for HMO benefits, the majority of these subscribers located in large metropolitan markets with a population base of one million or more.[1] Somewhat unexpected was the market penetration for these managed care plans remaining relatively flat during the 1998–99 period, with the large markets showing only a 2 percent increase in their average percentage of penetration. Small markets, those with a population of 250,000 or fewer, experienced a decline in average HMO market share, dropping from 18.2 percent in July 1997 to 17.6 percent in July 1998.

Managed care continues to be the most dominant form of health insurance coverage in California and Oregon. Twelve of the 29 metropolitan statistical areas in the United States with HMO penetration rates of 50 percent or more are located in these two west coast states.

This market-driven model is an outgrowth of Enthoven and Kronick's 1989 proposal that those not covered by Medicare or Medicaid should be eligible to purchase affordable coverage, either through their employer or through a "public sponsor."[2] Recommended was a strategy of managed competition whereby these sponsors would negotiate and then contract with competing health plans. This early HMO model assumed that an informed, cost-conscious public would reward those providers who delivered high-quality patient care at a reasonable cost. This market-driven approach, extremely attractive in a strong U.S. economy, was also meant to remedy the issues of lack of access to services among the underserved as well as to slow down increases in health expenditures. The theory of managed competition as envisioned early on by Ellwood,[3] Enthoven,[4] and others[5-6] has been most effective in a number of respects yet, when evaluated on the basis of other criteria, has proven to have been sometimes disappointing.

HMO Performance: An Overview

Some findings that compare the performance of managed care or HMOs to the earlier traditional fee-for-service plans might be briefly summarized as follows:

1. The percentage increase in national health expenditures has declined with the growth of managed care enrollment, although it is still rising at a rate roughly 50 percent higher than the consumer price index. The U.S. national health expenditure reached $1.1 trillion in 1997, a 4.8 percent increase over 1996. This rise represented the slowest growth in the last four decades and continues a trend of deceleration that started in 1991.[7] The 1994–97 annual growth has remained below 5 percent, a sharp contrast to the double-digit increases last seen in 1990. In fact, the annual growth in physicians' average net income dropped from 7.2 percent for the period from 1986 through 1992 to 1.7 percent from 1993 through 1996.[8]

This slowing down of health cost increases was influenced by such changes as the shift of large number of employees into managed care plans, more price competition among insurers, a more rigorous utilization review process, and much lower general and medical inflation. As a result, providers formed health networks and alliances to enhance negotiations with HMOs and to decrease the inflationary trend in their capital and operating costs. The popularity of the managed care concept among major industrialists and public officials is primarily related to its ability to constrain the rise in U.S. health expenditures, most of these savings being a direct result of a decrease in inpatient hospital use.

2. The fiscal incentives inherent in managed care have resulted in somewhat lower inpatient admission rates with shorter average lengths of stay. As outcomes, a lesser number of patient days per 1,000 persons per annum is experienced, and more procedures are now being performed on an outpatient basis.[9-12] Inpatient hospital care has become more intensive, and more patients are discharged needing additional posthospital care such as that provided by home health agencies, which more frequently are becoming subsidiaries of the same health network.

A decade ago there was a surplus supply of acute care beds and most tertiary services. Managed care's reducing the demand for these services has been a major factor in encouraging hospitals to merge and to form horizontally and vertically diversified health networks to reduce that excess capacity and to decrease expenses as a reaction to their revenue shortfalls.

Of considerable concern is that the utilization review process used by managed care plans to decrease utilization may not always be able to differentiate between services that are clinically superfluous and those that are clearly indicated. Incentives that decrease unnecessary services benefit patients and promote quality care. Yet managed care plans that use the review process to withhold clearly needed services creates serious ethical conflicts and results in poorer quality of care. Furthermore, such conflicts of interest may eventually erode patient trust in some physicians. Managed care is far more complicated than simply managing health expenditures.

3. Managed care enrollees use the same number as, or somewhat more physician office visits than, those enrolled in the fee-for-service plans, with the potential added advantage of those in HMOs receiving a greater use of preventive services to constrain future health costs.[13-15] Physicians often find themselves in a dilemma when patients demand more and more specialty care and the managed care plans discourage their subscribers from generating additional services and costs. Physicians are spending more time haggling with managed care plans when obtaining authorization from HMOs for their patients to receive clinically needed services than they had experienced under the previous fee-for-service arrangements.

4. There are mixed results when comparing the quality of care among the managed care and indemnity plans.[16-18] Studies comparing HMOs with fee-for-service care have generally found similar outcomes for the average health enrollee. Yet most studies have found worse outcomes among the managed care plans for vulnerable groups (i.e., the seriously ill, the mentally ill, and the poor). Overall the quality of care in the not-for-profit HMOs exceeds that in the investor-owned managed care plans, with a greater variation among those insurers that target the Medicare and Medicaid eligible.

5. Finally, somewhat lower subscriber and physician satisfaction is reported with HMO services, this being counterbalanced by the perception that managed care costs less than fee-for-service plans.[19-20] A 1999 National Committee for Quality Assurance survey[21] reported that 57 percent of the respondents rated their managed care plan an 8, 9, or 10 on a 10-point scale, and there was a strong correlation linking accountability, clinical performance, and customer satisfaction. Three-fourths of the consumers in this survey said that obtaining care was not a problem, while 17.9 percent said it was a small problem, and 8.6 percent indicated it was a major problem.

A 1999 Kaiser Family Foundation survey reported a strikingly negative view of managed care among physicians.[21] Ninety-five percent of the doctors said it had increased the amount of administrative paperwork. Seventy-two percent indicated that the quality of health care for people with managed care who were sick had deteriorated, and 77 percent said it had decreased the ability of patients to get the tests and treatments they needed.

The heated discussions at the federal and state levels among consumer groups, legislators, and the various special interests such as hospitals, physicians, and insurers reflect the difficulties and the need to reach some compromises in arriving at an equitable patient bill of rights.

Networks and HMOs: Facing Difficulties

Irrespective of the significant success of managed care in slowing down increases in U.S. health expenditures, and of the more socially oriented issues that are inherent in a market-driven approach, a health network's financial position is heavily dependent on how well it negotiates favorable reimbursement rates from the region's principal insurers. On the other hand, there are a number of reasons why the health leadership fostering the current market-driven strategies being used by the United States' powerful health networks, in some cases with their closely aligned HMOs, could in fact experience significant difficulties in guaranteeing that all Americans, including the aged, the indigent, and the currently uninsured, have ready access to an effective health system at an affordable price.

1. During the past half-century the effective implementation of the concept of regionalizing health services, with few exceptions, has been difficult to achieve (see chap. 1). Providers within a specific region generally exhibit greater interest in their own institutional or individual survival than in the community's overall long-term well-being.

2. Compared with the traditional fee-for-service payment system, HMOs have experienced to date only modest positive results in enhancing access, social equity, and quality of care. For managed care to continue as the preeminent approach to organizing, managing, and financing health services, it must play a more significant role in restructuring the U.S. health system than simply controlling U.S. health expenditures.

3. Managed care has the inherent fiscal incentive of limiting the choice of providers, encouraging physicians to order fewer tests and consultative services, and avoiding unnecessary hospitalizations. The long-term public acceptability of health networks offering less care when compared with a fee-for-service environment has yet to be evaluated in terms of the fact that HMOs (a) emphasize that free choice of providers negates their ability to guarantee quality care, yet physician contracts with HMOs can provide bonuses to limit care deemed unnecessary; (b) often require "gatekeepers" to approve all care by specialists, thereby limiting patients a direct access to other than their primary care physician; (c) sometimes ban physicians from disclosing the amount of money they receive when limiting care or discussing clinical treatment options that are not covered by a patient's managed care benefits; (d) can reject claims for emergency department (ED) care for nonemergencies, since doing so discourages the use of EDs when a visit to a primary care physician would suffice; (e) commonly urge new mothers and their newborns to leave the hospital within 24 hours of a normal delivery; and (f) sometimes allow those without clinical training to deny crucial services and then delay appeals for months.

4. Health networks and their affiliated HMOs have historically had difficulty in providing quality and affordable services to those who are hard to insure or those who live in poor inner-city or rural areas (see chap. 2). This shortfall is becoming more visible as additional HMOs are disenrolling those eligible for Medicare and Medicaid benefits.[22]

5. Although the Balanced Budget Act of 1997 has slashed reimbursement to health providers, public officials could, for political and fiscal reasons, potentially delay any further efforts to decrease Medicare and Medicaid payments to providers or to increase taxes to pay for these entitlements.[23]

6. Finally, antitrust officials in the Department of Justice (DOJ) and the Federal Trade Commission (FTC) can be expected, as they review the possible formation of various alliances and mergers, to continue to be relatively ineffective in playing a major role in the restructuring of the U.S. health system. These enforcement agencies have difficulty sorting out the appropriate balance between the two generally opposing concepts of consolidation and competition.[24]

Managed Care Serving Medicare and Medicaid Eligible

With HMOs experiencing such issues as limiting access and choice and guaranteeing overwhelming patient satisfaction, it is difficult to imagine that this competitive model alone will be able to produce an effective and efficient health system for more than 260 million Americans, thereby being almost the sole source of reimbursing health networks. With 46.4 percent of the total medical care dollar funded by the public sector,[7] it may be self-evident that the implementation of a solely market-driven strategy could face conceptual and operational complications in the delivery of services to the over 70 million Americans eligible for Medicare and Medicaid benefits.

What makes the potential melding of health networks, HMOs, and the entitlement programs for senior citizens and the indigent so complex is that there is insufficient evidence that the managed care concept, in terms of providing benefits to high utilizers of services (who are frequently encouraged to disenroll from HMOs),[25-26] cost,[27-28] utilization,[29-30] quality,[31-33] or consumer satisfaction,[25] is so superior to current fee-for-service arrangements that the competitive approach should be uniformly implemented for Medicare and Medicaid beneficiaries. The implication here is that health networks will continue to receive reimbursement from both the private (managed care) and public (Medicare and Medicaid) sectors and a combination thereof.

Perhaps the major conclusion to be drawn from this analysis is that there is no strong evidence available that lower costs or better care can be more readily anticipated for Medicare and Medicaid beneficiaries under managed care than under the traditional fee-for-service arrangements.[34] The more obvious scenarios that will therefore impact health networks in the foreseeable future are that Congress will provide less Medicaid funding by seducing the states into block grants that contain less federal guidelines; the Medicare program will be modified by raising deductibles, coinsurance, and the cost of supplementary insurance; and providers will be delivering services to Medicare and Medicaid beneficiaries at reduced reimbursement per unit of service.

Bias in the selection of risk, reduced utilization of services, higher costs per beneficiary to the government, and reasonable satisfaction by the providers would suggest that the managed care plans, hospitals, and physicians early on often "gamed" the governmental agencies that are anxious to pursue capitated payment for the Medicare and Medicaid eligible. As a result, it is inferred that the HMOs through the late 1990s provided roughly the same or slightly less care and in some cases ended up with more money in their pockets. By the late 1990s, however, many of the HMOs were experiencing significant fiscal shortfalls from their Medicare and Medicaid contracts and were canceling many of them with significant dispatch.

Some Remaining Issues with Prepayment

Current estimates of the fiscal viability of the nation's federal entitlements strongly suggest that in the next several decades health networks will be forced to achieve significant cost savings, or there will be limited resources left for most other governmental expenditures. Certainly the Balanced Budget Act of 1997 reflects the congressional thrust toward seriously curtailing health costs. The primary reason for these cutbacks is that, unless major cost reductions are implemented by the year 2007, as baby boomers start retiring and becoming eligible for Medicare benefits, the nation's spending will top $2.1 trillion, or 16.6 percent of the gross domestic product.[35]

An often cited hallmark of the U.S. health system is that it allows consumers the freedom of choice to select a provider and health insurance coverage, although the latter is a decision often assumed by the employer. The establishment of panels of providers by managed care plans, in an attempt to insure quality and to negotiate favorable reimbursement rates, restricts individual subscribers when selecting a provider. The HMOs may have more difficulty than they now expect as the public experiences increasing dissatisfaction with the limiting of free choice of providers, which interferes with long-standing relationships between patients and physicians and among physicians.[36] The HMOs' tightening up on choice of provider to enhance their bargaining position has in recent years resulted in more subscribers interested in point-of-service benefits.

Another concern is the potential adverse impact of HMO fiscal incentives on physicians' decisions for managed care patients, particularly as potentially more elaborate and more powerful approaches are implemented by case managers, thereby forcing providers to limit their services and costs further.[12, 37–38] The financial inducements inherent in managed care are potentially in direct conflict with Medicare, Medicaid, and the ability of the working poor and their dependents to obtain adequate health services.

The care of the sick and disabled has always had businesslike characteristics, since practicing physicians earn their livelihood through their professional efforts, and hospitals must remain solvent to be able to deliver services in their communities. It should be theoretically possible to modify both the organization and financing of health services so that managed care plans and other third-party payers are able to provide entitlements at a reduced cost. How to accomplish this within the context of the various vested interests has been a contentious issue for a number of decades.

What is most likely to happen with the remaining Medicare and Medicaid HMOs is the establishment of several nationwide systems of for-profit managed care plans focusing primarily on serving the aged, the indigent, and any newly insured, low-income families. In terms of utilization patterns and the level of quality of care, these HMOs might well replicate the earlier experiences with some inner-city Medicaid and Medicare mills in southern California and Florida, in spite of the fact that the public and private sectors now have available improved monitoring and measuring systems of quality and outcome.[39–40] Recent findings[18] concluded that the investor-owned HMOs provide significantly poorer quality of care than the not-for-profit managed care plans, suggesting the view that lower-income Americans could be expected to receive less than adequate health services.

Instead, the United States needs to use available resources in a more equitable and efficient manner to provide necessary services for all who need them. This is critical when public officials and health leaders consider that those eligible for Medicare, Medicaid, and those now without health insurance constitute almost half of the nation's population. As Relman clearly points out: "We cannot afford all the care a market-driven system is capable of giving."[41]

Interestingly, the antithesis of a competitive managed care plan model, with its micromanaging of physician services for individual patients and the negotiations of reduced reimbursement rates with hospitals, is the Canadian and European approach to establishing national health priorities and setting health expenditure targets by health sector and province or state.[42–44] There is, in fact, considerable empirical evidence that countries using some overall control of spending generally are more effective than those nations relying more on decentralized mechanisms of allocating resources.[45]

After considering the option of further privatizing the top teaching hospitals in the United States as an example of further pursuing the more market-driven, competitive model, this chapter concludes with a discussion of the Canadian and German health systems, which provide universal comprehensive health benefits but are also experiencing some operational and cost difficulties.

The Trend toward Privatization in the Health Industry

Fiscal pressures from managed care, Medicare, and Medicaid cutbacks; the ever-growing presence of the investor-owned healthcare corporations; and the competition for increased market share among health networks are quickly changing the landscape of the U.S. healthcare system. To survive in this current market-driven environment, many of the nation's "best" or "top" not-for-profit or state-supported academic health centers, most of them serving as the hub facility of a well-known health network, are clearly behaving like profit-oriented businesses.[46] This trend is vividly illustrated by their corporate restructuring, numerous joint ventures, and various horizontal and vertical acquisitions.

To be listed among "America's Best Hospitals,"[47] the "One Hundred Top Hospitals: Benchmarks for Success,"[48] the biggest healthcare systems,[49] or the 250 largest (based on revenues) investor-owned healthcare corporations is frequently sought after by our nation's healthcare leaders as a means to differentiate their health network's performance from that of competing alliances.[50] This entrepreneurial spirit is expected to continue irrespective of the fact that the canons of good medical care (i.e., enhanced access, social equity and quality of care, and the reduction of cost)[51] prescribe values often philosophically and conceptually inconsistent with the more profit-driven strategies that are now with increasing frequency being implemented in the health field.

For the past three decades teaching hospitals in the United States have been far more dependent than other acute care facilities on Medicare reimbursement. Unlike most other third-party payers, Medicare has paid academic health centers extra for their assuming some unique responsibilities: providing medical education and the training of house staff; treating patients who require more sophisticated care; and serving as the principal providers of health services for the nation's un- or underinsured.

As of 1994–95, competitive pressures generated by managed care plans had not yet eroded the financial position of U.S. teaching hospitals.[52–58] Academic health center representatives in 1999, however, indicated that current reimbursement constraints contained in the Balanced

Budget Act of 1997 (BBA) would place a crippling squeeze on their teaching facilities.[54] To preserve their traditional mission of teaching, research, and patient care, leaders of academic health centers lobbied Congress to restore indirect medical education and disproportionate-share payments (totaling $10.4 billion in 1998) to pre-BBA levels.

Pressure has been mounting on some hubs of major health networks so that they face such severe fiscal distress they may be forced to file for Chapter 11 bankruptcy protection and then possibly be acquired by an investor-owned hospital chain. One of the forerunners to this potential trend was the Allegheny Health, Education, and Research Foundation, a major health network with a medical school, 15 hospitals, and over 600 physicians (whose practices were previously acquired) located primarily in the Pittsburgh and Philadelphia metropolitan areas. In the summer of 1998 they filed for bankruptcy protection with $1.2 billion in debt. Several months later Tenet (the second largest investor-owned hospital group) purchased most of Allegheny's Philadelphia-based facilities.

Americans have generally supported academic health centers becoming the hub of politically and fiscally powerful health networks. At the same time, they have invested generously in publicly traded stocks offered by investor-owned hospitals, managed care plans, and physician management corporations. These trends raise a number of questions: Will America's best hospitals (selected by the 1998 *U.S. News & World Report* survey and all serving as hubs of a major health network) face serious fiscal distress when additional third-party payer cutbacks are implemented? Is the recent fiscal performance of major U.S. for-profit hospital systems, HMOs, and physician management corporations superior to that of the nation's best teaching hospitals? And should the current trend in the health field toward more privatization (i.e., more market-driven competition) be viewed as a preferred option for hub hospitals of health networks that are heading toward financial distress?

The Performance of Hubs of Health Networks

To insure that the analysis would include the most renowned hub facilities in the country, it was thought advisable to study in some depth the financial position of the nation's best teaching hospitals, as listed in the 1998 *U.S. News and World Report*.[47] New York City's Mount Sinai Medical Center, St. Louis University Hospital, and the University Medical Center in Tucson were somewhat arbitrarily added to the original 17 facilities to help verify the findings of health network hubs located in a similar geographic setting (table 9).

Financials are a mixed bag. For the year ending June 30, 1997, the University of Iowa Hospitals and Clinics experienced a 6.4 percent increase in net patient revenues from the previous year; a comfortable net margin of 12.4 percent; a current ratio of 10.3; and virtually no long-term debt. At the other end of the spectrum New York City's Columbia-Presbyterian Hospital for the year ending December 31, 1996, had a meager 1 percent increase in net patient revenues from the previous year; a slim 0.3 percent net margin; a current ratio of 1.7; and a disturbing long-term debt-to-equity ratio of 21.36. These data clearly illustrate an unhealthy disparity among the financial positions of the nation's best teaching hospitals.

Difficult to estimate is the fiscal impact that additional managed care, Medicare, and Medicaid cutbacks will eventually have on further decreasing net patient revenues. Considering the sizable investment the best hospitals are expending to become "more businesslike," a midpoint annual net revenue increase for these facilities of +6.5 percent compared

TABLE 9. Financial Data on the Top 20 Hospitals in the United States, 1996–97

Hospital	Latest Year's Revenue (in millions of dollars)	Percentage Change from Earlier Year	Percentage Operating Margin	Percentage Net Revenue	Debt to Equity Ratio
Johns Hopkins	615.9	+3.5	+9.4	+2.5	0.81
Massachusetts General	600.1	+4.0	−44.4	+4.6	0.66
Brigham and Women's	481.9	+5.7	−13.6	+4.4	0.79
University of Pennsylvania	604.0	+12.7	−1.1	+12.3	2.31
Columbia-Presbyterian	670.5	+1.8	−8.8	+0.3	21.36
Mt. Sinai, N.Y.C.	735.5	+3.7	−10.2	+2.7	1.09
Duke University	669.1	+7.6	−6.0	+9.2	0.63
Mayo Clinic (St. Marys)	255.3	+14.9	+10.9	−8.3	0.91
Cleveland Clinic	634.3	+1.0	+8.2	+8.8	0.83
University of Michigan	896.0	+0.1	+0.2	+6.1	0.47
Barnes-Jewish	588.5	+14.8	+1.6	+6.6	0.68
St. Louis University	187.0	−3.7	−45.1	+8.7	0.41
University of Iowa	394.0	+6.4	−2.6	+12.4	0.05
University of Chicago	909.4	+8.1	+52.3	+8.9	0.90
UCLA	520.3	+10.4	+3.6	+9.0	0.52
UC–San Francisco	454.1	+26.1	+18.4	+15.9	(0.55)
Stanford	552.3	+3.3	−5.3	+2.2	0.42
University of Washington	264.8	+7.6	−4.3	+2.4	0.39
UC–San Diego	266.1	+3.6	+1.9	+9.1	0.73
University of Arizona (Tucson)	202.3	+11.9	−6.0	+2.3	1.03

Sources: "America's Best Hospitals," *U.S. News and World Report,* July 27, 1998; and G. M. Pearl, *Financial Statements for U.S. Hospitals: 1999 Edition* (compiled from 1996–97 Medicare Reports) (Phoenix: Rate Controls Publications, 1999).

to a +4 percent rise in the hospital consumer price index (CPI) for the year ending May 1999 is not overly impressive.[55] Using as criteria for delineating the "poor cousins" less than a 3 percent net margin, and a debt-to-equity ratio of 0.42 percent or higher, six of America's best teaching hospitals should be considered in the foreseeable future to be potentially fiscally vulnerable (table 9). The six include what a national panel of clinicians consider to be the two very best hospitals—Johns Hopkins and the Mayo Clinic.

Is networking worth it? Attracting additional referrals for their sophisticated tertiary services, enhancing managed care negotiations, and potentially reducing costs by eliminating the duplication of clinical services are among the prime reasons for these teaching hospitals to expend considerable resources in major corporate restructuring, forming health networks, acquiring primary care physician practices, signing affiliation agreements, and engaging in other, similar strategic endeavors.[56] The New York Presbyterian Healthcare Network, which in 1997 consisted of 15 acute care hospitals, with net patient revenues of $3.1 billion, was only able to generate net operating revenues of $38.8 million (+1.2 percent). University of California–San Francisco (UCSF) Stanford Health Care's net patient revenues in 1998 were $1.2 billion, this San Francisco–based network (which in the winter of 1999 decided to divest) producing $16.2 million (+1.3 percent) in net operating revenues. The Johns Hopkins Health System in 1998 was slightly more fortunate with its $886.8 million in net patient revenues generating $23.6 million (+2.3 percent) in net operating revenues.

It is probably too early to judge whether all this corporate restructuring by the nation's best hub hospitals will pay off in more referrals, higher-quality patient care, cost reductions, and improved bottom lines. In the meantime networks with an academic health center as the hub are often experiencing difficulties in achieving a strategic fit, in finding a middle ground when differences in culture and values surface, in implementing operational efficiencies, in countering the inflexibility inherent in these large bureaucratic structures, and in adapting to the strategies necessary to insure their long-term survival as being among the best teaching hospitals.

Under-reimbursement or sloppy management. The leaders of these hub hospitals often claim that their fiscal woes are related to under-reimbursement, such as with Tennessee's experiment with Medicaid managed care (Tenncare),[57] while public officials and insurers frequently believe that their difficulties are related to "flabby" management. In an attempt to shed light on this traditional dispute, for each of the 20 teaching hospitals (table 10), the number of full-time equivalent employees (FTEs) was divided by the number of discharges adjusted by the facility's Medicare case-mix intensity to correct for differences in patient severity of illness.

The anticipated outcome was that hub hospitals experiencing fiscal distress would use fewer employee man-hours per adjusted discharge. Unexpected was a threefold range from 90.2 to 278.1 man-hours per adjusted discharge among these 20 teaching hospitals. Based on this analysis, the six facilities identified as being the most fiscally vulnerable could not be considered "overstaffed."

In an attempt to eliminate the bias of a hospital contracting out, operating expenses per discharge adjusted by Medicare case-mix intensity and wage index was calculated, the idea being that each teaching hospital

TABLE 10.   Financial Comparisons of the Top 20 Hospitals in the United States, 1996–97

Hospital	Current Ratio	Days Cash on Hand	FTE Man-hours / Discharge Adjusted by CHI[a]	Operating Expense / Discharge Adjusted by CMI and MWI[b] (in dollars)	Revenue / FTE Adjusted by CMI and MWI[c] (in dollars)
Johns Hopkins	1.4	122.7	173.6	6,243	59,200
Massachusetts General	2.4	194.7	278.1	7,962	48,889
Brigham and Women's	2.2	238.0	156.3	5,111	63,886
University of Pennsylvania	2.0	197.9	162.0	8,193	120,344
Columbia-Presbyterian	1.7	98.6	171.4	4,528	55,215
Mt. Sinai, N.Y.C.	2.2	103.7	171.7	4,485	47,161
Duke University	3.3	181.5	152.8	6,293	77,329
Mayo Clinic (St. Marys)	0.2	19.6	90.2	2,366	41,161
Cleveland Clinic	2.2	165.8	134.4	4,565	72,714
University of Michigan	1.0	65.8	226.9	7,556	67,324
Barnes-Jewish	3.1	217.7	174.6	5,219	95,290
St. Louis University	2.5	149.9	188.2	9,692	81,866
University of Iowa	10.3	252.3	273.2	6,815	58,359
University of Chicago	0.6	56.8	217.4	6,649	111,494
UCLA	2.0	167.7	196.1	7,076	102,126
UC–San Francisco	2.5	95.3	178.1	5,572	103,874
Stanford	1.3	181.6	138.9	4,979	86,616
University of Washington	3.6	269.3	179.8	5,145	53,368
UC–San Diego	1.9	163.1	189.0	4,715	86,039
University of Arizona	2.7	140.3	152.2	5,604	107,886

Sources: "America's Best Hospitals," *U.S. News and World Report,* July 27, 1998; and G. M. Pearl, *Financial Statements for U.S. Hospitals: 1999 Edition* (compiled from 1996–97 Medicare Cost Reports) (Phoenix: Rate Control Publication, 1999).

[a]Full-time equivalent man-hours per discharge adjusted by the Medicare case-mix intensity.

[b]Operating expense per discharge adjusted by Medicare case-mix intensity and wage index.

[c]New revenue per full-time equivalent employee adjusted by Medicare case-mix index and Medicare wage index.

should be evaluated on the basis of its total operating expenses adjusted by differences in the cost of labor locally and its patients' severity of illness. Reported again was a wide range of operating expenses per adjusted discharge. The hospitals with the second and third lowest operating expenses per adjusted discharge were New York City's Mt. Sinai and Columbia-Presbyterian Hospitals, suggesting that these two hub hospitals' financial woes are probably more related to inadequate reimbursement than slipshod management.

To further test whether some teaching hospitals' fiscal difficulties are related to under-reimbursement, the net patient revenue per full-time equivalent employee adjusted by Medicare case-mix intensity and wage index was calculated. Again, a wide range of values were experienced. What is difficult to explain is why four major California teaching hospitals (Stanford, UCLA, UCSD, and UCSF), vulnerable to managed care strategies, collect roughly twice the net patient revenues per FTE adjusted than Columbia-Presbyterian and Mt. Sinai Hospitals, whose income stream historically has been controlled by a state rate-setting approach.

What is obviously worrisome is that inherent in all of these revenue and expense analyses is that the United States has experienced a decade of unequaled prosperity. An almost inevitable economic recession sometime in the foreseeable future would be expected to result in a significant increase in the number of uninsured Americans and in major employers having more difficulty in paying their employees' health insurance premiums. Such an inauspicious economic downturn would have a perilous impact on roughly one-third of the nation's best hub hospitals, which are already fiscally fragile, particularly if simultaneously a public debate determined that the Medicare program, which was designed to finance healthcare for the aged, should be supporting broader societal objectives (e.g., the uninsured and medical education). The other two-thirds of the best teaching hospitals, having accumulated significant reserves, simply would need to tailor their teaching, research, and patient care programs to a somewhat more limited revenue stream.

Publicly Held Healthcare Corporations

Through 1998 pharmaceutical companies, drug distributors, biotech firms, and device manufacturers experienced double-digit earning gains and rising stock prices.[50] Meanwhile, other publicly traded health stocks, notably many managed care plans, physician practice management firms, investor-owned hospital chains, long-term care groups, and home health companies, evidenced significant slides in both earnings and stock prices.

In 1998 the United States' 250 largest healthcare corporations had an average revenue gain and stock appreciation of 14.6 percent and 14.3 percent, respectively. Usually, this would be considered an excellent return on investment, but it was far below the 32.1 percent increase witnessed by the Standard and Poor's (S&P) 500 index over the same twelve-month period. In fact, the health field's experience in 1998 was a far cry from its more vibrant days of 1995, when health stocks skyrocketed an average of 40 percent.

Investor-owned hospitals. Although during the past decade there has been a "graying" in how the not-for-profit health networks and the investor-owned chains are organized, financed, and managed, the latter have historically focused more on selecting patients with comprehensive health insurance benefits, charging more than the not-for-profits, and reducing operating costs so as to enhance their stockholders' return on investment.[58–59] Disappointment in the performance of these for-profit groups is evidenced by the nation's six largest investor-owned hospital chains in 1998 squeezing out net operating revenues of 4.3 percent. Thirteen of the 20 best teaching hospitals had a better bottom line than the average of the 6 for-profit chains.

Among the major reasons given for the investor-owned hospitals being unable to match the S&P 500 average net profit of 10.7 percent are being pressed by higher costs, lower third-party reimbursement, and the fact that several of them face serious federal fraud and abuse charges. Their inability to generate stock appreciation anywhere comparable to the 1998 S&P 500 average (+32.1 percent) is evidenced by three of the five chains experiencing a decline in their stock prices over this 12-month period.

A major factor in the struggle Tenet, Quorum, and HCA—The Healthcare Co. faced in the stock market is related not only to their low net margins, but to their debt-to-equity ratios as of December 31, 1998, which were 1.64, 1.45, and 0.89, respectively. Of no surprise, therefore, is that the June 1999 credit ratings of for-profits and not-for-profits looked quite different with the median for-profit rating of Ba and the median not-for-profit rating at A3.[60] To improve their performance the current strategy of these hospital chains is to divest themselves of unprofitable facilities rather than to consummate additional acquisitions, reflecting an attempt to consolidate their resources in areas in which they already enjoy reasonable market penetration and profitable operations.

HMOs. Starting in the early 1990s, providers experienced a major shift in third-party reimbursement from fee-for-service to managed care, a trend that immediately resulted in a shift in where patients were treated (i.e., from inpatient to ambulatory care). Although the nation's largest publicly held HMOs have served as an effective force in reducing increases in U.S. health expenditures and have witnessed significant growth in revenues by adding subscribers and acquiring smaller and frequently competitive plans, these managed care plans in 1998 were only able to squeeze out a 1.87 percent bottom line. Except for Wellpoint Health Networks, the major investor-owned managed care plans in 1998 delivered a return on equity that was far less than the average for the S&P 500 companies (+22.5 percent).

Physician Management Corporations. Due to the fiscal and management pressures generated by managed care, the reduction in Medicare reimbursement, and the formation of integrated health systems, an increasing number of physicians in the latter part of the 1990s chose to be acquired by a physician practice management corporation. The overall fiscal performance of these companies, formed primarily to allow doctors to earn more and work less, has been generally disappointing in terms of increases in revenues, net income (+2.79 percent), and stock appreciation. All of these companies experienced a sharp decrease (more than 40 percent) in their stock price in 1998.

Two of the seven companies (MedPartners and American Physician Partners) had six or more times debt than equity, the same ratio for the S&P 500 companies being 0.98. No wonder that some of the physician management companies have been forced to divest some of their large medical group practices and are considered among the most litigious companies in the health industry, primarily because a large number of physicians sold their practices for what is now almost worthless stock.

What this analysis demonstrates is that in terms of profitability these three sectors of the U.S. investor-owned health industry discussed earlier have not only experienced fiscal performance that is less impressive than the 20 best teaching hospitals, but also their stock appreciation is significantly below average for the S&P 500 companies. Moreover, those for-profit hospital chains, HMOs, and physician management companies that have incurred significant debt are also among those experiencing the most difficulties in generating operating surpluses and increases in their stock prices.

Privatization of Hub Hospitals

A combination of additional cutbacks in managed care, Medicaid, and Medicare reimbursement (particularly relating to indirect medical education and disproportionate share) would result in roughly a third of the nation's hub hospitals for health networks filing for bankruptcy by the year 2005 or so, unless these alliances make the decision and have the resources to cross-subsidize these teaching facilities. These "poor cousins" are already unable to generate adequate net operating margins, due most likely to being under-reimbursed for their present programs and services and being saddled with higher than average debt-to-equity ratios. Yet they appear to be managed with fewer full-time equivalent employees per discharge adjusted by case-mix intensity than those with greater fiscal resources.

Several key representatives in formulating health policy[61–65] have raised serious ethical issues concerning the way the health field functions more like a business. Because hospitals, physician services, home health care, and other facilities in investor-owned areas cost more;[66] for-profit HMOs deliver poorer quality of care than not-for-profits;[22] and in a continuing bullish economy the fiscal performance (based on their stock prices) during the first six months of 1999 of the publicly held hospital chains (–22.1 percent), HMOs (+3.3 percent), and physician management corporations (–27.7 percent) continued to deteriorate,[67] further privatization of the hub hospitals or most of the nation's not-for-profit health network would probably be detrimental to the public interest.

Tenet, which assumed fiscal responsibility for the merged Hahnemann Medical University and the Medical College of Pennsylvania and their related hospital facilities, reported a debt-to-equity ratio of 1.64 at the end of calendar year 1998. Of the 20 best hospitals this ratio is only exceeded by the University of Pennsylvania Hospital (2.31) and the Columbia-Presbyterian Hospital (21.36). In fact, some recent studies of the financial efficacy of health networks suggest that the nation's teaching hospitals might spend more time "tending to their knitting," although the strategy of becoming an oligopoly to better control market penetration and enhance negotiations with managed care plans will appear to them to be at least as compelling.[68–70] Based on this analysis, solely using further privatization of the health industry as the major theme of restructuring the field does not appear as an overly effective and efficient approach.

Replicating the Canadian Healthcare System

After the Clinton health reform plan was defeated in 1994, health dialogue in the United States shifted its major focus from concerns over universal access and social equity for the uninsured to the need for more stringent cost-containment efforts.[71–72] Even with a strong economy during most of the 1990s, the problems with managed care, and with out-of-pocket expenses for drugs and other health services, became critical fiscal and political issues.

Early in the 1990s there was a long litany of articles published in medical, hospital, and other journals espousing the virtues of the U.S. health system in terms of its technological superiority,[73-74] its pluralism,[75-76] and its conceptual consistency with our traditional values of individualism.[77] Most recommended solutions to achieve political consensus focused on such concepts as incrementalism,[78] a multipayer system,[79-80] the implementation of increased competition,[81] a limited increase in any taxes,[82] no ceiling on the total U.S. gross domestic product (GDP) expenditure for health,[83] and on the appeasement of most of the nation's key providers.

In contrast, the evidence from other Western countries[43-44, 84] clearly illustrates that, by gaining general agreement on national health policies and priorities and concurrently setting a maximum ceiling on total health expenditures, a universal comprehensive health insurance plan should be affordable in the United States. The Physicians for a National Health Program[85] estimated that $40 billion (1991) could be saved in administrative and related expenses by implementing a Canadian single-payer type plan. The projected cost reductions were thought to be sufficient to deliver comprehensive benefits to the then 36.6 million Americans who were uninsured, without any additional GDP expenditure for health. These conclusions were consistent with earlier findings[42, 86] indicating that the major differences between the Canadian (9.2 percent) and the United States (12.1 percent) system in the percentage of GDP expenditure for health (table 11) are related to the United States' higher prepayment and administrative costs.

Other corroborating evidence includes the fact that the current level of physicians' fees in the United States was estimated to be more than double that in Canada.[87] Physicians' incomes in the United States, however, were only about a third higher. This disparity was explained in part by the greater overhead expenses incurred in our health system[88] and, in addition, by the lower workload levels of the American procedure-oriented physicians when compared to their Canadian counterparts.

Canadian–U.S. Hospital Comparisons

Among the most frequent explanations given for the United States' higher per capita expenditure for health is that the U.S. system is technologically more sophisticated,[89-92] and other Western countries achieve considerable fiscal savings by rationing specialized services. Although Americans have available and use far more tertiary services than the Canadians and the Germans, our northern neighbors in 1990 spent on a per capita basis 27.6 percent less for health facilities construction and renovation than did the United States (table 11).

Even though Canada and the United States in 1990 had a relatively similar annual rate of inpatient admissions per person (table 11), Canadian hospitals had a longer average length of hospital stay (+47.9 percent). The data for their acute care days and their extended care days (19.3 percent of the total) are intermingled, and they have more limited fiscal incentives with their reimbursement methodology to encourage earlier discharges. In some ways this explains why Canadian hospitals manage with 3.3 full-time equivalent employees per occupied bed compared to the average of 5.5 FTEs per occupied beds in the United States.[93] In 1990, however, the number of paid hours per discharge in Canadian hospitals was only 11.2 percent less than that in the United States, which could instill some pride that our acute care facilities are relatively efficiently managed.

Unfortunately, the overall evidence of efficiency on a comparative basis suggests that perhaps the opposite is true.[94-95] In addition to Canadian hospitals in 1990 providing significantly more (+61.3 percent) patient

TABLE 11. **Comparative Hospital and Related Operating Data, Canada and the United States, 1990**

Variable	Canada	United States	Percentage Difference between Canada and the United States
Total population (millions)	26.6	248.7	−89.3
Health expenditures per GDP (percentage)	9.2	12.1	−24.0
Annual capital expenditure for health facility construction and renovation per person (dollars)	30.26	41.82	−27.6
Inpatient discharges per 1,000	136.5	125.5	+8.8
Inpatient days per 1,000	1,468.4	910.5	+61.3
Length of stay (days)	10.8	7.3	+47.9
Number of visits to surgical suite per 1,000	109.6	88.1	+24.4
Number of emergency department visits per 1,000	640.3	348.9	+83.5
Number of outpatient visits excluding emergency department visits per 1,000	927.6	868.1	+6.9
Full-time equivalent employees per occupied bed	3.3	5.5	−40.0
Average operating expense per discharge (dollars)	3,815	6,535	−41.7

Source: T. P. Weil, "How Do Canadian Hospitals Do It? A Comparison of Utilization and Costs in the United States and Canada," *Hospital Topics* 73, no. 1 (1995): 10–22.

Note: Values are in 1990 U.S dollars. Canadian figures were adjusted according to the purchasing power–parity exchange rate of $1.00 U.S. equals $1.31 Canadian.

days per person annually, they delivered more surgical procedures (+24.4 percent) and emergency department (+83.5 percent) and outpatient (+6.9 percent) visits per person per year. With these higher volumes of ambulatory care services, the Canadian average operating expense per discharge was $3,815 (−41.6 percent) versus $6,535 in the United States. These findings lead to the question, how all these free-standing Canadian hospitals deliver this increased volume of patient care services for fewer dollars per average discharge. More specifically, how are Canadian medium-size facilities able to manage their resources so they achieve a significantly lower average operating cost per discharge (table 12) than U.S. facilities of a similar average daily census?

Methodology Used in Comparing Hospital Performance

Since an earlier study had concluded that Canadian hospitals under 100 beds in 1989–90 were managed with a third fewer man-hours per discharge than similar-size American facilities,[96] medium-sized community hospitals with an average daily census of 200 patients in both countries were studied to determine whether a somewhat larger average daily census affected differences in staffing patterns. Purposefully excluded from this specific analysis are the regional medical and academic health centers, because of known differences between the two countries in terms of technological sophistication, although a study of their respective performances is reported elsewhere.[97]

All Canadian hospitals must complete and submit an operating and a financial report to the federal government. These annual submissions serve as the principal source of information on how acute care facilities there manage operations within the global budgetary allocation provided by their provincial governments.[98] The Canadian Center for Health Information within Statistics Canada processed the requested 1988–89 data (the latest information available then) from the reports submitted by all of the 59 Canadian hospitals with a total of 200 to 299 beds (table 12).

In the early 1990s the most readily available source of comparable departmentally oriented and fiscal information for hospitals in the United States was the American Hospital Association's (AHA) Monitrend data, which was subscribed to by 22.6 percent of the nation's acute care facilities. Medicare cost reports might have been a preferred source for this analysis, but they contained insufficient statistical and operating information on individual hospital departments to make the necessary detailed comparisons with these 59 Canadian facilities.

In using the AHA Monitrend information for comparative purposes, there are at least two limitations: (1) the operating and fiscal differences between the Monitrend and non-Monitrend hospitals are unknown; and (2) health executives have historically perceived that their colleagues too often maneuver the Monitrend data so that their internal operations appear as effective and efficient as possible to their facility's trustees and others.

The Monitrend "national" data used for comparative purposes included a sample of 87 hospitals with an average daily census of 227.5 patients for the quarter ending December 31, 1989. The AHA for 200–299-bed hospitals reported an average operating expense per discharge for 1988–89 of $5,336,[99] while the December 31, 1989, Monitrend sample, used for comparative purposes, had a $5,133 average operating expense per discharge. This 4 percent disparity suggests that the cost differences cited between Canadian and U.S. medium-size hospitals might be slightly overstated.

Since Canadian hospitals had a considerably longer (+47.9 percent) average length of stay (table 11), most nursing, support, administrative and fiscal, and similar services were analyzed on a per patient day basis. (The use of these resources is more often related to the facility's total patient days or its average daily census than its total number of discharges.) Professional services were studied on a per discharge basis, since the consump-

TABLE 12. General Operating and Fiscal Data of Medium-Size Canadian and U.S. Hospitals, 1988–89

Variable	Canada	United States
Total number of facilities	59	87
Total discharges per facility	6,736	12,815
Total patient days per facility	73,320	83,040
Average daily census per facility	200.9	227.5
Average length of hospital stay (days)	10.88	6.48
Number of emergency department visits per calendar day	98.6	81.6
Average operating expense per discharge (dollars)	3,018	5,133
Average operating expense excluding interest and depreciation per discharge (dollars)	2,918	4,673
Full-time equivalent (FTE) personnel per occupied bed	2.62	5.33
Paid hours per discharge	228.0	276.3
Salary per FTE (dollars)	25,576	25,043
Salary expense per discharge (dollars)	1,977	2,411

Source: T. P. Weil, "How Do Canadian Hospitals Do It? A Comparison of Utilization and Costs in the United States and Canada," *Hospital Topics* 73, no. 1 (1985): 10–22.

Note: Values are in 1988–89 U.S. dollars. Canadian data were adjusted according to the purchasing power–parity exchange rate of $1.00 U.S. equal to $1.315 Canadian.

tion of radiology, nuclear medicine, pathology, pharmacy, electrodiagnostics, and other similar clinically oriented modalities are frequently tied to a specific admission rather than how long the patient is hospitalized.

In making these micro-operational and fiscal comparisons between medium-size Canadian and U.S. hospitals, it is unlikely that case mix,[100] severity of illness,[94] surgical outcomes,[101] morbidity and mortality statistics,[84] and undergraduate and graduate medical education[102] can explain these differences. The number of sophisticated services offered by their respective facilities could be a contributing factor.[74] It is difficult to imagine, however, that these additional programs explain why the average operating expense per discharge at 200–299-bed Canadian hospitals was 37.6 percent less (excluding interest and depreciation expense) than in a U.S. acute care facility with a similar average daily census.

A microanalysis on a departmental/functional basis, using such variables as the volume of services provided to patients, direct expense, or paid hours, attempted to determine where there were significant differences in performance among the medium-size Canadian and American hospitals. More critical study was given where there were significant variations in volumes, paid hours, and direct expenses, since a 10 or 20 percent difference in a specific department/function between the two nations' hospitals could be readily explained by a host of factors (e.g., differences in definition, allocation of expenses).

General Operating and Fiscal Comparisons

The general operating and fiscal statistics of 59 Canadian and 87 U.S. community hospitals, which serve as the basis of this comparative analysis (table 12), confirm earlier findings that American hospitals experience a shorter average length of stay, fewer emergency department and outpatient visits, and greater average operating expense per discharge. This cost difference per discharge cannot be explained by Canadian hospitals having a higher (+2.1 percent) salary expense per FTE. A partial answer, however, is that Canadian medium-size hospitals utilize fewer paid hours per discharge (228 vs. 276.3 hours) with longer average lengths of hospital stay than similar-size American facilities. Canadian hospitals had a lower (−18 percent) salary expense per discharge, the most frequent explanation alleging that they provided less nursing and professional services.

Microanalysis of Nursing Service

The quality of nursing care at a patient's bedside is one of the hallmarks of any Western health system and is often evaluated on the basis of the number of nursing hours per patient day or other similar quantitative measures. Medium-size Canadian and U.S. hospitals experience virtually the same direct expense for nursing services per discharge (table 13). The Canadians, however, allocate considerably more of their total expenditures (25 vs. 19 percent) to these patient care activities.

The 59 Canadian hospitals provided an average of 56 hours of paid nursing hours per discharge compared to 67.4 hours in the United States. This difference (–16.9 percent) is usually explained by the Canadians having twice the supply of registered nurses (RNs) per 1,000 persons and therefore being able to staff the regular nursing units with a higher level of expertise. Also, with a higher ratio of registered nurses (RNs) to licensed practical nurses (LPNs) and certified nursing assistants (CNAs), the Canadians use half the number of ICU/CCU intensive care days to total days compared to U.S. hospitals.

TABLE 13.   Selected Comparative Nursing Service Data for Medium-Size Canadian and U.S. Hospitals, 1988–89

Variable	Canada	United States
Direct nursing service expense as a percentage of total operating expense	24.97	19.05
Direct nursing service expense per discharge (dollars)	744.56	962.09
Direct nursing service expense per patient day (dollars)	68.43	148.47
Total number of paid nursing hours per discharge	56.0	67.4
Total number of patient nursing hours per patient day	5.6	10.4
Total number of paid RN hours per discharge	35.1	34.8
RNs as percentage of total nursing staff	62.7	51.6
Medical CCU and surgical ICU total days per total patient days (percentage)	3.34	6.81
Total number of paid nursing hours in medical CCU and surgical ICU units per CCU and ICU patient days	16.50	21.43
Direct nursing administrative expense as percentage of total operating expense	1.67	1.29

Source: T. P. Weil and M. Stack, "Health Reform—Its Potential Impact on Hospital Nursing Service," *Nursing Economics* 11, no. 4 (1993): 200–207.

Note: Values are in 1988–89 U.S. dollars. Canadian data are adjusted according to the purchasing power–parity exchange rates if $1.00 U.S. equals $1.315 Canadian.

Microanalysis of Professional Services

The expected findings when comparing the use and the expense of professional services per discharge in Canadian and U.S. acute care facilities include: (1) a lower utilization of ancillary services per discharge in Canadian hospitals because of fewer torts, perceived differences in physician practice patterns, and a stronger public mandate there to conserve resources; (2) a lesser number of paid hours per unit of service in Canada because of a more industrious work ethic; (3) the ability to more prudently schedule procedures with a longer average length of stay; and (4) a lower expense per unit of service in Canada because their national health insurance plan has virtually eliminated the cost of processing third-party payer bills.

The overall evidence (table 14) is that medium-size Canadian hospitals were able to provide roughly the same number of units of professional or ancillary services per discharge both at slightly lesser paid hours and at a lesser cost per unit of service than similar-size U.S. facilities. These medium-size Canadian hospitals tended to provide not only more emergency department and outpatient visits but also more nuclear medicine, diagnostic radiology, and physical therapy and other rehabilitative services. Yet the same institutions provided fewer surgical procedures, deliveries, electrodiagnostics, and respiratory therapy and pulmonary function studies than similar American hospitals. Canadian hospitals using more diagnostic radiology and nuclear medicine services per discharge could be related to having fewer computer tomographic scanners (CTs) and magnetic resonance imaging machines (MRIs) available on-site.

The operating expense per unit of service or discharge for these ancillary modalities was either similar to or below those in the United States (except for therapeutic radiology). The most striking difference is that the pharmacy and drug expense per discharge was $141.74 in Canada compared to $258.70 in the United States. This finding is consistent with a General Accounting Office (GAO) study[103] that reported that the manufacturer to wholesaler prices for frequently prescribed items were on the average one-third less expensive in Canada than in the United States.

Canadian hospitals were not only able to provide a greater number of emergency department visits but also at significantly less expense ($19.04 vs. $38.90 per visit). These cost differences could generate roughly a $600,000 savings at then existing volumes at the average medium-size U.S. hospital.

The argument that medium-size Canadian hospitals' cost savings are based on providing their discharged patients with fewer professional services is not supported by these findings. In fact, there should be

TABLE 14. Selected Comparative Professional Services for Medium-Size Canadian and U.S. Hospitals, 1988–89

Variable	Canada	United States
Emergency department (ED)		
Paid hours per ED visit	1.31	2.46
Direct expense per ED visit (dollars)	19.04	38.90
Surgery and recovery		
Inpatient and surgical day care visits per calendar day	14.29	24.03
Paid hours per surgical visit	18.89	17.79
Direct expense per surgical visit (dollars)	154.56	513.12
Laboratory and pathology services		
Direct expense per discharge (dollars)	190.73	241.02
Paid hours per 100 workload units	2.36	2.76
Direct expense as percentage of total operating expense	6.32	5.08
Electrodiagnostics		
Paid hours per discharge	1.22	1.38
Direct expense per discharge (dollars)	19.41	20.57
Nuclear medicine		
Average number of exams per discharge	0.77	0.27
Paid hours per discharge	0.79	0.81
Direct expense per discharge (dollars)	20.22	19.28
Diagnostic radiology		
Average number of procedures per discharge	5.65	4.95
Paid hours per procedure	1.02	1.43
Direct expense per procedure (dollars)	23.23	27.06
Therapeutic radiology		
Paid hours per procedure	1.78	1.23
Direct expense per procedure (dollars)	34.23	25.05
Respiratory therapy and pulmonary function studies		
Paid hours per discharge	1.82	4.67
Direct expense per discharge (dollars)	26.25	69.77
Labor and delivery services		
Average number of deliveries per calendar day	2.5	5.1
Paid hours per delivery	27.57	22.57
Direct expense per delivery (dollars)	380.85	408.31
Pharmacy and drugs		
Direct expense per discharge (dollars)	141.74	258.70
Direct expense as percentage of operating expenses	4.68	5.06
Physical therapy and other rehabilitative services		
Paid hours per discharge	3.74	2.71
Direct expense as a percentage of operating expenses	1.67	1.22

Source: T. P. Weil, "How Do Canadian Hospitals Do It? A Comparison of Utilization and Costs in the United States and Canada." *Hospital Topics* 73, no. 1 (1995): 10–22.

Note: Values are in 1988–89 U.S. dollars. Canadian figures are adjusted according to the purchasing power–parity exchange rate of $1.00 U.S. equals $1.315 Canadian.

insignificant differences in utilization, since both countries offer similar undergraduate and postgraduate medical[102] and allied health education programs, which are a major factor in how patient care is delivered to the sick and disabled.

Microanalysis of Administrative and Support Services

Significant savings among Canadian hospitals were predicted in administrative, fiscal, and support services, because of their governmental, single-payer system versus the United States' competitive, pluralistic one. This perception was partially confirmed by the fact that their support services (e.g., dietary, housekeeping, plant operations, and laundry and linen) experience slightly lower expenses per day or per unit of services than in U.S. facilities.

Medium-size U.S. hospitals had far greater administrative and fiscal expenses per discharge or per patient day than among the 59 medium-size Canadian hospitals. The Canadian hospital, with an average daily census of 200 patients, had 48.1 FTEs in administrative and fiscal functions compared to 131.6 FTEs in a U.S. hospital. To implement such personnel reductions, American hospitals would need to eliminate almost all screening for determining eligibility for benefits, preparing detailed bills for insurers, responding to utilization review procedures, and marketing their services. If American acute care facilities in 1989–90 had administrative and fiscal expenses comparable to those in Canada, an estimated $8.9 billion would have been saved in total U.S. hospital expenditures. This is less than Shiels and his colleague's (1992) projected savings of $13.35 billion[104] and only a third of the amount that Grumbach and his colleagues (1992) estimated based on more macro-level assumptions.[85]

Often overlooked in previous Canadian–United States hospital cost comparisons is that acute care facilities north of our border have an average depreciation and interest expense of 3.3 percent of total operating expense in comparison to 9 percent in the United States, a difference of $360.84 per discharge. Most Canadian hospitals obtain outright grants from their provincial and other governmental agencies or generate support from local fund-raising activities for new construction, renovation, and the acquisition of new or the replacement of existing equipment.[105] In contrast, most U.S. acute care facilities use operating surpluses or need to borrow as their prime sources of funding for their major capital projects. Also, medium-size American hospitals generate greater depreciation expenses because of having more technologically sophisticated facilities than similar-size Canadian hospitals.

What's the Fiscal Outcome?

To obtain some insight into the fiscal position of the Canadian acute care facilities with their national health insurance system, the 1988–89 financial ratios of the 59 medium-size hospitals were compared to the 200–299-bed U.S. 1989 Healthcare Financial Management Association data.[106] This was to compare their facility's fiscal "wellness" or "sickness" under the single-payer system with that obtained under the U.S. pluralistic system.

Most noticeable was the average medium-size Canadian hospital experiencing a significant net operating loss (–6 percent) that was more than offset by nonoperating revenues. In 1988–89 the average Canadian hospital had a net margin of $722,478, suggesting that hospital officials tailored their expenses to the sum of the global budgetary amount received from the province and their available nonoperating revenues. Detsky suggests that the medical profession and the health executives implement an implicit rationing system whereby they allocate available resources to serve their community's health care needs most effectively.[98]

The Canadian health executives manage fiscally with low current ratios (1.17), days in net patient accounts receivable (24.4 days), and days cash on hand (15.2 days), reflecting a monolithic government-financed system. In addition, the Canadians demonstrate more favorable capital structure ratios since their long-term liabilities compared to their fund balance or fixed assets are far lower than among U.S. hospitals. Their activity ratios, which often are referred to as efficiency ratio, since they measure the relationship between outputs and inputs, suggest that Canadian acute care facilities use their assets more effectively than similar-size U.S. hospitals. A somewhat unexpected finding was that the average age of physical plant among medium-size Canadian hospitals (9.2 years) in 1988–89 was only a year and a half older than in the United States. There was only a half-year difference among all Canadian versus all American hospitals.[106]

In summary, operating data presented earlier suggest that the Canadian hospitals without developing health networks are able to deliver more care with fewer dollars per discharge, and the fiscal ratio analysis suggests that their national health insurance program has not yet bankrupted their acute care facilities.

What Can American Health Networks Learn from Canada?

Some political rhetoric heard during the 1992 presidential debates suggested that the Canadian "national socialized health insurance" program provided inadequate or drastically rationed care and resulted in deductions from payroll that were seriously out of control.[82] These statements are not supported by this microanalysis of their 59 medium-size hospitals nor by a GAO report[90] but were taken out of context in the heat of President Bush's reelection efforts. There are, however, some lessons that American health networks can learn from this comparative medium-size hospital study that are pertinent to achieving more effective and efficient U.S. health networks:

1. If Americans are willing to continue spending a quarter more of our GDP for health than Canadians, we can easily retain our technological sophistication while avoiding their queues for specialized services.

2. If the United States were to enact universal access, based on Canadian use rates, the existing acute care beds in American hospitals (in 1990) would experience a 128.1 percent occupancy. Congress's enacting universal access without some of the utilization constraints contained in managed care would result in the public clamoring for the construction of additional beds.

3. Inherent in most universal health insurance programs is that federal and state governments provide outright grants for new construction, renovation, and acquiring new equipment. This policy allows public officials to decide which and where health services will be provided, something quite alien to the United States' current competitive approach.

4. If the United States were to implement a single-payer health system, a somewhat unlikely occurrence, an anticipated reduction of 255,000 hospital positions (mostly in the business office) could be anticipated. Somewhat less severe personnel cutbacks could conceivably occur among other health facilities, in physicians' offices and among health insurers. These savings might well pay for the cost of establishing a U.S. comprehensive health insurance plan (multipayer) with a "core benefit package" for the uninsured.

5. If hospital pharmacy and drug expenses in the United States were similar to those in Canada, $3.6 billion annually would be saved here. More restrictive formularies and generic prescriptions, along with price regulation, would be required here to accomplish these cost reductions.[103] Enacting such measures would be met by negative reactions from the pharmaceutical industry and some physicians.

6. Although the global budgetary target concept often conjures up fear that government is inept or corrupt, or both, there are some

conceptual advantages for hospitals in obtaining such an annual appropriation and then deciding within the region and locally how to most appropriately allocate these resources. Global budgetary approaches as employed in most Western countries allow local leaders, health executives, physicians, and others the potential flexibility to implement the collaborative approaches inherent in health networking.

7. Finally, we instinctively recognize that additional cost reductions in U.S. hospitals will require them to provide more care with relatively less additional total reimbursement. The argument that Canadian hospitals accomplish this by providing inadequate nursing services or by adversely rationing professional services is not supported by this comparative analysis of Canadian and American hospitals. Any of the cost-containment approaches for the United States alluded to earlier, such as global budgetary targets and reviewing the pricing of drugs, if they are to be implemented, are neither painless nor easy.

Replicating the German Healthcare System

Americans have known for some time that the German multipayer system provides nearly universal comprehensive benefits and has a superior record to that of the United States in constraining health expenditures.[107-8] In 1997 Germany maintained its health spending at 10.4 percent of its gross domestic product, roughly one-quarter less than here.[84] Nevertheless, Germany, in comparison to U.S. averages, has an excessive supply of health resources: too many insurers (sickness funds), too many small specialty hospitals, approximately twice the number of beds, and about one-third more physicians per person. The federal republic has utilization rates for hospital services that Americans consider excessive—approximately 150 percent more inpatient days. Yet, despite such a comprehensive scope of benefits and high utilization rates, Germany's 1997 health expenditure per capita was $2,339, compared to $3,925 in the United States.

The German health system functions under a century-old social insurance concept that represents a middle ground in the spectrum of approaches currently being used by Western industrialized nations to protect their citizens from the economic consequence of illness, disability, unemployment, and old age. Germany could be most simply depicted as positioned near the midpoint between the U.S. private-oriented approach and the British "cradle to grave" program.

Among Western industrialized nations Germany's health insurance plan came closest during the 1980s to limiting increases in spending to a rate equal to the growth of its GDP. From post–World War II to the reunification with East Germany (roughly 45 years), West Germany achieved a blend of government-mandated financing by employees and employers, combined with the private provision of care by physicians, with controlled hospital expenditures, and with benefits administered by not-for-profit third-party payers.[109] The area's sickness funds paid the same negotiated per diem rate to a specific hospital, whatever the patient's diagnosis, an exception being made for a limited number of tertiary services. In Germany there are no health networks, no itemized patient bills, no cost shifting among payers, and virtually no one without health insurance.

All Germans have universal access to a comprehensive range of physician and hospital benefits and a free choice of doctor and acute care facilities. Practitioners enjoy a substantial degree of clinical autonomy, although doctors and hospitals are constrained by the caps established by global budgetary targets. Among its other virtues the German health delivery system has been traditionally decentralized, pluralistic, and self-governing.[110] Probably its major shortcoming is the separation between community- and hospital-based physicians, sometimes raising serious problems with the continuity of patient care.

What adds considerable flexibility to the German health system is the option to purchase private health insurance coverage. The roughly 10 percent of the population who earn the highest incomes opt out of the mandatory plan. The availability of private insurance for those with high incomes is expected to be viable for the foreseeable future, since pluralism, self-governance, and decentralization are traditional, ingrained elements of the German health system.

Limiting Physician Reimbursement

Under the 1993 health reform plan, total spending by the German sickness funds for all community-based physician services, which are reimbursed on a fee-for-service basis, was capped by an adjustment to any revenue increases experienced by the third-party payers. In addition, the Federal Ministry of Health proposed several controversial measures to decrease the utilization of physician services and to improve the geographic distribution of available doctors. Representatives from the regional associations of physicians and the sickness funds are continuing to oversee billing for patient services and will impose stricter financial sanctions on physicians who exceed average service volumes and prescribing levels.

Possibly the most controversial provision contained in the 1993 health reform law was the requirement that strict population-to-physician ratios (by specialty) be established for each municipality. Although the federal-level association for physicians has had the authority to limit a doctor from practicing in a specific geographic area with an excess supply of the doctor's specialty, it has not exercised this option. The group has instead focused on providing information about where physicians might most suitably establish new practices. Not surprisingly, Germany has rejected the option of limiting medical school enrollment because such a strategy would give rise to constitutional challenges and strong local opposition. In the next decades these issues of physician distribution, geographically and by specialty, obviously need to be resolved in Germany, as in the United States, to enhance our health delivery systems.

Reducing Hospital Expenditures

Historically, German hospitals, which for all practical purposes are free-standing, have been reimbursed almost exclusively on the basis of total days; as a result, average lengths of stay for most diagnoses have been approximately twice those in the United States (table 15). In Germany, however, the hospital's total operating costs are set annually primarily on the basis of the projected volume of surgical procedures, treatments, and discharges or a prospective global budgetary amount for each facility.

The potentially most far-reaching provision in the 1993 health reform plan for acute care facilities was allowing hospital-based physicians, who are almost always salaried, to consult with patients on an ambulatory basis. To provide increased continuity of patient care, hospital-based physician are now allowed "to counsel and to provide three treatment days within five days of admission, and seven treatment days within 14 days of discharge."[110]

Acute care facilities in the past decade have obtained an increasing percentage of the health dollar at the expense of community-based physicians. As a result, these practitioners have opposed a reform measure that allows hospital-based doctors to diagnose and treat patients on a more routine ambulatory care basis. To provide some equalization, as part of the 1993 reform plan, community-based surgical subspecialists for the first time obtained privileges to perform ambulatory surgery in hospitals.

With no immediate fiscal incentive to expand a service beyond the resources allocated through the global budgetary approach, German hospitals and their physicians have tended to work more collaboratively than U.S. providers to insure that patients are transferred from one facility to another when necessary.[109] Yet, if Germany moves toward a more clinically oriented, prospective payment system, as is now under way, it could anticipate some of the same problems experienced here with similar reimbursement incentives—the most obvious examples being the diagnostic related groups (DRGs) "creep" and the "dumping" of difficult and costly cases.

Comparative West German and U.S. Hospital Costs

In 1990 the average United States hospital provided 321.4 paid hours per discharge, twice as many as in the former West Germany (144.5 hours), which helps explain the significant difference in operating expense per discharge, $6,536 compared to $2,972 (see table 15). There are several reasons why the average 1990 discharge cost at a German hospital was 55 percent less than the average cost at a U.S. hospital:

1. German hospitals had an average of 1.4 full-time equivalent employees per occupied bed, compared with an average of 5.5 FTEs in U.S. hospitals. An average 400-bed hospital in Germany in 1990 had an 82 percent occupancy and employed only 25 FTEs for administrative and fiscal services.
2. The average 400-bed hospital in Germany annually has only 10,000 to 15,000 emergency room visits, mostly trauma patients or those requiring admission for complicated diagnostic problems. A German 400-bed hospital would have a CT scanner but generally would be without an MRI, cardiac catheterization, open-heart surgery, and radiation therapy, a significant shortfall in clinical capabilities compared to U.S. acute care facilities of a similar size. The amount of sophisticated medical technology per 100,000 persons in Germany is significantly less than in the United States but, in general, more than in Canada.[74, 111]
3. Patients and employees in German hospitals enjoy fewer amenities than those available in the United States. The average age in 1990 of a German hospital physical plant was 15 years, roughly twice that experienced among U.S. hospitals.
4. German hospital-based physicians are salaried, and they perform many functions that are provided in the United States by nursing service personnel. There are 40,000 to 45,000 unemployed or underemployed physicians in Germany, so there is intense compe-

tition for hospital positions and a willingness to work at a salary far below that provided in the United States.

5. Germany's governments pay for most hospital capital expenditures for construction and renovation via outright grants. In fact, the concept of borrowing for physical plant expansion is almost unheard of in Germany.

TABLE 15. Selected Health and Hospital Variables in West Germany and the United States, 1990

Variable	West Germany	United States
Health expenditures per total GDP (%)	8.7 (1992)	13.6 (1992)
Public spending per total health spending (%)	72.8	42.4
Per capita spending for health (dollars)	1,775 (1992)	3,094 (1992)
Acute care inpatient beds per 1,000	7.1	3.7
Acute care inpatient days per 1,000	2,237.0	910.5
Acute care admissions per 1,000 per year	173.6	125.5
Acute care average length of stay (days)	12.9	7.3
Surgical visits per 1,000	102.7	88.1
Outpatient visits excluding emergency department visits per 1,000	NA	868.1
Full-time equivalent employees per occupied bed	1.4	5.9
Operating expense per discharge (dollars)	2,972	6,535
Operating expense per day (dollars)	215	901
Paid hours per discharge	144.5	321.4
Number of physicians per 1,000	3.1	2.3
Annual physician contacts per person	11.5 (1988)	5.3 (1988)
Annual physician expenditures per person (dollars)	193 (1988)	414 (1988)
Expenditures for physician services per physician (dollars)	67,067 (1988)	183,281 (1988)
Infant mortality live births per 1,000	7.1	9.1
Perinatal mortality death per 1,000	6.4	9.6
Life expectancy at birth (years)	75.8	75.4
Percentage of population over 64 years of age	15.4	12.6
Dependency ratio	57.9	70.1
Pharmaceuticals as percentage of total health expenditures	16.1 (1992)	8.6 (1992)
	Outpatient only	
Pharmaceutical expenditures per person (dollars)	258 (1988)	182 (1988)

NA = Not available

Sources: G. J. Schieber, J.-P. Poullier, and L. M. Greenwald, "Health Spending Delivery and Outcomes in OECD Countries," *Health Affairs* 12, no. 2 (1993): 120–29; G. J. Schieber, J.-P. Poullier, and L. M. Greenwald, "Health Care Spending in Twenty-Four Countries." *Health Affairs* 10, no. 3 (1991): 22–38; T. P. Weil and W. H. Miller, "Germany's Health System—Clinton's Managed Competition with Global Budgets." *Healthcare Financial Briefs* 16, no. 2 (1993): 1–8; T. P. Weil and W. H. Miller, "West German Hospitals: Some Additional Data." *Healthcare Financial Briefs* 16, no. 4 (1993): 1–4; and, T. P. Weil, "An American Macromanaged Health Care System?" *Health Services Management Research* 7, no. 1 (1994): 43–56.

Note: Values are in 1990 or 1988 U.S. dollars. German data for 1990 were adjusted according to the purchasing power–parity exchange rate of U.S. $1.00 equals 1.598 DM.

Controlling Pharmaceutical Expenditures

A common political belief exists in Germany that the government should insure that prescribed drugs should be available to everyone.[112] The 1993 health reform plan imposed a budgetary cap at the 1991 expenditure level (with some inflationary adjustments) for drugs prescribed by community-based physicians. To keep spending below levels set by the global budget for drugs, the plan held the federal association of physicians and the pharmaceutical industry responsible for the portion of expenditures above the federally mandated cap. Physician fees were to be reduced to offset the first $175 million in potential overruns, the pharmaceutical industry was to cover the next $175 million in overruns, and the sickness funds were responsible for payments exceeding $350 million of overruns. In reality, because the $175 million potential penalty (which never needed to be utilized) is equivalent to only 1 percent of all physicians' expenditures, this provision in many ways was more "window dressing" than a means to reduce Germany's total health expenditures significantly.

By the end of 1996, however, Germany's drug budgets were overdrawn by $1.6 billion, and physicians in some states faced huge potential reimbursement claims from the sickness funds. The claims by the health insurance funds are being settled through agreements or arbitration. The long-term solution is for representatives of the associations of physicians and sickness funds to develop average prescription cost standards for doctors that will take into account their specialty, patient mix, use of technology, and region. German physicians who exceed these standards by specified percentages would then be penalized financially.

Why All This Cost Containment?

Germany's health reform initiatives are driven by the need for overall economic restructuring primarily due to its reunification efforts with East Germany, significant unemployment, and high labor costs, but are always undertaken in the context of its commitment to "social solidarity." In 1995 it was estimated that, for every dollar expended for salaries, another 36 cents was spent for retirement benefits, health and unemployment insurance, and other mandated coverage.[113] For the young German worker this is an alarming issue, particularly in light of estimates that by the year 2030 there will be more Germans drawing social security cash benefits than there will be workers in the active labor force.

Recent health reforms in Germany should be analyzed as an attempt to keep total healthcare expenditures, if possible, below 10 percent of GDP. Germany must tinker at the micromanagement level to obtain additional operating efficiencies, as this central European country continues to provide universal comprehensive benefits within global budgetary caps. These reform measures, and those now discussed, such as copayment and the more active management of patient care by insurers, are more a readjustment of the traditional German multipayer system rather than the package of major health reforms that was once envisioned by the Clinton plan. What is significant is the absence of any substantive discussion among German health policy experts or any health executives about developing health networks, although they experience what is obviously an excess supply of hospital beds and physicians.

A Single- versus a Multipayer System

A Canadian single-payer rather than a German multipayer system to constrain U.S. health costs makes little political and substantive sense. Proponents of the Canadian model focus on its monolithic approach and its operating efficiencies, but this country's ability to contain its health costs is based more on the power of its provinces to impose "tighter" global budgetary caps on their providers.[42]

Americans often overlook the fact that Canada *historically* has had the second most expensive health system in the world.[84] In 1997 three countries with multipayer systems maintained their expenditures for health as a percentage of their GDP slightly above and below Canada's 9 percent (France, at 9.6 percent; Germany, at 10.4 percent; and Japan, at 7.3 percent). The central issue is not the single- versus multipayer system but, rather, how tight to set global budgetary caps and how to allocate available health resources.

Government mandates that establish total healthcare expenditures pose a significant risk for any health provider, whether reimbursed in a single- or multipayer environment. A major argument against providing health networks with global budgets in the United States and thereby being able to reduce business office and related personnel significantly is that doing so may place the entire health delivery system and its health alliances in possible financial peril. Simply put, consumers and providers fear that U.S. public officials may fail to pass consistently the enabling legislation required to raise sufficient revenues to finance needed medical care services. Under such circumstances managing a health network would be further politicized, and several of the major virtues of the current market-driven environment (e.g., reducing cost increases and utilization) could well be lost.

More Competition or More Regulation?

Managed care during the past decade has been a major factor not only in controlling historical inflationary increases in U.S. health expenditures but in forcing providers to develop fiscally and politically powerful health networks. For managed competition, managed care, and further privatization as envisioned early on by Ellwood[3] and Enthoven[2] to continue playing a major role in restructuring the health system, the United States' health networks and HMOs must concurrently enhance access and social equity, improve quality, and reduce cost.

Constraints Imposed by Managed Care

Although the United States has experienced almost a decade of previously unprecedented economic growth, ready access to care provided by health networks is sometimes difficult to secure for those who are enrolled in some managed care plans and particularly among those who are uninsured. While the HMOs are now only slowly gaining additional market share,[1] almost a fifth of the nonelderly population (18.9 percent), or an estimated 44.6 million Americans, are without health insurance coverage.[115] Obtaining access to care can be particularly difficult among young adults, 34.6 percent of them without prepaid health insurance. The insurers would be anxious to enroll these potentially lower-risk subscribers, but many 19- to 24-year-olds, in particular, cannot readily afford to purchase such coverage or are desirous of using available funds for more consumer-oriented acquisitions.

Some HMO members can experience difficulties in obtaining access to care. If not all of the area's physicians are eligible providers, some subscribers no longer can utilize their previous physician or hospital without often experiencing a financial penalty. Managed care plans can use primary care physicians as "gatekeepers," and referrals to a specialist are only possible with their and the managed care plan's concurrence. Special diagnostic testing, outpatient surgery, inpatient care, and other expensive medical services almost always require prior authorization from the insurer. Consumers of health care seek to obtain the best care possible, while the HMOs prefer to minimize utilization and cost. With such conflicting incentives, even among the insured, access to health care can be restricted.

Social equity—frequently referred to in Europe as social solidarity—is not one of the hallmarks of the U.S. health system. The managed care plans try to be relatively selective when enrolling subscribers so as to enhance their bottom lines. In fact, during the latter part of the 1990s HMOs disenrolled many of their Medicare and Medicaid subscribers because they were unable to provide coverage to the aged and the indigent within the amount of dollars made available by Medicare and Medicaid. Managed care could well have the effect of sharpening the division of the three-tier health system in the United States: the wealthy receiving all the services they desire because of their ability to pay for care on a fee-for-service basis; the middle class obtaining managed care benefits with restrictions promulgated by the insurer concerning which provider and what services will be offered; and the uninsured, who receive most of their initial care at the hospital emergency department. The only known and proven way to bring about greater social equity in obtaining health services is through a universal compulsory health plan, which does not fit American political beliefs.

A careful analysis of the relationship between managed care and quality leads to the conclusion that managed care has not to date decreased overall effectiveness of patient care in the United States.[116] Evidence suggests, however, the position that current market-driven approaches may adversely affect the health of some vulnerable subpopulations,[117] and enrollees in managed care plans are generally less satisfied with their care and experience more problems accessing specialized services.[118–21] In addition, younger, wealthier, and healthier persons were more satisfied with their health plans than older, poorer, and sicker persons, even after adjusting for the type of HMO plan.

Unfortunately, there is a dearth of studies that provide definitive results about the effect of managed care on clinical outcome. Indeed, relatively few studies after 1990 compare the effectiveness of care among HMOs with that provided in traditional fee-for-service environments. Considering the rapid pace of change in the U.S. health system, the relevance of findings reported earlier may now be in some dispute. What is also missing is knowledge about how different types of financial incentives affect quality and cost in organizing, managing, and financing an effective and efficient HMO. In the absence of such knowledge, managed care plans likely will continue to use financial inducements to control costs without a full understanding of the effect that these incentives have on the quality of care. Managed care plans have been far more successful in controlling health costs than in managing their subscribers' health services.

While managed care plans thus far have not enhanced access or social equity and have achieved little to improve the quality of patient care, this market-driven approach has made a significant contribution in controlling health expenditures. In 1997 health spending in the United States increased just 4.8 percent, absorbing 13.3 percent of GDP, a share that has remained relatively constant for the past five years.[35] The pronounced recent slowdown in health expenditures as a result of managed care has certainly exceeded the expectations of most industry analysts. What this means for future health spending is of greater interest to employers, for whom the costs of providing their employees with health benefits increasingly affects their bottom lines; to public officials who are responsible for the Medicare, Medicaid, and other governmental programs; to insured Americans, who are sensing that an increasing percentage of their health care costs are now being paid for out-of-pocket; and to the general public, including the uninsured, who strive to be consumers of a more effective and efficient delivery of health services.

A continuing strong economy is expected to boost underlying demand for health services, and a higher inflation in medical costs might thereby fuel a rise in health spending. The current slowdown in the increase in private sector managed care enrollment and a pause in the downward trend for purchasing fee-for-service coverage can also be factors contributing to the acceleration in health spending growth. Although HMOs may not be as successful in the future as they have been in the past decade in slowing the inflationary trend in health services, managed care made a major contribution in restraining costs in the 1990s.

Privatization of the Health Field

Compatible with the market-driven managed competition model is the trend toward the privatization of health providers and insurers, most clearly evidenced by an increasing number of Americans in the early 1990s acquiring stock among the investor-owned hospitals, the for-profit managed care plans, and the physician management companies. More recently, the nation's teaching hospitals, in particular, have been concerned with decreases in reimbursement as outlined in the Balanced Budget Act of 1997.[122] To test the efficacy of the more market-driven approaches that are available, the financial positions of the nation's best teaching hospitals (tables 9–10) and some of the largest investor-owned health corporations were evaluated.[46] The significant difference in the fiscal outlook among some "well-off" academic health centers compared to their "poor cousins" is worrisome. Lack of reimbursement rather than sloppy management (i.e., excess number of paid man-hours) appears to explain why, unless additional monies are infused, a few of the most highly regarded referral centers in the United States could well be facing bankruptcy in the next few years.

Further privatization of the not-for-profit providers, more specifically the teaching hospitals facing fiscal distress, was evaluated. The fiscal performance of the largest hospital investor-owned corporations, for-profit managed care plans, and the physician management companies was disappointing in terms of increases in net revenues, net margins, debt-to-equity ratios, and recent stock appreciation.[46] The option of modifying the sponsorship of major not-for-profit providers to investor-owned, based on the current financial positions of these publicly held corporations, could not at this time be recommended as being in the public interest. In addition, the for-profits raise the ethical issues of whether health care should be considered a business, and the investor-owned providers and insurers have tended to be more concerned with bottom-line considerations than quality of care. The concept of further privatization of the health field seems more ideologically compatible with American values than with attaining a practical solution to improve the U.S. health system.

Universal Compulsory Health Insurance in the United States

When comparing the health spending, utilization, and outcomes of the Canadian, German, and U.S. health systems, possibly the simplest conclusion is that Americans spend the most, rely on a greater availability of technology, and do not necessarily achieve the best outcomes (see tables 15–16). Not only do Canada and Germany provide universal comprehensive health insurance at roughly 25 to 30 percent less of their GDP than the United States, but they deliver far more care with these lower expenditures. The Canadians and Germans achieve these results without forming U.S.-style health networks.

Canada and Germany are able to achieve savings in their health systems by a variety of means. First, they employ a simplified prepayment approach (the Canadian single-payer and the German multipayer systems) so that they are able to manage their facilities with considerably fewer administrative and business office personnel.

To determine differences in the use of hospital personnel, especially administrative and managerial, among Austrian, German, and U.S. hospitals, staffing of one Austrian, one German, and two U.S. academic health centers was analyzed.[123] The major findings (published in 1998) were that administrative categories included 19 percent of the full-time equivalent personnel in U.S. facilities compared to only 8 percent in the European hospitals. Among the administrative areas the largest absolute FTE differences were among the financial operations. U.S. hospitals for business office functions used more than five FTEs per 10,000 patient days versus less than one FTE among the Austrian and German academic health centers. The organization and financing of these countries' health systems were considered to be the key element in why Austrian and German hospitals use far fewer administrative-business office personnel than those in U.S. facilities.

Between 1968 and 1993 the U.S. health field labor force grew from 3.976 to 10.208 million FTEs, with the administrative categories increasing from 719,000 to 2.792 million persons.[124] Between 1971 and 1986 hospital employment per capita grew 29 percent in the United States (mostly because of administrative growth) and fell 14 percent in Canada. In 1986 Canadian hospitals still employed more clinical staff per million persons. Himmelstein and his colleagues concluded that, if U.S. hospitals and outpatient facilities adopted Canada's staffing patterns, 1.4 million fewer managers and related personnel would be required.[114] Possibly the most contentious finding is that, in spite of having a universal compulsory national health insurance program to balance spending per capita, Canadians overall receive slightly more nursing and other clinical care than Americans, if measured by labor inputs.

Second among the strategies employed by Canada and Germany to keep health costs down is simply reducing the number of available facilities, acquiring less medical technology, and centralizing tertiary services at major medical centers. Canada's health insurance system, the nation's most popular publicly financed service, has for years demonstrated a

TABLE 16.   Health Spending, Utilization, and Outcomes in Canada, Germany, and the United States, Various Years

Variable	Canada	Germany	United States
Health spending per person, 1997 (dollars)	2,095	2,339	3,925
Percentage of GDP spent on health, 1997	9.0	10.4	13.5
Percentage of population with government assured health insurance, 1997	100	92.2	33.3
Per capita spending on hospitals, 1996 (dollars)	918	796	1,646
Hospital days per person, 1996	1.9	2.8	1.1
MRI units per million persons	1.3 (1995)	5.7 (1996)	16.0 (1995)
CT scanners per million persons	7.9 (1995)	16.4 (1966)	26.9 (1993)
Per capita spending on physician services, 1996 (dollars)	298	375	761
Physicians per 1,000, 1996	2.1	3.4	2.6
Drug spending per person, 1996 (dollars)	258	289	344
Infant mortality per 1,000 live births, 1996	6.0	5.0	7.8
Life expectancy of males at birth, 1996	75.4	73.6	72.7

Source: G. F. Anderson and J.-P. Poullier, "Health Spending, Access, and Outcomes: Trends in Industrialized Countries," *Health Affairs* 18, no. 1 (1999): 178–92.

capacity to deliver universal, high-quality medical care for considerably less per capita than is achievable in the United States. But in recent years economic strains are testing Canada's commitment to maintaining its treasured system.

As Canada sought over the 1990s to eliminate its soaring budget deficit, the federal government reduced its financial commitment to the provincially administered health insurance plans. These state administered plans, in turn, sharply squeezed spending on their hospitals and sorely tested their physicians' and nurses' tolerance for major downsizing. In an unmistakable contrast with the United States, which has increasingly relied on market-driven methods to achieve the modest reductions in hospital capacity, Canada used a combination of fiscal and regulatory initiatives to undertake a radical restructuring of its hospital sector. This is evidenced by a significant decrease in the percentage of the Canadian health dollar being spent for hospital services (a 17.2 percent decline from 1987 to 1997), somewhat offsetting increases in drugs and home health services.[125]

As Canada faced serious fiscal pressures because of its overall economic outlook (including serious unemployment issues), a strategy was explored by Canada's provincial governments to regionalize or decentralize the delivery of health services. In order to achieve these objectives, the Ministry of Health requires each regional health authority to submit a business plan and an annual report, including performance information and underlying performance indicators. These criteria are then used to measure process and outcome and are useful in generating questions about the behavior or the performance of a specific provider. This is occurring, interestingly, in an environment in which a "system for defining systematic performance measures for a publicly funded healthcare system does not exist."[126]

As part of this "resizing," the Saskatchewan government in 1992 announced the closure and conversion of 52 small rural hospitals to wellness centers as part of a shift from institutional- to community-based care.[127] While the cost savings and benefits of this shift in policy are being contested, the paradox is that closing these rural hospitals may have created previously unrealized health, economic, and social distress, because of the psychological importance and public relations value of maintaining an acute hospital in each of these communities. Physicians hesitate to locate where an inpatient facility is not readily accessible to their patients, and downsizing a hospital usually means eliminating some well-paying positions, frequently in areas where "good jobs" are already scarce.

The federal and provincial or state governments in Canada and Germany are responsible for almost all capital funding for hospital construction and renovation and the acquisition of new or the replacement of old equipment. In a period of economic austerity there is limited funding to update physical plants already considerably outdated in comparison to those in the United States. The Canadians and Germans historically have provided less highly sophisticated medical technology per million persons than the United States and have centralized it in their major teaching hospitals.[84, 111] What is surprising to Americans is that there are teaching hospitals in Canada and Germany without open-heart surgery or MRI capabilities.

Against the background of a financial crisis and supposed inefficiencies due to the inappropriate or ineffective use of technologies in the German health system, increasing study has been given to how to limit providers from acquiring unnecessary new equipment.[128] In contrast to the situation in the United States under certificate of need legislation, the physician sector appears to be much more regulated than the hospitals, and, in general, the unavailability of capital and the financial infeasibility of obtaining sufficient patient revenues is slowing down German providers from acquiring more sophisticated equipment.

Although the Canadian and German health systems provide universal access and social equity, in a period of relatively high unemployment, public officials are attempting to reduce the number of available facilities and equipment and prevent providers from acquiring additional expensive technology. This approach may inconvenience patients and their families, and some physicians, but manages to provide reduced costs and higher-quality care, since sophisticated services are centralized where a high volume of these procedures and services can be provided.

A third approach to cutting the costs of health care in Germany and Canada involves their modifying the reimbursement system primarily to reduce health expenditures. Among the industrialized nations the former West Germany came closest during the 1980s to limiting health spending increases to a rate that equaled the growth of its national income, an achievement that the United States was nowhere close to fulfilling. But concerns over the impact of the reunification of East and West Germany on health costs prompted the Federal Republic to enact far-reaching reforms with lightning speed. These reforms, which were primarily started in 1993, were noticeable in terms of tightening up on all health expenditures, with some adjustments on how health services were to be delivered.

Seven private insurance companies in 1994 experimented with reimbursing providers on a fee-for-service basis with the co-insurance amount being paid by the patient.[129] Consumers became more cost conscious with this approach, but extending this pilot project to all Germans was considered to be inconsistent with their social solidarity principle. In 1997 Germany started to experiment with HMO type "gatekeepers," but to date this approach has not gained any significant following.[130]

German hospitals are now more aggressively competing with one another for the limited financial resources available in the healthcare sector. A major issue is that hospitals for the most part are reimbursed on the basis of a global budgetary amount, with the major component in the reimbursement methodology being the total number of patient days.[131] Therefore, German patients tend to have longer lengths of stay than in either Canada or certainly the United States. Beginning in 1996, certain procedures or therapies, primarily surgical procedures, earned a fixed fee. In 1998, 20 percent of the average hospital's budget was billed through such procedure-specific fees. But this is not a diagnostic-related group payment methodology, because nursing care is still reimbursed at a department-specific per diem rate. As in the United States, the DRG-type approach provides new opportunities for "upcoding" (using the diagnostic code generating the most reimbursement) and unbundling hospital services.[132]

Germans use twice as many prescribed drugs per year as do Americans. As a result of a three-year spending cap on the use of pharmaceuticals, promulgated in Germany in 1993, when doctors were held financially liable for spending overruns, there was a drastic drop in drug spending. German doctors, however, soon resumed their drug-intensive habits. The 1993 reform package called for a formulary to reduce significantly the number of drugs that insurers would be required to pay for, and such a list was eventually drawn up. The federal health minister eventually bowed to the pressures of the domestic pharmaceutical industry and in 1997 instituted a copayment system to curtail drug expenditures. Physician-specific drug budgets were introduced a year later in another attempt to control pharmaceutical expenditures.

The German insurers bargain with associations of providers and, because of legal constraints, are not able to negotiate fees with individual hospitals or physicians. Their only alternative at this point is to negotiate reimbursement rates with large groups of physicians or hospitals. The insurance companies are allowed to undertake some pilot experiments, but the overall picture in Germany is that change is coming to their health system much more slowly than in other countries.[107, 131–33]

The Canadians use their global budgetary targets as a means to set a limit on total health expenditures. There is little indication that quality of care or the deployment of personnel has improved there on the basis of forming a more regional approach to provide care and shuttering some facilities. What is far more noticeable in the case of these economic shortfalls in Canada is that local citizens give community leaders, physicians, and health executives more direction of how to provide the patient care needed in the community with less money.[134]

Why a Quasi-Private, Quasi-Public Appoach?

In summary, health expenditures can continue to be curtailed in the United States with managed care, but the only known and proven way to limit health spending increases to a rate equal to the growth of national income is to set global budgetary targets as used in Canada and Germany. The Germans do well with a multipayer system, which could be easily replicated in the United States.[135] The managed care plans, private insurance companies, Medicare, Medicaid, and other providers could still negotiate the level of reimbursement with providers; that part of the United States' competitive, market-driven system could remain intact.

Possibly the most contentious issue in the United States would be whether to enact a universal comprehensive health insurance system, in which access to care and social equity would be relatively comparable irrespective of income, race, and other demographic factors. Health care for the uninsured is already being cross-subsidized by the insured or by taxpayers. Universal access without the utilization review component of managed care in place could easily result in hospital inpatient and drug use patterns increasing to those experienced in Canada and Germany. By maintaining a market-driven rather than a regulatory approach, it is reasonably possible to provide universal access without bankrupting those paying the premiums, the insurers, or the providers.

Access to services and social equity might well be enhanced in the United States by again using the German model of providing everyone with a reasonable range of health insurance benefits and allowing those with significant incomes to opt out of the statutory (government) program and purchase private health insurance. Those in the statutory program also should be able to purchase supplementary coverage out of their own pockets or to negotiate with the employer for such benefits.

Quality of care and patient satisfaction are generally the highest among those who are young, healthy, and wealthy and can easily afford to seek care on a fee-for-service basis. If such an individual requires the most sophisticated technology available in the world, being a patient within the U.S. health system would be preferred. For the average person with an average illness, the difference among these countries is relatively minimal. Unfortunately, quality of care and patient satisfaction are lowest among those who are old, poor, or uneducated, have several chronic illnesses, or are living in a medically underserved community and in the United States can only afford to seek care as poorly insured or uninsured patients. These factors are more important than whether the patient is seeking care in a market-driven multipayer health system (United States) or a regulated single- (Canadian) or multipayer (German) one.

Health networks in the United States already function within a blended market-driven (managed care) and regulated (Medicare and Medicaid) environment. The idea that an entirely market-driven or a fully government-driven approach for the U.S. health system is not supportable has been reached after examining the options of solely managed care, further privatization, and the Canadian and German health systems. What would perhaps work the best is continuing with the United States' quasi-private, quasi-public approach, but one in which there is a compulsory, universal health insurance program; in which multipayers continue to negotiate reimbursement rates; in which the insurers have a vested interest in managing care; and in which consumers can select among all qualified providers. What would be achieved is improved access and social equity, probably little noticeable enhancement in quality of care, possibly some improvement in patient satisfaction, and a significant decrease in the percentage of the U.S. gross domestic product that is spent for health. Most of these savings would be incurred by reducing administrative-business office personnel among all providers and centralizing tertiary services.

The following chapter uses various existing "blended" models in the United States to explore how such a quasi-private, quasi-public system might be achieved and how it would affect the organization, management, and financing of health networks.

REFERENCES

1. www.hmodata.com (InterStudy Publications).

2. Enthoven, A., and Kronick, R. "A Consumer-Choice Health Plan for the 1990s: Universal Health Insurance in a System Designed to Promote Quality and Economy." *New England Journal of Medicine* 320, no. 1 (1989): 29–37.

3. Ellwood, P. M. "Shattuck Lecture—Outcomes Management: A Technology of Patient Experience." *New England Journal of Medicine* 318, no. 23 (1988): 1549–56.

4. Enthoven, A., and Kronick, R. "Universal Health Insurance through Incentives Reform." *Journal of the American Medical Association* 265, no. 19 (1991): 2532–36.

5. Butler, S. M. "A Tax Reform Strategy to Deal with the Uninsured." *Journal of the American Medical Association* 265, no. 19 (1991): 2541–44.

6. Caper, P. "Managed Competition That Works." *Journal of the American Medical Association* 269, no. 19 (1993): 2524–26.

7. Levit, K., Cowan, C., Lazenby, H., Sensenig, A., McDonnell, P., Stiller, J., Martin, A., and the Health Accounts Team. "Health Spending in 1998: Signals of Change." *Health Affairs* 19, no. 1 (2000): 124–33.

8. Bodenheimer, T. "The American Health Care System—Physicians and the

Changing Medical Marketplace." *New England Journal of Medicine* 340, no. 7 (1999): 584–88.

9. Rapoport, J., Gehlbach, S., Lemeshow, S. and Teres, D. "Resource Utilization among Intensive Care Patients: Managed Care vs. Traditional Insurance." *Archives of Internal Medicine* 152, no. 11 (1992): 2207–12.

10. Murray, J. P., Greenfield, S., Kaplan, S. H., and Yano, E. M. "Ambulatory Testing for Capitation and Fee-for-Service Patients in the Same Practice Setting: Relationship to Outcome." *Medical Care* 30, no. 3 (1992): 252–61.

11. Hillman, A. L. "Financial Incentives for Physicians in HMOs: Is There a Conflict of Interest?" *New England Journal of Medicine* 317, no. 27 (1987): 1743–48.

12. Hillman, A. L., Pauly, M. V., and Kerstein, J. J. "How Do Financial Incentives Affect Physicians' Clinical Decisions and the Financial Performance of Health Maintenance Organizations?" *New England Journal of Medicine* 321, no. 2 (1989): 86–92.

13. Dowd, B., Feldman, R., Cassou, S., and Finch, M. "Health Plan Choice and the Utilization of Health Care Services." *Review of Economic Statistics* 73, no. 1 (1991): 85–93.

14. Szilagyi, P. G., Roghmann, K. J., Foye, H. R., Parks, C., MacWhinney, J., and Miller, R. "The Effect of Independent Practice Association Plans on Use of Pediatric Ambulatory Medical Care in One Group Practice." *Journal of the American Medical Association* 263, no. 16 (1990): 2198–203.

15. Yelin, E. H., Criswell, L. A., and Feigenbaum, P. G. "Health Care Utilization and Outcomes among Persons with Rheumatoid Arthritis in Fee-for-Service and Prepaid Group Practice Settings." *Journal of the American Medical Association* 276, no. 13 (1996): 1048–53.

16. Miller, R. H., and Luft, H. S. "Does Managed Care Lead to Better or Worse Quality of Care?" *Health Affairs* 16, no. 5 (1997): 7–25.

17. Hellinger, F. J. "The Effect of Managed Care on Quality: A Review of Recent Evidence." *Archives of Internal Medicine* 158, no. 8 (1998): 833–41.

18. Himmelstein, D. U., Woolhandler, S., Hellander, I., and Wolfe, S. M. "Quality of Care in Investor-Owned versus Not-for-Profit HMOs." *Journal of the American Medical Association* 282, no. 3 (1999): 159–63.

19. Donelan, K., Blendon, R. J., Benson, J., Leitman, R., and Taylor, H. "All Payer, Single-Payer, Managed Care, No Payer: Patients' Perspective in Three Nations." *Health Affairs* 15, no. 2 (1996): 254–65.

20. Donelan, K., Blendon, R. J., Lundberg, G. D., Calkins, D. R., Newhouse, J. P., Leope, L. L., Remler, D. K., and Taylor, H. "The New Medical Marketplace: Physicians' View." *Health Affairs* 16, no. 5 (1997): 139–48.

21. Toner, R. "Many Doctors Tell of Denial of Coverage by HMOs." *New York Times,* July 29, 1999, A18.

22. Iglehart, J. K. "The American Health Care System—Medicare." *New England Journal of Medicine* 340, no. 4 (1999): 327–32.

23. Iglehart, J. K. "Support for Academic Health Centers—Revisiting the 1997 Balanced Budget Act." *New England Journal of Medicine* 341, no. 4 (1999): 299–304.

24. Whitesell, S. E., and Whitesell, W. E. "Hospital Mergers and Anti-Trust: Some Economic and Legal Implications." *Journal of Economics and Sociology* 54, no. 3 (1996): 305–21.

25. Langwell, K., and Hadley, J. P. "Insights from the Medicare HMO Demonstrations." *Health Affairs* 9, no. 1 (1990): 74–84.

26. Arnevitz, L. G. "Medicaid States Turn to Managed Care to Improve Access and Control Costs." Report GAO/HRD 93-46. Washington, D.C.: U.S. General Accounting Office, 1993.

27. Jaggar, S. F. "Medicare, Changes in HMO Rate Setting Method Are Needed to Reduce Program Costs." Report GAO/HEHS 94-119. Washington, D.C.: U.S. General Accounting Office, 1994.

28. Brown, R. S., Clement, D. G., Hill, J., Retchin, S., and Bergeron, J. W. "Do Health Maintenance Organizations Work for Medicare?" *Health Care Financing Review* 15, no. 1 (1993): 7–23.

29. Rossiter, L. F., Nelson, L., and Adamache, K. W. "Service Use and Costs for Medicare Beneficiaries in Risk-Based HMOs and CMPs: Some Interim Results from National Medicare Competition Evaluation." *American Journal of Public Health* 78, no. 8 (1988): 937–43.

30. Nadel, M. V. "Medicaid Prenatal Care States Improve Access and Enhance Services, but Face New Challenges." Report GAO/HEHS 94-152BR. Washington, D.C.: U.S. General Accounting Office, 1994.

31. Retchin, S. M., Clement, D. G., Rossiter, L. F., Brown, B., Brown, R., and Nelson, L. "How the Elderly Fare in HMOs: Outcomes from Medicare Demonstrations." *Health Services Research* 27, no. 5 (1992): 651–69.

32. Carey, T. S., Weis, K., and Homer, C. "Prepaid versus Traditional Medicaid Plans: Lack of Effect on Pregnancy Outcomes and Prenatal Care." *Health Services Research* 26, no. 2 (1991): 165–81.

33. Piper, J. M., Ray, W. A., and Griffin, M. R. "Effects of Medicaid Eligibility Expansion on Prenatal Care and Pregnancy Outcome in Tennessee." *Journal of the American Medical Association* 264, no. 17 (1990): 2219–23.

34. Weil, T. P. "Managed Care and Cost Reductions for Entitlements." *Managed Care Quarterly* 4, no. 4 (1996): 58–67.

35. Smith, S., Freeland, M., Heffler, S., McKusick, D., and The Health Expenditures Projection Team. "The Next Ten Years of Health Spending: What Does the Future Hold?" *Health Affairs* 17, no. 5 (1998): 128–40.

36. Emanuel, E. J., and Dubler, N. N. "Preserving the Physician-Patient Relationship in the Era of Managed Care." *Journal of the American Medical Association* 273, no. 4 (1995): 323–29.

37. Scovern, H. "A Physician's Experiences in a For-Profit Staff-Model HMO." *New England Journal of Medicine* 319, no. 12 (1988): 787–90.

38. Egdahl, E. H., and Taft, C. H. "Financial Incentives to Physicians." *New England Journal of Medicine* 315, no. 1 (1986): 59–61.

39. Bodenheimer, T. S. "Payment Mechanisms under a National Health Program." *Medical Care Review* 46, no. 1 (1989): 28–29.

40. U.S. Congress. House Committee on Government Operations. "Medicare Health Maintenance Organizations: The International Medical Center Experi-

ence." 100th Congress. Washington, D.C.: U.S. Government Printing Office, 1988.

41. Relman, A. S. "Shattuck Lecture—The Health Care Industry: Where Is It Taking Us?" *New England Journal of Medicine* 325, no. 12 (1991): 854–59.

42. Evans, R. G., Lomas, J., Barer, M. L., LaBelle, R. J., Fooks, C., Stoddart, G. L., Andersen, G. M., Feeny, D., Gafni, A., Torrance, G. W., and Tholl, W. G. "Controlling Health Expenditures—The Canadian Reality." *New England Journal of Medicine* 320, no. 9 (1989): 571–77.

43. Hurst, J. W. "Reforming Health Care in Seven European Nations." *Health Affairs* 10, no. 3 (1991): 7–21.

44. Pfaff, M. "Differences in Health Care Spending across Countries: Statistical Evidence." *Journal of Health Politics, Policy and Law* 15, no. 1 (1990): 1–68.

45. Iglehart, J. K. "Germany's Heath Care System: Parts I and II." *New England Journal of Medicine* 324, nos. 7 and 24 (1991): 503–9, 1750–56.

46. Weil, T. P., and Pearl, G. M. "America's Best Hospitals: Heading toward Fiscal Distress?" *Managed Care Interface* 14, no. 4 (2001): in press.

47. "America's Best Hospitals." *U.S. News and World Report,* 124, no. 4 (July 27, 1998): 65–91.

48. HCIA, Inc., and William W. Mercer, Inc. "One Hundred Top Hospitals: Benchmarks for Success, 1998." (1999).

49. Bellandi, D., and Kirchheimer, B. "Multi-Unit Providers Survey: For-Profits Report Decline in Acute-Care Hospitals." *Modern Healthcare* 29, no. 21 (1999): 23–36.

50. Serb, C. "The Health Care 250." *Hospital and Health Networks* 73, no. 4 (1999): 38–48.

51. Donabedian, A. *Aspects of Medical Care Administration: Specifying Requirements for Health Care.* Cambridge, Mass.: Harvard University Press, 1973.

52. Reuter, J., and Gaskin, D. "Academic Health Centers in Competitive Markets." *Health Affairs* 16, no. 4 (1997): 242–52.

53. Anderson, G. F., Greenberg, G., and Lisk, C. K. "Academic Health Centers: Exploring a Financial Paradox." *Health Affairs* 18, no. 2 (1999): 156–67.

54. Iglehart, J. K. "Support for Academic Health Centers—Revisiting the 1997 Balanced Budget Act." *New England Journal of Medicine* 341, no. 4 (1999): 299–304.

55. Cys, J. "CPI: Medical Care Increases Slightly." *AHA News* 35, no. 24 (1999): 2.

56. Topping, S., Hyde, J., Barker, J., and Woodrell, F. D. "Academic Health Centers in Turbulent Times: Strategies for Survival." *Health Care Management Review* 24, no. 2 (1999): 7–18.

57. Meyer, G. S., and Blumenthal, D. "TennCare and Academic Health Centers: The Lessons from Tennessee." *Journal of the American Medical Association* 276, no. 9 (1996): 672–76.

58. Gray, B. H. *For-Profit Enterprises in Health Care,* 182–208. Washington, D.C.: National Academy Press, 1986.

59. Woolhandler, S., and Himmelstein, D. U. "When Money Is the Mission—

The High Costs of Investor-Owned Care." *New England Journal of Medicine* 341, no. 6 (1999): 444–46.

60. Lee, D. "For-Profit Hospitals versus Not-for-Profit Hospitals." New York: Moody's Investors Service, June 3, 1999.

61. Andreopoulos, S. "The Folly of Teaching Hospital Mergers." *New England Journal of Medicine* 336, no. 1 (1997): 61–64.

62. Kassirer, J. P. "Managing Managed Care's Tarnished Image." *New England Journal of Medicine* 327, no. 5 (1997): 338–39.

63. Lundberg, G. D. "National Health Care Reform: The Aura of Inevitability Intensifies." *Journal of the American Medical Association* 267, no. 18 (1992): 2521–24.

64. Relman, A. "Medical Practice under the Clinton Reforms—Avoiding Domination by Business." *New England Journal of Medicine* 329, no. 21 (1993): 1574–76.

65. Rodwin, M. A. "Conflicts in Managed Care." *New England Journal of Medicine* 332, no. 9 (1995): 604–7.

66. Silverman, E. M., Skinner, J. S., and Fisher, E. S. "The Association between For-Profit Hospital Ownership and Increased Medicare Spending." *New England Journal of Medicine* 341, no. 6 (1999): 420–26.

67. www.healthcare markets.com/2q99stock.htm.

68. Clement, J. P., McCue, M. J., Luke, R. D., Bramble, J. D., Rossiter, L. F., Ozcam, Y. A., and Pai, C.-W. "Strategic Hospital Alliances: Impact on Financial Performance." *Health Affairs* 16, no. 6 (1997): 193–203.

69. Melnick, G., Keeler, K., and Zwanziger, J. "Market Power and Hospital Pricing: Are Non-Profits Different?" *Health Affairs* 18, no. 3 (1999): 167–73.

70. Connor, R. A., Feldman, R., Dowd, B. E., and Radcliff, T. A. "Which Types of Hospital Mergers Save Consumers Money?" *Health Affairs* 16, no. 6 (1997): 62–74.

71. Rice, T. "Containing Health Care Costs in the United States." *Medical Care Review* 49, no. 1 (1992): 19–65.

72. Jencks, S. F., and Schieber, G. J. "Containing U.S. Health Care Costs: What Bullet to Bite?" *Health Care Financing Review,* annual supplement (1991): 1–12.

73. Blendon, R. J., Edwards, J. N., and Hyams, A. L. "Making the Critical Choices." *Journal of the American Medical Association* 267, no. 18 (1992): 2509–20.

74. Rublee, D. A. "Medical Technology in Canada, Germany, and the United States: An Update." *Health Affairs* 13, no. 4 (1994): 113–17.

75. Levey, S., and Hill, J. "National Health Insurance—The Triumph of Equivocation." *New England Journal of Medicine* 321, no. 25 (1989): 1750–54.

76. Kinzer, D. M. "Universal Entitlement to Health Care: Can We Get from Here to There?" *New England Journal of Medicine* 322, no. 7 (1990): 467–70.

77. Butler, S. M. "A Tax Reform Strategy to Deal with the Uninsured." *Journal of the American Medical Association* 265, no. 19 (1991): 2541–44.

78. Shortell, S., and McNerney, W. J. "Criteria and Guidelines for Reforming

the U.S. Health Care System." *New England Journal of Medicine* 322, no. 7 (1990): 463–67.

79. Rockfeller, J. D., IV. "A Call for Action: The Pepper Commission's Blueprint for Health Reform." *Journal of the American Medical Association* 265, no. 19 (1991): 2507–10.

80. Clinton, B. "The Clinton Health Care Plan." *New England Journal of Medicine* 327, no. 11 (1992): 804–7.

81. Enthoven, A., and Kronick, R. "A Consumer-Choice Health Plan for the 1990s: Universal Health Insurance in a System Desired to Promote Quality and Economy." *New England Journal of Medicine* 320, no. 2 (1989): 94–101.

82. Sullivan, L. W. "The Bush Administration's Health Care Plan." *New England Journal of Medicine* 327, no. 11 (1992): 801–4.

83. Todd, J., Seekins, S. V., Krichbaum, J. A., and Harvey, L. K. "Health Access America—Strengthening the U.S. Health Care System." *Journal of the American Medical Association* 265, no. 19 (1991): 2503–6.

84. Anderson, G. F., and Poullier, J.-P. "Health Spending, Access, and Outcomes: Trends in Industrialized Countries." *Health Affairs* 18, no. 3 (1999): 178–92.

85. Grumbach, K., Bodenheimer, T., Himmelstein, D. U., and Woolhander, S. "Liberal Benefits, Conservative Spending: The Physicians for a National Health Program Proposal." *Journal of the American Medical Association* 265, no. 19 (1991): 2549–54.

86. Himmelstein, D. U., and Woolhandler, S. "Cost without Benefit: Administrative Waste in U.S. Health Care." *New England Journal of Medicine* 314, no. 7 (1986): 441–45.

87. Fuchs, V. R., and Hahn, J. S. "How Does Canada Do It? A Comparison of Expenditures for Physicians' Services in the United States and Canada." *New England Journal of Medicine* 323, no. 13 (1990): 884–90.

88. Hughes, J. S. "How Well Has Canada Contained the Costs of Doctoring?" *Journal of the American Medical Association* 265, no. 18 (1991): 2347–51.

89. Linton, A., and Naylor, C. D. "Organized Medicine and the Assessment of Technology: Lesson from Ontario." *New England Journal of Medicine* 323, no. 21 (1990): 1463–67.

90. Nadel, M. V. "Canadian Health Insurance: Lessons for the United States." Report HRD-91-90. Washington, D.C.: U.S. General Accounting Office, 1991.

91. Linton, A. L. "The Canadian Health Care System: A Physician's Perspective." *Journal of the American Medical Association* 323, no. 3 (1990): 197–99.

92. Katz, D. M., Mizgala, H. R., and Welch, H. G. "British Columbia Sends Patients to Seattle for Coronary Artery Surgery: Bypassing the Queue in Canada." *Journal of the American Medical Association* 266, no. 8 (1991): 1108–11.

93. Weil, T. P. "Preparing for Increased Hospital Use in a Reformed System." *Health Affairs* 11, no. 4 (1992): 258–60.

94. Newhouse, J. P., Anderson, G., and Roos, L. L. "Hospital Spending in the United States and Canada: A Comparison." *Health Affairs* 7, no. 5 (1988): 6–16.

95. Redelmeier, D. A., and Fuchs, V. R. "Hospital Expenditures in the United States and Canada." *New England Journal of Medicine* 328, no. 11 (1993): 772–78.

96. Weil, T. P., and Miller, W. H. "Canadian-U.S. Comparisons of Capital Expenditures for Health." *Healthcare Financial Briefs* 15, no. 7 (1992): 1–4.

97. Weil, T. P. "How Do Canadians Do It? A Comparison of Utilization and Costs in the United States and Canada." *Hospital Topics* 73, no. 1 (1995): 10–22.

98. Detsky, A. S., O'Rourke, K., Naylor, C. D., Stacey, S. R., and Kitchens, J. M. "Containing Ontario's Hospital Costs under Universal Insurance in the 1980s: What Was the Record?" *Canadian Medical Association Journal* 142, no. 6 (1990): 565–72.

99. American Hospital Association. *Hospital Statistics: 1989–90.* Chicago: Association, 1989–90.

100. Carter, G., and Ginsburg, P. B. "The Medicare Case-Mix Index Increase: Medical Practice Changes, Aging and DRG Creep." Publication No. R-3292-HCFA. Santa Monica, Calif.: Rand Corp., 1985.

101. Roos, L. L., Fisher, E. S., Brazanskas, R., Sharp, S., and Shapiro, E. "Health and Surgical Outcomes in Canada and the U.S." *Health Affairs* 11, no. 2 (1992): 56–72.

102. Whitcomb, M. E. "The Organization and Financing of Graduate Medical Education in Canada." *Journal of the American Medical Association* 268, no. 9 (1992): 1106–9.

103. Shikles, J. L. "Prescription Drugs: Companies Typically Charge More in the United States than Canada." Report GAO/HRD-92-100. Washington, D.C.: General Accounting Office, 1992.

104. Shiels, J. F., Young, G. J., and Rubin, R. J. "O Canada: Do We Expect Too Much from Its Health Care System?" *Health Affairs* 11, no. 1 (1992): 7–20.

105. Smith, K. "Capital Funding of Canada's Hospitals: Policy versus Practice." Ottawa: Canadian Hospital Association Press, 1990.

106. Weil, T. P., and Miller, W. H. "Comparison of Canadian-U.S. Hospital Financial Ratios." *Healthcare Financial Briefs* 15, no. 9 (1992): 1–6.

107. Weil, T. P. "Health Reform in Germany: An American Assesses the New Operating Efficiencies." *Health Progress* 75, no. 7 (1994): 24–29.

108. Iglehart, J. K. "Germany's Health Care System." *New England Journal of Medicine* 324, no. 7 (1991): 503–8; and 324, no. 24 (1991): 1750–56.

109. Thompson, L. H. "1993 German Health Reforms: New Cost Control Initiatives." Report GAO/HED-93-103. Washington, D.C: General Accounting Office, July 1993.

110. Weil, T. P. "The German Health Care System: A Model for Hospital Reform in the United States?" *Hospital and Health Services Administration* 37, no. 4 (1992): 533–47.

111. Weil, T. P. "Comparisons of Medical Technology in Canadian, German, and U.S. Hospitals." *Hospital and Health Services Administration* 40, no. 4 (1995): 524–35.

112. Huttin, C. "Drug Price Divergence in Europe: Regulatory Aspects." *Health Affairs* 18, no. 3 (1999): 245–49.

113. Jost, T. "German Health Care Reform: The Next Steps." *Journal of Health Politics, Policy and Law* 23, no. 4 (1998): 697–711.

114. Himmelstein, D. U., Lewontin, J. P., and Woolhandler, S. "Who Administers? Who Cares? Medical Administrative and Clinical Employment in the United States and Canada." *Journal of the American Public Health Association* 86, no. 2 (1996): 172–78.

115. Vistnes, J. P., and Zuvekas, S. H. "Health Insurance Status of the Civilian Noninstitutional Population." AHCPR Publication no. 99-0030. Rockville, Md.: Agency for Health Care Policy and Research, 1999.

116. Hellinger, F. J. "The Effect of Managed Care on Quality: A Review of Recent Evidence." *Archives of Internal Medicine* 158, no. 8 (1998): 833–41.

117. Ware, J. E., Bayliss, M. S., Rogers, W. H., Kosinski, M., and Tarlov, A. R. "Differences in 4-Year Health Outcomes for Elderly and Poor. Chronically Ill Patients Treated in HMO and Fee-for-Service Systems: Results from the Medical Outcomes Study." *Journal of the American Medical Association* 276, no. 13 (1996): 1039–47.

118. Davis, K., Collins, K. S., Schoen, C., and Morris, C. "Choice Matters: Enrollees' Views of Their Health Plans." *Health Affairs* 14, no. 2 (1995): 99–112.

119. Greenfield, S., Rogers, W., Mangotich, M., Carney, M., and Tarlov, A. R. "Outcomes of Patients with Hypertension and Non-Insulin Dependent Diabetes Mellitus Treated by Different Systems and Specialties: Results from the Medical Outcomes Study." *Journal of the American Medical Association* 274, no. 18 (1995): 1436–44.

120. Brown, R. S., Clement, D. G., Hill, J., Retchin, S. M., and Bergeron, J. W. "Do Health Maintenance Organizations Work for Medicare?" *Health Care Financing Review* 15, no. 1 (1993): 7–23.

121. Greenfield, S., Nelson, E. C., Zubkoff, M., Manning, W., Rogers, W., Kravitz, R. L., Keller, A, Tarlov, A. R., and Ware, J. E., Jr. "Variations in Resource Utilization among Medical Specialties and Systems of Care. Results from the Medical Outcomes Study." *Journal of the American Medical Association* 267, no. 12 (1992): 1624–30.

122. Anderson, G. F., Greenberg, G., and Lisk, C. K. "Academic Health Centers: Exploring a Financial Paradox." *Health Affairs* 18, no. 2 (1999): 156–67.

123. Koeck, C. M., Minnick, A., Roberts, M. J., Moore, K., and Scholz, N. "Use of Administrative Personnel in Hospitals: A Three Nation Study." *Wien Klinic Wochenscribe* 111, no. 22 (1998): 789–95.

124. Hiles, D. R. H. "Health Services: The Real Jobs Machine." *Monthly Labor Review* 2, no. 11 (1992): 3–16.

125. Naylor, C. D. "Health Care in Canada: Incrementalism under Fiscal Duress." *Health Affairs* 18, no. 3 (1999): 9–26.

126. DeRosario, J. M. "Healthcare System Performance Indicators: A New Beginning for a Reform Canadian Health System." *Journal of Healthcare Quality* 21, no. 1 (1999): 37–41.

127. James, A. M. "Closing Rural Hospitals in Saskatchewan: On the Road to Wellness?" *Social Science in Medicine* 49, no. 8 (1999): 1021–34.

128. Perleth, M., Busse, R., and Schwartz, F. W. "Regulation of Health-Related Technologies in Germany." *Health Policy* 46, no. 2 (1999): 105–26.

129. Konig, H. H., Seitz, R., and Arnold, M. "The Cost Reimbursement Trial Regulation in Mandatory Health Insurance: Results of a Survey of Participants." *Gesundheitswesen* 61, no. 1 (1999): 13–19.

130. Schucht, C., and Kochen, M. M. "Managed Care—A Model Also for Ambulatory Medical Care in Germany?" *Zeitung Arztl Fortbild Qualitatssich* 92, no. 10 (1998): 685–95.

131. Betzler, M., and Hann, P. "Hospital Comparisons—Status Quo and Prospects." *Chirurg* 69, no. 12 (1998): 1300–1304.

132. Scholte, M., and Doherty, J. "German Health System Slow to Change." *Managed Care Quarterly* 6, no. 2 (1998): 68–70.

133. Brown, L. D., and Amelung, V. E. "Manacled Competition: Market Reforms in German Health Care." *Health Affairs* 18, no. 3 (1999): 76–91.

134. Markham, B., and Lomas, J. "Review of the Multi-Hospital Arrangements Literature: Benefits, Disadvantages, and Lessons for Implementation." *Healthcare Management Forum* 8, no. 3 (1995): 24–35.

135. Jackson, J. L. "The German Health System: Lesson for Reform in the United States." *Archives of Internal Medicine* 157, no. 2 (1997): 155–60.

7

Blending Competitive and Regulatory Approaches

ABSTRACT. The American public demands a pluralistic health system since it has limited trust in either a totally private or a totally public approach to the delivery of health services. By discussing the establishment of a health services commission in each state that functions as a public utility; replication of the Telecommunications Act of 1996, thereby allowing for both "regulated" competition and consolidation to occur; and the public disclosure of each provider's clinical and fiscal performance, this chapter suggests that continuing to use a blended quasi-private, quasi-public approach is the only viable and sensible option for achieving any significant changes in how health networks will deliver medical care in the United States. Such a strategy is predicted eventually to gain acceptance, legitimacy, and momentum, since this hybrid design is more consistent with U.S. cultural and political values and the inherent complexities of successfully implementing any major health reform proposals in the United States. In addition, this conclusion is consistent with the current trend of the federal government's devolution of its overall authority in achieving significant changes in how networks provide Americans with health services.

The United States during the past two decades has arrived at a new consensus of how health services will be organized, managed, and financed. Instead of expanding the government's role as in the 1960s and 1970s, the focus is now on how well medical care can be delivered with the more competitive model and particularly, whether this approach has the potential of continuing to constrain costs. In fact, until recently the general public believed that its interests were being reasonably well protected through these market-driven forces, and, as a result, the health field experienced limited additional regulation.

Government is no longer seen as a means to substitute the regulative processes for the workings of a more market-driven environment but, rather, to insure that a suitable framework is in place to guarantee competition. Yet, paradoxically, the diminution of regulating mergers and HMOs during the 1990s was offset by increased government intervention in the marketplace through social-value regulation, the explosive increase in numbers of individuals and groups seeking claims of rights and social entitlements, and an unprecedented increase in the machinery of litigation within the courts at all levels.

The current balance between market-driven competition and government regulations (the former being more dominant today) will be judged in the long run by what it delivers, by its fairness to the general public, and by the quality and cost of the services it provides. Americans are willing to tolerate more insecurity against the cost of healthcare than those in other industrialized nations, but there are still limits to how much uncertainty they will accept. While Americans are not anxious for government to extend its reach, neither do they want this prosperous country to abandon its U.S.-style safety net as now provided by Medicare, Medicaid, and public welfare programs.

When it comes to the profit motive, there are limits as well. It seems, for instance, that faceless managers of HMOs, in the name of quality and profits, have been overruling doctors on whether treatments and medications are clinically indicated. There can be little doubt, as was illustrated in the fall of 1999 with the congressional debate over whether subscribers can sue their managed care plan, that the public is increasingly demanding that these organizations be subjected to increased scrutiny, regulation, and restriction.

If the investor-owned companies, for example, notwithstanding the quarterly requirements for dividends made by Wall Street, do not participate in meeting the broader needs of their communities and society, they will find themselves more on the defensive, and government will extend its control over their operations. Although it is not yet a critical topic among the general public, the U.S. market system eventually will also be judged by its ability to include that part of the population that is now either uninsured or underinsured. Continuing to add one million annually to the number of uninsured Americans in the long term will result in an unacceptable disparity between the rich, who are becoming richer (and for the most part desire to maintain the status quo), and the poor, who in a relative sense are becoming poorer. After the United States has experienced 10 years of economic prosperity, it could well be that a recession might swing the pendulum back to more government regulation and a greater concern for such issues as access and social equity.

The purpose of this chapter is to explore various options for the health field that might provide the appropriate balance between too much competition and too much government control, so that health networks might most effectively and efficiently meet community and regional health needs. The models used for discussion purposes are: state health services commissions that function as a public utility; the federal telecommunications–type approach being applied to the health industry, so that providers are governed by something similar to the Federal Communications Commission with an overall theme of regulated competition; and, finally, the proposal of more open public disclosure on how well individual providers perform on such parameters as quality and cost so that more consumer information might be available. After examining both the competitive and regulatory themes in chapter 6 and studying the three models evaluated herein, a rather detailed competitive-regulatory approach to enhance the performance of health networks is proposed. The argument is that, if a relatively sound approach to organizing, managing, and financing the health networks can be appropriately designed, then enhanced access, social equity, and quality of care and reduced health expenditures should be forthcoming.

Establishing State Health Care Commissions

During the past decade federal and state antitrust enforcement in the health industry has not been a serious barrier in restraining health networks from gaining powerful control over the delivery of services in most major metropolitan areas.[1] Of the 397 acute hospital mergers reviewed by the Department of Justice and the Federal Trade Commission during the 13-year period from fiscal year 1981 through fiscal year 1993, less than 4 percent were challenged.[2] Although these regulatory agencies might continue attempting to derail some mergers (e.g., the only two hospitals in the same community), the overall view is that anti-trust enforcement is not a major deterrent in health networks eventually managing as oligopolies.[3]

Lack of competition among providers already exists in most rural areas where only one hospital is located and is economically sustainable, and a limited number of physicians practice. With one large alliance (or several in a large metropolitan area) dominating most regions in the United States, classical economics has taught us that in a highly competitive marketplace the goal of an oligopolist is to secure a monopoly posture or what is more accurately called a "managed oligopoly" or a "monopolistically competitive position."

But, as these immense health networks, with an increasing concern about their bottom lines, begin to exhibit insensitivity about access, social equity, and lowering their costs, the public could become increasingly incensed.[4] To curb such practices and to protect the public interest from these possible abuses of "big business," Ray Brown,[5] an early leader in hospital administration, recommended in 1959 the use of a state health services commission to allocate a region's capital resources. In fact, this public utility concept was the model used in 1971 when the Maryland Health Services Cost Review Commission was established.[6]

While most providers and insurers in the United States think that our current market-oriented approach will generate a more competitive environment, there is growing evidence that more health networks are portraying the traditional characteristics of an oligopoly. Under such circumstances Americans may raise the question of whether the health industry and particularly health networks might be best regulated as a public utility with federal guidelines and state administration. There are several reasons why this concept might have some appeal:

1. By establishing a Federal Health Board and promulgating guidelines for state health services commissions, federally elected and appointed officials could set the broad framework of how the health industry would function and yet would insulate themselves from the process of allocating specific resources within their state or district.
2. Many regions in the country are already dominated by one or a few regional networks managing as oligopolies, and the leadership of these politically and fiscally powerful alliances may not always act in the public's best interest.
3. The public utility concept has been used in other service-oriented industries (e.g., power, telecommunications), all of which have similar "natural monopoly" economic status. This precedent suggests the advisability of maintaining some statutory regulations in place of pure competition; and this principle is particularly applicable where costs can be potentially lowered, if there is a single supplier.
4. The term *public utility* is more acceptable to elected officials and the media than are such earlier cost constraint methodologies as price controls,[7] rate setting,[8] and certificate of need (CON).[9]

The Federal Health Board Setting State Standards

The formation of a Federal Health Board, which would set the guidelines for a multipayer system where each state has a quasi-private, quasi-public health services commission, is politically more acceptable than replicating Canada's provincial statutory authorities. The Federal Republic of Germany has a pluralistic approach to delivering universal, comprehensive healthcare and with its federal-state structure is able to constrain costs (see chap. 6). A Federal Health Board, structured similarly to the Securities and Exchange Commission or the Federal Reserve Board, could meet quarterly and advise Congress and the President on health priorities and overall expenditure targets for various sectors of the U.S. healthcare system.

Congress could use the Board's counsel in a similar manner to the Defense Base Closure and Realignment Commission when enacting legislation that includes such provisions as eligibility for coverage, scope of benefits, how the various plans are to be financed, and the overall administrative guidelines that could be used by the state public utility commissions responsible for allocating limited health resources. Again, the German model could be followed, where over 1,000 third-party payers (sickness funds) negotiate rates with groups of providers without direct government involvement, but within federally established global budgetary targets.

The Use of the Public Utility Model

Independent regulatory commissions are a unique American institution. In most other countries public utilities are owned and operated by the government. In the United States during the late 1800s it became apparent that competition among railroad, power, and other public services was ineffective in protecting the consumer's interest, and public utility commissions were established.[10] Private ownership of these resources was thereby maintained as the U.S. economy fostered a fundamentally competitive, free enterprise system. As more of these independent federal and state regulatory commissions evolved in this century, they became our major organizational agent to regulate services that enjoy a natural monopoly and are associated with a sizable share of our nation's GDP.

Possibly the most fundamental issue surrounding the use of this public utility model for the health field and particularly for health networks is to find the appropriate balance between the rights of consumers and providers, and the appropriate extent of governmental control. What is disconcerting to those supporting the concept of separation of powers is that when our nation's public utility commissions regulate an industry, they merge the powers of the legislative, judicial, and executive branches. Advantages assumed to accrue to such regulatory organizations include continuity of policy, expertise, impartiality, experimentation, flexibility, and the isolation from politics enjoyed by the judiciary branch.[11] In recent decades, however, these supposed virtues have been seriously challenged.

A regulatory commission's independence is thought to isolate its members from undue political pressures, thereby insuring its dedication to the public interest and its impartiality in carrying out needed statutory tasks. But commissions, like most other branches of government, operate within a political environment. They are dependent on the executive branch for their appointed members; their budgets must be approved by the executive and legislative branches; in some instances their court cases must be initiated by the attorney general's office; and their authority and decisions are subject to judicial review.

True independence in a commission's decision-making process is difficult to achieve; even if it were obtainable, some would question its wisdom. Our state regulatory commissions often have been subject to improper outside pressures from both the executive and legislative branches, thereby delivering rulings tainted with political partisanship rather than unprejudiced determinations. Because the commissioners and their staffs must keep in constant contact with the organizations under their jurisdiction, the line between proper and improper ex parte contacts is frequently worth drawing.

A health services commission working closely with providers would almost inevitably have a life cycle of four periods: gestation, youth, maturity, and old age.[12] The gestation phase includes the period during which legislation is enacted to establish the regulatory commission. Because most legislative statutes that call for the regulation of an activity or industry have their genesis in a publicly recognized problem, time is required to create appropriate law and precedent. And, during this gestation period, forces are often at work to lessen the effect of regulation.

The youth phase is illustrated by a crusading commission with strong public support and a highly qualified staff; the issues are challenging; and the organization is presented with opportunities for initiative and imagination. As the commission matures, its original political support deteriorates as high-profile issues start to be resolved, and maintaining its own existence and power base becomes more critical. During the old-age phase, both public support and political leadership diminish more, as most of the commission's actions become more of a routine nature, and the agency becomes more closely identified with the industry it regulates. Those supporting this cycle theory would suggest that a state health services commission would be systemically transformed over several decades from the vigorous protector of the public interest in delivering quality medical care into an organization captured by the providers it purports to regulate.

Operational Issues of Regulatory Commissions

One of the major operational problems with these regulatory commissions during their early years is their inability to develop definitive standards to permit decisions to be fairly predictable and the rationale for them to be clearly understood. Regulatory bodies operate under broad statutes resulting largely from the difficulty of the state legislators to resolve critical issues themselves and from the need for these commissions to have flexibility in meeting changing conditions. It would therefore be difficult to visualize how a state health services commission can always be expected to make creditable policy decisions when a legislature, because of conflicting political and economic forces, is unable to do so in the authority's enabling legislation.

There are other difficulties with state health services commissions regulating health networks. Delay in granting approval could deny to patients their share of the benefits flowing from advances in medical sciences and organizational efficiencies. These commissions would be expected to have power over entry, market share, the scope of services offered, reimbursement rates, profit margins, and exit. Delays could be costly in terms of human energies expended by the health providers when obtaining approval to make beneficial changes. Not the least of the problems is for the goals of (1) the state departments charged with regulating insurance and public health and (2) these proposed new health services commissions to be at odds with one another. These drawbacks have been illustrated by the added costs incurred and the overall failure nationwide of earlier attempts to restrain health expenditures.[7-9]

What is of concern with the formation of state health services commissions is that the regulatory body—not the health network's management—is often responsible for a health organization's programmatic and financial success or failure. As the regulators affect the providers' management decisions, entrepreneurial initiatives are discouraged and the sense of any operational responsibilities can be diminished. Or, by providing a monopoly to a specific provider (e.g., a health network, an academic health center, a prestigious multi-specialty group practice), such public utility protection may be a haven for all aspiring monopolists, who previously found it too difficult, too costly, or too precarious to provide effective and efficient healthcare.

The Experience of Selected Regulatory Commissions

Potential criticisms of using state health services commissions to regulate health networks are numerous. The major shortcomings include political control, ex parte influences, industry favoritism, the failure to develop meaningful policy standards, diseconomies, and undue delays. If all of these specific defects were remedied, the performance of these commissions would probably still fall short, because the difficulties with regulation are largely in the contentious nature of the undertaking itself.

During the 1960s and 1970s regulation in the nontransport industries contributed to the nation's economic prosperity.[13] The growth of the regulated utilities in the postwar period has far exceeded that of the nonregulated industries—nearly double the growth rate of the economy as a whole. The regulated utilities' productivity increased faster than that of any other industrial sector, with utility rates having risen far less than prices generally. As a result, from 1968 to 1980, Congress voted for the strongest extension of regulations since the 1930s, and perhaps in our nation's history.[14] That twelve-year period witnessed the creation of the Environmental Protection Agency, the National Highway Transportation Safety Administration, and the Occupational Safety and Health Administration.

Regulatory reform was one of Ronald Reagan's major planks in his bid for the presidency. Once assuming office and setting out to deliver on his campaign promise, President Reagan found that the easiest reforms had already occurred in the Ford administration and that "life was much more comfortable for surviving firms and industries with regulations than without them."[15] When focusing on the experience of deregulation in the United States during the 1980s and only on five industries—trucking, railroad, airlines, telecommunications, and savings and loan associations (S&Ls), one sees that four of them have been successful.[16] The fifth case, deregulation of the S&Ls, was a disaster and not because of deregulation, but because of how and when the deregulation was implemented.[17] The possibility of a debacle in the health field similar to the S&L industry was considered to be relatively remote, although an increasing number of bankruptcies are starting to occur.[18]

The effect of deregulation on the structures of these five industries has been dramatic. Mergers continue to occur, and monopolistic levels may have increased during the 1980s, as deregulation was accompanied by the lack of vigilance of federal anti-trust policy. Bankruptcy was a conspicuous aspect of this deregulation period, and to some extent it should be, as some inefficient organizations spawned and protection by regulations were eliminated.[19–21]

Although this deregulation period was relatively successful, its redistribution effects have not always been equitable. Redistribution has been regressive particularly with telephone services, where low-income local users pay more, while more affluent long-distance callers pay less. Banks have often closed their inner-city branches serving the poor.

If we assume that cost containment, improved access, and quality of care are among the major issues that face most health networks, these proposed health services commissions would be expected for several reasons to achieve limited results. For example, these regulatory bodies will seek to require providers to reduce expenses and to reallocate some of their resources to inner cities and poor rural areas, and both concepts will be fraught with contention. Moreover, the widely accepted paradigm of management theory that competition lowers prices or costs is difficult to replicate in the health field.[22] Managed care plans have serious difficulties in negotiating favorable prices in markets where one network supplies almost all general inpatient services and there is a single provider of tertiary services. The most powerful alliances may well preclude future price reductions and even discourage the entry of additional managed care plans.

If a major economic downturn occurs in the United States, what should not be entirely discounted is the potential for health networks, functioning as oligopolies not seriously objecting to the establishment of a new federal-state regulatory environment, to prevent entry of new suppliers of services. This probably would start the process of forming several state health services commissions. What is undoubtedly unexpected is that today's aggressive competitive environment may ultimately evolve into the need to protect the public's interest by forming quasi-public, quasi-private bodies, which are expected to experience significant difficulties in achieving cost reductions and improvements in either access or quality of care. Certainly, the notion of establishing state health services commissions is alien to those who propose that cost containment efforts in the United States should be implemented almost solely by competitive forces.

Replicating the FCC Regulatory Powers

In an era when government intrusion into our daily lives is under increasing attack, the suggestion of instilling more competition within a highly regulated industry such as telecommunications, which historically has been under the aegis of the Federal Communications Commission (FCC), might be heralded as a great idea.[23] On February 8, 1996, President Clinton signed the Telecommunications Act of 1996, just one week after the U.S. Congress passed it with overwhelming bipartisan support. A few key elements of the act follow:

1. The FCC was mandated to encourage and to create enhanced competition in the communications field. To accomplish this, the Congress gave the FCC the power to forbear (i.e., refrain from applying any former or past regulations it had imposed on the industry because of its prior rules and regulations or because of the

requirements of the Communication Act of 1934, which the Congress in 1996 amended.).

2. If the FCC determines that any regulation it may have enforced in the past is not a necessary action to protect consumers (or competitive carriers from each other), the forbearance authority that the Congress granted to FCC and its exercised forbearance is per se in the public interest.

3. Any carrier may submit a petition to the FCC requesting its forbearance. After one year, if the FCC has not acted on the petition or has not specifically denied it, the petition will be held to be granted.

Congress decided to legislate so that the telecommunications industry would be best served by competition and corporate consolidations (i.e., mergers), both being justified. In order to pursue this new concept, Congress required that all telecommunications carriers interconnect directly or indirectly with the facilities and equipment of all other telecommunications carriers. They were further instructed not to install network features that do not permit the users of these facilities and other information suppliers "seamlessly and transparently to transmit and receive information between and across telecommunications networks." These congressional mandates were designed to correct industry practices that formerly inhibited or actually prohibited any semblance of competition and had at one time been used primarily by American Telephone and Telegraph (AT&T) to foster its monopoly.[24]

The foregoing is not to say that all is well and without difficulties since the passage of the act.[25] There are problems of regional carriers (principally the Baby Bells) entering the long-distance business in addition to rendering their local service. Also, "universal services" is under FCC scrutiny, just as the health field seeks to provide coverage to Americans without health insurance. Congress wants every person, no matter how remote, to have a communication link to the world, but is unwilling to fund such a program. In addition, the cable companies have taken advantage of the act and many have gone too far in raising prices to users.

The act does deserve some credit for removing legal barriers to competition; however, in many areas, the act failed to recognize that deregulation means freedom. A statute that makes it illegal for Company A to compete with Company B is not a good thing. But allowing competition only if Company A spends two years wrestling with regulators and subsidizes Company C is not much better. Markets need freedom to operate, and only when they perceive less regulatory red tape will there be the necessary and significant investment in the telecommunications industry.

Interestingly, three decades ago, when a special committee of the American Hospital Association (AHA) studied the future organization of the health industry, this group of health leaders made some recommendations that are consistent with the overall objectives of the Telecommunications Act of 1996. The AHA report, "Ameriplan: A Proposal for the Delivery and Financing of Health Services in the United States,"[26] suggested "a substantial restructuring of our delivery system to make it truly an organized, cohesive system designed to make health care more accessible, more comprehensive and more relevant to the needs of the community." With the Ameriplan, government would "act as the control agency through regulations for the scope, standards of quality, and comprehensiveness of health services." Individual health organizations were to be organized statewide and would be mandated to follow federal guidelines.

Why this plan did not attract wider health industry attention can be explained at least in part by the concern of insurers and providers being subjected to a more severe regulatory environment. Also, it was widely thought that the politicization of the financing, organization, and management contributed significantly to the Ameriplan's demise. If the health networks were to function in a quasi-private, quasi-public approach, along the lines of the Ameriplan or the Telecommunications Act of 1996 paradigm, then bipartisanship at the congressional and health field leadership level needs to be the industry's highest priority. It is doubtful whether any of the various interest groups, certainly not among the health networks, will in the foreseeable future provide the direction to promulgate such a model of competition and consolidation. The major reasons are the lack of significant accomplishment to date of the Telecommunications Act of 1996 and other similar endeavors, and primarily the health field's overall inherent fear of further governmental encroachment.

Expanding the Public Disclosure Concept

Today's entrepreneurship by overtly profit-seeking providers and insurers, including health networks, hint at the possible need for a more thorough public disclosure of clinical and financial information as a possible strategy to enhance access, improve quality of care, and reduce health expenditures.[27] Particularly for those patients with serious acute or chronic illnesses and those who require enormous quantities of health services, the high-visibility scandals (e.g., National Medical Enterprises and HCA— The Healthcare Co.) and bankruptcies (Allegheny Health, Education, and

Research Foundation in Philadelphia) among the investor-owned and not-for-profit health networks create understandable concerns.[28-29]

The public disclosure of a provider's clinical and financial performance is complicated because the United States has a highly politicized pluralistic approach to the delivery of health services; self-interest among consumers and providers is pervasive; there is a lack of agreement among professionals when arriving at the critical quantitative measures to evaluate community healthcare needs; and there is an intense fear among most Americans that additional regulations in the health field could result in restricting one's ability to obtain quality healthcare as well as infringing on one's political freedom. In comparison, the Securities and Exchange Commission's (SEC) rules and regulations, which have insured since 1933 that investors have access to the disclosure of all material information concerning publicly traded securities,[30] provide a significant amount of data concerning major investor-owned hospital chains, HMOs, and physician management companies in the United States.

Public Disclosure of Quality of Care Data

One of the major problems historically with quality measurement has been the lack of valid indicators that can accurately reflect the performance of various providers over a broad spectrum of healthcare services. During the past several years, the range of quality-assurance measures has significantly expanded and their reliability has improved.[31-36]

JCAHO

The country's oldest, best established, and largest accreditor of healthcare providers is the Joint Commission on the Accreditation of Healthcare Organizations (JCAHO), which now surveys more than 18,000 hospitals, long-term and ambulatory care facilities, home care agencies, and clinical laboratories. Tarred with the perception that its accreditation criteria emphasize structural and process standards rather than quality of care and health outcomes, the JCAHO in January 1997 initiated a new program called "ORYK." This addendum is designed to incorporate quality-assurance measures and performance improvements directly into the survey processes.

Since JCAHO accreditation is already considered too expensive, bureaucratic, subjective, and slow in weeding out marginal facilities, the commission for the past decade has been under fire, particularly by the state hospital associations "for being too tough" and inconsistent, and by the federal Health Care Financing Administration "for being too lenient." Since JCAHO findings to the public are limited to whether the specific facility is either accreditated or not, consumers and insurers gain limited information from the nation's largest healthcare surveyor upon which to make quality comparisons.

HEDIS

Continuing to be the most frequently utilized resource in assessing a health plan's performance is the Health Plan Employers Data and Information Set (HEDIS) (using clinical records and administrative data) developed by the National Committee for Quality Assurance (NCQA). More than 330 plans, covering three-quarters of the nation's HMO enrollees, provided data for the second edition of NCQA's *Quality Compass*.[37]

Early fears that only health plans with perceived outstanding performances would provide information appear to be unsubstantiated. Potentially more troublesome is that the HEDIS findings include no risk adjustments and most of its indicators assess the process of care rather than patient outcomes. Although major corporations, health networks, and insurers until now have been the driving force behind pursuing these performance measures, it is expected that in the future, public payers are more likely to insist that such data be made available, to evaluate quality versus cost.

With the large number of health networks expending considerable resources in the JCAHO, HEDIS, and other similar survey processes, the question of whether their findings influence either improving quality or reducing cost has encouraged further study.[38–39] In a Kaiser Family Foundation / Agency for Health Care Policy and Research survey,[40] 42 percent of the respondents said that quality of care was their most important concern in choosing a health plan; however, 61 percent said they had not seen any sort of comparative data on quality during the previous year. Of the 39 percent who had seen information on quality, only about one-third said they utilized such findings to select a health insurer or providers. Anecdotal information suggests that recommendations from their physician, family, and friends had considerably more influence on their choice than all the published findings on quality and cost.

CABG Studies

Probably the most revealing information compiled over the last decade on the potential impact of public disclosure of quality of care and financial data can be derived from the California Health Outcomes Project and the New York state and Pennsylvania "report cards."[41] The latter two studies evaluate in these two states every cardiac surgeon and hospital (most of which are the hub facility for a health network) providing coronary artery bypass graft (CABG) surgery. Early on the publication of these findings prompted individual hospitals to undertake efforts to improve quality and to decredential low-volume surgeons who had higher mortality rates.[42–44]

With comparative CABG surgery information so readily available in these two states, one might expect that consumers would be likely to use these report cards to select a surgeon and hospital, but the opposite appears to be true.[45] A survey of 500 patients in Pennsylvania who underwent CABG surgery reported that only 12 percent were aware prior to their operation of the availability to the public of comparative CABG studies. Less than 1 percent knew the correct rating of their hospital or surgeon; and, furthermore, only a few respondents said that the CABG findings had a "moderate" or "important" impact on their decision about where to have such surgery. With a fivefold variation in the unadjusted CABG mortality rates in Pennsylvania, it would have been expected that cardiovascular specialists and prospective open-heart surgery patients would give more heed to where the best CABG clinical outcomes would most likely be achieved.

A study interestingly published in the *Journal of Accounting, Auditing, and Finance*[46] reported that the public disclosure in 1990 of poor CABG report cards for specific Pennsylvania providers had by 1992 a positive effect on reducing mortality rates among these earlier "marginal" hospitals. Improvement were most marked in highly competitive environments suggesting that market pressures strongly encourage quality initiatives. These findings were replicated by Bentley and Nash,[43] who demonstrated that some Pennsylvania hospitals, particularly those where other providers were available nearby, made significant changes in their clinical care programs as a result of these CABG disclosures to the public.

Although the release of HEDIS, JCAHO, and other similar survey findings made available to the public has generally had only a modest impact on improving quality of care and virtually none on clinical outcomes, the question arises whether the standard of patient care among U.S. providers would have been significantly less if such report cards were unavailable. Unfortunately, consumers and providers give these performance reports limited attention. Where these surveys have apparently generated the most beneficial effect is among marginal providers and in highly concentrated environments where there is probably already intense competition for tertiary-type patients.

Public Disclosure of Financial Information

Reporting to the public on quality of patient care has always been considered somewhat vague and amorphous, and there has always been difficulty in finding an acceptable middle ground in this pursuit among those who believe that information on individual providers is critical and those who believe it is harmful (e.g., confidentiality, reliability, reporting misinformation). Interestingly, Ellwood,[47] often considered the founding father of the managed care concept, recently suggested that the uneven quality of healthcare provided in the United States should be corrected by some type of government regulation; and proposed that the SEC and the Federal Aviation Administration (FAA) be considered as possible models. The information provided to the SEC by the investor-owned hospital chains, HMOs, and physician management companies; and the Medicare cost reports submitted annually to the Department of Health and Human Services provide the necessary data for the public to analyze the financial position of almost all providers (most physician services being the major exclusions).

Selected Investor-Owned Health Corporations

In the 1993 to 1997 period the investor-owned hospitals compared to the not-for-profits significantly increased their number of admissions, average daily census, and ambulatory care visits (see table 17). The American Hospital Association reports that during this four-year period, the for-profits were able to decrease their total adjusted cost per admission by 8.8 percent, while the expense per discharge among the not-for-profits increased by 2.5 percent. These findings suggest that the investor-owned hospital

TABLE 17.   Percentage Change in Operating and Fiscal Data, Not-for-Profit versus Investor-Owned Hospitals, 1993 to 1997

Variable	Not-for-Profit Hospitals	Investor-Owned Hospitals
Number of hospitals	−4.9	+11.2
Number of admissions	+6.8	+34.1
Average daily census	−13.1	+17.2
Number of ambulatory care visits	+12.2	+64.1
Full-time equivalent employees	+2.0	+32.8
Total adjusted cost per admission	+2.5	−8.8

Source: American Hospital Association (AHA), *Hospital Statistics, 1994 and 1999* (Chicago: AHA, 1994 and 1999).

chains should be experiencing significant growth in both earnings and stock prices.

In spite of these volume increases, the disappointing performance of the for-profit hospital group is evidenced by the nation's six largest investor-owned hospital chains squeezing out a bottom line of only 4.4 percent in 1998,[48] below that experienced by most of the nation's best hub hospitals (table 9). But the impact on the average consumer of these investor-owned hospital chains having either poor financial or quality performance has been minimal.[49–50] The choice of hospital for inpatient care is usually made when selecting a specific physician and is further influenced by the ease of access to needed services by the patient and the convenience to the family to visit. Even if rather horrendous findings are made available to the public relating to the quality of patient care and overcharging (e.g., Charter's psychiatric facilities), such providers usually experience some short-term setbacks, but are able to continue providing health services for a relatively extended period. The most noticeable outcome of publicly disclosing adverse information about a hospital or physician is witnessing affected health executives within the region scurrying either to maintain or to add to their market share.

What is obviously worrisome is that inherent in all the above discussions is the recent decade of unequaled prosperity experienced in the United States. An economic downturn would result in more Americans being without health insurance coverage, and major corporations would be trimming their employee fringe benefits as their revenues decline. After the United States experiences an economic recession, health policy makers might recommend instituting the broad public disclosure of a relatively comprehensive amalgam of information on health providers that includes both quality of care and fiscal performance data.

Relatively predictable is that public officials would be expected to use comparative quality of care and cost information more to ratchet down Medicare and Medicaid reimbursement to providers than to improve access, social equity, or quality of care. Since consumers in a recessionary period might be responsible for paying more of their health costs out-of-pocket, the public disclosure of provider report cards might thereby gain more public attention. No doubt health providers in such an environment would be particularly sensitive about government agencies releasing such information to the public, if for no other reason than protecting their own self-interest.

What is questionable is whether health consumers can count on their elected or appointed officials to provide the necessary leadership so that regulatory mechanisms outperform the competitive market-driven forces, when determining the relative value of the not-for-profit versus the for-profit forms of delivering effective and efficient health services. For example, the investor-owned HMO plans increased their market share between 1980 and 1998 from 26 percent to 62 percent, but the for-profit managed care plans delivered a lower quality of care than the not-for-profit plans.[50] Nor can the public expect that those responsible for shaping health policy, when weighing the benefits and costs of either a governmentally or a privately directed action, to remain unaffected by various special interest groups. The point is that policy making by either the government or the market is both an imperfect mechanism and with either option there could well be roughly an equal chance to "get it right."

Within a continually changing competitive-regulatory U.S. health marketplace, what will be increasingly critical is for employers to use performance data, such as HEDIS, when selecting health plan options for their employees; and, thereafter, providing their workers with sufficient information so they are able to make some informed decisions among the various plans offered. Some employers experience difficulty in implementing these principles and place the blame on HEDIS, since their published findings are not considered by most employees to be particularly user friendly. Furthermore, the sheer volume of performance information generally provided when making purchasing decisions is considered by most employees to be a serious barrier in the selection process.[51]

More cynical observers say that most employers really never cared about quality, but were only interested in the HMOs minimizing their companies' fringe benefit costs. In addition, major corporations have used these quality of care surveys primarily to smooth over employees' concerns about the transition from fee-for-service to managed care.[52] Irrespective of the desirability of more public disclosure relating to health services, a substantive question is whether employers are the best choice to take the lead to enhance quality of patient care.

Although consumers, public officials, purchasers, and providers have expressed interest in the public disclosure of healthcare performance information, it is primarily the hospitals (particularly those with the most negative findings) that have taken the most heed to these surveys.[41] An evaluation of the impact of an obstetrical consumer-oriented survey conducted by the Missouri Department of Health reported significant operational and policy changes among hospitals within one year of releasing their study results.[53] Hospitals in competitive markets were found to be about twice as likely to consider improving process indicators and patient satisfaction, and to address the appropriateness of their patient charges, than those facilities that are their area's sole provider. In addition, hospitals located in communities where there is more than one provider of obstetrical services were twice as likely to improve quality indicators as those in far less competitive environments.

More recently a Pennsylvania survey[44] assessed how hospital executives utilized a comparative CABG quality and cost study, the results of which were publicized widely. Since most open-heart surgery patients have health insurance coverage, the hospitals' management team assigned low ratings of importance to published comparative charge information. Hospital executives in highly concentrated areas, however, assigned significantly higher relevance to the CABG ratings relating to quality. The major finding in both the Missouri and Pennsylvania studies is that public disclosure of quality information has the most beneficial impact in communities where there is inter-institutional competition for patients.

Public Disclosure—Today and the Future

During the last decade merger mania resulting in politically and fiscally powerful networks has been a striking trend in the health field. The strategy encouraging the formation of these huge alliances, often then functioning as oligopolies, is to improve the integration of services, to reduce expenses, and to increase the ability of providers to manage risk-based payment. During the past quarter-century, however, limited operational and fiscal evidence has been published in either the health or the general management literature that strongly supports the efficacy of these mergers.[54]

In spite of disappointments among these amalgamations in effecting significant cost reductions,[55-56] the nation's health networks are expected to continue to acquire additional providers and insurers. And, because more health networks eventually will be managed as a monopoly, these alliances will be able to position themselves so they must only give minor heed to the usual public disclosures relating to their quality of care or their financial position.

When the United States eventually experiences an inevitable economic downturn, the health networks in almost every metropolitan area will be forced to achieve their earlier projected enhancements in the delivery of health services. The health field's leadership will be forced to implement such cost-cutting measures as: more vigorously coordinating the network's key clinical services to reduce competition for revenues among the partners within an alliance; shuttering superfluous hospitals and centralizing expensive tertiary services; and providing direction towards integrating carefully the best elements of what the competitive and regulatory strategies are able to offer to improve access, social equity, and quality of care and to reduce total health expenditures. Quality of care and financial information that has already been disclosed to the public and additional data requested from providers by the insurers and government officials will undoubtedly be used to facilitate this major "downsizing" strategy.

In the short term some modest incremental steps can be expected in improving report cards by adding data sets and by significantly enhancing public knowledge about which plan to select and the quality of care to be expected in the delivery of specific health services.[57] Both an effective use and some abuse of these performance reports of physicians, hospitals, and other providers can be anticipated.[58]

It will be during a major downsizing in the health field, caused by external economic forces, that the public disclosure of quality of care and the financial position of providers and insurers can be expected to play a far more major role than it does today in reshaping U.S. health services. Since health is such a major industry in terms of its societal importance and its share of the U.S. gross domestic product, it is conceivable that a federal-type Securities and Exchange Commission might be established regulating all major health providers and focusing on the public disclosure of a broader spectrum of quality of care, fiscal, and other similar information than is currently available. Such a commission's legislative mandate with respect to its role in shaping the organization, management, and financing of health services as proposed by Congress would be a highly partisan issue, but would be very critical in how the public disclosure of patient care, fiscal, and other data, now commonly available or added to later on, would be utilized in the future.

Blending Competition and Regulation

Although annual increases in health expenditures are currently increasing in the United States at a historical low (3 percent), their ascent is still slightly greater than that of the overall consumer price index.[59] When judged against the backdrop of numerous earlier failed governmental policies to curtail health spending, this is an impressive achievement, but it does not go far enough, particularly if the United States were faced with economic difficulties such as a lengthy recession. Serious macroeconomic pressures such as the nation's trade deficit, the inability to appropriately fund Social Security and Medicare, and the increasing cost of entitlements require implementing additional cost containment efforts.

Any meaningful restructuring of the health field, however, is fraught with conflict since it involves clear-cut winners and losers, where some providers and insurers benefit at the expense of others. The speed with which any further discipline can be imposed on health spending depends primarily on the extent to which unavoidable conflict can be lessened when accomplishing what is now perceived to be much needed structural reform.

Although admittedly messy and open to inconsistent, contradictory impulses, what may be needed is the acknowledgment of the public and the health professionals that the blending of two generally adversarial theories, competition and regulation, might well be the most appropriate compromise now available in the way health services might be provided in the United States.[60] A mixed approach is more compatible with how the U.S. health system now functions, the pluralistic character of U.S. culture and politics, and the complex manner in which health services are currently organized, managed, and financed. The inherent common sense of a search for the best features of both competition and regulation could be consistent, moreover, with the United States' cultural fascination with innovation and a preference for what works as compared with an inflexible attachment to abstract theory and utopian ideas.

After reviewing both highly competitive and regulatory approaches to delivering healthcare (see chap. 6) and several quasi-private, quasi-public models (e.g., the health services commission as a public utility) to enhance health services in the United States, the following strategy is proposed: U.S. leaders should reject the approach that simply demands a choice between competition or regulation, when competition means "more market driven" and regulatory means "more government." Instead, policy makers should strive to implement a competitive healthcare model that is blended with sufficient regulatory safeguards to protect the public and enough competitive features to reduce unnecessary utilization and cost, and improve quality of care. To outline how such a strategy might be achieved, this chapter's concluding section explains the rationale and describes some fundamental conditions that would be required to implement this proposed hybrid solution.

A More Societal Perspective

Failure throughout this century to recognize and then to adapt to the intensity of popular support for the efficacy of market-driven forces is perhaps the major reason why the proponents of a compulsory national health insurance plan have been unable to gain its passage.[61] Those proposing a "stronger safety net" persist in arguing for more and bigger government spending on the grounds that the United States has an increasing number of persons "in need" and is wealthy enough to spend more on social insurance programs.

Advocates of higher social spending could be more sensitive to some disturbing new fiscal realities. Key issues are the nation's increasing trade deficits since the 1970s, the inability to gain consensus on how to reform the Medicare program, strong public support to reduce public welfare expenditures, and a lack of agreement on how to provide and finance health services to the un- and underinsured.[62-65]

Achieving higher standards of living, particularly among the lowest quartile, requires focusing U.S. resources on increasing household income through the creation of more and better-paying jobs. A strong performing economy is key to alleviating the pain of prudent debt management and to averting the possibility of a "meltdown" of Social Security, Medicare, Medicaid, and related endeavors. Of particular concern is the projected dramatic rise in the size of the retiree population in conjunction with the long-term affordability of the nation's social insurance programs due to a shrinking work force and the inherent resistance to higher payroll taxes. Even if the economy continues to prosper in the 2000s, tomorrow's workers will have to shoulder considerably higher taxes if the public sector is to fulfill its currently prescribed obligations to the elderly and the poor. Otherwise, current eligibility and benefit levels will be substantially reduced.

These imperatives underline the transfiguration of the federal government's role in health and welfare services, whereby greater responsibility is being delegated to the states, so that Washington can concentrate more on strengthening the general economy and meet international commitments. The states, therefore, now have an opportunity to formulate new ways to deal with the old dilemma that has bedeviled federal policy makers—how to control health costs while simultaneously expanding access to services and improving the quality of care. Although some states will falter in this process, there is good reason to be optimistic that the benefits of these additional innovations outweigh the risks.

The United States is not alone in grappling with the future of entitlement as virtually all highly developed countries are struggling to curtail the cost of social welfare benefits. It is against the backdrop of similar macroeconomic exigencies that governments are expressing interest in various forms of market-driven strategies to scale back public expenditures and to shift more of the cost of health and social services either to state and local government or to the private sector in order to better target budgetary resources for the nation's overall improved economic growth. A major appeal of managed competition as a cost containment strategy is its ability to facilitate change by circumventing bureaucratic barriers and the politically powerful status quo adherents, notably health providers and organized labor.[66]

Knowledgeable policy makers generally agree that health services restructuring is best achieved through the co-optation of market forces that unleash entrepreneurial energies strong enough to overcome the formidable special interest groups opposed to meaningful reform. At the same time, these experts recognize that it is necessary to curtail any perverse effects accompanying unfettered competition through the imposition of intelligent regulatory controls.[67]

The Option of a Regulatory Approach

A regulatory-oriented model by itself for the U.S. health system is deemed inappropriate for the reason that it has simply not worked.[68–69]

The experience of states that have enacted legislation to control hospital spending by the setting of prices is illustrative. When adjusted for differences in case mix intensity, wage rates, and admission rates per 1,000 persons, hospital costs per capita are substantially higher in rate-setting states than they are in states where market forces have been encouraged to play a major role in establishing hospital reimbursement rates. In Massachusetts, Maryland, and New York, for example, the average annual hospital cost per person was 49.1 percent higher than in Arizona, California, and Oregon, where competition among HMOs has been the principal weapon to promote cost containment.[70]

The regulatory approach is inescapably burdened by political considerations and the special interest groups that can be at odds with the principles of managerial efficiency. Government mandates personalize responsibility for unpopular actions in a way that inhibits, if not precludes, elected officials from participating in decision-making that leads to major staffing layoffs or hospital closures. This is frequently a significant issue because of the current surplus of hospital inpatient facilities and specialist physicians. The reluctance of most politicians (sometimes because of campaign contributions) to enact unpopular but necessary measures to constrain costs is further compounded in the United States' inner cities and rural areas, where any downsizing of health resources exacerbates the problems of already poorly performing local economies and of high unemployment levels.

Vulnerability to voter backlash and the ire of powerful special interests (e.g., provider groups, insurers, drug companies) leads politicians to prefer settlements that discriminate against establishing more centers of excellence in favor of allowing inefficient and ineffective providers to "remain open." Concerns about being reelected and the unknowns in implementing a serious programmatic shift predispose politicians to follow collective decision-making processes that avoid letting the full consequences of cost containment fall on their health providers wherever possible.

Bureaucratic "red tape," which is also experienced both in the private and public sectors, is a further drag on managerial efficiency. In addition to the fulfillment of lengthy due process safeguards and vulnerability to delay because of the legal tactics of reform opponents, regulatory agencies suffer from an inability to successfully compete for qualified staff. Although there are some exceptions, private sector employment is usually more attractive in terms of compensation, flexible working conditions, and opportunities for career advancement. It is problematic, therefore, whether regulatory agencies, federal or state, can recruit and retain sufficient numbers of quality and dedicated civil servants to competently implement and monitor government mandates.

Perhaps the most serious flaw of the regulatory process is its susceptibility to being captured by the interests that it is supposed to control. The regulatory approach could be made more efficient by simply infusing private industry approaches within a quasi-public framework, as exemplified by the public utility model. This quasi-private, quasi-public approach is very often preferred by critics of conventional regulation, who nevertheless continue to believe in the indispensability of modest governmental control. Unfortunately, the capture thesis suggests that the transformation of a health services commission into a public utility would systemically occur over time from a vigorous protector of the public interest into an organization dominated by the very providers and insurers it is supposed to regulate.[71,72]

The Option of a Competitive Approach

Unlike regulation, the competitive model is attractive in the way it depoliticizes responsibility and conflict, and frees management to make decisions on the basis of what is doable, affordable, and profitable. The accompanying numerous advantages of conducting a large-scale and controversial reorganization of the U.S. health system within the framework of market-driven dynamics, notwithstanding the use of a purely competitive approach to constrain costs and to improve access, is not a panacea either. Ideally suited to attain efficiency, competitive forces are far less responsible to the objectives of universal coverage and social equity.[73-74]

The current enthusiasm for market-oriented reforms, such as the use of the competitive model to shrink excess capacity and to deploy fiscal incentives that alter provider and consumer behaviors, is enormously appealing within a short-term context; however, when these reforms are assessed over a larger period of time their attractiveness tends to fade. In this connection competition among health insurers for market share and profitability through more selective enrollment is bound to compound the already serious problem of uninsured Americans. This and other socially insidious dynamics that fuel the managed care movement are a source of serious concern.

There are a number of other reasons why the current market-driven strategies that have evolved into powerful health networks capable of generating annual revenues of $1 billion or more, could face significant barriers in insuring that all Americans have an effective health system at an affordable cost:

1. Managed care plans have yet to demonstrate conclusively that the financial parameters within which they function enable them to successfully enroll high-risk Medicare and Medicaid populations, including the inner-city and rural poor.[75–79] Unfortunately, their capacity and willingness did not improve as the managed care industry matured, and was encouraged by government policy to cover the Medicare and Medicaid eligible.

   In principle, fewer plans each with an increased number of enrollees should be better positioned to assume more risk. Because of the protective actuarial effect of more subscribers and political pressures, the HMOs should be more willing to underwrite higher-risk insurees without increasing premiums. But they have not done so to date, if for no other reasons than being unable to significantly increase premiums to help meet the additional cost of providing such coverage and the inability of investors because of thin operating margins to share much of their return on investment with broader community welfare objectives.

2. HMOs offer a somewhat mixed proof of cost reductions. Reported savings may be illusory due to selective enrollment and higher administrative expenses.[80] On the other hand, more recent evidence suggests that a properly structured competitive approach can play a significant role in controlling and, in fact, reducing health expenditures.[81–83] Some larger corporations and business coalitions already have been quite successful in forcing HMOs to compete on quality as well as on price.

3. Along with the potential perverse effects of selective enrollment, the financial incentives that many HMOs use to stimulate physician productivity present troublesome conflict of interest issues when the clinicians' income is tied to the withholding of services

which may be medically appropriate and necessary. Managed care plans sometimes use their gatekeepers to approve all care provided by specialists, thereby restricting their enrollees direct access to more sophisticated care. In addition, HMOs sometimes reject claims for emergency department (ED) services for nonemergencies. In the absence of a clear definition of what constitutes a non-reimbursable ED visit, this and related fiscal practices can adversely affect quality of patient care.

4. It is disturbing that some HMOs ban doctors from disclosing the income they derive when limiting care or from discussing clinical treatment options that are not covered by the plan's benefits. Also troublesome is the practice of allowing persons without any clinical training to delay services that are perceived by either the patient or the primary care practitioner to be appropriate. Appeal procedures which allow for reversals only after months of delay compound doubts about whether managed care is always in the public's best interest.

In light of the above concerns, it is difficult to imagine that the competitive model alone will be able to implement an effective and efficient health system for over 260 million Americans. With 43.9 percent of the total medical care dollar in the United States funded by the public sector,[85] it becomes more apparent that implementing a singularly market-driven strategy would face substantial conceptual and operational difficulties.

Ingredients of a Blended Approach

Ideological purists will scoff at the suggestion that such theoretically discordant principles as competition and regulation can be harmonized in actual practice, but most pragmatists will tend to perceive this hybrid as a worthy challenge.[86–87] Subject to the qualification that perfect solutions are seldom, if ever, attainable in the real world, the aim of public policy in the health field should be to move from what is unsustainable to a more sustainable position. It is within this context that what follows outlines how the competitive and regulatory models can be successfully blended to enhance access, social equity, and quality of care, and to constrain health costs.

What is envisioned here is an enlightened private-public partnership in which both parties concentrate on what they do best. Thus, in the broadest terms the private sector with the virtues of the competitive model would bear principal responsibility for curtailing unnecessary utilization, and for improving efficiency and quality of health services, whereas the regulatory focus of government would be constraining total health expenditures and insuring social equity.[88] Such a balanced arrangement is more conducive to resolving the issues facing the U.S. health system than a total government takeover or a purely market-driven system would be.

One major advantage of a blended approach is the alleviation of the fiscal burdens on government, freeing the federal budget for investments in economic growth and improving the quality of life without detracting from its responsibility for promoting and maintaining the general welfare. More specifically, this proposed blended approach could include these factors:

1. Overall policy established at the federal level that eventually might include a global budgetary target or something similar for each state.
2. Administration at the state level, most realistically a health services commissions functioning as a public utility.
3. Competition among providers for contracts from insurers that focus on curtailing unnecessary utilization and cost, and improve quality of care.
4. Government oversight to assure access to clinically needed care, social equity, and reasonable patient satisfaction.

The experiences of the Arizona Medicaid program illustrate a creative way that state government can respond to the opportunity to blend competitive and regulatory forces for the public interest during a period when the federal government is granting more discretionary authority to the states. The incorporation of most of the above hybrid policy features is largely responsible for why Arizona has achieved both lower costs and improved accessibility of services to needy persons in administering its Medicaid program.

The Arizona Health Care Cost Containment System's (AHCCCS) annual fiscal increase per capita from 1983 to 1991 was 6.8 percent versus 9.9 percent for the traditional Medicaid program nationwide.[89] In 1994, 21 health plans, some not-for-profit and others investor-owned, submitted 95 bids to provide Medicaid services in Arizona's 15 counties for the 1995–97 contract period. This number of third-party payers was more than double the number of bids (44) submitted in 1993, the start of the previous contract cycle. The AHCCCS health plans in 1994 earned $56 million in operating surpluses (representing 6.7 percent of their total revenues), thereby creating increased interest in securing the succeeding Medicaid contracts.

Nearly 90 percent of the Medicaid beneficiaries surveyed were satisfied with the care they received through AHCCCS. In addition, the plan in 1991 netted savings of $70.7 million for the state. Arizona's indigent care program is only one example of how competitive and regulatory strategies could be blended and successfully utilized to constrain health expenditures. Other western states (e.g., California, Oregon) have embarked in a similar direction.[70, 81]

What is occurring in the United States, moreover, is consistent with the general trend now evident in other industrialized societies encountering comparable dilemmas in financing entitlement. Demographic and fiscal realities are moving countries with extensive social insurance programs (e.g., Canada, France, Germany, and Japan) to try to adopt formerly out of favor competitive practices such as pitting the purchasers of services against the providers of care. Market-oriented measures are being injected both within and outside the confines of government programs; and privatization increasingly is viewed as an acceptable adjunct or alternative to public services. As in the United States, lower levels of government (states and provinces) are now assuming a larger and more independent role in holding insurers, hospitals, physicians, and others more accountable to providing access and social equity, while simultaneously constraining costs and improving quality of patient care.[90-91]

Where Do We Go from Here?

Within the broad goal of blending competitive and regulatory approaches, there are a number of unresolved public issues that need to be addressed in any health reform agenda. More specifically, they include such options as:

1. Setting global budgetary targets such as in Canada and Germany (see chap. 6);
2. Reducing regional differences in utilization and cost, so that hospital expenditures are not twice as high in the northeast as they are in the far west;
3. Eliminating superfluous overhead by simplifying reimbursement and reducing excess capacity by centralizing tertiary services;
4. Enacting enabling legislation that forms state health services commissions as public utilities in order to place more control over oligopolistic concentration; and
5. Implementing regulations that foster competition to lower cost and enhance quality of care, but protect the public without crippling innovation and efficiency.

Global Budgetary Targets

Although disliked by providers and insurers, and certainly not compatible with current competitive concepts, some approach to set health expenditure ceilings might be established. Countries where this concept is practiced do a much better job than the United States in managing total health expenditures relative both to GDP and the budgetary allocations made by federal and state government.[92–93]

Setting global budgetary caps by state and by health sector is the most customary methodology used in other highly developed nations.[94] Interestingly, the United States is moving in a similar direction. Members of Congress have enacted Medicaid block grants by which each state receives a specific payment from Washington to provide health services to its indigent, the details of which are causing disputes between Capitol Hill and the White House, and at the state level.[95]

Capitated payment for a large employer group or for Medicare and Medicaid beneficiaries is another example of a global budgetary target, in the sense that the total expenditure (premiums) is capped for a given insured population. Under such circumstances physicians and hospitals are those most affected by fiscal risk. Providers are thereby induced to behave in a more disciplined manner when they allocate resources, compared to a fee-for-service environment. Since there is an almost insatiable demand for medical care services, it is anticipated that unless a "fiscal lid" is placed on total expenditures, Americans will spend a continuing larger share of this nation's GDP on health services, to the detriment of other worthy goals.

Regional Differences

Regional differences in health costs, adjusted for variations in the local cost of living and in use rates for specific medical treatments, are so pronounced in the United States that Medicare expenditures per capita in Miami, for example, are twice those in Lincoln, Nebraska. As indicated in the Dartmouth atlas study,[96] there is no evidence that those patients who receive more services or those who pay more for them experience improved clinical outcomes.

Although there will continue to be regional variations (e.g., far longer average lengths of hospital stay in the northeast than on the west coast primarily because of variations in physician practice patterns), these differences will narrow as managed care plans insist that providers follow more rigid treatment protocols. Hospitals and physicians located in high-cost, high use regions like Baltimore, Birmingham, Los Angeles, Nashville,

New Orleans, New York City, and Pittsburgh would be most adversely affected by global budgetary targets, by competitive bidding wars for additional subscribers, and by restrictions on what services should be approved for payment by managed care plans.

Reducing Superfluous Overhead and Excess Capacity

Growth of employment in the health field is another manifestation of the inability of regulation to curb expansion. Between 1968 and 1993 the number of employees in the health field grew from 4 to 10.3 million persons. Some of these increases were exacerbated by technologic advances, excess capacity, and the compliance standards imposed by the regulatory agencies on hospitals, nursing homes, and physicians.

During this quarter-century, the number of administrative jobs grew from 18.1 percent to 27.1 percent of the total.[97] Significant reduction in administrative costs could be obtained by simplifying prepayment, by requiring providers to "self-police" their own peers, by abolishing as many regulatory provisions as possible without removing the necessary safeguards required by the general public to avoid fraud and abuse, and by imposing fiscal incentives that force the relocation of health manpower from where it adds little value to places where it meets community health needs.

Eliminating surplus capacity requires more severe measures than merely cutting red tape and reallocating underutilized resources. The closure of redundant facilities and unnecessary educational programs (where there is an excessive supply of such health manpower) is imperative.[98] Other appropriate measures include: refusing eligibility for third-party reimbursement to physicians who want to locate their offices in areas that are already overstaffed with that specialty; and limiting the number of approved post-graduate residency training positions by medical specialty in accordance with supply-demand projections.

Considering the resiliency of hospitals and medical schools in thwarting earlier regulatory attempts to constrain spending through the management of supply, the few subsequent closures stimulated by exposing the hospitals to market-driven forces are noteworthy. The pace of recently completed and ongoing mergers among major medical centers and community hospitals and the implications of these consolidations on health delivery patterns are unprecedented.[99]

Control of Oligopolistic Concentration

Concentration of insurers and providers is an inevitable outcome of the continuing trend toward mergers and consolidations, with the ironic consequence that competition no longer will continue to promote the public interest by forcing providers to compete on the basis of price and quality.

In the near future, the elimination of weak competitors could culminate in a single or few networks dominating each region's health services by segmenting the market (geographically and clinically) into virtual monopolies (i.e., oligopolies). Giant-sized providers would then be in a position to exercise regional dominance to further their own self-interest rather than applying their fiscal and managerial resources to such broader social objectives as expanding access for low income population, or providing more and better care at little or no additional costs.

These oligopolistic concentrations in the health field present serious problems worthy of further comment. The Minneapolis/St. Paul Business Coalition's dissatisfaction with the performance of local HMOs led them to contract with providers directly.[100] What happens, however, when there are few "survivors" left, and the employers are no longer able to play one managed care plan against another? At that juncture do state governmental officials have the responsibility to step in and provide the necessary additional regulations to protect the public? Or, does state government threaten the providers with a health services commission as a public utility to be established soon? In this connection, it is not far fetched to expect that the further expansion of the managed care approach will serve as a back door to further government control of the health field in the future.

Regulations That Protect the Public Interest

Our current competitive environment must be accompanied by well-thought-out regulations that protect the public interest without crippling innovation and efficiency (e.g., safe harbors and anti-kickbacks). Of particular concern are the huge networks that might engage in antisocial behavior to the disadvantage of patients, their community, those who are responsible to pay their third-party benefits, and various lenders. There are a number of serious difficulties in enacting legislation that enhances access, social equity, and quality of care, and reduces utilization and cost.

Unlike the European "social solidarity" concept, the Americans in the simplest terms foster a three-tier health system where the wealthy primarily use the fee-for-service system; the middle-class has access to care through the managed care system; and the poor, who are not covered by Medicaid, use the hospital emergency department as their primary care physician. As a result of the delay in obtaining care and other social and economic barriers, in general those without health insurance benefits experience poorer clinical outcomes.

One obvious option is for Congress to enact universal access and provide the monies from taxes to subsidize the currently un- or underinsured. There is no growing political swell in the United States that the increasing number of uninsured Americans should have health insurance benefits. When the question of subsidy is introduced there are immediate concerns about the huge cost, and that employers with few employees will be encouraged to drop their current coverage and will suggest to their workers that they join the "subsidized" plan.

Another alternative is to use the cost savings generated by simplifying the American prepayment system and centralizing tertiary services to pay the premiums for the current un- or underinsured. This proposal, aside from overcoming strong political opposition from the providers and insurers, would cause major disruption in terms of: eliminating a large number of employees in the health field who are now responsible to process patient billing and related information and data; and shuttering a large number of tertiary programs in primarily nonteaching hospitals, requiring patients and their families to travel greater distances to obtain specialized care. What would be accomplished is that the monies saved by health systems reducing paperwork and centralizing sophisticated services could be reallocated to pay for more clinically oriented personnel providing hands on care to the un- and underinsured.

Quality of care needs to be a major concern when designing or operating any health network. The clinical outcomes of the Canadian and German universal comprehensive national health insurance plans show no evidence of being inferior to the outcomes in the United States. In fact, in terms of infant mortality and life expectancy, the opposite is true. Interestingly, there is no overwhelming evidence that managed care provides a higher quality of care than do fee-for-service plans. And there is no overpowering demand by the public to obtain comparative quality and cost information even in the case of obtaining open-heart surgery. Most Americans rely on their physician, family, and friends to make quality of care decisions, not empirical evidence processed by health professionals.

The most effective way to reduce health expenditures is to decrease either utilization or price paid per unit of service. Once having made the decision to blend competitive and regulatory concepts to reduce cost, the question arises of whether to rely more on market-driven principles or government regulations to reduce cost. To study the efficacy of the current market-driven approaches to constrain health expenditures in the United States, an analysis was undertaken of 1993 hospital discharge costs and related data (e.g., Medicare case-mix intensity and wage index) of the 15 states in the United States with the highest percentage of HMO market penetration.[101] The study's major finding was that the number of paid hours for a facility was more critical in reducing average expense per discharge than whether the hospital was located in a "competitive" or a "regulated" state. The implication is that health networks that are able to manage with a low number of man-hours per discharge are those who in terms of cost might well be judged as being most effective and efficient.

Broader Implications of a Blended Strategy

Americans by and large are politically uncomfortable with any vast increases in the scope of regulatory authority over the delivery and financing of health services. Public opinion has historically favored private over publicly sponsored health services and continues to do so.[102] Clearly there is a strong preference by Americans for the "buying in" principle whereby governmental programs and services are administered and rendered within the private sector.

Skepticism toward the public sector is understandable in light of the failure of numerous post–World War II regulatory strategies to achieve any appreciable headway when dealing with cost containment. Although enthusiasm for the private sector and competition is understandable given the rapid pace of health services restructuring following the introduction of market incentives, the intoxication of unconditional approval must not be allowed to obscure recognition that competition is not, as discussed earlier, a major elixir. While market-driven approaches unquestionably have done more to speed the attack on many erstwhile intransigent issues, competition has serious shortcomings and limitations conducive to the multiplication of socially unacceptable problems. Like regulation, competition is inherently imperfect.

While perfection in the real world of healthcare may be an unobtainable goal, a balanced approach combining the best of what competition and regulation have to offer provides a practical compromise. Pluralism is one of the defining cultural characteristics of U.S. society. Within the framework of multiple competing values and beliefs, neither regulation nor competition functioning separately is sufficient for dealing with the many complex and diverse aspects of what currently ails health reform. In this connection a mixture of the two concepts appears far more practical and advantageous.

Because of the redirection of federal spending described earlier, the states now are in a position to exercise leadership in developing new and improved ways for making health services more efficient without detracting from enhanced effectiveness, while simultaneously resolving the problem of the uninsured. In this process some states can be expected to do better than others. Indeed some, for whatever reason, may actually regress and engage in a "race to the bottom."

Given that not all states will deliver on the promise of devolution, it is incumbent on Washington and the health networks to exercise proper oversight. Consistent with the judicious use of regulatory powers advocated herein, the federal government should seek to formulate minimal uniform standards based on the results obtained from the best performing states, while sustaining an intergovernmental climate favorable to the continuation of innovations in health services delivery that rewards superior provider efficiency, effectiveness, and quality of patient care services. In fact, Chapter 9 focuses on how this might all be accomplished in conjunction with the nation's health networks.

REFERENCES

1. Weil, T. P. "How Health Networks and HMOs Could Result in Public Utility Regulation." *Hospital and Health Services Administration* 41, no. 2 (1996): 266–80.

2. Jaggar, S. F. "Health Care: Federal and State Antitrust Actions Concerning the Health Industry." Report GAO/HEHS-94-220. Washington, D.C.: U.S. General Accounting Office, 1994.

3. Bloch, R. E., and Falk, D. M. "Antitrust, Competition and Health Reform." *Health Affairs* 13, no. 1 (1994): 206–23.

4. Donelan, K., Blendon, R. J., Schoen, C., Davis, K., and Binns, K. "The Cost of Health System Change: Public Discontent in Five Nations." *Health Affairs* 18, no. 3 (1999): 205–16.

5. Brown, R. E. "Let the Public Control Hospitals through Planning." *Hospitals* 33, no. 23 (1959): 34–39,108–9.

6. Cohen, H. A. "Experience of a State Cost Control Commission." In Zubkoff, M., Raskin, I. E., and Haft, R. S. *Hospital Cost Containment,* 401–28. New York: Prodist, 1978.

7. Anderson, O. W. *Health Services in the United States: A Growth Enterprise since 1875,* 205–6. Ann Arbor: Health Administration Press, 1985.

8. Eby, C. L., and Cohodes, D. R. "What Do We Know about Rate-Setting?" *Journal of Health Politics, Policy and Law* 10, no. 2 (1985): 299–327.

9. Salkever, D. S., and Bice, T. W. *The Hospital Certificate of Need Controls: Impact on Investment, Costs, and Use.* Washington, D.C.: American Enterprise Institute for Policy Research, 1979.

10. Keller, M. *Regulating a New Economy: Public Policy and Economic Change in America, 1990–1993.* Cambridge, Mass.: Harvard University Press, 1990.

11. Krislov, S., and Musolf, L. D. *The Politics of Regulation: A Reader.* Boston: Houghton Mifflin, 1964.

12. Bernstein, M. H. *Regulation Business by Independent Commission,* 74. Princeton: Princeton University Press, 1955.

13. Phillips, C. F., Jr. *The Economics of Regulation: Theory and Practice in the Transportation and Public Utility Industries.* Homewood, Ill.: Richard D. Irwin, 1969.

14. Reagan, M. D. *Regulation: The Politics of Policy.* Boston: Little, Brown, 1987.

15. Meiners, R. E., and Yandle, B. *Regulation and the Reagan Era: Politics, Bureaucracy, and the Public Interest.* New York: Holmes and Meier, 1989.

16. Mueller, D. C. "Symposium: Deregulation in Retrospect." *Southern Economic Journal* 59, no. 3 (1993): 436–37.

17. White, L. J. *The S & L Debacle: Public Policy Lessons from Bank and Thrift Regulation.* New York: Oxford University Press, 1991.

18. Weil, T. P. "Any Possibility of an S & L–Type Debacle Occurring in the Health Industry?" *Health Care Management Review* 20, no. 4 (1995): 34–41.

19. Morrison, S. A., and Winston, C. "The Dynamics of Airline Pricing and Competition." *American Economic Review* 80, no. 2 (1990): 389–93.

20. McFarland, H. "The Effects of United States Railroad Deregulation on Shippers, Labor, and Capital." *Journal of Regulatory Economics* 1, no. 2 (1989): 259–70.

21. Ying, J. S., and Keeler, T. E. "Pricing in a Regulated Environment: The Motor Carrier Experience." *Rand Journal of Economics* 22, no. 2 (1991): 264–73.

22. Dranove, D., Shanley, M., and White, W. D. "Price and Concentration in Hospital Markets: The Switch from Patient-Driven to Payer-Driven Competition." *Journal of Law and Economics* 36, no. 2 (1993): 179–204.

23. Jorgensen, N. E., and Weil, T. P. "Regulating Managed Care Plans: Is the Telecommunications Industry a Possible Model?" *Managed Care Quarterly* 6, no. 3 (1998): 7–16.

24. Olsin, G. P. *The Story of Telecommunications.* Macon, Ga.: Mercer University Press, 1992.

25. Bell, T. W., and Singleton, S. *Regulators' Revenge: The Future of Telecommunications Deregulation.* Washington, D.C.: Cato Institute, 1998.

26. American Hospital Association (AHA). *Ameriplan: A Proposal for the Delivery and Financing of Health Services in the United States.* Chicago: AHA, November 1970.

27. Weil, T. P. "Public Disclosure in the Health Field: Why Not a SEC Commission?" *American Journal of Medical Quality* 16, no. 1 (2000): in press.

28. Waxler, C. "A Nasty Conglomerate." *Forbes* 162, no. 11 (1998): 55–56.

29. Goldsmith, J. "Columbia/HCA: A Failure of Leadership." *Health Affairs* 17, no. 2 (1998): 27–29.

30. www.sec.gov/asec/asecart.htm provides a discussion on what the U.S. Securities and Exchange Commission is and what it does.

31. Borowksy, S. J., Goertz, C., and Laurie, N. "Can Physicians Diagnose Strengths and Weaknesses in Health Plans?" *Annals of Internal Medicine* 125, no. 3 (1996): 239–41.

32. Borowsky, S. J., Davis, M. K., Goertz, C., and Laurie, N. "Are All Health Plans Created Equal? The Physicians View." *Journal of the American Medical Association* 278, no. 11 (1997): 917–21.

33. Foundation for Accountability. *Accountability Action* 1, no. 1 (Fall 1996).

34. U.S. General Accounting Office. "Health Care Reform 'Report Cards' Are Useful but Significant Issues Need to Be Addressed." Report GAO/HEHS 94-219. Washington, D.C.: U.S. General Accounting Office, 1994.

35. Berwick, D. M., and Wald, D. L. "Hospital Leaders' Opinion of the HCFA Mortality Data." *Journal of the American Medical Association* 263, no. 2 (1990): 247–49.

36. Luce, J. M., Thiel, G. D., Holland, M. R., Swig, L., Curring, S. A., and Luft, H. S. "Use of Risk-Adjusted Outcome for Data for Quality Improvement by Public Hospitals." *Western Journal of Medicine* 164, no. 5 (1996): 410–44.

37. Epstein, A. M. "Rolling Down the Runway: The Challenge Ahead for Quality Report Cards." *Journal of the American Medical Association* 279, no. 21 (1998): 1691–96.

38. Jewett, J. H., and Hibbard, J. H. "Comprehension of Quality Care Indicators: Differences among Privately Insured, Publicly Insured, and Uninsured." *Health Care Financing Review* 18, no. 1 (1996): 75–94.

39. Gibbs, D. A., Sangl, J. A., and Burras, B. "Consumer Perspectives on Information Needs for Health Plan Choice." *Health Care Financing Review* 16, no. 1 (1996): 55–73.

40. Robinson, S., and Brodie, M. "Understanding the Quality Challenge for Health Consumers: The Kaiser/AHCPR Survey." *Joint Commission Journal on Quality Improvement* 23, no. 5 (1997): 239–44.

41. Romano, P. S., Rainwater, J. A., and Antonius, D. "How Hospitals in California and New York Perceive and Interpret Their Report Cards." *Medical Care* 37, no. 3 (1997): 239–44.

42. Hannan, E. L., Siu, A. L., Kumar, D., Kilburn, N., Jr., and Chassin, M. R. "The Decline in Coronary Artery Bypass Graft Surgery Mortality in New York State: The Role of Surgeon Volume." *Journal of the American Medical Association* 273, no. 3 (1995): 209–12.

43. Bentley, J. M., and Nash, D. B. "How Pennsylvania Hospitals Have Responded to Publicly Released Reports on Coronary Artery Bypass Graft Surgery." *Joint Commission Journal on Quality Improvement* 24, no. 1 (1998): 40–49.

44. Maxwell, C. I. "Public Disclosure of Performance Information in Pennsylvania: Impact on Hospital Charges and the Views of Hospital Executives." *Joint Commission Journal on Quality Improvement* 24, no. 9 (1998): 491–502.

45. Schneider, E., and Epstein, A. M. "Public Use of Public Performance Reports: A Survey of Patients Undergoing Cardiac Surgery." *Journal of the American Medical Association* 279, no. 20 (1998): 1638–42.

46. Evans, J. H., Hwang, Y., Nagaraju, N., and Shastri, K. "Involuntary Benchmarking and Quality Improvement: The Effect of Mandated Public Disclosure on Hospitals." *Journal of Accounting, Auditing, and Finance* 12, no. 1 (1997): 315–46.

47. Ellwood, P., Jr. "Harvard Outcomes Symposium." Summarized in *Healthcare Briefings* 16, no. 11 (1999): 5.

48. Weil, T. P., and Pearl, G. M. "America's Best Hospitals: Heading toward Fiscal Distress?" *Managed Care Interface* 14, no. 4 (2001): in press.

49. Serb, C. "The Health Care 250." *Hospitals and Health Networks* 73, no. 4 (1999): 38–48.

50. Himmelstein, D. U., Woolhandler, S., Hellander, I., and Wolfe, S. M. "Quality of Care in Investor-Owned vs. Not-for-Profit HMOs." *Journal of the American Medical Association* 282, no. 2 (1999): 159–63.

51. Hibbard, J. H., Jewett, J. H., Legnini, M. W., and Tusler, N. "Choosing a Health Plan: Do Large Employers Use the Data?" *Health Affairs* 16, no. 6 (1997): 172–80.

52. McNeil, D. "What's Happened to Employers' Push for Quality?" *Business and Health* 17, no. 4 (1999): 26–32.

53. Longo, D. R., Land, G., Schramm, W., Braas, J., Hoskins, B., and Howell, V. "Consumer Reports in Health Care: Do They Make a Difference?" *Journal of the American Medical Association* 279, no. 19 (1997): 1579–84.

54. Weil, T. P. "Horizontal Mergers in the United States Health Field: Some Practical Realities." *Health Services Management Research* 13, no. 3 (2000): 137–51.

55. Clement, J. P., McCue, M. J., Luke, R. D., Bramble, J. D., Rossiter, L. F., Ozcan, Y. A., and Pai, C.-W. "Strategic Hospital Alliances: Impact on Financial Performance." *Health Affairs* 16, no. 6 (1997): 193–203.

56. Connor, R. A., Feldman, R., Dowd, B. E., and Radcliff, T. A. "Which Types of Hospital Mergers Save Consumers Money?" *Health Affairs* 16, no. 6 (1997): 62–74.

57. Knudson, D. J., Kind, E. A., Fowles, J. B., and Adlis, S. "Impact of Report Cards on Employees: A Natural Experiment." *Health Care Financing Review* 20, no. 1 (1998): 5–27.

58. Kassirer, J. P. "The Use and Abuse of Practice Profiles." *New England Journal of Medicine* 330, no. 9 (1994): 634–36.

59. American Hospital Association. "Consumer Price Index." *AHA News* 35, no. 46 (1999): 3.

60. Weil, T. P., and Battistella, R. M. "A Blended Strategy Using Competitive and Regulatory Models." *Health Care Management Review* 23, no. 1 (1997): 37–45.

61. Battistella, R. M., Bergun, J. W., and Buchanan, R. J. "The Political Economy of Health Services: A Review of Major Ideological Influences." In Litman, T., and Robins, L. S., eds. *Health Politics and Policy,* 66–92. 2d ed. Albany, N.Y.: Delmar Publishing, 1991.

62. Bipartisan Commission Entitlement Performance. *Interim Report to the President.* Washington, D.C.: Government Printing Office, 1994.

63. Concord Coalition. *The Zero Deficit Plan: A Plan for Eliminating the Federal Budget Deficit by the Year 2002.* Washington, D.C.: Concord Coalition and U.S. Government Printing Office, 1995.

64. Congressional Budget Office. *Reducing Entitlement Spending.* Washington, D.C.: Government Printing Office, 1994.

65. Madrick, J. *The End of Affluence.* New York: Random House, 1995.

66. Ellwood, P. M., Anderson, N. N., Billings, J. E., Carlson, R. J., Hoagberg, E. J., and McClure, W. "Health Maintenance Strategy." *Medical Care* 9, no. 3 (1971): 291–98.

67. Enthoven, A. C. "The History and Principles of Managed Competition." *Health Affairs* 12, supp. (1993): 24–48.

68. Hackney, R. B. "Trapped between State and Market Regulating Hospital Reimbursement in the Northeastern States." *Medical Care Review* 49, no. 3 (1992): 355–88.

69. Levit, K., Lazenby, H. C., Cowan, C. A., and Letsch, S. W. "Health Spending by State: New Estimates for Policy Making." *Health Affairs* 12, no. 3 (1993): 7–26.

70. Weil, T. P. "The Blending of Competitive and Regulatory Strategies: A Second Opinion." *Journal of Health Care Finance* 23, no. 2 (1996): 46–56.

71. Stigler, G. E. "The Theory of Economic Regulation." *Bell Journal of Economics and Management Science* 2, no. 2 (1971): 2–21.

72. Bernstein, M. H. *Regulation of Business by Independent Commission,* 74. Princeton: Princeton University Press, 1955.

73. Arrow, K. J. "Uncertainty and the Welfare Economics of Medical Care." *American Economic Review* 53, no. 5 (1963): 941–73.

74. Battistella, R. M., and Weil, T. P. "Procompetitive Health Policy: Benefits and Needs." *Frontiers of Health Services Management* 2, no. 4 (1986): 3–36.

75. Rossiter, L. F., Langwell, K., Wan, T. T., and Rivnyak, M. "Patient Satisfaction among Elderly Enrollees and Disenrollees in Medical Health Maintenance Organizations: Results from the National Medicare Competition Evaluation." *Journal of the American Medical Association* 262, no. 1 (1989): 57–63.

76. Retchin, S. M., Clement, D. G., Rossiter, L. F., Brown, B., Brown, R., and Nelson, L. "How the Elderly Fare in HMOs: Outcomes from the Medicare Competition Demonstrations." *Health Services Research* 27, no. 5 (1992): 651–69.

77. Brown, R. S., Clement, D. G., Hill, J., Retchin, S. M., and Bergeron, J. W. "Do Health Maintenance Organizations Work for Medicare?" *Health Care Financing Review* 15, no. 1 (1993): 7–23.

78. Arnevitz, L. G. "Medicaid States Turn to Managed Care to Improve Access and Control Costs." Report GAO-HRD-93-46. Washington, D.C.: U.S. General Accounting Office, 1993.

79. Sisk, J. E., Gorman, S. A., Reisinger, A. L., Glied, S. A., DuMouchel, W. H., and Haynes, M. M. "Evaluation of Medicaid Managed Care. Satisfaction, Access, and Use." *Journal of the American Medical Association* 276, no. 1 (1996): 50–55.

80. Miller, R. H., and Luft, H. S. "Managed Care Plan Performance since 1980: A Literature Analysis." *Journal of the American Medical Association* 271, no. 10 (1994): 1512–19.

81. Melnick, G. A., and Zwanzinger, J. "State Health Care Expenditures under Competition and Regulation: 1980 through 1991." *American Journal of Public Health* 85, no. 10 (1995): 1391–96.

82. Robinson, J. C. "HMO Market Penetration and Hospital Cost Inflation in California." *Journal of the American Medical Association* 266, no. 19 (1996): 2719–23.

83. Robinson, J. C. "Decline in Hospital Utilization and Cost Inflation under

Managed Care in California." *Journal of the American Medical Association* 276, no. 13 (1996): 1060–64.

84. Kerr, E., Mittman, B. S., Hays, R. D., Leake, B., and Brook, R. H. "Quality Assurance in Capitated Physician Groups." *Journal of the American Medical Association* 276, no. 15 (1996): 1236–39.

85. Burner, S. T., and Waldo, D. R. "National Health Expenditure Projections, 1994–2005." *Health Care Financing Review* 16, no. 4 (1995): 221–42.

86. Steinfels, P. *The Neoconservatives: The Men Who Are Changing America's Politics.* New York: Simon and Schuster, 1979.

87. Battistella, R. M. "Health Services Reforms: Political and Managerial Aims—An International Perspective." *International Journal of Health Planning and Management* 8, no. 4 (1993): 265–74.

88. Wallack, S. S., Skwara, K. C., and Cai, J. "Redefining Rate Regulations in a Competitive Environment." *Journal of Health Politics, Policy and Law* 21, no. 3 (1996): 489–510.

89. Scanlon, W. J. "Arizona Medicaid Competition among Managed Care Plans Lowers Program Costs." Report GAOHEHS-95-2. Washington, D.C.: U.S. General Accounting Office, 1995.

90. Wilsford, D. "States Facing Interests: Struggles over Health Policy in Advanced, Industrial Democracies." *Health Politics, Policy and Law* 20, no. 3 (1995): 571–613.

91. Organization for Economic Cooperation and Development (OECD). *Health Care Reform: The Will to Change.* Paris: OECD, 1996.

92. Schieber, G. J., Poullier, J.-P., and Greenwald, L. M. "Health System Performance in OECD Countries, 1998–1992." *Health Affairs* 13, no. 4 (1994): 100–112.

93. Organization for Economic Cooperation and Development (OECD). *New Orientations for Social Policy.* Paris: OECD, 1994.

94. Pfaff, M. "Differences in Health Care Spending across Countries: Statistical Evidence." *Journal of Health Policy, Politics and Law* 15, no. 1 (1990): 1–68.

95. Rotwein, S., Boulmetis, M., Boben, P. J., Fingold, H. I., Hadley, J. P., Rama, K. L., and Van Hoven, D. "Medicaid and State Health Care Reform: Process, Programs, and Policy Options." *Health Care Financing Review* 16, no. 3 (1995): 105–20.

96. American Hospital Association. *The Dartmouth Atlas of Health Care in the United States.* Chicago: American Hospital Association, 1996.

97. Himmelstein, D. U., Lewontin, J. P., and Woolhandler, S. "Who Administers? Who Cares? Medical Administrative and Clinical Employment in the United States and Canada." *American Journal of Public Health* 86, no. 2 (1996): 172–78.

98. Pew Health Professions Commission. *Critical Challenges: Revitalizing the Health Professions for the Twenty-first Century.* San Francisco: UCSF, Center for the Health Professions, 1995.

99. Kassirer, J. P. "Mergers and Acquisitions—Who Benefits?; Who Loses?" *New England Journal of Medicine* 334, no. 4 (1996): 722–23.

100. Weissenstein, E. "Cut Out of the Middleman: Coalition Seeks Big Savings by Taking the Direct Approach." *Modern Healthcare* 25, no. 27 (1995): 28–30.

101. Weil, T. P. "Competition versus Regulation: Constraining Hospital Discharge Costs." *Journal of Health Care Finance* 23, no. 3 (1996): 62–74.

102. Blendon, R. J., Leitman, R., Morrison, L., and Donelan, K. "Satisfaction with Health Systems in Ten Nations." *Health Affairs* 9, no. 2 (1992): 185–92.

8

Leadership for Health Networks: What's Needed?

ABSTRACT.   The increasing number of mergers that have taken place during the past decade among health providers has created a leadership crisis. Public opinion and turnover statistics suggest that an insufficient number of qualified leaders are currently available who possess the necessary vision and operational skills. This chapter, therefore, focuses on the attributes, knowledge, and competencies required to provide the leadership now needed by the United States' increasingly complex health networks. Furthermore, it discusses: the critical intangibles required by these CEOs; some impediments experienced in mounting sound educational programs to train these leaders; criteria that governing boards might utilize when selecting and evaluating their health network CEO; and the advisability of appointing "outside directors" to broaden a governing board's policy decision-making capabilities in order to facilitate its CEO to behave as a "true" leader.

Providing effective leadership to U.S. health networks is a particularly complex task. These roles require sound business acumen and a profound understanding of how the health field functions. In today's highly competitive environment, health network leaders must constantly balance their constituents' demands for more and improved health services with the increasing pressures being advanced by the various powerful business coalitions and public officials that are insisting on stiffer cost constraints. When deciding between what makes the most clinical sense and what might be the most fiscally prudent, health network leaders must not only demonstrate stewardship by doing things the right way, but must also convince the communities they serve of their CEO's (chief executive officer) wise and forthright judgment to do the right things.[1]

In the practice of medicine, those at the most eminent levels of clinical expertise tend to concentrate on narrower and narrower disciplines. This is a trend consistent with the establishment of additional board certification categories among the medical subspecialties. In contrast, in the leadership of health networks, the higher the level of responsibility, the greater the need for a broader knowledge of business practices, of the organization and management of health services, and of the most appropriate ways of adding value to the delivery of health services.[2-3]

Health alliance CEO roles are awfully complicated and differ in a number of ways from those in other industries: medical services are of critical concern to any person with significant illness or disability; the patient-physician relationship is intensely personal; providers are surrounded by a conglomeration of legal, moral, and ethical standards; and sensitivity is required to such potentially conflicting demands on resources as enhancing access to care, social equity, quality, and cost containment efforts.[4-5]

The words *leader, executive,* and *manager* are frequently used interchangeably. Leaders and leadership, the central foci of this chapter, are terms derived from the old English word for *travel,* connoting giving direction or heading. Executives, on the other hand, are those who are more directly immersed in management (from the Italian word for handling) or administration (from the Latin word for executing).[6] A number of Peter Drucker's disciples have a somewhat different definition: a leader diverges from an executive or manager in terms of the former's emphasizing such difficult to measure intangibles as vision, community-oriented values, trust, participation, and integrity.[7] Kotter refers to these slightly vague concepts more simply as the three subprocesses of establishing direction, aligning people, and motivating.[8] In any case, in pursuing an alliance's goals and objectives, these somewhat abstract concepts become pivotal when a leader weighs the various tradeoffs of enhancing the region's health delivery system versus reducing its healthcare expenditures.

That these health network CEO positions are so complicated and the basic attributes required to succeed are so abstruse may help explain at least partially why it is so difficult to initiate highly effective training programs for leadership roles. Theoretically, a broad spectrum of health-related and business-oriented knowledge and experience is required that should be most readily obtainable by interdisciplinary and joint academic and practical ventures organized by major research universities. There are some obvious difficulties in initiating such training as illustrated by the difficulty of teaching future health network leaders in the classroom about how to respond in pragmatic terms to such issues as reducing cost in the face of advances in scientific medicine and an aging population consuming more and more health resources.

Rather than simply trying to focus on the intangibles of leadership and the various complexities inherent in integrating the enormous body of knowledge necessary to train future leaders of health networks, this chapter discusses criteria that governing boards can employ when selecting and evaluating CEOs for these roles; and the advisability of appointing outside directors to broaden the governing board's policy decision-making processes in order that the CEO can function as a true leader. Trustees and their CEOs might find it prudent to jointly review these various performance measures. Their frank discussion should enhance leadership opportunities, and they are among the most pressing issues currently faced by many U.S. health networks.

The Intangibles of Health Network Leadership

Being the leader of a health network is a demanding role and requires that a CEO possess a number of intangible qualities. Some factors appear more crucial than others and their individual importance is often dependent on the organization's current and future needs. The more essential intangibles to consider when selecting a health network leader follow:

Vision. A key role for a leader is to articulate a thoughtful, clear, and compelling vision for the health alliance. What are the short- and long-range role and goals of this health network? What are its values and what corporate culture does the health network wish to articulate to its internal and external publics? Where is the health network heading and how will it in the future achieve these objectives? What factors are the most critical to an alliance's eventual success, so that its various stakeholders can believe in and set forth a similar vision?

Effective leaders must be charismatic and able to articulate those pretty global pictures of how the health network's various components will interact with each other to effectively and efficiently meet the region's healthcare needs. In addition, an alliance's CEO must create: (1) an understandable and common purpose that is compatible with the organization's culture; and (2) a meaningful and eventually attainable mission statement that provides the health network with stability, the reasons for its existence and potentially enhancing its value, and concurrently allows its employees to become part of something greater than each of their respective roles.

One of the more recurrent CEO failings, which causes relatively frequent turnover among medical school deans and health network CEOs,[9-10] has been the CEO's inability to implement that overriding vision. Governing boards and physicians expect their leaders not only to lay out the overall plan, but also to be relatively decisive in implementing the doable and in creating commendable results with reasonable dispatch. In that process, it is critical for health network leaders to build some rallying points for their various communities, trustees, medical staffs, and employees.

Community-oriented values. Successful leaders for the nation's health networks should have community-oriented values that contain a broader and deeper societal prospective on life generally and their role as a CEO than how much power they are able to muster or how much money they can earn. These CEOs must possess a deep sense of personal and professional gratification and self-fulfillment when providing the leadership to enhance a region's health delivery system. They must evaluate their achievements by such factors as: (1) contributing to the prevention of illness and in restoring wellness to the region's sick and disabled; (2) creating something of significant value for their fellow men, such as designing and implementing a broader range of services that are easily accessible and affordable; and (3) acting as a responsible corporate citizen by delivering health services based more on clinical need than on an individual's ability to pay for care.[11]

In 1997 the United States spent 13.5 percent of its gross domestic product on health followed by Germany (10.4 percent), Switzerland (10.1 percent), France (9.6 percent), and Canada (9 percent). But Americans fared far worse on some critical health outcomes. For instance, in 1995, the United States' infant mortality rate ranked 23d and the life expectancy for men ranked a disappointing 21st among the world's 29 leading industrialized nations.[12]

Among the most frequently encountered stumbling blocks to the improvement of the delivery of health services is the fact that 44.8 million Americans are without health insurance and an additional 29 million are seriously underinsured.[13-14] This sizable number of persons lacking insurance coverage suggests that the health networks should be far more aggressive in initiating such options as Medicaid HMOs to provide health insurance coverage for poor rural and inner-city residents. But, realistically, these alliances must also generate sufficient demand for care from patients with health insurance coverage to satisfy the organization's financial objectives. It is critical that these recently restructured corporations are also able to continue to exist within that same community, as solvent health providers. Current issues in access, societal inequalities, and the ability to pay for quality healthcare require that leaders of U.S. health alliances seriously and continually evaluate the depth of their community-oriented values.

Trust. Leaders know that trust provides a significant competitive edge in a world of massive and complex adversarial relationships. Trust is the glue that holds positive relationships together. Any major change, such as the CEO announcing that the health network will experience a huge employee layoff, threatens trust and can ultimately destroy confidence in the organization's leadership. Particularly in a period of internal crisis or because of a major threat generated by a competitor, ineffective or nonexistent communications frequently result in an enormous increase in mistrust, confusion, and cynicism, and a huge decline in morale and confidence in an alliance's leadership.

Trust takes a long time to earn, often by a leader developing deep listening skills and maintaining an open-door policy. It can be easily lost in one moment of thoughtlessness. Leaders must be genuine, believable, dependable, predictable, and benevolent. Although we rarely talk about it, we all need to trust our leaders. We all know in our hearts when we do and when we don't. If we trust our leaders and each other, the process of building meaningful relationships and an effective and efficient health network becomes far easier.

Leaders can get entangled in the trappings of their power, and in the pomp and the prestige of their role. Sometimes these CEOs become greedy and lose sight of their own imperfections. In doing so, they become isolated from their colleagues. The synergy of the health network's common vision or purpose thereafter slowly dissolves and the result in the ranks is almost always a combination of distrust, resentment, disillusionment, and apathy.

Participation. If among the leadership intangibles vision provides the direction, community-oriented values establish the broad societal perspectives, and trust creates the solid foundation, then participation is the energy that potentially drives the health network forward. A leader's challenge is to unleash that power and then to focus that initiative on achieving the alliance's goals and objectives.

Active participation in the decision-making process is particularly important today because in the current pro-competitive health environment driven by managed care forces, most providers need to deliver more services, in less time, and with fewer resources. In fact, for an alliance to achieve a competitive edge it must significantly expand the workload and the personal and professional commitment of each employee within the health network. Integrated systems need leaders who will take the necessary initiative, be accountable for results, support the health network's values and mission statement, and actively mentor the next generation of leaders. Meanwhile, their employees want a voice in deciding on operational policies and procedures and, thereby, gain some sense of ownership within the organization. The alliance's employees need to believe in themselves and feel like winners, since all workers long to invest in something that really matters such as enhancing the delivery of the region's health services.

By sharing power and also sharing all the tools that go along with it—information, data, responsibility, and rewards—effective leaders are able to create full participation and a working environment wherein employees contribute freely and to the best of their ability. When leaders succeed in creating a participative corporate culture, employees are able to act as mature partners. They can take initiative, make appropriate decisions after evaluating potential options, provide competent feedback, accept responsibility, and assist in designing and implementing a smoothly operating and efficient health network.

Integrity. The kind of leader that health network employees want to follow is driven by fundamental, undeniable principles. These principles are deeply ingrained in the leader's makeup, shaped over a lifetime of mentoring and introspection. They serve as a moral compass, an internal guidance system that has fairness and justice at its magnetic north. It is important to note that integrity has nothing to do with a leader's personal view or political agenda. It is more fundamental than that since it is about the leader's being an appropriately centered and grounded person.

Leaders with integrity have the courage to be themselves. They are not afraid of making tough decisions and stand firm in the face of adversity. Their integrity grows out of their own sense of self-worth, but this does not mean they are necessarily naive. Effective leaders know that people possess a mixture of altruism and self-interest, and cannot always be counted on to do the right thing. To them, how we produce things is just as important as what we achieve.

The real test comes when the leader must put the principles of ethics and equity into practice. Ultimately, by employing these precepts of integrity, a CEO builds a culture of institutional fairness, a place where employees have the courage to voice their opinions, where pay is equitable, and where reputation matters. The end result is an ethical health network, where as an overriding goal there is a fair and balanced return for all the alliance's stakeholders—the community, patients, trustees, physicians, and employees.

Training Future Health Network Leaders

Most leaders of American health networks are now being drawn from those who completed a graduate program awarding a master's degree in health services administration or equivalent. In more recent years, an increasing percentage of those recruited for these roles are physicians who often have also completed formal management training. Those appointed to these positions generally have many years of experience in various healthcare environments such as health systems or alliances, academic health centers, medical group practices, and managed care plans. Although the intangibles of health network leadership (that are exceedingly difficult to evaluate in an interview or by checking the applicant's references) such as vision, community-oriented values, trust, participation, and integrity are sometimes woven into the existing curricula and off-campus training endeavors, most often discussions concerning their relevance occur by simply happenchance rather than in any explicit fashion.

Most of the arguments in the past concerning training future health executives have focused on whether the most appropriate core curriculum for such roles should be sought from a school of public health or a school of business administration.[15-17] More recent discussions center on the necessity for U.S. health leaders to become more familiar with clinical-fiscal methodologies that simultaneously improve quality of care and reduce health expenditures.[3, 18] These approaches measure the trade offs of expending more clinical resources and therefore adding cost, compared to the potential increments of improved patient outcomes.

Resources available in schools of medicine, public health, nursing, business administration, allied health sciences, and others need to be integrated into programs of health administration or other similar endeavors, to start weighing specific patient care options compared with fiscal contingencies. Those health network leaders who are most familiar with the medical care production process and can generate clinical and management benefits in terms of effectiveness and efficiency should be the most successful in an era that focuses on cost constraint and quality patient care. More familiarity with the "clinical-fiscal productivity" methodologies should enable CEOs to implement lower cost labor and material substitutes to further reduce healthcare expenditures, without significantly compromising quality patient care.

A strong clinical background can be helpful to a leader in identifying appropriate ways of adding value to the provision of care, thereby encouraging the alliance toward pursuing the most cost-effective approaches to patient treatment. Previous hands-on patient care experience also can be exceedingly valuable when evaluating expensive new technologies and procedures. For the past several decades, the expansion of the medical sciences has been a strong driving force behind the nation's rising healthcare costs and, unfortunately, has sometimes yielded questionable gains in clinical outcomes.

A number of factors may hinder the implementation of developing educational programs for future health network leaders at major research universities. These include:

1. most full-time faculty members in academic health centers and other similar environments resist the concept of joint venturing with colleagues, such as schools of business, to start such meaningful interdisciplinary efforts;
2. most clinical protocols and outcome studies have been designed

and utilized to date to constrain costs rather than to enhance the quality of patient care;[19] and

3. most health network leaders are absorbed in strategic and fiscal macro-type deliberations and decisions, while the long-term success of their leadership is dependent on improvements in access and quality of care, and the reduction in the cost of care.

Therefore, it could well be that we expect too much from even the best academic institutions in the United States when we ask them to produce health leaders who are comfortable and effective in weighing the tradeoffs of incremental increases or decreases in cost versus improving the region's healthcare delivery.

This task of training health network leaders might be significantly aided if more of the country's most effective CEOs were strongly committed to mentoring or tutoring generally younger, less experienced professionals.[20-21] A mentor is expected to share his or her professional expertise, wisdom, and knowledge about the field as well as about the professional life passage and other career-related topics. Such one-on-one training and informal experience can sharpen the knowledge, skills, and experience of an emerging neophyte. Unfortunately, mentoring is less prevalent today for several reasons: (1) leaders are under significantly more pressure to achieve immediate positive outcomes; (2) spouses are often also employed outside the home, so the CEO must share more family responsibilities and therefore has less time to tutor young colleagues; and (3) a more rapid turnover of CEOs causes more difficulties in arranging which staff members are most responsible to train the next generations of leaders.

It is simply more difficult to become a top professional without having worked closely with one or preferably more leaders with outstanding abilities. The health field, the academic programs, and their faculties, with the student taking a vigorous role, have a vested interest and must jointly assume the responsibility to help place bright, young, well-trained, and thoughtful neophytes in environments where they are not only tutored so they have the opportunity to expand their horizons but where they can also eventually become so well prepared that in several decades they are able to succeed their mentors.

Criteria for Selecting a Health Network Leader

There are a number of challenges that almost all health networks and their leaders now face as they develop corporate restructuring strategies. Avoiding these potential entanglements should be among the criteria used (in addition to the intangibles enumerated earlier) by the search committee to evaluate whether a specific candidate is well qualified to fill a specific leadership role.

One selected for a health network CEO position should demonstrate a clear and in-depth understanding of the following factors. First, he or she must recognize that the goals and objectives agreed upon by the community, governing board, physicians, and the management team must be structured to be consistent with the region's healthcare needs and must be aligned to insure a *smooth integration of the disparate operating cultures* that were generated by the previous corporate amalgamations. Achievable and realistic strategies proposed by the CEO and his or her senior advisors and then reviewed, possibly modified, and finally ratified by the various medical staffs and trustees of the major subsidiaries are among the prime driving forces that enhance the long-term operational and fiscal successes of any health network. This point of view has particular relevance when one or more of the new partners within the alliance were, prior to a recent corporate restructuring endeavor, relatively independently minded.

Because of the possibility of creating morale problems among physicians, employees, and affected citizens, often the most difficult decision for leaders of health networks to implement is to consolidate clinical services or close an acute care facility. While downsizing generally offers the greatest potential to achieve significant fiscal savings, such approaches frequently require enormous skill in blending diverse self-interested operating cultures.

Second, and often underestimated among the key conditions a CEO must understand, is the *critical importance of physician input and counsel* in planning and then in ongoing decision making after the corporate restructuring has been consummated. Gaining any physician consensus is often a laborious process and requires the successful integration of the professional concerns of the competing medical staffs within an alliance.

Frequently overlooked by a governing board's trustees is that physicians more often than patients determine the slope of the demand curve for services rendered by most health providers. Consolidating clinical services among fewer facilities typically provides a major portion of projected cost reductions underlying the economies created by a merger. In combining services, physician dialogue and their reluctant acceptance are required in order for the health network leadership to effect a smooth transition. Other similarly sensitive issues include: operational and fiscal interrelationships among physicians, hospitals, and managed care plans; and the acquisition of numerous primary care and other physician practices. Physician discontent can occur on these and other issues and can result in decreased patient numbers and operating cash flows, which have already contributed to the faltering of several health networks.

Obtaining physician agreement within a health network on such major issues as consolidating tertiary-type services at fewer sites, acquiring or divesting physician practices, or negotiating with HMOs on reimbursement is seldom easy. And it is far more complicated when an academic health center or one of its affiliated teaching hospitals are partners. Facilities involving in-house staff training usually bring a high cost structure to the discussions. In addition, there is often difficulty in integrating the practice patterns and culture of faculty physicians, whose primary focus is teaching and research, with those of community-based physicians, whose primary interest is patient care. After obtaining physician input and counsel, still the most capable health network leadership is needed when shuttering tertiary or other major patient care sites as well as when integrating the interests of academic and private practicing physicians.

Third, there are several potential strategies available to a CEO once the health network *has secured significant market penetration* within the region:

1. Simply reducing the region's healthcare costs by lowering payroll and overhead expenditures. Such a cost-containment effort usually requires centralizing various clinical and administrative services, eliminating one layer of management, or implementing other similar measures;
2. Using its market clout during reimbursement negotiations to significantly increase its leverage on managed care plans; or,
3. Maintaining the status quo and utilizing the alliance's oligopolistic posture to control within the region the availability of services and the setting of prices, with the prime objective of enhancing the health network's bottom line.

So when selecting a CEO, it is critical that the governing board and a new CEO at the very outset agree on the strategies to achieve the health network's goals and objectives. The implications of such policy discussions are overwhelming.

There is increasing concern among elected officials, physicians, and consumer watchdog groups that the primary reason for this merger mania now under way in the health field is that these alliances seek to gain oligopolistic capabilities. Some mergers appear to be consummated to enhance a provider's market penetration. This consolidation of resources is usually justified by the improved economies of scale (e.g., in terms of lower costs) that are theoretically possible among these hospitals, physicians, and HMOs by all this current corporate restructuring, but the projected positive outcomes have not yet become clearly apparent.[22–23] In fact, there is increasing evidence that most of the corporate restructuring that has been consummated is intended to control market share, prices, and managed care negotiations.[24–25]

What happens when there are few providers left in the region and a managed care plan is no longer able to negotiate prices as theorized in a competitive marketplace? In most underserved inner-city and rural areas, there is already a limited number of physicians and hospitals available. But, of far greater concern to the usual competitive theory is a metropolitan area that is dominated by one powerful network functioning as a cartel. Do state officials or others have the responsibility to step in and enact the necessary rules and regulations to protect consumers, insurers with mostly adverse risks, and other providers who are being squeezed out? If so, by whom, at what point, and how should it be accomplished?

A critical question in the CEO selection process is whether a health network leader views horizontal integration as a means to improve health services at a reduced cost, or as a means to control prices and to increase the organization's bargaining capabilities with managed care plans and others. In such discussions with various CEO applicants, an increasing long-term concern for communities, trustees, physicians, the organizations' employees and others should be whether the nation's health networks eventually will, because of their oligopolistic tendencies, become regulated as monopolies by their respective state department of health or similar agency.

Fourth, a CEO must recognize that many health networks have sought without significant success *vertical diversification strategies* (i.e., expanding into other related healthcare businesses) as a means to securing additional patient referrals and thereby improving market share. In many communities hospitals have pursued this option by acquiring primary care and other physician practices through ownership or equity models. Some alliances have paid exorbitant prices for these acquisitions, and have signed long-term contracts without appropriate productivity incentives. These agreements have now resulted in some health networks (e.g., HCA—The Healthcare Co., Tenet Healthcare Corporation, Allegheny Health, Education, and Research Foundation) experiencing declining cash flows and divesting themselves of some of their earlier acquisitions. Some healthcare providers have pursued establishing HMOs, other similar insurers or have purchased an equity position in an existing health insurance plan, all approaches that generally require significant capital outlays.

While these vertical integration strategies have the potential of resulting in improved market share and enhanced reimbursement rates, a CEO needs to be cognizant of the fact that these growth strategies can be costly. In some instances the increases in market penetration and revenues by using such an option have not offset the associated financial losses. Among the frequent explanations for the failures in using this approach are that many health network staffs are not particularly experienced in managing these nonhospital business ventures, and that there are high additional overhead costs associated with becoming a partner of a major health network.

Leaders of health networks are often anxious to replicate one of the more effective horizontally and vertically integrated alliances, such as the Henry Ford Health System (Detroit), Intermountain Health Care Inc. (Utah), and Sentara Health System (Norfolk), health alliances that evolved over several decades. Among the underpinnings of each of these alliances are integrated clinical programs that have coalesced over time as part of a truly successful health network that historically has experienced favorable patient care and financial outcomes.

Criteria for Evaluating a Leader

The kind of leadership required by a specific organization varies and often changes over time. Governing boards can use certain criteria to evaluate the leadership of their health networks. First, a good leader exhibits *vision,* or *insight,* that makes a lot of practical sense, is achievable, and, most of all, enhances the effectiveness and efficiency of the region's existing healthcare system. Such foresight requires leaders to possess a thorough knowledge of healthcare trends and legislation, the inner workings of the health system, and the capability to effortlessly conceptualize what possible impact various proposals might have on a health network's organization, management, and financing.

This complicated balancing act could well include the CEO's stepping back, taking a hard look at the alliance, and, on this basis, finding ways to improve the current and future horizontal integration of the region's major clinical services, since a vast majority of health service deliveries are a relatively local matter (i.e., one-hour travel time). Also, the leadership must consider that hospital (horizontal) mergers have been significantly more successful compared to health networks acquiring physician practices, developing HMOs, and other similar vertically diversified endeavors.[26-27]

What should be avoided by network governing boards is furthering a health network CEO who has any inclination toward pursuing power and greed rather than what is good for the residents served. The nation's most highly regarded leaders in the health field, most of whom have experienced relatively long tenure in their current position, have been productive since they foresaw early on what changes are needed to improve their region's delivery of healthcare services and were highly successful in implementing their visions with the support of the network's trustees, physicians, and management colleagues.

Second, a good leader seeks *consensus,* or *establishes alignment,* toward shared objectives by (1) seeking out promising opportunities; (2) carefully evaluating possible alternatives by paying attention to community-oriented values, among others; (3) soliciting participation in the decision-making process from the various interested parties; (4) analyzing the fiscal and political risks; and (5) implementing options that have a reasonable chance of success. If within a network trust and integrity are givens, the network CEO can then commence dialogue that should result in bringing the key trustees and physicians to a shared understanding of how various options for the delivery of health services might play out in reducing costs and improving access and quality of care.

This consensus-building process is often complicated by the fact that nonphysician leaders may occupy an elegant office with a spectacular view, but it is attending physicians who make individual patient care decisions and determine the related use of the alliance's resources. Therefore, it is not unusual for a CEO to be repeatedly tested on addressing complex cross-cutting issues, on his or her ability to attend to a variety of issues simultaneously, and on whether he or she consistently incorporates a view that the health network's overall role is to enhance the region's healthcare.

Third, health network leaders should be *emphasizing improvements in access, social equity, quality, and cost reduction* rather than encouraging their alliances to become the sole or major provider for the region's healthcare services. The latter strategy is so appealing since it offers the opportunity for a network to control the availability of services and to set prices, and thereby provides an upper hand in managed care negotiations. By 2005 there could be fewer than 850 health networks in the United States, suggesting that many freestanding or solo providers will be squeezed out and that an increasing number of alliances will be functioning as oligopolies or possibly as cartels.[28]

If many health networks display limited admiration for the public interest, elected officials will be forced to evaluate whether the health field should be monitored as a regulated monopoly. Some will argue that with the rules and regulations inherent in Medicare and Medicaid, and with those enforced by state departments of health and insurance, providers and insurers are already experiencing too much governmental control. The options that elected officials might examine when attempting to make the health field "more consumer friendly" are forming state health services commissions, regulating the health field like the telecommunications industry (quasi-competitive, quasi-regulatory), or using a combination of capitated payment and global budgetary targets to control healthcare expenditures (the latter is applied by most of the world's industrialized nations).[29]

The outcome of discussions now under way in Congress and among many state legislatures concerning the HMO patients' bill of rights might set the tone of whether in the United States there will be a shift toward protecting the patient's interest at the expense of the managed care plans and possibly some providers. What is somewhat worrisome in this regard is that historically the regulatory approach, in terms of providing improved access, greater social equity, higher quality, and decreases in cost, has generally not been any more successful than the competitive strategy.[30]

Fourth among the qualifications to be considered in evaluating a health network leader, in addition to rating his or her prior track record, are such *personality traits and attitudes* as having patience in the process of gaining consensus, being open to diverse points of view and differing cultures, being able to act decisively, and taking pride in the accomplishments of others.[31] The CEO also must be able to respond effectively to the inherent clash of values between business and the provision of healthcare. Among key business values are achieving overwhelming success in meeting competitive pressures and increasing the organization's bottom line, while among the health field's traditional values are service, advocacy, and altruism. Pecuniary interests have already gained a stronghold in healthcare, so the current challenge for most leaders is how to use the positive elements of the entrepreneurial spirit to improve health services within their region.

Outside Directors Can Enhance the Evaluation Process

Trustees of most health networks evaluate their leaders on the basis of the organization's financial performance and his or her ability to get along with the physicians on the various medical staffs. Yet the principal objective of an alliance is to deliver effective and efficient healthcare to the region.

Trusteeship of a not-for-profit health network is frequently sought after because it involves community service, prestige, power, special ties with some of the region's most influential physicians, and participation in the policy-making of one of the area's major employers. Unlike in smaller publicly held corporations, generally few board members have experienced being responsible for an annual budget of $250 million or more. A possible change in a governing board's composition, by adding more professional expertise, potentially would result in a broader based policy-making process and thereby improve the chances for creative leadership.

When measuring the alliance's or the CEO's ability to enhance quality of patient care and to meet regional health needs, a governing board relies heavily on the information provided by its own medical staffs and management team, outside experts, and various accrediting agencies. The question arises of whether the governing board's ability to make decisions would be enhanced if a minority of the board's membership was made up of: an industrialist from outside the area, who is currently serving as a trustee of a major health network; a current or retired CEO of another health network; a physician(s) with proven leadership skill practicing in a nearby state; and a few outside experts (e.g., lawyer, accountant, architect, engineer, and consultant), who have specialized in the health field, but who are not currently or who have not provided in the recent past professional services to the health network. To encourage their attendance, these outside board members could receive a fee for attending each meeting with the total remuneration for a trustee probably not to exceed $30,000 per year.

Bringing more and broader know-how into the board room by using outside directors could make it possible to more effectively appraise the leader's performance. Also, it would more readily allow the alliance to think on a more global basis; to be more forward looking, with greater precision in programmatic and fiscal terms when studying various options and developing specific plans; and then to implement strategies to deliver the most effective and efficient care to the region. The outside physician(s) could be a major resource to other board members in evaluating the quality of care provided by the health network's various subsidiaries as well as the efficacy of acquiring specific medical technologies.

A few health network CEOs could be expected to resist appointing outside directors, feeling that his or her role thereby would be somewhat diminished. It is hoped that more CEOs would be in favor of such a proposal, since it would better insure a higher level of expertise on the governing board that should result in enhancing his or her leadership opportunities.

Producing More Leaders Is Critical

The biggest threats to a health network's success in the next decade are expected to be: the political-type barriers to effectively integrating their acquired partners; the fiscal cutbacks resulting from the Balanced Budget

Act of 1997; the difficulty in adequately responding to managed care; the weakening of the nation's overall economy; and, in some cases, the inability of the alliance's trustees, medical staffs, and management to sort out its own problems.[32–33] But the bigger issue, as suggested by the national polls, could well be the public's becoming concerned with the networks' oligopolistic positioning in the marketplace and, particularly, their losing sight of the primary mission of delivering quality, cost-effective health services.[34]

There is a relatively high turnover among health network CEOs,[9] deans of medical schools (an average tenure of 3.5 years),[10] and Fortune 500 CEOs (an average tenure of 4 years). If you look ahead five years, a great number of our current leaders in the health field will be retiring. What should be of additional concern is that many senior executives, who are frequently identified as our future leaders, often think they have a better chance to be appointed a CEO at some other health network. This lack of continuity and succession within an organization can often be explained by the high turnover among those in leadership positions, now caused by increased pressures for immediate results by trustees and physicians. Meanwhile, various community-based organizations are more focused on solving regional healthcare needs; and the network's employees meanwhile often have opinions of how to potentially enhance patient care and reduce costs that are frequently overlooked.

While all the current merger mania resulting in fiscally and politically powerful health networks inevitably bears new difficulties to overcome and a sense of loss of some individual or institutional identity, it also brings the opportunity to help reshape the healthcare delivery system to better meet community needs. Sound academic training and mentoring to be a leader becomes even more meaningful if the CEO can speak from the heart; can solicit ideas, criticisms, and opinions from various layers in the organization; can be candid, respectful, and responsible, even if a new project he or she fostered fails; and can be a team player when choosing between competing healthcare and entrepreneurial ideas and strategies. The challenge now is to how to produce more of this type of leader.

REFERENCES

1. Warden, G. L. "Leadership—An Introduction." *Journal of Healthcare Management* 44, no. 1 (1999): 9–10.

2. Kinding, D. A., and Kovner, A. *The Role of the Physician Executive: Cases and Commentary.* Chicago: Health Administration Press, 1992.

3. Weil, T. P. "Health Services Management Manpower and Educational Needs with American Health Reform." *Health Services Management Research* 9, no. 2 (1996): 79–89.

4. Donabedian, A. *Aspects of Medical Care Administration: Specifying Requirements for Health Care,* 1. Cambridge, Mass.: Harvard University Press, 1973.

5. Wennberg, J. E. "Outcomes Research, Cost Containment, and the Fear of Health Care Rationing." *New England Journal of Medicine* 323, no. 17 (1990): 1202–4.

6. Talbot, J. A. "Management, Administration, Leadership: What's in a Name?" *Psychiatry Quarterly* 58, no. 2 (1987): 229–42.

7. Hesselbein, F., Goldsmith, M., and Bechard, R., eds. *The Leader of the Future: New Visions, Strategies, and Practices for the Next Era.* San Francisco: Jossey-Bass, 1996.

8. Kotter, J. *A Force for Change: How Leadership Differs from Management.* New York: Free Press, 1990.

9. Weil, P. A. "High Hospital CEO Turnover Continues." *Healthcare Executive* 14, no. 4 (1999): 34.

10. Yedidia, M. J. "Challenges to Effective Medical School Leadership: Perspectives of 22 Current and Former Deans." *Academic Medicine* 73, no. 6 (1998): 631–39.

11. Shalowitz, J. "The Healthcare System and Medicine—Current Status." In LeTourneau, B., and Curry, W. *Search of Physician Leadership,* 15–38. Chicago: Health Administration Press, 1998.

12. Anderson, G. F., and Poullier, J.-P. "Health Spending, Access, and Outcomes: Trends in Industrialized Countries." *Health Affairs* 18, no. 3 (1999): 178–92.

13. Rice, D. P. "The Cost of Instant Access to Health Care." *Journal of the American Medical Association* 279, no. 13 (1998): 1030.

14. Vistnes, J. P., and Zuvekas, S. H. "Health Insurance Status of the Civilian Noninstitutional Population: 1997." AHCPR Publication No. 99-0030. Rockville, Md.: Agency for Health Care Policy and Research, 1999.

15. Joint Commission on Education. *The College Curriculum of Hospital Administration.* Chicago: Physician's Record Co., 1948.

16. Commission on University Education in Hospital Administration. *University Education for Hospital Administration.* Washington, D.C.: American Council on Education, 1954.

17. Chester, T. E. *Graduate Education for Hospital Administration in the United States: Trends.* Chicago: American College of Hospital Administrators, 1969.

18. O'Neil, E. H. *Health Professions Education for the Future: Schools in Service to the Nation.* San Francisco: UCSF Center for the Health Professions, 1993.

19. American College of Physicians. "The Oversight of Medical Care: A Proposal for Reform." *Annals of Internal Medicine* 120, no. 5 (1994): 423–31.

20. Mahayosnand, P. P., and Stigler, M. H. "The Need for Mentoring in Public Health." *American Journal of Public Health* 89, no. 8 (1999): 1262–63.

21. Wickman, F., and Sjodin, T. *Mentoring: The Most Obvious yet Overlooked Key to Achieving More in Life than You Dreamed Possible.* Chicago: Irwin Professional Publications, 1997.

22. Clement, J. P., McCue, M. J., Luke, R. D., Bramble, J. D., Rossiter, L. F.,

Ozcan, Y. A., and Pai, C.-W. "Strategic Hospital Alliances: Impact on Financial Performance." *Health Affairs* 16, no. 6 (1997): 193–203.

23. Feldman, R., Wholey, D. R., and Christianson, J. "Effect of Mergers on the Health Maintenance Organization Premiums." *Health Care Financing Review* 17, no. 3 (1996): 171–89.

24. Melnick, G., Keeler, E., and Zwanziger, J. "Market Power and Hospital Pricing: Are Nonprofits Different?" *Health Affairs* 18, no. 3 (1999): 167–73.

25. Connor, R. A., Feldman, R., Dowd, B. E., and Radcliff, T. A. "Which Types of Hospital Mergers Save Consumers Money?" *Health Affairs* 16, no. 6 (1997): 62–74.

26. Walston, S. L., Kimberly, J. R., and Burns, L. R. "Owned Vertical Integration and Health Care: Promise and Performance." *Health Care Management Review* 21, no. 1 (1996): 83–92.

27. Robinson, J. C. "Administered Pricing and Vertical Integration in the Hospital Industry." *Journal of Law and Economics* 19, no. 1 (1996): 357–78.

28. Weil, T. P., and Jorgensen, N. E. "A Tripartite Regulation of Health Networks." *Journal of Public Health Management and Practice* 2, no. 3 (1996): 46–53.

29. Wolfe, P. R., and Moran, D. W. "Global Budgeting in OECD Countries." *Health Care Financing Review* 14, no. 3 (1993): 55–76.

30. Melnick, G., and Zwanziger, J. "State Health Care Expenditures under Competition and Regulation, 1980 through 1991." *American Journal of Public Health* 85, no. 10 (1995): 1391–96.

31. Hosmer, L. T. "The Importance of Strategic Leadership." In Levey, S., and Loomba, N. P. *Health Care Administration: A Managerial Prospective,* 87–99. Philadelphia: Lippincott Co., 1984.

32. Topping, S., Hyde, J., Barker, J., and Woodrell, F. D. "Academic Health Centers in Turbulent Times: Strategies for Survival." *Health Care Management Review* 24, no. 2 (1999): 7–18.

33. Iglehart, J. K. "Support for Academic Health Centers—Revisiting the 1997 Balanced Budget Act." *New England Journal of Medicine* 341, no. 4 (1999): 299–304.

34. Donelan, K., Blendon, R. J., Schoen, C., Davis, K., and Binns, K. "The Cost of Health System Change: Public Discontent in Five Nations." *Health Affairs* 18, no. 3 (1999): 206–16.

9

Can Health Networks Be the Solution?

During the 1990s, the increased enrollment in managed care plans, merger mania among providers and insurers, and the formation of politically and fiscally powerful health networks, often referred to as integrated delivery systems (IDS), resulted in profound changes in the health field. In the new millennium these closely interrelated trends, which serve as the major themes explored in this book, are expected to continue and to generate a significant impact on how health services will be organized, managed, and financed in the United States.

When attending a press conference announcing a new merger between either providers or HMOs, it is hard to resist being swept up by the righteous dialogue of how much this new amalgamation will benefit a particular region: the two CEOs' comments are often so impressive in their soaring strategic vision about why this new combination of resources will significantly enhance access, equity, and quality, and above all reduce costs. Also noteworthy is the infectious camaraderie that radiates from the podium, suggesting that these two organizations now consummating a merger possess such similar culture and values. Still, among the questions most frequently being raised concerning the efficacy of consummating these health networks are:

1. Whether such laudable objectives as enhancing regional health services are readily achievable by the formation of these politically and fiscally powerful health networks.
2. Whether the current merger mania being pursued by the leadership of these alliances is primarily aimed at reducing cost and at improving patient care or at increasing a network's market penetration as a means to more easily increase its bottom line.
3. What additional strategic and operational endeavors will be required in the next decade by the leadership of these health networks to improve the delivery of health services within their region.

A shift from a regulatory to a more market-oriented environment, and the continuing restructuring of health resources, have frequently been viewed as playing pivotal roles in reducing the double-digit healthcare inflation experienced in the 1980s.[1] As the HMOs imposed stricter controls on the use of sophisticated and sometimes unnecessary services, and behaved as tougher negotiators in setting reimbursement rates with providers, annual premium increases for health insurance benefits have tended to level off. In turn, HMO subscribers and providers are questioning the wisdom of the potentially divisive patient care and fiscal incentives contained in managed care. Particularly worrisome for social welfare planners are the 44.6 million Americans who are uninsured, a number that has been increasing until recently at the annual rate of one million persons.[2]

Health networks, the central focus of this book, could potentially serve as a major vehicle to restructure the U.S. health delivery system, a topic that is closely intertwined with the efficacy of the large number of mergers and acquisitions that have occurred during the past decade. The leaders of the nation's most innovative networks have formed various entities and in the process have restructured their total organization to more effectively and efficiently deliver healthcare. But these corporate changes have frequently resulted in the formation of huge health alliances that are then often managed as oligopolies. In most of the nation's major metropolitan areas these amalgamations are starting to control the exit of existing services and the entry of new ones as well as the prices charged for health services.

That some divestitures would occur, to date consisting mostly of physician groups and provider-sponsored HMOs, was initially unanticipated from these alliances. As a result, most alliances are giving more diligent study than was undertaken in the past when pursuing additional horizontal and vertical diversification. Possible explanations for their proceeding with more caution include the increasing number of health networks that are encountering fiscal distress (e.g., Allegheny Health Education and Research Foundation) and the divestiture of major stakeholders (e.g., UCSF-Stanford Health Care and Penn State Geisinger Health System).

In understanding how to achieve the successful long-term financing and effective overall operation of the nation's health networks, it is critical to understand the objectives, the benefits provided, and the fiscal incentives inherent in the managed care plans and the Medicare and Medicaid programs, since these are the prime insurers and third-party payers of U.S. health services. In fact, curtailing hospital inpatient utilization by the HMOs, when the health industry was already experiencing too many available beds, has to be considered among the principal reasons for creating the health field's merger mania and the rapid formation of health networks throughout the United States during the 1990s.

Purposes and Outline of Chapter

With the fiscal incentives inherent in managed care plans and the massive corporate restructuring now under way in the health field serving as important background variables, this chapter first summarizes the major findings contained earlier in this book. Thereby, it is possible to structure a framework to respond to the question whether health networks in the next decade can realistically be expected to provide the solution in the United States to enhance access, social equity, and quality and to reduce healthcare costs. This inquiry is relevant because in many metropolitan areas politically and fiscally powerful health networks are well on their way to controlling the day-to-day delivery of health services. In attempting to shape an appropriate response, the discussion here focuses on a number of external and internal variables that are critical in evaluating the overall design that would encourage these alliances to serve as the major players in restructuring the U.S. healthcare system.

Several elements crucial in arriving at some assessment of the future efficacy of the U.S. health networks, discussed at length earlier in this book, are now briefly summarized as follows:

1. The conceptual and pragmatic evolution of regionalization and networking in the health field (chap. 1), and the appropriate steps that need to be considered by an alliance in achieving a strategic fit (chap. 2).
2. The theory and the day-to-day performance of both horizontal and vertical diversification in the health field as a means to evaluate the potential effectiveness and efficiency of health networks in enhancing the delivery of health services (chaps. 3–4).
3. The ability of a health network to attract additional qualified physicians into underserved rural and inner-city communities to enhance access, social equity, and quality of care for the nation's disenfranchised (chap. 5).
4. The potential impact of using either the competitive or the regulatory strategies to improve the performance of U.S. health networks (chap. 6).
5. The advisability of blending competitive and regulatory approaches so that health networks can improve the delivery of health services in the United States (chap. 7).
6. The leadership skills that are required to enhance the performance of the nation's health networks (chap. 8).

Throughout this book, one of the major themes is that health networks are finding it increasingly difficult in this current environment to focus on cost-containment efforts, which concurrently allow them to renew themselves in terms of acquiring new technology, replacing outdated facilities, establishing new and innovative programs, and maintaining the previous year's bottom line. To avoid experiencing increasingly serious operational and fiscal shortfalls, the leaders of health networks (including trustees, physicians, and particularly the management team) need to allocate more resources to the organization's overall strategic planning activities; more critically, to tailor their expenses to decreasing revenues; and to enhance their clinical and business-oriented information systems.

In attempting to find some pragmatic remedies within what is already a highly competitive and politically charged healthcare environment, the latter part of this chapter specifies some major steps that the leadership of these alliances might heed in the next decade to curtail their expenditures and to better position themselves and their communities for the future. Since "rightsizing" is not feasible in the long run without some changes in the financing of care, the discussion turns to how the reimbursement for health services might be modified in the next 10 years in order to show how some proposed "new" payment mechanisms might potentially affect networks and, therefore, the future delivery of medical care.

It is assumed in this chapter's analysis that many of the cutbacks proposed here will be eventually effected in the context of a more fiscally constrained environment than the current competitive marketplace, and one that falls short of a federally mandated universal comprehensive health insurance plan. This is because Americans strongly favor a pluralistic, multipayer approach, primarily because they fear an environment in which their health services are solely controlled by either the private or the public sector.

This chapter's major contribution is its focus on some key organizational and financing changes that will be required by these health networks in order for them to enhance access, social equity, and quality of care and to reduce cost. More simply stated, it outlines how health networks could potentially make a major contribution to solve some of the underlying issues now facing the delivery of health services in the United States.

How Did Networks Become What They Are Today?

The concept of health networks or networking is modeled on the same framework as that suggested over sixty-five years ago in the final report of the 1929–33 Commission on the Cost of Medical Care (CCMC).[3] This earlier study recommended that healthcare services be organized so that primary care physicians and smaller community hospitals provided care for routine illnesses and disabilities, and referred more complicated cases to secondary providers. Tertiary services were to be offered at major medical centers with quality teaching and research capabilities (see chap. 1). Over the next half-century the original CCMC concept was embellished in the United States with the advent of the Hill-Burton program, comprehensive health planning, the regional medical program, health systems agencies, multihospital systems, health systems, integrated delivery systems, health networks and many other similar endeavors.

A number of reasons are cited why the implementation of the CCMC recommendations and health networking have been so tedious:

1. Self-interest is pervasive among consumers and providers, who are anxious to develop the most comprehensive range of health services affordable within their own community. A well-planned array of available health services and facilities not only generates local pride and greater accessibility to care, but creates additional well-paying jobs. Modest cost savings can be generated by a hospital eliminating a major clinical service. Shuttering an entire facility results in significant cost reductions, but almost always such strategic planning efforts have serious political repercussions from the local community, physicians, and employees.

2. The European or Canadian concept of social solidarity that consists of universal access, social equity, and a more even handed way of levying the costs of social insurance is alien to American culture and values. A three-tier, highly politicized, pluralistic approach is preferred in the United States, where the wealthy obtain most of their medical care on a fee-for-service basis; middle-income Americans are most frequently enrolled in managed care plans; and the un- or underinsured receive a majority of their initial care in hospital emergency departments.

3. Although there is often resistance to community health planning among those with powerful vested interests or with strong ties to the status quo, the process is now generally recognized as a critical activity to gauge the region's health needs. Limited funding has been available to date for such purposes except for that made available by providers, insurers, and various interested public entities. Simply asking the community, through consumer surveys, what additional health services it now needs and how existing resources might be more effectively provided is the type of information rarely readily available to many networks today.

4. Unfortunately, there is a lack of agreement among professionals on setting the critical quantitative norms to be used in determining the need for specific health services. The number of inpatient days per person per

year in the major metropolitan areas in the northeast is twice that on the west coast. The cost of care for Medicare recipients with the same diagnosis, after being adjusted for severity of illness and differences in wage scales, is twice as high in Miami as it is in Omaha.[4]

5. There is intense fear among many Americans that health planning endeavors can only result in restricting a person's ability to obtain quality healthcare as well as infringing on one's political freedom. Major factors why the public has arrived at this decision include the fact that providers and elected officials having gained the upper hand in this health planning process and that most of these agencies' governing boards are plagued with self-interest. Historically, there has been a shortage of experienced health planners; most funding has come from government grants or hospitals within the region; and most state health planning review agencies have lacked sufficient clout to follow through on politically sensitive rulings.

A three-tier regional system with prepaid group practice, as outlined in the CCMC report over six and a half decades ago, is being rejuvenated with greater perseverance than ever before by the trends of merger mania, health networking, and the HMOs, these concepts being implemented primarily due to far tougher cost containment pressures by government officials and major corporate leaders.

How to Put a Health Network Together

The virtues in conceptual terms of regionalizing services and thereby potentially reducing costs and the early experiences with health networking are well documented (see chap. 1). Limited attention has been given to date to the most effective strategies to be used by a provider when evaluating the possibility of a merger with a major network or when a health alliance is interested in acquiring an additional partner (see chap. 2). Too often overlooked in such an analysis is the need to undertake at the very outset a careful and comprehensive assessment of where your organization is now and where it might be heading in the future.

Concurrently with such broad-based strategic planning activities, pertinent data gathering and evaluation need to be undertaken. The scope of these endeavors might include regional and local population and demographic information; patient origin and market penetration data; historical and comparative utilization statistics; the composition and utilization patterns of the facility's medical staff; the determination of physician needs by specialty in the region; surveys of consumer, major employer, and physician preferences; a physical plant assessment to determine where some possible functional consolidations are feasible without significant capital expenditures; and a detailed financial evaluation. Possibly more critical than any of these quantitative-type analyses is an appraisal of the similarities and differences in corporate culture and how human resources might be most appropriately managed by the new merged entity, the importance of which is usually underestimated.

Once the decision to consummate a merger has been made, there are a number of practical issues that need to be evaluated:

First, there are usually major issues surrounding institutional control and governance. The organization being acquired desires not to lose any control over its future destiny, but to receive from the health network significant additional resources. Conversely, usually an alliance hesitates to lend its good name and to provide substantial money and manpower resources unless it can dominate the governing board's policy-making powers, if the "deal starts to turn sour."

Second, health networks when consummating a merger are anxious to gain considerable net worth, but the organization being acquired often demands as part of the merger agreement some fiscal concessions so that its balance sheet and revenue and expense statements will be significantly enhanced. After these initial discussions concerning who needs to bring how much money to the table, similarities and differences in management styles between the two organizations often come to the forefront. Of particular concern are instances when there is pressure to centralize a satellite's perceived critical patient care activities as a major vehicle to reduce cost. Heated discussions are to be expected when the health network's leadership desires to make major strategic changes and the satellite historically has had a forceful governing board and medical staff, and an aggressive management team.

Third, difficult to evaluate are the specific outcomes of any potential merger or of a major health network proceeding with another acquisition. In the final analysis, most of today's corporate restructuring is resulting in some compromises in the delivery of health care, fiscally, politically, and in other ways. What should always be paramount in the formation of a new health network or the expansion of an existing one is whether the proposed solution will realistically improve the delivery of health services to the area's residents.

Fourth, when undertaking any long-range planning endeavor, it is worthwhile considering what might occur if the United States experienced within the next decade almost inevitable economic difficulties. An anticipated outcome of a recession in the United States would be for the health networks to decide quickly to divest themselves of their "losers."

Fifth, hospitals have been most anxious to bond with their primary care physicians and particularly with their major admitters. Some of these arrangements between health networks and groups of physicians were destined from the very outset to result in highly contentious disputes since: (1) physicians once having been "bought out" expect to work less and earn more; and (2) hospitals, having made sizable expenditures when acquiring these practices, anticipate additional inpatient admissions from these doctors and expect to obtain a reasonable return on their capital investment.

Simply, more physicians will become disenchanted working for health networks; and, in turn, health alliances, particularly in a recessionary period, will find how difficult it is to successfully manage physician practices at a reasonably profitable level for the individual doctors and the network. Even more complicated, and requiring some skillful management, is how a health network can maintain a physician's loyalty after divesting his or her group from the alliance.

How effectively and efficiently a health network eventually delivers healthcare to the region is greatly dependent on its initial planning efforts. This process usually starts with a self-assessment of its current position, the collection and analysis of pertinent data and information, and the evaluation of the similarities and differences in organizational culture and management style. A higher probability of success for a merger or acquisition should be forthcoming when each organization carefully studies whether a proposed amalgamation will result in an appropriate fit—one that does the community and the providers some actual good and does not later result in a divestiture where both parties often lose out.

What Type of Horizontal Diversification Achieves Success?

Putting aside all the theoretical arguments for advocating mergers and the formation of health networks, there is frequently a practical reason: an increasing number of hospitals, physicians, and other providers sense that they are becoming operationally and fiscally vulnerable, as is most vividly illustrated by the adverse effects of managed care and by their shortfalls at the bottom line. A freestanding provider, realizing that its organization is becoming somewhat less competitive, but under the impression that it is easily repairable with some corporate restructuring, will expend significant resources in evaluating how to most appropriately "survive" in the 21st century.

Health networking creates the opportunity to generate some sizable economies. There is always a concern, because of the potential monopoly it creates, particularly when two geographically contiguous hospitals that were highly competitive for decades decide to merge so that a new consolidated organization has 75 percent or greater market penetration within their previous service areas (see chap. 3). Some of these mergers have occurred because one facility fears that its historical competitor will be acquired by an out-of-town health network. Others are consummated because when the two institutions tacitly decide to consolidate, the new entity is expected to be in a far stronger position to control competitive forces. Once the new network can function as an oligopoly, HMOs could well experience more difficulty in negotiating attractive reimbursement rates for their local subscribers; and doctors will lose some of their flexibility when demanding that the network acquire additional new technology in their specialty or requesting reappointment with all their previous privileges.

Efficacy of Horizontal Mergers in the Health Field

Serious study of the efficacy of horizontal mergers among hospitals began in the early 1970s. The evidence of whether such corporate restructuring actually achieved projected economic efficiencies was then judged to be mixed at best.[5] More recent studies have focused on the financial performance of U.S. health networks and alliances.[6-7] On the basis of a significant number of research endeavors, horizontal mergers and health networking have been evaluated as being most effective and efficient under these general terms and conditions:

1. Cost reductions are more readily demonstrable where labor-saving technologies can be effectively applied and where the health network leadership can avoid turf battles with physicians. There is general agreement, moreover, that far greater cost savings can potentially be realized through the centralization, integration, and coordination of clinical services.[8]
2. Cost reductions and improvements in the bottom line are most easily achievable by merging two medium-size, high case-mix intensity, nonteaching, not-for-profit hospitals that are located in the same community (service area), where both historically experienced a low percentage of occupancy.[9-11] The new consolidated entity has the potential ability to implement an improved bottom line in its operations by shuttering specific clinical services in one of the two institutions, by eliminating inter-institutional competition and by controlling prices within its marketplace.
3. Health networks can potentially achieve modest cost reductions (−7.1 percent), except in more concentrated market areas where there seems to be a slight increase (+1.3 percent) rather than the anticipated decrease in expenses.[6] This finding suggests that there

is a potential need for a tightening up of antitrust policies in the health field, where networks have the opportunity to function as oligopolies.

4. Cost savings among health networks are reported to be most evident in environments where there is a high concentration of group model HMOs.[6] The merger mania occurring in the last decade might well represent a direct response to providers sensing increasing fiscal difficulties in "cutting deals" with price-sensitive managed care plans, particularly where local physician groups are already well organized.

5. Finally, and probably most critical, the question whether a network or a specific provider within an alliance can generate cost savings may well be highly dependent on its executive team's management skills. After controlling for market, environmental, and hospital operational variables, differences in cash flow and expenses between network and nonaligned facilities surprisingly were reported not to be statistically significant.[7]

Unfortunately, little is actually known about whether mergers and health networks enhance access, social equity, and quality of patient care. The reason is that almost all of the research concerning mergers and alliances in the health field has focused on cost containment, since major industrial leaders and public officials have called for a far slower inflationary trend in medical expenditures than was witnessed in earlier decades.

Cost studies of mergers and health networking completed over the last three decades suggest that how effectively and efficiently health services are delivered within a specific region is highly dependent on the management skills of its leadership, and on the amount of competition experienced from other physicians and hospitals located nearby that are offering somewhat similar services. While managed care plans have been relatively successful in decreasing inpatient utilization and reducing inflationary increases in health expenditures, once a health network is positioned to function as an oligopoly, it is likely to raise prices in order to improve its bottom line.

The merger mania of the 1990s theoretically could well slow down to little more than a trickle in the new millennium, since health networks are having difficulty in clearly demonstrating that these huge alliances are more effective and efficient than well-managed freestanding organizations. In spite of these shortcomings now being experienced by the alliances, it is anticipated that the current trend toward consolidation will continue. Further corporate restructuring is predicted to be particularly prevalent where health networking is primarily used to obtain control over the marketplace rather than to improve access to healthcare and to lower cost.

Studies of mergers among HMOs illustrate similar conclusions to those experienced by health networks dominated by hospitals. Despite the entry of additional insurers, there has been a trend toward more subscribers being enrolled among fewer managed care plans. This concentration should be of concern, since managed care plans that experienced more competition were reported to offer lower premiums.[12] The unexpected outcome is that a merger of managed care plans reduces competition in a specific marketplace, allowing the remaining HMOs to raise premiums. In fact, several studies suggest that HMO mergers have not benefited consumers by the expected result of premium reductions.[13–14]

Experience of Non–Health Field Mergers

Since hospital and HMO amalgamations to date have been less than impressive in their fiscal and operational outcomes, the question arises whether the non-health fields are experiencing similar experiences with their horizontal integration. Somewhat surprisingly, a number of non-health merger studies have revealed limited improvement over time in the acquired organization's operational and fiscal performance.[15–16]

As a corporation diversifies with a merger that is strategically further from its major revenue stream, its productivity tends to decline.[17] A major exception to this rather dismal performance experienced after mergers in all U.S. industries is among mergers of equals, particularly those involving management buyouts. These outperform their control group and their pre-merger performance, primarily because the existing management knows how to make the "deal work."[18] The analogy in the health field might well be two similar-size hospitals in the same community deciding to merge, and it is noteworthy that the results of such amalgamations have been equally successful.[10]

Steps Necessary to Enhance Merger Performance

If health networks, once formed, are not yet achieving their earlier projected cost reductions, what steps can be expected to be necessary to improve their bottom lines, which are required to react to an environment where managed care, Medicare, and Medicaid reimbursement continues to deteriorate? Among those cost-cutting measures that the leadership of health networks will need to evaluate with increasing frequency are: (1) shuttering superfluous hospitals within a health network, since the closing of an entire acute care facility results in considerable cost savings; (2) centralizing virtually all tertiary services at major medical centers to reduce cost and enhance quality; (3) eliminating a layer of management in every facility, an option more readily achievable with a simplified reimbursement system; (4) divesting of physician practices or medical group practices because of "misfit of objectives" and fiscal shortfalls for both the physicians and the alliance; (5) divesting of provider-sponsored HMOs, PPOs, IPAs, and other similar plans because of insufficient capitalization, inability to appropriately assess risk, and conflict between filling beds and reducing the insurer's costs; and (6) proposing better structured regulations, to be easily implemented by capable regulators who are able to protect the public interest without crippling innovation and efficiency. For reasons discussed at greater length later in this chapter, it is highly dubious whether a significant portion of these merger strategies can be implemented in the current environment, in which the battle between the marketplace and the government is already complicating the process of trying to restructure the health field.

A quick and naive reading of these arguments concerning horizontal mergers is that most hospitals, physicians, and insurers would be just as well off remaining freestanding rather than merging. A more accurate conclusion from these discussions is that far more attention should be directed to making mergers function more effectively and efficiently. In fact, a more positive outcome from these amalgamations is more likely to be achieved in a recessionary environment where it is fiscally necessary and more politically acceptable to make some hard decisions that cut costs but result in a minimal adverse effect on accessibility, social equity, or quality of healthcare.

Should Networks Pursue Vertical Diversification?

Unlike horizontal integration, where frequently two or more hospitals consummate a merger, vertical diversification in the health field (chap. 4) attempts to bring under one corporate umbrella additional, or in a few cases almost all, healthcare services that are necessary to the community for the provision of improved patient care.

Vertical integration as defined herein can encompass a continuum of care that starts with primary care physicians' offices, extends through all acute in- and outpatient services, provides for institutional and home-bound long-term care, and even establishes an appropriate provider-sponsored health insurance mechanism so that residents within the region can prepay a majority of their health expenditures. The presumed benefits of such a consolidation of health resources include enhancing the region's health status by improving clinical and administrative integration, centralizing clinical information, creating marketplace efficiencies when shuttering unnecessary capacity, eliminating unnecessary care, and concentrating responsibility for the provision of a broad continuum of care.

Performance of Vertical Diversification

Unfortunately, most studies report that increased profitability was not generally associated with a health network undertaking vertical diversification approaches.[19] Integration that focused on more acute care hospital–related strategies such as the ownership and operation of an ambulatory care center, an ambulatory surgical center or a satellite radiation therapy unit resulted in far better short-term financial performance than a somewhat unrelated posthospital diversification such as a nursing home or a wellness-rehabilitation center.[20–21] The most successful vertically integrated endeavors are usually those services related to the health network's existing acute care, clinical and managerial competencies. Unrelated diversification projects require different governance structures and greater autonomy in their overall management for the subsidiary to succeed, and usually are health services that historically were less profitable.

Among all the vertically diversified options available to health networks, acquiring and managing physician practices so that the doctors remain loyal to their affiliated hospitals while their offices remain "profitable" is terribly important and demands the greatest level of skill by the alliance's senior executives. The struggle for power, control, and monies is often related to the tension experienced between physicians and those responsible for the management of these health networks. Such differences are continually being tested because of their need to serve two masters—patients or the community and the organizations that employ them.

Studies published by the Health Care Advisory Board,[22] the Hospital Financial Management Association,[23] and Coopers and Lybrand[24] found that physician practices acquired by hospitals during the 1995–97 period were losing an average of $80,000 to $100,000 per physician. In spite of these losses, some health networks are continuing, at a much slower rate than in the past, to acquire physician practices as a vertically diversified strategy. In fiscal terms the logical solution for health networks is for members of their medical staffs to continue to admit their patients to alliance-sponsored facilities and forget about vertically integrating these practices through their acquisition.

Some health networks started their own HMO or similar plan as a means to control the "premium dollar." Aside from a relatively few provider-owned HMOs, health network-sponsored managed care plans have experienced fiscal difficulties due to their low enrollment, their lack of understanding about risk selection, their inability to control costs, and, unfortunately, the fact that they were not the region's dominant managed care plan.[25] The failure of health networks to vertically diversify into HMOs is directly related to the difficulty of gaining entry into a complex and competitive prepayment business, and then trying to mesh competing interests within the same alliance. This is most easily explained by the conflicting fiscal incentives of decreasing inpatient utilization to make the HMO more profitable and yet filling more of the network's inpatient beds.

Interestingly, the marginal performance of vertical integration in the health field is generally echoed in other industries. Among highly diversified nonhealth industry corporations, frequently reported were increased costs of production without any savings in overhead costs.[26] Those firms that primarily implemented "backwards" integration (e.g., hospitals acquiring long-term care facilities rather than an ambulatory surgery center) incurred higher overall costs and lower profits. The corporations most likely to succeed most effectively are those where coordination, production scheduling, and planning are relatively straightforward, where demand is certain and increasing, and where the company has a few very large plants.[27] Obviously, this description does not portray today's average, vertically diversified health network.

Why Vertical Diversification Fails

Vertical diversification in the health field often fails, and may indeed be destined to fail, for a number of reasons: (1) physicians rather than health facilities in the final analysis control the flow of patients to the various providers of health services; (2) vertical integration usually requires huge capital investments, with the fiscal rewards forthcoming over a long rather than a short period of time; (3) complicated organizational structures are often required, with the chain of command and the sharing of risk and operating surplus being difficult to define and then to appropriately execute; and (4) in spite of closer integration of various health resources within the region, there are no guarantees that by using vertical integration improved fiscal or clinical outcomes will emerge. What happens too frequently is that operating losses from these vertical ventures begin to pile up, and for the alliances to divest themselves of some of these subsidiaries becomes the most appropriate fiscal solution.

Although there may be a large number of barriers when health networks implement vertically diversified projects, they are not all necessarily doomed from the outset. Whether the overall effects of vertical integration for the health network are positive, neutral, or negative depends greatly on who is at the controls—the quality of the health network's leadership.

The major conclusion from this analysis is that each potential vertically diversified acquisition needs to be evaluated in terms of whether it enhances access, quality of care, and profitability, and reduces regional health expenditures. Health networks might well be cautioned to slow down on the number of acquisitions they consummate, unless the results can achieve a larger market share in one of their existing or related programs and services where traditionally they have experienced significant operational and fiscal success.

Can Health Networks Attract Physicians into Underserved Areas?

Many health network executives are evaluating various proposals of how to attract qualified physicians to practice in their region's poor rural or inner-city communities in order to enhance their market share and thereby encourage additional Medicaid enrollees and other residents to use their physicians and hospitals (see chap. 5). Conventional approaches used over the last decades to supply more physicians to underserved areas include: increasing the number of medical schools and as a result supplying more doctors,[28] expanding the National Health Service Corps (NHSC) program,[29–30] and allowing more international medical graduates (IMGs) to pursue residency training in the United States.[31] Medical educators, and the leaders in U.S. hospitals that provide the majority of care for the urban poor and those officials sponsoring community health centers in rural areas,[32] are among those most supportive of these alternatives that could potentially improve the current geographic maldistribution of doctors.

There are several other approaches that health networks might use to increase their market penetration and at the same time provide enhanced health services to their area's underserved: (1) provide eminent leadership in the overall design and governance of soundly conceived Medicaid HMOs;[33] (2) strengthen existing or develop additional community health/primary care centers specifically designed to meet the needs of the poor; (3) interface more effectively with local schools to foster Medicaid managed care plans for children of low income families;[34] and (4) reimburse at premium rates primary care physicians who are willing to practice in underserved areas. A health network desirous of expanding its activities to more directly focus on those persons currently underserved might find these strategic options worth exploring. The last approach possibly creates the most controversy since it raises the issue of whether by simply being offered more money, doctors will relocate to less attractive locations to practice.

A growing surplus of doctors in the United States now offers the opportunity to attract more qualified physicians to provide care to the underserved, by offering these MDs and DOs (osteopathic physicians) premium working conditions and higher than customary incomes. The level of reimbursement that would be necessary to achieve these proposed results is a matter of some conjecture, but conventional wisdom suggests that payment that is roughly 30 percent higher than the area's average for that specialty is necessary to achieve the proposed objectives. The Arizona experience with Medicaid HMOs provides some positive findings for such an approach.[35] The Title XIX Medicaid "mills" in Florida and California[36] and the "tweaking" of Medicaid rates for physicians in Maryland, New York, and Tennessee[37–39] suggest that the states may end up paying more with the underserved obtaining minimal additional quality healthcare.

The inability to date to successfully implement a proposal of "overpaying" physicians to locate in underserved areas clearly illustrates the difficulty that health networks face in the United States in improving social equity in the delivery of health services. The barriers are many and varied: (1) the additional billions needed to attract physicians into these underserved areas; (2) the reluctance of physicians to locate to these areas for cultural and social reasons; (3) the weak political voice of those most adversely affected, the poor; and (4) the practical problem of a high turnover of those eligible for Medicaid coverage.[40–41] Possibly the major reason is the reluctance of middle- and upper-income taxpayers to consider the geographic maldistribution of physicians as an issue of major social or economic consequence.[42] Those health networks faced with an increased number of uninsured, and with declining operating margins, may decide, however, that it is in their own self-interest to expend more resources in fostering Medicaid HMOs for children, and developing primary care centers to attract more physicians and other health services to the United States' underserved communities.

The Battle between More Competition and More Regulation

At the center stage of this country's health policy debate is the question of whether health networks would be made more effective and efficient in meeting their community needs by more market-driven competition or by more government regulation (see chap. 6). At the forefront of these deliberations is managed competition, or the managed care plans that were touted early on as a way to enhance access, social equity, and quality of care, and reduce health expenditures. The growth in enrollment among HMOs, IPAs, PPOs, and other similar plans has been a major precipitating factor in forcing the formation of health networks and now continues to play a major role in how health services are organized, managed, and financed.

The major contribution of the HMOs has been the decline in the percentage increase in national health expenditures, although it is still rising at a rate of roughly 50 percent more than the Consumer Price Index.[43] HMOs have achieved control of health costs by reducing inpatient utilization and by requiring prior approval from plan officials for other than primary care–type services. Whether such barriers to care eliminate unnecessary services or are used primarily to reduce an insurer's costs continues to be debated. Studies comparing HMOs with fee-for-service care have generally reported similar outcomes for the average, healthy enrollee. Most studies, however, have found worse outcomes among managed care plans for the vulnerable groups (i.e., the seriously ill, the mentally ill, and the poor).[44–45]

Somewhat lower subscriber and physician satisfaction is reported with HMO services, this being counterbalanced by the perception that managed care coverage costs less than fee-for-service plans. Current heated discussions among patients, physicians, hospitals, and the HMO plans reflect the conflicting interests that are inherent in the health field (e.g., patients demanding more care from physicians and insurers, who want to control unnecessary services and expense), and the need to reach some compromises at the state and federal level on an equitable patients' bill of rights.

Some Issues Facing Managed Care

There are a number of reasons why the current market-driven strategies that are being used by the nation's powerful health networks and managed care plans could in fact experience significant difficulties in guaranteeing that all Americans, including the indigent, uninsured, and aged, have ready access to an effective health system at an affordable price.

1. Regionalization of resources and access to care for the poor and underserved tend to break down, since institutions and individual providers consider their survival to be more important than the community's overall long-term well-being.

2. How HMOs are currently organized and managed is incompatible with improved access (e.g., a million more persons each year become uninsured), social equity, or quality of care, since the sickest and those with chronic illnesses experience the most difficulty with the managed care plans.

3. What is problematic in the long run is whether the American public will accept an arrangement whereby there are inherent fiscal incentives that limit the choice of providers and encourage physicians to order fewer tests and consultative services, and avoid inpatient care.

4. Although providers are focusing in the public media on the shortfalls in the Balanced Budget Act of 1997, their actual fiscal problems may be more related to HMOs being able to cut deals below a hospital's or physician's historical cost. The reason for signing such agreements is the providers' fear of losing market share, as well as the fact that some previously consummated horizontal and vertical mergers are creating significant negative operating margins.

5. There is no conclusive evidence that lower costs or better healthcare can be provided for Medicare and Medicaid beneficiaries with HMOs than under fee-for-service arrangements.[46]

Further Privatization in the Health Industry

To survive in this current market-driven, managed care environment, many of the country's top not-for-profit or state-supported academic health centers, most of them serving as the hub facility of a well-known health network, are clearly behaving like profit-oriented businesses. Frequently sought after by our nation's health leadership as a means to differentiate their health network's performance from other competing alliances is inclusion in the listings of "America's Best Hospitals,"[47] the "One Hundred Top Hospitals: Benchmarks for Success,"[48] the biggest healthcare systems,[49] or the 250 largest (based on revenues) investor-owned healthcare corporations.[50]

As one possible way to evaluate the efficacy of the trend toward privatization in the health field, the fiscal performance of the nation's best teaching hospitals was compared to its major for-profit hospital chains, HMOs, and physician management corporations. This analysis assesses whether more privatization should be viewed as a preferred option for those health networks' hub hospitals that are heading toward fiscal distress.

The most general finding concerning the financial positions of the nation's 20 best teaching hospitals was an unhealthy disparity between those with significant operating surpluses and virtually no debt, and those which might be considered to be the poor cousins. Using as criteria for designating poor cousins, a total margin of less than 3 percent and a debt-to-equity ratio of 0.42 or higher, six of America's best teaching hospitals, including Johns Hopkins and the major hospital affiliate of the Mayo Clinic, should be considered to be now or in the foreseeable future potentially fiscally vulnerable (table 9).

It is probably premature to evaluate whether all the corporate restructuring now being undertaken by these hub hospitals will pay off in terms of more referrals, in higher quality of patient care, in cost reductions, and in improved bottom lines. In the meantime, networks with an academic health center as their hub are frequently experiencing difficulties in achieving an appropriate strategic fit, in finding a middle ground when differences in culture and values surface, in implementing operating efficiencies to counter the inflexibility inherent in these large bureaucratic structures, in developing compatible information systems throughout the network and in adapting to the strategies necessary to insure their long-term survival among the best teaching hospitals.

Although during the past decade there has been a "graying" in the way that the not-for-profit health networks and the investor-owned chains are organized, financed, and managed, the latter have historically focused more on selecting patients with comprehensive health insurance benefits, charging more than the not-for-profits, and reducing operating costs so as to enhance their stockholders' return on investment.[51-52] Disappointment in the performance of these for-profit groups is evidenced by the nation's 6 largest investor-owned hospital chains in 1998 squeezing out net operating revenues of only 4.3 percent. Thirteen of the 20 best teaching hospitals had a better bottom line than the average of the 6 for-profit chains.

Although the nation's largest publicly held HMOs have served as an effective force in reducing increases in U.S. health expenditures, and have witnessed significant growth in revenues by adding subscribers and by acquiring smaller and frequently competitive plans, these managed care plans in 1998 were only able to squeeze out a 1.87 percent bottom line. Nine of the 10 major investor-owned managed care plans (Wellpoint Health Networks being the major exception) in 1998 delivered a return on equity that was far less than average for the S&P 500 companies (+22.5 percent).

An increasing number of physicians in the latter part of the 1990s chose to be acquired by a physician practice management corporation. The overall fiscal performance of these companies, formed primarily to allow doctors to compete more favorably in the managed care environment and to earn more and work less, has been generally disappointing in terms of increases in revenues, net income (+2.79 percent), and stock appreciation. All of these companies experienced during 1998 and 1999 a sharp decrease in their stock price. A large number of physicians sold their practices for what is now almost worthless stock.

What this analysis demonstrated was, first, that in terms of profitability these three sectors of the U.S. investor-owned health industry discussed earlier have not only experienced fiscal performance that is less impressive than the 20 best teaching hospitals, but also that their stock appreciation was until recently significantly below the average for the S&P 500 companies. Second, that those for-profit hospital chains, HMOs, and physician practice management companies that have incurred significant debt are among those experiencing the most difficulties in generating operating surpluses and increases in their stock prices.

A combination of additional cutbacks in managed care, Medicaid, and Medicare reimbursement (particularly relating to indirect medical education and disproportionate share) could result in roughly a third of the nation's hub hospitals for health networks filing for bankruptcy by the year 2005 or so, unless these alliances make the decision and can allocate resources to cross-subsidize these teaching facilities. These poor cousins are already unable to generate adequate net operating margins, due most likely to being under-reimbursed for their present programs and services, and being saddled with higher than average debt-to-equity ratios. Based on this analysis, relying solely on further privatization of the health industry to restructure the field and its alliances and, in particular, the nation's best hospitals does not appear to be an overly effective and efficient option.

Summary of Experiences of the Canadian and German Health Systems

America's health dialogue shifted its major focus, after the Clinton health reform plan was defeated, from concerns with universal access and social equity for the uninsured to the need for more stringent cost containment efforts.[53–54] In fact, there was a long litany of papers published in the early 1990s espousing the virtues of the U.S. health system in terms of its technologic superiority,[55–56] its pluralism,[57–58] and its conceptual consistency with our traditional values of individualism.[59] Most proposed solutions for achieving political consensus focused on such concepts as incrementalism,[60] a multipayer system,[61–62] the implementation of increased competition,[63] a limited increase in any taxes,[64] no ceiling on the total U.S. gross domestic product (GDP) expenditure for health,[65] and the appeasement of most of the nation's key providers. In contrast, the evidence from other Western industrialized nations[66–67] clearly illustrates that by gaining general agreement on national health policies and priorities, and concurrently setting a maximum ceiling on total health expenditures, a universal comprehensive health insurance plan should be affordable in the United States.

When comparing the health spending, utilization, and outcomes of the Canadian, German, and U.S. health systems (see chap. 6), possibly the simplest conclusion is that the Americans spend the most, rely on a greater availability of technology, and do not necessarily achieve the best out-

comes. Not only do Canada and Germany[68] provide universal comprehensive health insurance at roughly 30 percent less of their GDP than the
United States, but they deliver far more services with these lower expenditures. Interestingly, the Canadians and Germans are able to achieve these
superior results operationally without forming U.S.-style health networks.

The major factors to explain why Canada and Germany are able to
achieve more care "for the dollar" from their health systems than the
United States follow:

1. They have simplified their prepayment system (the Canadian single-payer and the German multipayer) so that they are able to
   manage their facilities with considerably fewer administrative and
   business office personnel.
2. They have centralized all their tertiary services at major medical
   centers to enhance quality and to reduce cost.
3. They have limited annual increases in health spending to a percentage that is equal to the growth of their national income.
4. They have established patent medicine review boards to control
   pharmaceutical expenditures.

None of these four strategies could be implemented in the United States
with any great ease without an economic downturn that might force public
officials and major industrialists to support these options at least in part.

Since there are inherent difficulties in both the market-driven and the
regulatory approach to delivering health services, it is predicted that
health networks in the United States will continue to function with a
blended competitive (managed care) and regulated (Medicare and Medicaid) configuration. A review of the managed care approach and the Canadian and German health systems suggests that possibly what would work
the best is to continue on with the nation's quasi-private, quasi-public
approach, but one in which there is a compulsory, universal health insurance program, in which multipayers continue to negotiate reimbursement
rates, in which the insurers have a vested interest in managing care, and in
which consumers can select among all qualified providers.

What might be achieved by such a blended approach is improved
access and social equity, probably little noticeable enhancement in quality
of care, possibly some improvement in patient satisfaction, and no
increase in the percent of the U.S. GDP that is spent for health. Most of
the fiscal savings required to finance this proposed endeavor are envisioned to be obtained by reducing the number of administrative–business
office personnel among all providers and insurers and by the centralization
of tertiary services.

Blending Competitive and Regulatory Approaches to
Enhance Future Health Networking

The current balance between market-driven competition and government regulation (the former being more dominant today) will be judged in the long run by what it delivers, by its fairness to the general public, and by the quality and cost of the services it provides. Americans are willing to tolerate more uncertainty about the cost of healthcare than those in other industrialized nations, but there are still limits to how much uncertainty they will accept. While Americans are not anxious for government to extend its reach, neither do they want this prosperous country to abandon the safety net now provided by Medicare, Medicaid, and the existing public welfare programs.

Chapter 7 focused on the various options available for the health field that might provide the appropriate balance between too much competition and too much government control, so that health networks might most effectively and efficiently meet community and regional health needs. The models used for discussion purposes include: state health services commissions that function as public utilities; a federal commission, enabled by a mandate similar to that of the Telecommunications Act of 1996, to oversee healthcare providers in an atmosphere of regulated competition; and, finally, more open public disclosure of how well individual providers perform on such parameters as quality, cost, and safety, so that more consumer information might be available.

Health Services Commissions

Independent regulatory commissions are a unique American institution. In most other countries public utilities are owned and operated by the government. In the United States during the late 1800s, it became apparent that competition among railroad, power, and other public services was ineffective in protecting the consumer's interest, and so public utility commissions were established.[69] Private ownership of these resources was thereby maintained as the U.S. economy fostered a fundamentally competitive, free-enterprise system.

Possibly the most fundamental issue surrounding the possible use of this public utility model for the health field, and particularly for health networks, is to find the appropriate balance between the rights of consumers and providers and the extent of governmental control. What is disconcerting to those supporting the concept of separation of powers is that when our nation's public utility commissions regulate an industry, they merge the powers of the legislative, judicial, and executive branches. Advantages assumed to accrue to such regulatory organizations include continuity of policy, expertise, impartiality, experimentation, flexibility, and the isolation from politics enjoyed by the judicial branch.[70] In recent decades, however, these supposed virtues have been seriously challenged.

One of the major operational problems with these regulatory commissions during their early years was their inability to develop definitive standards to permit decisions to be fairly predictable and to allow the rationale for them to be clearly understood. Regulatory bodies operate under broad statutes resulting largely from the difficulty that state legislators find in resolving critical issues themselves and from the need for these commissions to have flexibility in meeting changing conditions. It would therefore be difficult to visualize how a state health services commission can always be expected to make credible policy decisions when a legislature, because of conflicting political and economic forces, is unable to do so within the authority's enabling legislation.

There are several other difficulties that health networks could envision with the formation of state health services commissions. These could include delays in granting approval that could prevent some patients from receiving their share of the benefits flowing from advances in medical sciences and from organizational efficiencies. These commissions would be expected to have power over entry, market share, the scope of services offered, reimbursement rates, profit margins, and exit. Delays could be costly in terms of human energies expended by the health providers when obtaining approval to make beneficial changes. Not the least of the potential problems is that of having the goals of the state departments charged with regulating insurance and public health, and those proposed by the new health services commissions, at odds with one another. Those drawbacks have been illustrated by the added costs incurred and the overall failure nationwide of earlier regulatory attempts to restrain health expenditures.[71–73]

What is of concern with the formation of a state health services commission is that the regulatory body, not the health network's management, is often responsible for the organization's programmatic and financial success or failure. As the regulators influence the providers' management decisions, this discourages entrepreneurial initiatives and can diminish the sense of any operational responsibilities. Or, by providing a monopoly to a specific provider (e.g., a health network, an academic health center, a prestigious multispecialty group practice), such public utility protection may become a haven for all aspiring monopolists, who previously found it too difficult, too costly, or too precarious to provide effective and efficient healthcare.

If a major economic downturn occurs in the United States, it is possible that those health networks functioning as oligopolies will not seriously object to the establishment of a new federal-state regulatory environment to prevent entry of new suppliers of services. This probably would start the process of forming several state health services commissions throughout the United States. The unexpected outcome may be that today's aggressive competitive environment may ultimately evolve into the need to protect the public's interest by forming quasi-public, quasi-private bodies, which are expected to experience significant difficulties in achieving cost reductions and improvements in either access or quality of care. Certainly, the outcome of establishing state health services commissions is alien to those who propose that cost containment efforts in the United States should be implemented almost solely by competitive forces.

The Telecommunications Act of 1996 as a Model

In an era where government intrusion into our daily lives is under increasing attack, the suggestion of instilling more competition within a highly regulated industry such as telecommunications, which historically has been under the aegis of the Federal Communications Commission (FCC), might be heralded as a great idea.[74] On February 8, 1996, President Clinton signed the Telecommunications Act of 1996, just one week after the U.S. Congress passed it with overwhelming bipartisan support.

Congress decided to legislate so that the telecommunications industry would be best served by competitive forces and corporate consolidations, both of them being justified. In order to pursue this new concept, Congress required that all telecommunications carriers interconnect directly or indirectly with the facilities and equipment of all other telecommunications carriers. They were further instructed not to install network features that did not permit the users of these facilities and other information suppliers "seamlessly and transparently to transmit and receive information between and across telecommunications networks." These congressional mandates were designed to correct industry practices that formerly inhibited or actually prohibited any semblance of competition and had at one time been used primarily by American Telephone and Telegraph (AT&T) to foster its monopoly.[75]

The foregoing is not to say that all is well and without difficulties since the passage of the telecommunications act.[76] There are problems of regional carriers (principally the Baby Bells) entering the long-distance business in addition to rendering their local service. Also the provision of "universal services" is under FCC scrutiny, just as the health leadership seeks to provide coverage to Americans without health insurance. Congress wants every person, no matter how remote, to have a communication link to the world, but is unwilling to fund such a program. In addition, most cable companies have taken advantage of the act and many have gone too far in raising prices to their users.

It is rather doubtful whether any of the various interest groups in the health field, especially among the health networks, will provide in the foreseeable future the direction to promulgate such a model of competition and consolidation as now being implemented by the telecommunications industry. The major reasons for this are the lack of significant accomplishment to date of the Telecommunications Act of 1996 and other similar endeavors, but primarily the health field's overall inherent fear of further governmental encroachment.

Expanding the Public Disclosure Concept

Today's entrepreneurship by overtly profit-seeking providers and insurers, including health networks, hints at the possible need for a more thorough public disclosure of clinical and financial information as a possible strategy to enhance access, improve quality of care, and reduce health expenditures.[77] Particularly for those patients with serious acute or chronic illnesses and those who require enormous quantities of health services, the high-visibility scandals (e.g., National Medical Enterprises and HCA—The Healthcare Co.) and bankruptcies (Allegheny Health, Education and Research Foundation in Philadelphia) among the investor-owned and not-for-profit health networks create understandable concerns.[78–79]

The public disclosure of a providers's clinical and financial performance is complicated, because the United States has a highly politicized pluralistic approach to the delivery of health services; self-interest among consumers and providers is pervasive; and there is a lack of agreement among professionals how to arrive at the critical quantitative measures with which to evaluate community healthcare needs. In addition, there is an intense fear among most Americans that additional regulations in the health field could result in restricting one's ability to obtain quality healthcare, as well as infringing on one's political freedom.

In comparison, the Securities and Exchange Commission's (SEC) rules and regulations, which since 1933 have guaranteed investors access to the disclosure of all material information concerning publicly traded securities,[80] provide a significant amount of data concerning the nation's major investor-owned hospital chains, HMOs, and physician practice management corporations. Recently, the Institute of Medicine in its well-publicized report[81] proposed a comprehensive strategy for government, industry, consumers, and health providers to reduce medical errors. The study called on Congress to create a national patient safety center to develop new tools and systems needed to address persistent issues.

One of the major problems historically with measuring quality has been the lack of valid indicators that can accurately reflect the performance of various providers over a broad spectrum of health services. During the past several years, the range of quality measures has significantly expanded and their reliability improved.[82-86] The country's oldest, most established, and largest accreditor of healthcare providers is the Joint Commission on the Accreditation of Healthcare Organizations (JCAHO), which now surveys more than 18,000 health facilities and services. The Joint Commission continues to be under pressure since it is considered to be too expensive, bureaucratic, subjective, and slow in weeding out marginal facilities. Probably its major shortcomings relate to its inability to measure clinical outcomes and its practice of limiting information to the public concerning its findings.

The most frequently used resource to assess a health plan's performance is the Health Plan Employers Data and Information Set (HEDIS) which is based on both clinical records and administrative data. The value of such data and conclusions is somewhat suspect since a Kaiser Family Foundation/Agency for Health Care Policy and Research survey[87] suggested that recommendations from colleagues at work, physicians, family, and friends had considerably more influence on a patient's choice of provider than all the published findings on quality and cost.

Probably the most revealing information compiled over the last decade on the potential impact of the public disclosure of quality of care and financial data can be derived from the California Health Outcomes Project and the New York and Pennsylvania "report cards."[88] With comparative coronary artery bypass graft (CABG) surgery information so readily available in these two states, one might expect that consumers would be likely to use these report cards to select a surgeon and hospital, but the opposite appears to be true.[89]

Although consumers, public officials, purchasers, and providers have expressed interest in the public disclosure of healthcare performance information, it is primarily the hospitals (particularly those with the most negative findings) that have taken the most heed of these disclosures.[90] An evaluation of the impact of an obstetrical consumer-oriented survey conducted by the Missouri Department of Health reported significant operational and policy changes among hospitals within one year of releasing their results.[91] Hospitals in competitive markets were found to be about twice as likely to consider improving process indicators and patient satisfaction, and to address the appropriateness of their patient charges, than those facilities that are the area's sole provider.

Careful review of both competitive and regulatory approaches to delivering healthcare (chap. 6), and of several quasi-private, quasi-public models (e.g., health services commission as a public utility) (chap. 7) to improve health services in the United States, leads to the following proposal: the nation's leaders should reject the approach that simply demands a choice between competition and regulation, when competition means "more market driven," and regulation means "more government." Instead, policy makers should strive to implement a competitive healthcare model that is blended with sufficient regulatory safeguards to protect the public and enough competitive features to reduce utilization and cost, and improve quality of care.

Blending Competitive and Regulatory Approaches

Ideological purists will scoff at the suggestion that such theoretically discordant principles as competition and regulation can be harmonized in actual practice, but most pragmatists will tend to perceive this hybrid as a worthy challenge.[92–93] Subject to the qualification that perfect solutions are seldom, if ever, attainable in the real world, the aim of public policy in the health field should be to move from what is unsustainable to a more sustainable position. It is within this context that what follows outlines how the competitive and regulatory models could be successfully blended, so that health networks are in an improved position to enhance access, social equity, and quality of care, and to constrain health costs.

What is envisioned here is an enlightened private-public partnership in which both parties concentrate on what they do best. Thus, in the broadest terms, the private sector with the virtues of the competitive model should bear principal responsibility for curtailing unnecessary utilization, and for improving efficiency and quality of health services. The regulatory focus of government, on the other hand, would be on constraining total health expenditures and insuring social equity.[94] Such a blended approach is more conducive to solving the issues facing the U.S. health system and the management of health networks than a total government takeover or a purely market-driven system.

More specifically, the ingredients of this proposed blended approach could include these factors:

1. Overall broad health policy established at the federal level, as it is in Canada and Germany, which might eventually include a global budgetary process or something similar for each state.
2. Administration solely at the state level, most realistically by some agency similar to a health services commission functioning as a public utility that focuses on controlling oligopolistic concentra-

tion. The commissions in the northeast states might address the issue of why hospital expenditures there were often twice those experienced on the west coast.
3. Competition among providers for contracts from insurers, focusing on curtailing utilization and cost and on improving the quality of care. This objective might include eliminating superfluous overhead by simplifying reimbursement and reducing excess capacity by centralizing tertiary services.
4. Government oversight to assure access to clinically needed care, social equity, and reasonable patient satisfaction. This approach would require implementing regulations that foster competition to lower cost and enhance quality of care, but protect the public without crippling innovation and efficiency.

How these factors mesh in making health networks the potential solution to the U.S. health delivery system's problems of access, social equity, quality, and cost is the general focus of the remaining portions of this chapter.

Leadership for Health Networks: What's Needed?

The large number of mergers that have taken place during the past decade among health providers have produced a leadership crisis, as well as creating increasing difficulty in evaluating a chief executive officer's performance (see chap. 8). Public opinion[95] and turnover statistics[96–97] among the health field's leadership suggest that an insufficient number of qualified leaders are currently available who possess the necessary vision and operational skills to pilot these powerful integrated delivery systems, which manifest so many vested interests.

To function effectively in today's complex environment, health networks' CEOs must have sound business sense, an understanding of the healthcare environment, an ability to balance their constituents' demand for more services with increasing fiscal constraints imposed by third-party payers, and a commitment to the community that the alliance will continue to provide needed health services. In this context, network trustees must be prepared to ask themselves a number of questions concerning the health network's overall objectives and whether their management team is fulfilling the organization's commitments to its various constituents.

When evaluating a potential or a current health network CEO, trustees will need to consider the merger mania and enormous managed care issues that are today roiling the U.S. health system. In such an environment, it is very likely that a CEO will need to find ways to enhance revenues and decrease expenses, and at the same time to lead the system into partnerships of various types with other organizations. Such complexities being major factors, the successful CEO will need to posses certain characteristics and training:

A CEO Must Establish Critical Objectives

A CEO must, with the support of the community, governing boards, physicians, and the executive team, outline the health network's overall objectives as well as those of each of its subsidiaries. In this process of goal setting, the CEO must be sensitive to the needs of the various cultures that, through mergers or acquisitions, often become an integral and critical part of any health network.

Competition among various subsidiaries becomes even more apparent when the network's central office attempts to restructure available resources, as in the case of centralizing information systems, closing redundant facilities or consolidating services, to achieve significant fiscal savings and to improve quality of patient care. Unfortunately, shuttering a facility or service can also cause serious political and morale problems among employees, physicians, and community residents. Such cost containment measures usually require great skill by the health network executives in reconciling diverse interests and cultures.

Necessary Personal Attributes of an Effective CEO

An effective CEO will be decisive, open to diverse points of view, patient in working for consensus, and able to take pride in the accomplishments of others. He or she will work for the community, rather than for narrow personal rewards. The effective CEO will base his or her actions on fundamental principles, thereby helping to build an institutionally fair culture, one where pay is equitable, reputation matters, and employees have the courage to voice their opinions.

An effective health network CEO will also value trust, recognizing it as a kind of glue holding together trustees, physicians, the management team, and employees. The effective CEO, in addition, will acknowledge that trust can give an organization an advantage over its competitors, since the health field contains such complex adversarial relationships.

A health network CEO must never underestimate the importance of physician input and advice, especially when making major decisions such as in restructuring, downsizing, and launching a new venture that affects its revenue stream. In such situations, particularly those involving other organizations within the region, a wise CEO will provide the system's medical staffs with forthright progress reports. Achieving physician consensus is often a laborious task that requires compromises by all interested parties, since the medical staffs within a system all have their own, sometimes competing interests. It is especially vital when shuttering a facility, program or service that the CEO bring concerned physicians into discussions involving specific fiscal savings, and any improvements in patient care such cost reductions might eventually make possible.

Do a CEO's Operational Strategies Fit the Network's Mission?

The public expects certain things from a health network that has achieved significant market penetration in its region—namely, higher-quality care and enhanced access, and at a lower cost to the community. Given such expectations, the trustees should continually question the CEO closely about his or her views concerning operating strategies such as horizontal and vertical diversification.

Trustees will certainly want to know whether the CEO considers controlling costs through horizontal integration as primarily a means to improve healthcare in the community or as merely a way to enhance the system's position in negotiating reimbursement rates with managed care plans. A system that dominates its marketplace should provide the community with the benefits of being positioned as an oligopoly.

For better or worse, increased regulation in some form is likely to occur in the next decade, to achieve additional cost containment and to protect patients' access to health services. Recent hearings in Congress and state legislatures are evidence of a growing movement eventually to protect patients' rights vis-a-vis managed care. Unfortunately, history suggests that regulation will be no more successful than competition in improving access, increasing quality, or reducing costs in healthcare (chap. 1). A wise CEO candidate must, nevertheless, be prepared to deal with both competitive and regulatory approaches, as they are both present in today's healthcare environment.

The health network's trustees should continually question the candidate's views on vertical diversification. Although many systems have sought additional patient referrals and market penetration by acquiring physician practices, few have done so successfully (see chap. 5). Too often health networks not only pay too much for the practices, they also lock themselves into long-term contracts without appropriate productivity incentives. As a result, some systems have experienced declining cash flows, and a few have been forced to divest themselves of such acquisitions as physician practices and provider-sponsored managed care plans.

How the CEO Demonstrates Effective Leadership

The CEO must possess a practical, achievable vision for strengthening the region's healthcare. To do this, he or she must know the inner workings of the healthcare system, including legislation affecting it, and be able to predict how various healthcare trends might impact the health network's organization, management, and financing. In addition, a capable CEO will exploit the integrated delivery system's strengths, address its shortcomings, and build meaningful bridges to its community. In this process, trustees must determine whether the CEO pursues these projects to improve the delivery of the region's healthcare or simply for his or her self-aggrandizement.

The effective health network CEO must be able to build consensus, which requires seeking out promising opportunities that contain shared values. In addition, he or she must carefully evaluate possible alternatives; involve all interested parties in the decision-making process; analyze the fiscal, operational, and political risks and determine which options have a reasonable chance of success; and then implement these options. In that process, it is not unusual for a health network CEO to be required to address several complex, interconnected problems at the same time. Trustees should evaluate his or her ability to do so successfully.

It is natural for a CEO to dream of making his or her system the dominant one in its region or even the only one in the region. Some experts believe that in the United States by 2005 there will be fewer than 850 systems functioning as oligopolies or cartels, most freestanding providers having been squeezed out of the market. The surviving health systems will have a good deal of leverage with patients, physicians, and insurers. But a truly first-rate CEO will want the health network to prosper not simply to attain added market penetration but to be in a position to use an improved competitive position to increase access to high-quality, cost-effective healthcare for the region.

The Education and Mentoring for CEOs

Most leaders of the nation's health networks have completed a graduate program awarding a master's degree in health services administration or the equivalent. In more recent years an increasing percentage of those recruited for these roles are physicians, who often have also completed formal management training.

In the past, most of the arguments concerning training future health executives have focused on whether the most appropriate core curriculum for such roles should be sought from a school of business administration or a school of public health. More recent discussions[98] center on the need for the United States' health leadership to become more familiar with the clinical-fiscal methodologies that simultaneously improve quality of care and reduce health expenditures. It is for this reason that a strong clinical background can be helpful to a leader in identifying appropriate ways of adding value to the provision of care. Previous hands-on patient care experience also can be exceedingly helpful when evaluating expensive new technologies and procedures.

Resources available in schools of medicine, public health, nursing, business administration, allied health sciences, and others need to be integrated into programs of health administration or other similar endeavors to start weighing specific patient care options against existing fiscal constraints. Those health network leaders who are most familiar with the medical care production process, and can generate clinical and management benefits in terms of enhancing effectiveness and efficiency, should be most successful in an era that focuses on cost containment and improving the quality of patient care.

A genuinely successful CEO will spend time on leadership development. First, the CEO will recruit a strong executive staff to carry out the health network's current operations. Second, he or she should mentor junior executives, sharing expertise and wisdom with them, preparing them to lead the system in the future. Unfortunately, many health CEOs today are so caught up in the daily demands of running a competitive organization that they think they have limited time for building staff and training future leaders. They are mistaken. Indeed, in failing to prepare new leaders they endanger the health network's future.

It is simply more difficult to become a top professional without having worked closely with one or preferably more leaders with outstanding abilities. The health field, the related academic programs, the faculty, and the students taking an active role have a vested interest and must jointly assume the responsibility to help place bright, young, well-trained, and thoughtful neophytes in environments where they are tutored so that they have the opportunity to expand their horizons.

Need to Find True Leaders

Although the current merger mania and the growth of managed care can often be disconcerting, in the long run they have the potential to build stronger health networks. Those alliances should theoretically be in a better position to meet their regions' health needs.

Today's and tomorrow's health networks will need true leaders, men and women who speak from the heart, solicit ideas, opinions, and criticisms from all layers of the organization; are candid, respectful, and responsible even in difficult circumstances; and are team players when choosing among competing options and strategies. The challenge for communities and trustees lies in finding and keeping CEOs with these qualities to lead their health network.

Advantages of Health Networking

Over the last six and a half decades there have been innumerable attempts by the nation's health leadership to regionalize health services in the United States (see chap. 1), a concept that is consistent with the current day formation of health networks in every metropolitan area. Some of the many, sometimes interrelated motives that help explain why experts in health policy and management[99-102] express an affinity toward consummating health networks may be briefly summarized as follows:

1. To improve efficiency and effectiveness, because by combining available resources and operations, it is possible to exploit cost-reducing synergies and to take a fuller advantage of risk-spreading managed care opportunities.
2. To enhance access by providing a broader range of sophisticated programs and services; and to improve the quality of patient care offered in the region.
3. To gain market share and thereby the increased revenues that eventually flow from becoming the sole or one of the dominant providers in the region's health delivery system.
4. To overcome the fear whether a freestanding hospital or a solo practitioner is able to survive in an increasingly aggressive, market-driven environment where huge and powerful networks are also experiencing cutbacks in managed care, Medicare, and Medicaid reimbursement.

When negative conclusions concerning the efficacy of health networks and networking are publicized, it is often argued that: (1) insufficient time has elapsed for these alliances to demonstrate their potential prowess in enhancing efficiency and effectiveness;[103] and (2) these health networks are not solely responsible for reorganizing the U.S. health system in terms of enhancing access, social equity and quality of care, and reducing national health expenditures. Yet can these arguments alone explain why most health networking endeavors to date have been relatively disappointing in achieving their earlier projected outcomes?

Forming Health Networks: A Complex Process

There are a number of reasons why integrated delivery systems encounter such significant obstacles in realizing their theoretical value. Among the most frequently cited are difficulties related to achieving an effective strategic fit, loss of too much power and fiscal control to the local governing board, problems in achieving operating efficiencies, challenges in realigning resources between the hub (i.e., the medical center with the tertiary services) and the satellites, and public concern of whether the network will be managed as an oligopoly. A detailed discussion now follows:

Health networking is much easier to achieve in theory than in practice. The United States has expended enormous resources for two-thirds of a century in developing regional health networks (chap. 1), but the implementation of this concept has failed primarily because: (1) community and provider have been driven by self-interest rather than a concern about what might make better sense for the region; and (2) Americans, being culturally wedded to pluralism, continually proclaim an inherent fear of substantial government control over their health system.

Insufficient attention is given in the initial analysis to merging or to establishing a new business entity. Chapter 2 delineates in some detail an outline of the initial analysis that a freestanding provider might pursue when seeking a merger, or the approach that a health network might utilize in evaluating an acquisition. The author's review of feasibility studies for potential mergers suggests that most providers have used these reports as "negotiating" documents, since few of them express any downside implications of such amalgamations (e.g., closing part of a facility to make the merger financially feasible). To date the nation's health networks have illustrated their greatest lack of conceptual and analytical evaluation in the acquisition of physician practices and of long-term care facilities, and the formation of provider-sponsored HMOs or similar managed care plans.

Horizontal mergers do not necessarily lead to operating efficiencies. A review of the health and nonhealth literature (chap. 3) clearly illustrates that the most successful horizontal mergers consummated by health networks are those between two previous competitors (e.g., two similar hospitals serving the same population base); and where management at the very outset knows how to implement major cost reduction efforts, and the barriers to accomplishing this are insignificant.[104] Health networks that are organized with an academic health center or major medical center at the hub, and many satellites, all with relatively similar culture and values, serving as spokes, within 90 minutes travel time from the tertiary facility, offer the opportunity to render cost savings and improved access to care. What is of some concern is that health networks in highly concentrated regions tend to enhance their bottom lines rather than to pass potential cost savings on to their constituents.

Vertical integration is only fiscally effective in closely related endeavors. A review of the health and nonhealth literature (chap. 4) illustrates that the most successful vertical diversification efforts occur among similar or closely related programs and services. Acute care hospitals do well in acquiring ambulatory care centers and radiation therapy centers; and home healthcare services do well in acquiring durable medical equipment suppliers. The performance of health networks in vertically integrating less closely aligned services (e.g., rehabilitation centers, nursing homes, wellness centers, physician practices, sponsoring managed care plans) is far less impressive.

There are difficulties in improving distribution of physicians to enhance health networking. Strategies such as establishing additional medical schools, expanding the National Health Service Corps program, and allowing more international medical graduates (IMGs) to pursue residency training in the United States have been relatively unsuccessful in attracting qualified physicians to practice in the nation's poor rural or inner-city communities (chap. 5). Even the option of reimbursing primary care physicians who would be willing to practice in underserved areas at premium rates was evaluated. The reluctance of physicians, for social and economic reasons, to open their offices in these areas; and of middle- and upper-income taxpayers to support increased spending to provide improved healthcare for the poor, helps explain the difficulty health networks face in providing adequate care to the nation's disenfranchised.

Health networks prefer market-driven approaches to more regulations. Whether health networks should experience more market-driven competition or more government regulation continues to be at the center stage of the U.S. health policy debate. Since the financing of healthcare is so critical in assessing how medical care is organized, managed, and delivered, various competitive and regulatory approaches are evaluated (chaps. 6–7). The conclusion is that either extreme makes little sense and that an appropriate blended approach with emphasis on practicality rather than ideological exactness provides the greatest advantages, since Americans are so strongly tied to pluralism. A quasi-private, quasi-public system delivering healthcare makes managing an alliance even more complex and contentious.

A need for more leadership among health networks. Public opinion and turnover statistics suggest than an insufficient number of qualified leaders are currently available who possess the necessary vision and operational skills to lead the nation's health networks (chap. 8). What is equally questionable is whether the nation's major research universities are up to the task of training additional leaders who are familiar with the "clinical-fiscal productivity" methodologies that should enable networks to implement lower-cost labor and material substitutes, as a means of further reducing health expenditures without significantly compromising quality of patient care. Another critical issue is whether today's health network leaders are really interested in mentoring the next generation of national leaders who will be required by the health field.

Difficulties in achieving a strategic fit. More likely to consummate a merger are those providers who are expected in the foreseeable future to experience a fiscal crisis because of the current highly competitive, managed care environment; who already have concluded that shortfalls in Medicare and Medicaid reimbursement will become an increasing issue; and whose overall operational and financial outlook as freestanding entities suggests serious difficulties.[105–7] Some amalgamations consummated might well represent two relatively weak providers who have mutually decided that their best option (because they can thereby project significant reductions in expense) is to simply consolidate their resources. An equally frequent explanation, often overlooked, is that health providers have relatively high fixed and low variable costs. A merger of two weak entities offers no guarantee of creating a new organization that is an effective strategic fit or one that can operate well and at a high level of efficiency.

Possibly an equally frequent explanation for these alliances' weak performance has been the fact that the region's dominant health system often targets for acquisition (merging is the more politically acceptable term) one or more of the area's weaker providers. In such situations, what is so often problematic is whether a large, well-functioning medical center and its various existing satellites can relatively expeditiously achieve improved operating and clinical outcomes when integrating into their network other new and previously not particularly productive related and unrelated providers. In some cases, these acquisitions can be expected to adhere to a different culture and set of values, and incompatible information systems. In this regard, vertical integration appears to raise more operational difficulties than horizontal diversification.[108–9]

Giving away too much money and governance. The newly acquired organization may well be blessed with a sound business plan, potentially a seamless integration of clinical services, and a harmonious blend of values, all elements that are so essential for synergies. Yet, in order that almost all patient referrals continue to be sent to the network's specialists rather than to those of a competitor, the integrated health system too frequently overpays for the primary care physician practices[110–12] and for a satellite hospital, and concedes in the governance arrangement that most of its major policies will be framed at the local level.

Another example possibly of giving away too much occurs when a health network, in order to consummate a deal, makes a sizable contribution to a local charitable foundation.[113] Or the smaller facility, as part of the merger agreement, receives from the health network significant capital funding for a new building or additional equipment. Under normal circumstances such an expenditure would not be affordable; and, in fact, it may not even be needed to meet the area's healthcare needs. These "unnecessary" capital outlays simply add cost to the region's health delivery system.

The medical center's specialty and subspecialty physicians are usually ecstatic about such acquisitions, since they thereby can expect to obtain significantly more tertiary referrals. Meanwhile, the physicians at the former freestanding facility are often far less sanguine about the new arrangement, since they fear that eventually the amalgamation could result in more external controls over their practice of medicine.

Difficulties in achieving operating efficiencies. Once it has paid a premium for an acquisition, and without immediately experiencing cost savings, the health network's leadership usually needs to implement cost reductions within the alliance, and could concentrate its efforts to produce savings at the recently merged facility. A system will experience increasing overhead expenditures as a direct result of its expansion activities. Gaining economies in business and related functions is usually far easier for a health network to achieve than consolidating clinical services, which conceivably could result in far greater dollar savings. The leaders of most health networks want to avoid controversies with their own medical staffs.

The feasibility of shuttering a hospital or a major clinical service depends on overcoming such local, politically laden issues as the natural wishes of consumers and physicians to maintain ease of access to as many services and to preserve as many jobs as possible. In many cases the practicality of such options is dependent on the travel time between the system's various partners. A carefully designed regionally oriented network has a far better chance of achieving clinical integration, and thereby effecting major cost reductions, than one that is spread out over several counties or states.[114]

Realigning resources between the hub and its satellites. In attempting to maximize a network's overall objectives, what is often more time consuming than expected is the process of arriving at some strategic and operational compromises between a system's central office and its satellites.

The network's leadership often experiences barriers in appropriately realigning the resources of its newly acquired facility with its other related entities because of the fuzziness built into the merger's governance arrangement in order to consummate the deal. Moreover, other issues often arise where clinical services overlap and the fiscal incentives and programmatic concerns for the satellite and its hub may well be in conflict. A smaller institution may well oppose shuttering a clinical service that creates marginal operating surpluses for the facility itself, but can more efficiently and with more consistent high quality be provided at the system's medical center.

There are also frequent problems relating to integrating the business and clinical information systems of the hub with all the satellites; satisfying the egos of the physician leadership at the local level without antagonizing the medical center's specialists and sub-specialists; and implementing the appropriate and compatible clinical protocols and total quality management initiatives. Under such circumstances, it is often difficult to generate both system-wide operating efficiencies and local goodwill, as more patients may need to be referred and then travel out of the immediate area to other providers within the health network.

Impact of networks functioning as oligopolies. Projected operating savings are sometimes also elusive because the system's central office staff has found that some of its earlier cost reduction proposals are in conflict with significantly more public, physician, and employee self-interest than previously anticipated. The system, once having achieved a high percentage of market penetration within the region, may then find it simply easier to enhance its bottom line by assuming an aggressive posture with HMOs during reimbursement negotiations than by cutting expenses.[115] The managed care plan in these discussions may have no other alternative, if it can afford to, but to pay a premium. The integrated health system representing the region's major providers can thereby manage their patient care and fiscal affairs as an oligopoly (i.e., controlling the flow of patients and price).

With all of the impediments outlined earlier, it is difficult to foresee that health networks will play a major role, at least in the short term, in achieving their theoretical goal of enhancing access, social equity, and quality, and significantly reducing the nation's total health expenditure.

A Practical Case: Thirty-Three Jewish-Sponsored Hospitals

The closure of San Francisco's Mt. Zion Medical Center as an acute care facility by the University of California San Francisco Medical Center and the shuttering of the Sinai Hospital of Detroit by the Detroit Medical Center in late 1999 offered a "natural" experiment to study the impact of managed care, mergers, and health networking on the 33 Jewish-sponsored hospitals that were providing general, acute care in 1975. This case study (outlined in more detail following this chapter) is presented to clearly illustrate that many conceptual findings reported earlier in this book have already occurred in the health field with reasonable frequency. The conclusions reached, based on the information and data collected from these 33 hospitals, may even suggest to some readers that there could be considerable disparity between the theoretical underpinnings of health networking and the more pragmatic findings "from the trenches."

The chief executive officers of several Jewish-sponsored hospitals recognized in 1979 the need to undertake more joint planning, and 16 of them embarked on the formation of the Consortium of Jewish Hospitals. Their primary objectives were to negotiate national purchasing contracts and to hire an insurance broker to study the feasibility of group insurance contracts.[116] This group grew rapidly into a 26-hospital consortium that was structured as a member-owned cooperative. Early in 1985, it was renamed the Premier Hospitals Alliance to attract a wider constituency and to expand into additional endeavors.[117] The Premier Hospitals Alliance continued to prosper and became a major force in facilitating cooperative ventures among health networks throughout the United States.

A short historical brief on each of these 33 Jewish-sponsored facilities in operation in 1975 and the average daily census (when reported) of those that remained viable until 1997 or 1998 are provided in table 18. These synopses illustrate that each organization tended to follow a slightly different course of action that was most often contingent on its patient activity volumes and on available local options. Forming a not-for-profit, national Jewish-sponsored hospital network or a Jewish investor-owned hospital chain similar to HCA—The Healthcare Co. or Tenet today did not make much practical sense nor was the concept politically acceptable.

Of the 33 Jewish-sponsored hospitals providing general acute care in 1975, eight of these facilities have been shuttered for short-term inpatient care. Some of the hospitals in 1975 provided a significant amount of care, as illustrated by the average daily census of Pittsburgh's Montefiore Hospital (380 patients), Sinai Hospital of Detroit (587), and San Francisco's Mt. Zion Hospital and Medical Center (281). Each was a teaching hospital affiliated with a local medical school and would be difficult to assess as a "marginal" facility.

A frequent strategy actually employed by 13 of the Jewish-sponsored hospitals was to form or join an existing partnership made up of a nonsectarian, not-for-profit facility, sometimes as an "equal" and sometimes as a subordinate partner of a larger and fiscally more viable organization. Major exceptions were Hartford's Sinai Hospital, which merged with a Catholic facility; and Cleveland's Mt. Sinai, Chicago's Michael Reese, and Denver's General Rose hospitals, which were acquired by an investor-

TABLE 18. Selected Information Concerning Jewish Hospitals, 1975–2000

Name of Facility, Location, and Average Daily Census	Selected Information
Beth Israel Hospital, Boston ADC: 336 (1975); NR (1998)	Merged with Deaconess Medical Center and became Beth Israel Deaconess Medical Center under CareGroup, which owns six area hospitals totaling 1,270 beds.
Miriam Hospital, Providence ADC: 217 (1975); 168 (1998)	Merged with Rhode Island Hospital and then eventually became part of Lifespan Corp., which includes the New England Medical Center, Boston.
Mt. Sinai Hospital, Hartford ADC: 269 (1975); Closed	Affiliated and then merged with St. Francis Hospital and Medical Center, Hartford, and eventually closed as an acute inpatient facility.
Mt. Sinai Medical Center, New York City ADC: 1059 (1975); NR (1998)	Established a new medical school in the mid-1960s. In 1998 merged with the New York University Hospital (NYU) and became the Sinai-NYU Hospitals and Health System.
Beth Israel Medical Center, New York City ADC: 869 (1975); 1,006 (1998)	Beth Israel Medical Center and St. Luke's–Roosevelt Hospital Center formed an alliance in 1997 as Continuum Health Partners, Inc., and in 1998 were joined by Long Island College Hospital.
Montefiore Medical Center, New York City (Includes the Hospital of the Albert Einstein College of Medicine ADC: 1,241 (1975); 805 (1998)	One of the earliest hospitals to vertically diversify with a prepaid, multispecialty group practice, long-term care facilities, and home health services, all tied to a medical school environment.
Hospital of Joint Diseases, New York City ADC: 311 (1975); Closed	Relocated from Manhattan's Harlem and became an integral part of Beth Israel Hospital, New York City.
Maimonides Medical Center, New York City ADC: 610 (1975); 557 (1998)	Remains as an independent teaching facility with 600 ambulatory satellites serving south Brooklyn and focusing on providing care for Orthodox Jews.
Bronx-Lebanon Hospital, New York City ADC: 524 (1975); 505 (1997)	In 1962 the Bronx Hospital merged with the Lebanon Hospital. Originally serving an eastern European Jewish population who began moving into the suburbs after World War II. Now governed and provides care for a heterogeneous population primarily eligible for Medicaid or who are uninsured.
Jewish Hospital, New York City ADC: 174 (1975); Closed	Located in Manhattan's Washington Heights, now closed.

TABLE 18. *Continued*

Name of Facility, Location, and Average Daily Census	Selected Information
Jewish Hospital and Medical Center of Brooklyn ADC: 585 (1975); Merged	Merged with the St. John's Episcopal Hospital and formed a two-site Interfaith Medical Center, now facing serious fiscal difficulties.
Long Island Jewish Hospital, New York ADC: 835 (1975); 706 (1998)	Merged with North Shore Hospital and became part of the North Shore–Long Island Jewish Health System, which includes 13 affiliated acute care facilities.
Beth Israel Medical Center, Newark, N.J. ADC: 400 (1975); 383 (1998)	Now part of New Jersey's largest and most diversified integrated system, Saint Barnabus Health Care System, consisting of 10 hospitals, 9 nursing homes, and other resources. Newark Beth Israel performs heart and lung transplants.
Beth Israel Hospital, Passaic, N.J. ADC: 177 (1975); 132 (1998)	Serves the facility's local communities in accord with the "Jewish tradition of its founders."
Barnert Memorial Hospital, Paterson, N.J. ADC: 236 (1975); 102 (1998)	Struggling fiscally as a freestanding facility.
Albert Einstein Medical Center, Philadelphia ADC: 725 (1975); NR (1998)	Merger of the Jewish Hospital and Mt. Sinai Hospital in 1951; the latter facility was eventually sold and then closed for acute inpatient care.
Sinai Hospital of Baltimore ADC: 419 (1975); NR (1998)	Early in the 1960s relocated to the suburbs after being adjacent to Johns Hopkins Hospital.
Mt. Sinai Medical Center, Miami ADC: 566 (1975); 507 (1998)	Serves an increasing number of Jews relocating from the Northeast and the Midwest to Florida's east coast.
Jewish Hospital, Louisville ADC: 351 (1975); 447 (1998)	Serves as the "hub" facility for the Jewish Hospital Health Care Services system that includes the ownership of three satellite hospitals.
Jewish Hospital, Cincinnati ADC: 550 (1975); 139 (1998)	One of the six hospitals (1,520 beds) of the Health Alliance of Greater Cincinnati system that includes Christ Hospital and University Hospital.
Montefiore Hospital, Pittsburgh ADC: 380 (1975); Closed	Affiliated then was sold for $75 million in 1993 to the University of Pittsburgh Medical Center System and eventually was closed as an acute inpatient facility.
Mt. Sinai Medical Center, Cleveland ADC: 451 (1975); NR (1998)	Considered relocating to the suburbs in the 1960s; purchased by investor-owned Primary Health Systems (PHS) in April 1996; filed for Chapter 11 bankruptcy

(continued)

TABLE 18. *Continued*

Name of Facility, Location, and Average Daily Census	Selected Information
	protection in 1999; attempted to be reorganized by PHS; and closed 400-bed University Circle and 98-bed East in Richmond Heights in March 2000.
Sinai Hospital, Detroit ADC: 587 (1975); 364 (1997)	Founded in 1953. Merged in 1998 as part of the Detroit Medical Center system and in 1999 was closed as an acute care inpatient facility.
Michael Reese Hospital and Medical Center, Chicago ADC: 71 (1975); NR (1998)	Was acquired in 1991 by investor-owned Humana and later became part of HCA— The Healthcare Co., the nation's largest investor-owned corporation.
Mt. Sinai Hospital Medical Center of Chicago ADC: 357 (1975); 232 (1997)	Has continued since the 1960s as a major provider of health services to the poor living on Chicago's south side.
Mt. Sinai Hospital, Milwaukee ADC: 239 (1975); Merged	Merged with the Good Samaritan Medical Center (Lutheran) in 1987 and became the Sinai-Samaritan Medical Center. Then the two institutions were merged with St. Luke's Hospital, forming the nucleus of the Aurora Healthcare system.
Mt. Sinai Hospital, Minneapolis ADC: 189 (1975); Closed	Merged in 1988 with the Metropolitan Medical Center owned by Health One Corp.; Health One and LifeSpan merged to form Health Span Health Systems; within that system the Phillips Eye Institute in 1991 became the "replacement" for the Mt. Sinai Hospital, Minneapolis, and in 1994 Health Span and Medica merged and became Allina Health System.
Jewish Hospital of St. Louis ADC: 478 (1975); NR (1998)	Merged with Barnes Hospital and became an integral part of the Barnes-Jewish-Christian Health System, which now owns 11 hospitals in the region and thereby serves as St. Louis' major health provider.
Menorah Medical Center, Overland Park, Kans. ADC: 284 (1975); 76 (1998)	Relocated from Kansas City, Missouri, to a suburban site in Kansas; merged with Health Midwest, the region's largest health system.
Touro Infirmary, New Orleans ADC: 410 (1975); 202 (1998)	Served for decades as the preferred inpatient facility for the private patients of the Louisiana State University and Tulane full-time and clinical faculty

TABLE 18. *Continued*

Name of Facility, Location, and Average Daily Census	Selected Information
	members, and is where Drs. DeBakey and Ochsner started their clinical careers.
Rose Memorial Hospital, Denver ADC: 281 (1975); NR (1998)	Sold to for-profit interests and is now part of HCA—The Healthcare Co.
Mt. Zion Hospital and Medical Center, San Francisco ADC: 327 (1975); NR (1998)	Merged with the University of California–San Francisco system and was closed in 1999 as an acute inpatient facility.
Cedars-Sinai Medical Center, Los Angeles ADC: 533 (1975); 636 (1998)	Cedars of Lebanon Hospital merged with Mt. Sinai Hospital in 1961, and then the latter facility was eventually closed.

Sources: American Hospital Association, *Hospital Statistical Guide* (Chicago: American Hospital Association, 1979 and 1999); and information obtained from the websites of each of the hospitals listed here.
Notes: ADC = Average Daily Census. NR = Not Reported.

owned group. In almost every case, the partner sought was known for its strong teaching programs and for the quality of its patient care, and often was considered the region's most prestigious health system.

This case study illustrates that when a hospital as a strategy decides to merge, but for all practical purposes is acquired by the region's dominant provider, there is a reasonable likelihood that as one of the smaller facilities within the integrated delivery system, it eventually may be shuttered for acute inpatient services. The experience among the Jewish hospitals is that a health network will only keep a facility open as long as it remains fiscally viable. Unlikely in today's competitive environment is the prospect of a health network cross-subsidizing an acquired hospital for any extended period of time.

Twelve of the 33 Jewish-sponsored hospitals are still freestanding, either because they were unable to consummate a suitable partnership, because they wanted to control their own destiny, because they had developed a workable "niche" or for a combination of these reasons. Some of these freestanding facilities with relatively modest average daily censuses and severe fiscal difficulties can be expected to either merge or close their facility.

Those Jewish hospitals that are part of a health network should be more favorably positioned in financial terms than the freestanding institutions. A far more critical issue based on this case study might well be the specific facility's payer classification mix and where the facility is located. Louisville's Jewish Hospital Health Care Services (a health network) and Los Angeles' Cedars-Sinai Medical Center, which is free standing, might be examples of two organizations with reasonable operating surpluses and relatively low debt-to-equity ratios. Less sound financially in contrast are the New York City based teaching centers and the Detroit Medical Center, which with an annual revenue of $1.5 billion, needed to shutter Sinai Hospital of Detroit, because of a system-wide net operating loss of $76.5 million in 1999 (tables 19 and 20).

On the basis of this case study it is difficult to make the argument that health networks are significantly more effective and efficient in providing healthcare than freestanding providers. A more accurate summary might be:

1. Hospitals, even those of some stature, can expect to be shuttered as a result of further reductions in third-party reimbursement, regardless of whether they are freestanding or part of a health network.
2. It is critical for a provider, whether freestanding or part of a network, to find an appropriate niche to meet local and regional health needs; to build meaningful relationships with local patients, highly qualified physicians, and nearby institutions in order to obtain, when appropriate, tertiary referrals; and to establish a track record of carefully and prudently focusing on its core operations.
3. Outstanding leadership and top-flight management that can appropriately balance clinical and fiscal tradeoffs might be far more critical than whether the provider is freestanding or a subsidiary within a major health network.
4. Health networking is not necessarily "a road paved with gold," nor does it automatically provide enhanced access, social equity, quality and reduced costs. Being a community-oriented, effective, and efficient provider of health services requires careful analysis of regional health needs, diligent leadership, and a willingness by various vested interests to compromise for an area or region's overall good.

The Economic and Political Climate of the United States: A Major Determinant

During the 1990s managed care, merger mania, and the performance of the U.S. health networks were, as was to be expected, compatible with the country's economic and political climate. What is often overlooked is that the organization, financing, and quality of care provided by the nation's networks must be closely linked to the nation's overall economic prosperity and to the public's attitude toward social solidarity (e.g., Social Security, Medicare, Medicaid, public welfare, and public housing), a concept well accepted in Canada and in western and central Europe. In comparison with other industrialized nations, the United States, a country respected for its technological and economic innovations and for its unexcelled standard of living, has been slow to enact broad social insurance programs that will safeguard a family against the threat of economic insecurity arising from the costs of illness and disability.[118]

In fact, the concept of an unfettered free enterprise economy, as illustrated by the lack of a meaningful regulatory review of health mergers, is now nowhere in the industrialized world so firmly rooted as in the United States. Possibly relevant as an example is the protracted struggle for some form of national health insurance as far back as 1912, when it was an important issue in the presidential campaign of Teddy Roosevelt.[119]

The competitive, market-driven managed care plans and the recent welfare reform measures, aside from their conceptual and political appeal to the American voter, have attracted such overwhelming public support because of their compatibility with a bullish economy now spanning almost a decade. At other times during the second half of the twentieth century, when the United States experienced a recession, the costs of illness and disability surfaced as more critical concerns for elected officials and political parties, irrespective of whether the Democrats (e.g., Truman) or the Republicans (e.g., Nixon) controlled Congress and the White House.[120] The U.S. health system may have been tweaked as a result of these economic downturns, but its basic tenet of retaining a quasi-private, quasi-public approach is deeply ingrained in our culture. Americans are simply resistant to a complete government or private takeover of the delivery of health services.[121]

Nothing could potentially more dramatically reshape how the health networks currently function than a major economic recession that adversely affects the stock market; causes a sizable increase in personal bankruptcies due to unemployed workers no longer being able to repay their earlier incurred consumer debt; and has major corporations complaining at some length as they experience increasing difficulty in defraying the costs of their employees' health insurance and other fringe benefits.

Since the United States for several centuries has witnessed normal business cycles, it is predictable that an economic recession will occur here sometime in the next decade. Obviously, it is difficult to forecast when such a recession will occur, how seriously it will affect most Americans, and how long it will last. During such an onerous economic period, it is predicted that health networks and their patients will encounter a major shift in public policy that requires a significant curtailment of health expenditures.

During such a recessionary period when money is "tight," health networks are expected to have more of an opportunity to solve some of the underlying problems now facing the U.S. health system. The remaining sections of this book outline what steps might be taken by health networks, particularly in difficult economic times, to play a far more major role in enhancing access, social equity, and quality, and reducing cost.

Proposals for Health Networks to Achieve Improved Efficiencies

As the public demands more affordable health services, the networks experience more fiscal constraints as a result of managed care, Medicare, and Medicaid cutbacks; and, particularly when the United States faces the impact of an economic recession, leaders of health networks can be expected to implement a significant number of downsizing or rightsizing measures.

Divestiture of Physician Practices

Among all of the vertically integrated options available for health networks to implement, acquiring and then managing physician practices so that they are effective and profitable have demanded the highest skill level. This activity requires that the alliance has the ability to manage clinical and financial risk, properly align financial incentives, and implement total continuous quality management practices.

The struggle for power, control, and monies is often reflected in the tension observed between physicians and health network executives. The strain manifests itself in such issues as agreeing on vision, mission, leadership, control over decision-making, and managing conflict. These are particularly troublesome problems when both parties are continually being tested concerning their loyalty to the two masters that they serve: patients or the community, and the organization that employs them.

In spite of these impediments when health networks acquire primary care physician practices, there have been some notable successes. Some alliances have experienced favorable results by organizing these physician groups in combination with less integrated arrangements such as physician-hospital organizations (PHOs) and independent practice associations

(IPAs). When a large, rural-based multispecialty group practice has dominated the hub care facility for decades (e.g., Fargo, Geisinger, Packard, and Marshfield clinics), the formation of an integrated health system has coalesced their somewhat diverse interests into a more effective and efficient health delivery system.

The divestiture by networks of unprofitable physician practices, and the firing of many employed physicians, regrettably will become a relatively frequent occurrence in the next decade for a number of reasons: negative financial margins already ranging from 15 percent to 40 percent of net revenues;[111] inherent economic and philosophical conflicts between the practice of medicine and the fiscal well-being of a network; and the fact that physicians who are bought out by networks anticipated working less and increasing their income, while the systems projected additional admissions and a fair return on their investment.[122–24]

Other explanations why networks may need to divest physician practices include these: the splitting of the network's managed care payment between the physicians and the hospitals is becoming an enormously politicized process; more physicians are focusing on unionization and IPAs (independent practice plans) as alternatives to better control their practice of medicine; and a small percentage of physicians with many high-income patients will opt out of all their managed care contracts and only accept fee-for-service or point-of-service payment. The leadership of health networks may even start talking publicly about an integrated delivery system's business being fundamentally different from that of the private practice of medicine, since these divestitures could cause considerable wrath among those physicians adversely affected.

Shutter Programs, Services, and Facilities

Most health networks experience an excess number of inpatient beds and sites where various sophisticated programs and services are offered. Since the health industry is characterized as having such high fixed costs, significant savings can be achieved by closing a total facility or at least a major service.

After a health network experiences unusually severe fiscal shortfalls, the alliance's weaker financial position can be used as the excuse to shutter programs, services, and facilities that are not particularly productive, that have incurred significant operating losses for several years, and that are recognized as providing "questionable" or "marginal" quality of care. Some senior executives of networks potentially could prepare for their trustees a listing of options for "closing," each with a projected dollar saving, although some estimates will require initial capital expenditures. This

approach is similar to that used by Congress in shutting down military bases.

Not only are most of these poorly performing health resources a major source of employment for these communities, but they create significant local pride. If an acute facility closes in a rural or inner-city location, some of the existing physicians there could be expected to relocate, and the recruitment of new doctors to such communities certainly becomes far more arduous.[125]

Centralizing Tertiary Services

Considerable cost savings and higher quality of care can be achieved by the centralization of tertiary services at major medical centers, where a high volume of such procedures are performed and where quality residency training and related programs are under way. For many of the nation's community hospitals, however, eliminating these sophisticated services would not only modify an institution's case mix but would adversely affect its public image. In addition, some of the facility's subspecialists would need to relocate elsewhere and might even find it difficult to obtain appropriate hospital privileges because of an existing glut of physicians with similar training.

The experience of Canada and Germany would suggest that if health networks consolidated tertiary services at fewer facilities a significant cost savings and an improved quality of patient care would result. The Canadians and Germans have centralized their high-technology services at regional medical centers, mostly teaching facilities, with clinical outcomes consistent with those in the United States.[126-27] Patients in Canada and Germany are more often required to travel out of town for such services; families are inconvenienced; and there is frequently a queue for elective procedures (the length of the waiting period is often a matter of considerable dispute).

The cost savings in the United States by decreasing by half the number of facilities offering tertiary services (roughly comparable to that in Canada and Germany) would be significant (three to five billion dollars annually).[128-29] Some closures of marginal tertiary programs are to be expected with the further cutbacks in reimbursement. Shuttering these sophisticated programs would change the clinical landscape and in some cases the financial viability of a significant number of community hospitals in the United States. The political power base of the nation's academic health centers would be expected to be significantly enhanced by this reshuffling of where sophisticated services are provided.

Eliminate Many Administrative and Business Office–Related Positions

The Canadians (with a single-payer system) and Germans (with a pluralistic approach) spend a third and a quarter less, respectively, of their gross domestic product (GDP) for health services than the United States. In making comparisons among Canadian, German, and U.S. physicians and hospitals,[130-33] there are at least four areas of significant difference:

1. There is a far higher utilization of hospital days and physician visits per person in Canada and Germany than in the United States because their reimbursement incentives encourage longer average lengths of stay and more follow-up visits to physician offices.
2. There are far fewer man-hours for administrative and business-office and related personnel per hospital discharge in Canada and Germany than in the United States because of their less complicated reimbursement strategies.
3. Somewhat fewer man-hours are spent on medical technologic support (e.g., clinical pathology, diagnostic radiology, physical therapy) per discharge in Canada and Germany than in the United States, but a relatively comparable number of nursing service hours per discharge. Irrespective of how a nation finances its health services, decreasing costs among clinical patient care activities becomes increasingly arduous.
4. Physician incomes are far higher in the United States than in either Canada or Germany.

Based on these experiences in Canada and Germany, a simplified reimbursement methodology in the United States, with the implementation of a state-administered global budget process (discussed at length later), could result in two million fewer workers employed (mostly in hospitals and physician offices) in the U.S. health field. Positions in the health industry are among the most sought after in many communities, and laying off 15 percent of the industry's labor force during a recession would have serious political and social implications. Those who claim that the health field has an excess number of nonclinically oriented personnel would feel, however, that such a downsizing is long overdue.[134]

The specific number of administrative and business office–type employees who would be terminated in a recessionary period is certainly a matter of considerable conjecture. Since less funding would be available, and in a comparative sense fewer employees involved in direct patient care could be terminated, it is only logical to argue that a large number of "white-collar" positions eventually would be eliminated because of a less complicated reimbursement system.

Reimbursement of Pharmacy Expenses

Whether prescriptions filled at local pharmacies should be included as a benefit for all Medicare-eligible patients has received considerable attention from The National Bipartisan Commission on the Future of Medicare.[135] To date the integrated delivery systems have been able to sidestep the issue of an annual increase of 10 to 14 percent in nonhospital pharmaceutical drug expenditures.[136] A number of reasons are given for this significant rise: an additional number of prescriptions are being dispensed; more costly new drug therapies are being introduced that provide patients with enhanced well-being; antidepressant drugs are being substituted for more expensive psychotherapy; narcotic analgesics and other prescriptions filled at local pharmacies are being used to avoid or to shorten hospital inpatient stays; and some patients demand that their physicians prescribe by trade name, or they will demand such a prescription from another more willing practitioner.

Interestingly, the drug utilization incentives for physicians under managed care contracts can act in various directions.[137-39] On the one hand, studies on the number of pills per managed care prescription versus the fee-for-service prescription suggest that HMO physicians are trying to keep their patients out of the office by increasing the number of pills per prescription. On the other hand, managed care plans offering drug benefits constrain pharmacy costs by holding physicians responsible for exceeding a preestablished drug benefit amount. In 1996, drugs accounted for 10 percent of the HMOs' budgets but generated 50 percent of their cost increases, possibly explaining why managed care plans continue to experience sluggish bottom lines and why drug costs are becoming an issue of increasing concern for insurers.

The managed care plans, Medicare and other third-party payers in the United States have historically avoided providing benefits for prescriptions filled at a local pharmacy.[140] Western and central European countries provide coverage for prescription drugs, usually with a modest deductible or coinsurance provision, and the number of prescriptions per capita filled is at least twice that in the United States or Canada.[141] With an increasing aged population on modest fixed incomes here, many of whom have one or more chronic illness, the cost of drugs purchased at the local pharmacy has become a serious problem for those without such drug benefits.

The United States eventually could follow the example of the Canadians and Germans in establishing a patent medicine review board that focuses on pricing new drugs.[142–44] Such a proposal would be strongly opposed by the pharmaceutical industry, an exceedingly powerful lobby in the United States, but Congress could expect to receive strong endorsement from an equally powerful group, the American Association of Retired Persons. Since it is unlikely that either the integrated delivery systems or the managed care plans by themselves will want or be able to force the pharmaceutical industry to lower drug costs, the providers and insurers, with the endorsement of consumer groups, should be expected to eventually lobby federal public officials to step in with some form of patent medicine review board. Such a regulatory process could be expected to have a significant impact, as in other countries, on reducing the cost of pharmaceuticals dispensed by hospital pharmacies and other providers.

Tying Together These Proposals

The proposals offered here for generating enhanced effectiveness and efficiencies in the performance of health networks will be critical whether or not the United States experiences a recession. Overall, these proposals express a desire to provide greater access and social equity (to improve the healthcare provided to the nation's disenfranchised) and to reduce the annual rate of inflation of healthcare costs. It is unlikely, based on comparative Canadian, German, and U.S. studies reviewed herein and in chapter 6, that significant cost savings can be generated by reducing direct patient care activities. Therefore, the emphasis needs to be on simplifying reimbursement strategies used in this country, to reduce the number of administrative and business office–related personnel; centralizing sophisticated tertiary-type services (with the realization that this could inconvenience some physicians, patients, and families); and reducing pharmaceutical costs, the most likely approach being a federal patent medicine review board.

Unfortunately, these proposals may require more "big government," an approach that has not been particularly popular in the past. In contrast, an obvious concern is that health networks will use their market concentration to limit entry of competitors, to control price, and to increase their bottom lines (i.e., to function as oligopolies). Therefore, maintaining the concept of a balanced competitive and regulatory approach (i.e., pluralism) to delivering health care services is critical in allowing health networks to play a more major role in solving some of the nation's underlying health system problems.

The variable that tends to influence most which, to whom, and how health services are delivered is the way in which they are financed. This phrase "how they are financed" includes who actually pays for the health services (e.g., corporate fringe benefits, payroll taxes, general public subsidies, individuals out-of-pocket); who administers the benefits (e.g., managed care plans, government); the benefits provided under the various plans offered (e.g., limitations on inpatient admissions will increase ambulatory care activities); and the fiscal incentives inherent in the reimbursement methodology (e.g., the difference in volume of care provided in a total fee-for-service versus a capitated approach would be noticeable). Selecting any of these options, alone or in tandem, leads to significant compromises. It is in this context that the last section of this book focuses on possible options to modify the way the United States reimburses health networks for providing health services.

Future Changes in the Financing of Health Services

There is little assurance in the long run that increasing competition among managed care plans, the improved operations of health networks, and the halfhearted implementation of the proposals outlined herein will result by say 2005 in an economically acceptable growth rate for total health spending in the United States. During an inevitable recessionary period within the next decade, the pendulum between competition and regulation could be expected to swing back toward more regulation. At least temporarily, Congress could try in some way to simultaneously improve access to health services and try to impose a ceiling on total health expenditures, with any future increases in total reimbursement tied to improvements in the nation's productivity or other similar indices.

Price controls,[145] rate setting,[72] and certificate of need[73] will not be considered as viable options, since they previously failed to control increases in health expenditures or to enhance access to health services. As a result, discussion could heat up again on some of the same issues contained in the Clinton and other health reform plans: (1) providing universal, comprehensive health insurance benefits; (2) implementing a single- or a multipayer system; (3) controlling the utilization and cost of health services; and (4) having a federal agency set global budgetary targets by state for each sector of the U.S. health system. Since it is commonly thought that how health services are financed has a major impact on the delivery of medical care, a brief discussion of each and how these traditional issues in the organization and payment of healthcare might conceivably affect the management of health networks in the next decade now follows:

Universal Comprehensive Health Insurance Benefits

It is rather problematic whether the United States and, therefore, the health networks will witness a significant enhancement in access to care among the uninsured, or in social equity, even if Congress mandates a basic range of health insurance benefits. The major reason is that the United States has a different cultural-social philosophy than most other Western industrialized nations (chap. 1). One possible exception might be the expansion of the State Children's Health Insurance Program (CHIP) that was enacted as part of the Balanced Budget Act of 1997, an enhancement to the Medicaid program that to date has experienced isolated success.[146]

Based on the values held by most Americans and on past experience, it would be difficult to envision health networks taking an aggressive leadership role in seriously pressuring for universal comprehensive health insurance. In operational terms, most providers are unable to embrace the concept of universal access and social equity in the provision of health care. Hospitals and physicians are innately opposed to the idea that government officials should promulgate more regulations and take a more vigorous role in the delivery of personal health services. Although these networks publicly espouse the importance of meeting community healthcare needs, their executives are more often judged by their trustees and peers on how many deals they consummate, how well they get along with their medical staffs, and on their bottom lines at the end of the year than on whether they deliver adequate health services to the region's disenfranchised.

Americans have traditionally rationed health services by family income and the ability to pay for care. Therefore, they instinctively expect integrated health networks to perpetuate a three-tier healthcare system whereby the uninsured poor will continue to receive care in urgent circumstances; the middle-class will obtain coverage for almost all medically needed services through managed care plans that more often in the future will limit choice of provider or expect the subscriber to copay; and the wealthy will continue to opt for the flexibility of using providers of choice (e.g., upper-income Medicare-eligible individuals will select fee-for-service or point-of-service plans).

Single- or Multipayer System

A single-payer top-down health system controlled by the federal and state governments is not only alien to American culture and values but is not necessarily the most efficient option and would be expected to create serious political consequences.

The experience of states that have enacted legislation to control spending by the setting of prices is illustrative. After they were adjusted for differences in case-mix intensity, wage rates, and admission rates per 1,000 persons, hospital costs per capita were substantially higher in rate-setting states compared to where market forces have been encouraged to play a major role in establishing hospital reimbursement rates.[147] In Massachusetts, Maryland, and New York, for example, the average annual hospital cost per person in 1994 was 49.1 percent higher than in Arizona, California, and Oregon, where competition among managed care plans has been the principal weapon to promote cost containment.

The percentage of the gross domestic product spent for health in 1997 for Canada (9 percent), Sweden (8.6 percent), and the United Kingdom (6.7 percent) with a single-payer system is only slightly less than in France (9.6 percent), Germany (10.4 percent), and Japan (7.3 percent) with a multipayer system.[131] The difference between a single- and multipayer system could well be the percentage of a nation's GDP that federal legislative and executive branch officials decide to spend for health services. Most often this decision is based on affordability, historical precedents, consumer demands, and the political clout of various providers.

What should be of particular concern to the public and the management of health networks is the possibility of implementing a single-payer approach. A top to bottom regulatory endeavor would be at odds with establishing and managing the most effective and efficient network in the region because of the inescapable political considerations (e.g., local elected officials trying to gain favor before crucial elections) and various pressures from special interest groups (e.g., labor unions protecting jobs that need to be eliminated). What the general public might consider the most serious possible flaw in a single-payer system is the threat that a state regulatory agency, established to control the supply of available services and the level of reimbursement, might eventually be dominated by the most politically and fiscally powerful providers that it is suppose to regulate.[148–49]

Controlling the Utilization and Cost of Health Services

Regional differences in health expenditures, adjusted for variations in the local cost of living and in use rates for specific medical treatments, are very pronounced in the United States. There are, for example, far longer average lengths of hospital stay in the northeast than on the west coast, primarily because of variations in physician practice patterns and the fiscal incentives inherent in third-party reimbursement. These differences are expected to narrow as managed care plans insist that providers follow more rigid treatment protocols.

An analysis was undertaken of 1993 U.S. hospital discharge costs and related data of the 15 states with the highest percentage of HMO market penetration.[150] Interestingly, a lesser number of paid hours was more critical in reducing average expense per discharge than whether the hospital was located in a competitive or a regulated environment. What is obvious, but sometimes overlooked, is that for an integrated delivery system to be able to enhance its bottom line, the network's management must focus on becoming productive by simply finding ways to reduce man-hours per adjusted discharge.

What might be the preferred multipayer approach, since it focuses concurrently on controlling utilization and cost, is for health networks to encourage the formation of an enlightened private-public partnership in which both parties concentrate on what they do best. Thus, the private sector, with the virtues of the competitive model, would bear principal responsibility for curtailing unnecessary utilization and improving overall efficiency, whereas the regulatory focus of government would be to curtail total health expenditures and insure access and social equity. Such a blended strategy might be more conducive to many issues facing the health networks than either a total government takeover, as with a national health insurance plan, or a purely market-driven approach that has already led to having more uninsured Americans and can more easily encourage fraud and abuse.

Global Budgetary Targets by State and by Health Sector

Typically, the primary objective of global budgetary targets is to establish a desired level of spending through various regulatory controls over insurers and providers. A number of models have been proposed: (1) global fees (i.e., total reimbursement by diagnosis, adjusted by age and severity, for a comprehensive range of health services);[151] (2) global budget targets with all-payer rate-setting, with premium regulation or with managed competition;[152] and (3) a global budget process, structured around a competitive, multipayer approach that allows the region's total health expenditures to be arrived at on the basis of market conditions rather than by some statutory authority.[153]

Global Fees
Using global fees would be the option most consistent with the Medicare diagnostic-related group reimbursement methodology and would require

the health networks to negotiate dividing the global revenues among physicians, hospitals, and other providers. Such an approach raises a number of issues such as (1) the ability of the official agencies to construct a valid and reliable prepayment methodology by diagnosis, age, severity, and other pertinent factors related to the patient care resources required; (2) the increased cost of installing and operating more sophisticated information systems to keep track of such a payment system; and (3) the potential "cherry picking" by providers of patients with a favorable versus unfavorable illness and disability, based on the reimbursement provided for a specific perspective global fee. It is also doubtful whether this option would provide a sufficiently powerful incentive for integrated health systems to centralize tertiary services or allow them to significantly reduce administrative, business office, and related positions.

Global Budgetary Targets

Having less appeal to the leadership of the nation's health networks would be for the government to implement global budgetary targets with an all-payer rating setting, with premium regulation, or with managed competition, a concept used in almost every Western industrialized nation[66-67] and which has some precedence in the United States. The most visible current examples include the Medicare and Medicaid HMOs, where insured persons obtain a voucher (coverage) to obtain specific benefits.

A total global budgetary amount for an integrated health system could then be arrived at theoretically by multiplying the number of persons in its service area with a specific voucher (those insured) times the reimbursement rate for each voucher. Public officials could tweak the incentives contained in these global budgetary target arrangements to include as part of their long-term strategy the objectives of simultaneously expanding access to medical care, improving social equity, controlling healthcare costs, and enhancing quality of patient care.

Trends such as the potential rebirth during the next decade of the capitated payment reimbursement methodology as a means to constrain health costs, the lump-sum payments made by the federal government to the states to provide Medicaid and eventually other health benefits, and the impact of an almost inevitable major economic downturn in the United States during the next decade could in toto easily set the stage for a global budgetary approach to financing our nation's health services. Interestingly, these elements tied together could some time in the future provide the major ingredients of the "back door" approach to global budgetary targets used by almost all other industrialized nations, closely paralleling the German multipayer approach.[154] Such an outcome would surprise supporters of the market-driven strategies to organize health services.

Global budgetary targets are not without some significant drawbacks: how to set the total dollar ceiling for health expenditures, a given when utilizing this approach; how to insure that patients will receive necessary and quality medical care; how to appropriately reimburse providers; how to achieve the appropriate balance among the rights of various consumers and providers; and how to determine the extent of governmental control that is needed over the actual delivery of health services (e.g., establishing national protocols of care by diagnosis, to reduce resource allocation and to improve quality of care).

Although expenditure caps and targets function well in constraining health costs throughout the industrialized world,[155] this option's aggressive regulatory overtones at this time are simply too politically contentious to be applied in the United States.

Global Budget Process
A possible option exists to implement a blended competitive-regulatory, more patient-provider friendly approach. A global budget process could conceivably be structured on a state basis that would enhance access to healthcare and promote social equity, using multipayers (managed care plans), a capitated payment reimbursement methodology, price and quality competition among integrated health systems for prospective subscribers (patients), and the determination of the region's total health expenditures on the basis of market conditions (competitive bids). Such a market-driven process could be implemented with minimal government oversight, by relying on HMOs and other insurers to negotiate with employers and public officials the cost (premium) for specific coverage, and with providers concerning the capitated payment amount necessary to provide specific benefits.

An example of such an approach with a single payer is the Arizona Health Care Cost Containment System (AHCCCS), a government-sponsored model for allocating health services across multiple providers for those covered by Medicaid and for employees of small companies (chap. 7). All Medicaid-eligible are required to obtain health benefits from managed care plans selected in a competitive bidding process, while insurers are paid by the state on a capitated payment basis. This plan guarantees consumer choice across a broad range of providers (except in rural areas) and offers fiscal incentives for hospitals and physicians to provide quality care and at the same time to be highly efficient.[156–57]

Arizona has achieved with AHCCCS both lower costs and improved accessibility of services to needy persons. It has also established a global budget process that allows the cost of benefits to be arrived at from the bottom up rather than promulgated from the top down by a state statutory authority. Health networks can readily improve their bottom lines by effecting operating economies such as shuttering underutilized facilities and programs, and centralizing sophisticated services, as long as they are able to satisfy the needs of a majority of their subscribers (i.e., so they only experience a few disenrollees). Although now losing favor nationally to point of service contracts, the capitated payment reimbursement methodology with relatively simple, valid, and reliable severity adjustments, should allow providers and insurers to employ far fewer managerial and business office–type personnel.

The global budget process, too, has its serious drawbacks: a major concern is that the cumulative dollar amount for health services of the low bidders may still end up being greater than what major corporations, smaller employers, and public agencies can afford or at least are willing to spend for health insurance benefits. Also, how do you avoid the issue of a hospital, the only one in the region and part of a health network, suggesting to its central office that it submit a bid (capitated payment) to provide benefits for its area residents at a price significantly above facilities in other similar areas providing roughly the same range of services? In addition, methods for health networks to predict insurance risks must be retooled to prevent "cream skimming," and discriminating against the sick, to reduce stinting (undercare), and to reward quality providers.

There are other issues with the global budget process: Are providers willing to assume the fiscal risk related to capitated payment? If so, how do you divide a capitated payment arrived at by a global budget process equitably and amicably among hospitals, physicians, and other providers within a large and complex health network?[158–59] Patients traditionally have trusted their physicians to act in their best interests in matters relating to their health and overall well-being.[160] If, however, physicians are reimbursed on the basis of a capitated payment and profiled by an insurer on their utilization of services: how can patients be assured that with these fiscal incentives, they will receive adequate care?, and how can participating doctors be assured that high-cost utilizers will not be excluded from the plan's eligible panel after the next contract negotiations occur?

Since mergers have already led to price increases at hospitals that have amalgamated as well as among their competitors (even when those have a not-for-profit or government sponsorship),[161] providers in the next decade could simply be expected to raise their bids (prices) as they exploit their market power. Thus, if a global budget process or similar approach is implemented, the leadership of health networks should anticipate that federal and state antitrust regulators eventually will become more diligent.[162]

What makes the global budget process so attractive is that it establishes total expenditures through a flexible interaction of supply (providers) and demand (consumers). Moreover, if a health network obtains a majority of its revenues in a lump-sum payment through a global budget process, its governing board would have far more discretion in allocating available resources on the basis of community need rather than what might enhance the organization's bottom line. In the long term, health networks should find this approach preferable to the current circumstances in the United States where expenditures are driven primarily by supplier costs. Finally, for providers and insurers a global budget process is certainly far superior to being controlled and dictated to almost solely by a government agency, with respect to the supply of services made available and to the placing of a "lid" on operating expenditures, which is often experienced abroad with top down global expenditure limits.

Future Outlook for Health Networks

There are blended competitive and regulatory approaches available, for example, the global budget process, through which health networks could potentially enhance access, social equity, and quality, and reduce health costs. Therefore, a national health insurance program with universal access and global budgetary targets such as is the pattern in Canada and western and central European countries should not be expected to be forthcoming in the United States for at least a decade. The reasons for this conclusion are that for the government to be solely responsible for health is alien to American values and culture; and, more important, that some workable quasi-private, quasi-public alternatives already exist for averting an almost exclusively regulatory-oriented solution.

The idea that health networks will play a major role in advocating an affordable, multipayer, universal comprehensive health insurance plan with something similar to a global budget process is not now nor in the foreseeable future to be anticipated. This view could be explained in terms of the health networks' governing board, medical staff leadership, and management teams over the last several decades demonstrating limited interest in being the driving force to reshape the U.S. health delivery system. The health systems and networks have instead tended to react to rather than to originate specific reform proposals. This is primarily because the major trade organizations in the health field represent such a diverse constituency, all with strong vested interests. A proposal favored by the urban teaching hospitals and physicians usually causes difficulties for the nation's small rural facilities and their physicians. There are often impediments in gaining consensus between not-for-profit and investor-owned health systems on any significant changes in reimbursement.

More realistically, health networks and their management teams will try to continue business as usual, while at the same time enhancing their "strategic fit"; will be forced to implement more cost-cutting measures, as they become less effective in bargaining with managed care plans and with various federal and state third-party payers; will position themselves when possible so they can behave as oligopolists; and, if a serious recession occurs, may reluctantly agree to something similar to a global budget process, since this makes more sense and is less threatening than the Canadian-European regulatory approaches. If this scenario for health networks is reasonably correct, it is predicted that the poor may find it increasingly difficult to gain access to care, because providers will be more fiscally constrained; the middle class will depend on managed care, with fewer choices of providers and with the capitated payment being determined by a global budget process or something similar; and the wealthy will continue to use and pay for health services as in the past and will reluctantly support the status quo.

The answer to the question of whether health networks, which are becoming fiscally and politically powerful oligopolies in every metropolitan area, *will* be the solution to the problem of access, social equity, and quality, and succeed in reducing cost, unfortunately, has to be no. If some of the precepts outlined earlier in this book were to be carefully followed, what might evolve is a quasi-private, quasi-public approach to the delivery of health services that is somewhat more responsive to the country's disenfranchised and would more effectively use for healthcare the correct percentage of GDP.

As long as the U.S. economy flourishes the way it did during the 1990s, no significant changes in the organization, management, and financing of health services and the health networks can be envisioned. More simply stated, there are reasons to believe that health networks can make some kind of difference, but right now and in the foreseeable future they are not expected to make nearly enough.

REFERENCES

1. Burner, S. T., and Waldo, D. R. "National Health Expenditure Projections, 1994–2005." *Health Care Financing Review* 16, no. 4 (1995): 221–42.
2. Vistnes, J. P., and Zuvekas, S. H. "Health Insurance Status of the Civilian Noninstitutional Population, 1997." Report AHCPR No. 99-0030. Rockville, Md.: Agency for Health Care Policy and Research, 1999.

3. Perkins, B. B. "Economic Organization of Medicine and the Committee on the Costs of Medical Care." *American Journal of Public Health* 88, no. 11 (1998): 1721–26.

4. The Center for Evaluation of Clinical Services. *The Dartmouth Atlas of Health Care, 1998.* New York: Oxford University Press, 1998.

5. Zuckerman, H. S. "Multi-Institutional Systems: Promise and Performance." *Inquiry* 16, no. 4 (1979): 291–314.

6. Connor, R. A., Feldman, R., Dowd, B. E., and Radcliff, T. A. "Which Types of Hospital Mergers Save Consumers Money?" *Health Affairs* 16, no. 6 (1997): 62–74.

7. Clement, J. P., McCue, M. J., Luke, R. D., Bramble, J. D., Rossiter, L. F., Ozcan, Y. A., and Pai, C. W. "Strategic Hospital Alliances: Impact on Financial Performance." *Health Affairs* 16, no. 6 (1997): 192–203.

8. Shortell, S. M. "The Evolution of Hospital Systems: Unfulfilled Promises and Self-Fulfilling Prophesies." *Medical Care Review* 45, no. 2 (1988): 177–214.

9. Bogue, R. J., Feldman, R., Dowd, B. E., and Radcliff, T. A. "Which Types of Hospital Mergers Save Consumers Money?" *Health Affairs* 16, no. 6 (1997): 62–74.

10. Alexander, J. A., Halpern, M. T., and Lee, S.-Y. D. "The Short-Term Effects of Merger on Hospital Operations." *Health Services Research* 30, no. 6 (1996): 827–47.

11. Ermann, D., and Gabel, J. "Multihospital Systems: Issues and Empirical Findings." *Health Affairs* 3, no. 1 (1984): 50–64.

12. Wholey, D. R., Feldman, R., and Christianson, J. B. "The Effect of Market Structure on HMO Premiums." *Journal of Health Economics* 14, no. 1 (1995): 81–105.

13. Feldman, R. "The Welfare Economics of a Health Plan Merger." *Journal of Regulatory Economics* 6, no. 1 (1994): 67–86.

14. Feldman, R., Wholey, D. R., and Christianson, J. B. "Effect of Mergers on Health Maintenance Organization Premiums." *Health Care Financing Review* 17, no. 3 (1996): 171–89.

15. Scherer, F. M., and Ross, D. *Industrial Market Structure and Economic Performance.* Boston: Houghton Mifflin, 1990.

16. Gunn, E. P. "Premium Prices." *Fortune* 139, no. 2 (1999): 99–102.

17. Stewart, J. F., and Kim, S.-K. "Merger and Social Welfare in U.S. Manufacturing, 1985–86." *Southern Economic Journal* 59, no. 4 (1993): 701–20.

18. Jansen, M. C. "The Takeover Controversy: Analysis and Evidence." In Coffee, J. C., Jr., Lowenstein, L., and Ackerman, S. R., eds. *Knights, Raiders and Targets: The Impact of the Hostile Takeover.* Cambridge: Oxford University Press, 1988.

19. Weil, T. P. "Is Vertical Integration Adding Value to Health Systems?" *Managed Care Interface* 13, no. 4 (2000): 57–62.

20. Clement, J. P., D'Anunno, T., and Poyzer, B. L. M. "The Financial Performance of Diversified Hospital Subsidiaries." *Health Services Research* 27, no. 6 (1993): 741–63.

21. Cody, M. "Vertical Integration Strategies: Revenue Effects in Hospital and Medical Markets." *Hospital and Health Services Administration* 41, no. 3 (1996): 343–57.

22. Health Care Advisory Board. "American Healthcare 1997 State of the Union." Washington, D.C., 1997, 37.

23. Hill, J., and Wild, J. "Survey Profiles Data on Practice Acquisition Activity." *Healthcare Financial Management* 49, no. 9 (1995): 54–60.

24. Finders, G. "Hospitals That Gobbled Up Physician Practices Fell Ill." *Wall Street Journal* 17 (June 17, 1997): B4 BE(W).

25. Rauber, C. "Market Deflates for Provider-Owned HMOs." *Modern Healthcare* 29, no. 24 (1999): 34–46.

26. D'Aveni, R., and Ravenscraft, D. J. "Economies of Integration versus Bureaucracy Costs: Does Vertical Integration Improve Performance?" *Academy of Management Journal* 37, no. 5 (1994): 1167–1206.

27. Stuckey, J., and White, D. "When and When Not to Vertically Integrate." *Sloan Management Review* 34, no. 3 (1993): 71–83.

28. Iglehart, J. K. "Health Care Reform and Graduate Medical Education." *New England Journal of Medicine* 330, no. 16 (1994): 1167–71.

29. Cullen, T. J., Hart, L. G., Whitcomb, M. E., and Rosenblatt, R. H. "The National Health Services Corps: Rural Physician Service and Retention." *Journal of the American Board of Family Practice* 10, no. 4 (1997): 272–79.

30. Pathman, D. E., and Konrad, T. R. "Minority Physicians Serving in Rural National Health Service Corps Sites." *Medical Care* 34, no. 5 (1996): 439–54.

31. Iglehart, J. K. "The Quandary over Graduates of Foreign Medical Schools in the United States." *New England Journal of Medicine* 333, no. 25 (1996): 1679–83.

32. Nadel, M. V. "Rural Health Clinics Rising Program Expenditures Not Focused on Improving Care in Isolated Areas." Report GAO/HESS-97-24. Washington, D.C.: U.S. General Accounting Office, 1996.

33. Kongstvedt, P. R. *The Managed Health Care Handbook.* 3d ed. Gaithersburg, Md.: Aspen Publishers, 1996.

34. Coulam, R. F., Irvin, C. V., Calore, K. A., Kidder, D. E., and Rosenbach, M. L. "Managing Access: Extending Medicaid to Children through School-Based HMO Coverage." *Health Care Financing Review* 18, no. 3 (1997): 149–75.

35. Silverstein, G., and Kirkman-Liff, B. "Physician Participation in Medicaid Managed Care." *Social Science in Medicine* 334, no. 17 (1995): 355–63.

36. Iglehart, J. K. "Medicaid and Managed Care: The Evolution of Medicaid and Managed Care." *New England Journal of Medicine* 332, no. 25 (1995): 1727–31.

37. Adams, E. K. "Effect of Increased Medicaid Fees on Physician Participation and Enrollee Service Utilization in Tennessee, 1985–1988." *Inquiry* 31, no. 2 (1995): 173–87.

38. Fanning, T., and de Alteriss, M. "The Limits of Margin Economic Incentives in the Medicaid Program: Concerns and Cautions." *Journal of Health Politics, Policy and Law* 18, no. 1 (1993): 27–42.

39. Fox, M. H., Weiner, J. P., and Phua, K. "Effect of Medicaid Payment Levels on Obstetrical Care." *Health Affairs* 11, no. 4 (1992): 150–61.

40. Ellinger, J. "The Little Engine That Could and Slowly Will: A Bureaucrat's View." *Frontiers of Health Services Management* 14, no. 4 (1998): 27–30.

41. Carrasquillo, O., Himmelstein, D. U., Woolhandler, S., and Bor, D. H. "Can Medicaid Managed Care Provide Continuity of Care to New Medicaid Enrollees? An Analysis of Tenure on Medicaid." *American Journal of Public Health* 88, no. 3 (1998): 464–66.

42. Hurley, R. "From Trickle Down to Paying Off: Making Money Talk." *Frontiers of Health Services Management* 15, no. 2 (1998): 29–32.

43. American Hospital Association. "Consumer Price Index." *AHA News* 35, no. 46 (1999): 3.

44. Hellinger, F. J. "The Effect of Managed Care on Quality: A Review of Recent Evidence." *Archives of Internal Medicine* 158, no. 8 (1998): 833–41.

45. Himmelstein, D. U., Woolhandler, S., Hollander, I., and Wolfe, S. M. "Quality of Care in Investor-Owned versus Not-for-Profit HMOs." *Journal of the American Medical Association* 282, no. 3 (1999): 159–63.

46. Weil, T. P. "Managed Care and Cost Reductions for Entitlements." *Managed Care Quarterly* 4, no. 4 (1996): 58–67.

47. "America's Best Hospitals." *U.S. News and World Report* 124, no. 4 (July 27, 1998): 65–91.

48. HCIA, Inc., and William W. Mercer, Inc. "One Hundred Top Hospitals: Benchmarks for Success, 1998." Chicago and Baltimore, 1999.

49. Bellandi, D., and Kirchheimer, B. "Multi-Unit Providers Survey: For-Profits Report Decline in Acute Hospitals." *Modern Healthcare* 29, no. 21 (1999): 23–36.

50. Serb, C. "The Health Care 250." *Hospital and Health Networks* 73, no. 4 (1999): 38–48.

51. Gray, B. H. *For-Profit Enterprises in Health Care,* 182–208. Washington, D.C.: National Academy Press, 1986.

52. Woolhandler, S., and Himmelstein, D. U. "When Money Is the Mission—The High Costs of Investor-Owned Care." *New England Journal of Medicine* 341, no. 6 (1999): 444–46.

53. Rice, T. "Containing Health Care Costs in the United States." *Medical Care Review* 49, no. 1 (1992): 19–65.

54. Jencks, S. F., and Schieber, G. J. "Containing U.S. Health Care Costs: What Bullet to Bite?" *Health Care Financing Review,* annual supplement (1991): 1–12.

55. Blendon, R. J., Edwards, J. N., and Hyams, A. L. "Making the Critical Choices." *Journal of the American Medical Association* 267, no. 18 (1992): 2509–20.

56. Weil, T. P. "Comparisons of Medical Technology in Canadian, German, and U.S. Hospitals." *Hospital and Health Services Administration* 40, no. 4 (1995): 525–34.

57. Levey, S., and Hill, J. "National Health Insurance—The Triumph of Equivocation." *New England Journal of Medicine* 321, no. 25 (1989): 1750–54.

58. Kinzer, D. M. "Universal Entitlement to Health Care: Can We Get from Here to There?" *New England Journal of Medicine* 322, no. 7 (1990): 467–70.

59. Butler, S. M. "A Tax Reform Strategy to Deal with the Uninsured." *Journal of the American Medical Association* 265, no. 19 (1991): 2541–44.

60. Shortell, S. M., and McNerney, W. J. "Criteria and Guidelines for Reforming the U.S. Health Care System." *New England Journal of Medicine* 322, no. 7 (1990): 463–67.

61. Rockfeller, J. D., IV. "The Pepper Commission's Blueprint for Health Reform." *Journal of the American Medical Association* 165, no. 19 (1991): 2507–10.

62. Clinton, B. "The Clinton Health Care Plan." *New England Journal of Medicine* 327, no. 11 (1992): 804–7.

63. Enthoven, A., and Kronick, R. "A Consumer-Choice Health Plan for the 1990s: Universal Health Insurance in a System Desired to Promote Quality and Economy." *New England Journal of Medicine* 320, no. 1 (1989): 29–37.

64. Sullivan, L. W. "The Bush Administration's Health Care Plan." *New England Journal of Medicine* 327, no. 11 (1992): 801–4.

65. Todd, J., Seekins, S. V., Kirchbaum, J. A., and Harvey, L. K. "Health Access America—Strengthening the U.S. Health Care System." *Journal of the American Medical Association* 265, no. 19 (1991): 2503–6.

66. Hurst, J. W. "Reforming Health Care in Seven European Nations." *Health Affairs* 10, no. 3 (1991): 7–21.

67. Pfaff, M. "Differences in Health Care Spending across Countries: Statistical Evidence." *Journal of Health Politics, Policy and Law* 15, no. 1 (1990): 1–68.

68. Anderson, G. F., and Poullier, J.-P. "Health Spending, Access, and Outcomes: Trends in Industrialized Nations." *Health Affairs* 18, no. 3 (1999): 178–92.

69. Keller, M. *Regulating a New Economy: Public Policy and Economic Change in America, 1990–1933.* Cambridge, Mass.: Harvard University Press, 1990.

70. Krislov, S., and Musolf, L. D. *The Politics of Regulation.* Boston: Houghton Mifflin, 1964.

71. Anderson, O. W. *Health Services in the United States: A Growth Enterprise since 1875.* Ann Arbor: Health Administration Press, 1985.

72. Eby, C. L., and Cohodes, D. R. "What Do We Know about Rate Setting?" *Journal of Health Politics, Policy and Law* 10, no. 2 (1985): 299–336.

73. Salkever, D. S., and Bice, T. W. *The Hospital Certificate of Need Controls: Impact on Investment, Costs, and Use.* Washington, D.C.: American Enterprise Institute for Policy Research, 1979.

74. Jorgensen, N. E., and Weil, T. P. "Regulating Managed Care Plans: Is the Telecommunications Industry a Possible Model?" *Managed Care Quarterly* 6, no. 3 (1998): 7–16.

75. Oslin, G. P. *The Story of Telecommunications.* Macon, Ga.: Mercer University Press, 1992.

76. Bell, T. W., and Singleton, S. *Regulators' Revenge: The Future of Telecommunications Deregulation.* Washington, D.C.: Cato Institute, 1998.

77. Weil, T. P. "Public Disclosure in the Health Field: Why Not a SEC-Type Commission?" *American Journal of Medical Quality.* 16, no. 1 (2001): 23–33.

78. Waxler, C. "A Nasty Conglomerate." *Forbes* 162, no. 11 (1998): 55–56.

79. Goldsmith, J. "Columbia/HCA: A Failure of Leadership." *Health Affairs* 17, no. 2 (1998): 27–29.

80. www.sec.gov/asec/asecart.htm provides a discussion on what the U.S. Securities and Exchange Commission is and what it does.

81. Institute of Medicine (IOM) of the National Academies. *To Err Is Human: Building a Safer Health System.* Washington, D.C.: IOM, 1999.

82. Borowksy, S. J., Goertz, C., and Laurie, N. "Can Physicians Diagnose Strengths and Weaknesses in Health Plans?" *Annals of Internal Medicine* 125, no. 3 (1996): 239–41.

83. Foundation for Accountability. *Accountability Action* 1, no. 1 (Fall 1996).

84. General Accounting Office. "Report Cards Are Useful but Significant Issues Need to Be Addressed." Report GAO/HEHS 94-219. Washington, D.C.: Government Printing Office, 1994.

85. Berwick, D. M., and Wald, D. L. "Hospital Leaders' Opinion of the HCFA Mortality Data." *Journal of the American Medical Association* 263, no. 2 (1990): 247–49.

86. Luce, J. M., Thiel, G. D., Holland, M. R., Swig, L., Curring, S. A., and Luft, H. S. "Use of Risk-Adjusted Outcome for Data for Quality Improvement by Public Hospitals." *Western Journal of Medicine* 164, no. 5 (1996): 410–44.

87. Robinson, S., and Brodie, M. "Understanding the Quality Challenge for Health Consumers: The Kaiser/AHCPR Survey." *Joint Commission Journal on Quality Improvement* 23, no. 5 (1997): 239–44.

88. Romano, P. S., Rainwater, J. A., and Antonius, D. "Grading the Graders: How Hospitals in California and New York Perceive and Interpret Their Report Cards." *Medical Care* 37, no. 3 (1999): 295–305.

89. Schneider, E., and Epstein, A. M. "Public Use of Public Performance Reports: A Survey of Patients Undergoing Cardiac Surgery." *Journal of the American Medical Association* 279, no. 20 (1998): 1638–42.

90. Bentley, J. M., and Nash, D. B. "How Pennsylvania Hospitals Have Responded to Publicly Released Reports on Coronary Artery Bypass Graft Surgery." *Joint Commission Journal on Quality Improvement* 24, no. 1 (1998): 40–49.

91. Longo, D. R., Land, G., Schramm, W., Frass, J., Hoskins, B., and Howell, V. "Consumer Reports in Health Care: Do They Make a Difference in Patient Care?" *Journal of the American Medical Association* 278, no. 19 (1997): 1579–84.

92. Steinfels, P. *The Neoconservatives: The Men Who Are Changing America's Politics.* New York: Simon and Schuster, 1979.

93. Battistella, R. M. "Health Services Reforms: Political and Managerial Aims—An International Perspective." *International Journal of Health Planning and Management* 8, no. 3 (1993): 265–74.

94. Wallack, S. S., Skwara, K. C., and Cao, K. "Redefining Rate Regulations in a Competitive Environment." *Journal of Health Politics, Policy and Law* 21, no. 3 (1996): 489–510.

95. Donelan, K., Blendon, R. J., Schoen, C., Davis, K., and Binns, K. "The

Cost of Health System Change: Public Discontent in Five Nations." *Health Affairs* 18, no. 3 (1999): 206–16.

96. Weil, P. A. "High Hospital CEO Turnover Continues." *Healthcare Executive* 14, no. 4 (1999): 34.

97. Yedidia, M. J. "Challenges to Effective Medical School Leadership: Perspectives of 22 Current and Former Deans." *Academic Medicine* 73, no. 6 (1998): 631–39.

98. Weil, T. P. "Health Services Management Manpower and Educational Needs with American Health Reform." *Health Services Management Research* 9, no. 2 (1996): 79–89.

99. Shortell, S. M., Giles, R. R., Anderson, D. A., Erickson, K. M., and Mitchell, J. B. *Remaking Healthcare in America: Building Organized Delivery Systems.* San Francisco: Jossey Bass, 1996.

100. Zuckerman, H. S., and Kuluzny, A. D. "The Management of Strategic Alliances in Health Services." *Frontiers of Health Services Management* 7, no. 3 (1991): 3–23.

101. Conrad, D. A., and Shortell, S. M. "Integrated Health Systems: Promise and Performance." *Frontiers of Health Services Management* 13, no. 1 (1997): 3–35.

102. Brown, M. "Multihospital Systems: Trends, Issues, and Prospects." In Becker, G. E., Jr., ed. *Multihospital Systems: Policy Issues for the Future,* 1–21. Chicago: Hospital Research and Trust, 1981.

103. Bogue, R. J., Shortell, S. M., Sohn, M.-W., Manheim, L. M., Bazzoli, G., and Chan, C. "Hospital Reorganization after Merger." *Medical Care* 33, no. 7 (1995) 676–86.

104. Lynk, W. J. "The Creation of Economic Efficiencies in Hospital Mergers." *Journal of Health Economics* 14, no. 5 (1995): 507–30.

105. Mullner, R. M., and Andersen, R. M. "A Descriptive and Financial Ratio Analysis of Merged and Consolidated Hospitals: United States, 1980–85." *Health Services Research* 7, no. 1 (1987): 41–58.

106. Robinson, J. C., and Casolino, J. P. "Vertical Integration and Organizational Networks on Health Care." *Health Affairs* 15, no. 1 (1996): 7–22.

107. Robinson, J. C. "Administered Pricing and Vertical Integration in the Hospital Industry." *Journal of Law and Economics* 39, no. 1 (1996): 357–78.

108. Walston, S. L., Kimberly, J. R., and Burns, L. R. "Owned Vertical Integration and Health Care: Promise and Performance." *Health Care Management Review* 21, no. 1 (1996): 82–92.

109. Coddington, D. C., Moore, K. D., and Fisher, E. A. "Vertical Integration: Is the Bloom Off the Rose?" *Healthcare Forum Journal* 39, no. 5 (1996): 42–47.

110. Zuckerman, H. S., Hilberman, D. W., Andersen, R. M., Burns, L. R., Alexander, J. A., and Torrens, P. "Physicians and Organizations: Strange Bedfellows or a Marriage Made in Heaven?" *Frontiers of Health Services Management* 14, no. 3 (1998): 3–34.

111. Zismer, D. K., and Lund, D. E. *Health System Sponsored Primary Care Networks: Achieving Best Practice Financial Performance.* Chicago: Towers Perrin, 1998.

112. Burns, L. R., and Robinson, J. C. "Physician Practice Management Companies: Implications for Hospital-Based Integrated Delivery Systems." *Frontiers of Health Services Management* 14, no. 2 (1997): 3–30.

113. Milbank Memorial Fund. *New Foundations in Health: Six Stories.* New York: Milbank Memorial Fund, 1999.

114. Brooks, G. R., and Jones, V. G. "Hospital Mergers and Market Overlap." *Health Services Research* 31, no. 6 (1997): 701–22.

115. Pauly, M. V. "Managed Care, Market Power, and Monopsony." *Health Services Research* 33, no. 5, pt. 2 (1998): 1439–60.

116. DiPaolo, V. "16 Large Jewish Hospitals Form a Group Purchasing Consortium." *Modern Healthcare* 9, no. 11 (1979): 12–13.

117. Graham, J. "Consortium of Jewish Hospitals Plans National Hospital Alliance." *Modern Healthcare* 15, no. 24 (1985): 40.

118. Battistella, R. M., Begun, J. W., and Buchanan, R. J. "The Political Economy of Health Services: A Review of Major Ideological Influences." In Litman, T., and Robins, L. S. *Health Policy and Politics,* 66–92. 2d ed. Albany: Delmar Publishers, 1991.

119. Starr, P. *The Social Transformation of American Medicine,* 243–54. New York: Basic Books, 1982.

120. Stevens, Rosemary. *American Medicine and the Public Interest.* New Haven: Yale University Press, 1971.

121. Weil, T. P., and Battistella, R. M. "A Blended Strategy Using Competitive and Regulatory Models." *Health Care Management Review* 23, no. 1 (1997): 37–45.

122. Ernst and Young, "PHOs: Physician Hospital Organizations—Profile 1995." Washington, D.C.: Ernst and Young, 1995.

123. Project HOPE. "Hospital-Physician Relations: A Multivariate Analysis of Hospital Financial Performance." Extramural Report E-96-02. Washington, D.C.: Prospective Payment Assessment Commission, 1996.

124. Goes, J. B., and Zhan, C. L. "The Effects of Hospital Physician Integration Strategies on Hospital Financial Performance." *Health Services Research* 30, no. 4 (1995): 507–30.

125. Mick, S. S., Morlock, L. L., Salkever, D. S., deLissovoy, G., Malita, F. E., Wise, C. C., and Jones, A. S. "Horizontal and Vertical Diversification in Rural Hospitals: A National Study of Strategic Activity, 1983–1988." *Journal of Rural Health* 9, no. 2 (1993): 99–119.

126. Weil, T. P. "Comparisons of Medical Technology in Canadian, German, and U.S. Hospitals." *Hospital and Health Services Administration* 40, no. 4 (1995): 524–34.

127. Ross, L. L., Fisher, E. S., Sharp, S., Newhouse, J. P., Anderson, G., and Bubolz, T. A. "PostSurgical Mortality in Manitoba and New England." *Journal of the American Medical Association* 263, no. 18 (1990): 2453–58.

128. Weil, T. P. "Health Reform in Germany: An American Assesses the New Operating Efficiencies." *Health Progress* 75, no. 7 (1994): 24–29.

129. Weil, T. P., and Hunt, R. S. "Canadians Write a New Rx for Health Care Reform." *Health Progress* 75, no. 7 (1994): 32–40.

130. Fuchs, V. R., and Hahn, J. S. "How Does Canada Do It? A Comparison of Expenditures for Physician Services in the United States and Canada." *New England Journal of Medicine* 323, no. 13 (1990): 884–90.

131. Schieber, G. J., Poullier, J.-P., and Greenwald, L. M. "Health Spending, Delivery, and Outcomes in OECD Countries." *Health Affairs* 12, no. 2 (1993): 120–29.

132. Iglehart, J. K. "German Health Care System: Parts I and II." *New England Journal of Medicine* 324, no. 7 (1991): 503–8; and 324, no. 24 (1991): 1750–56.

133. Redelmeier, D. A., and Fuchs, V. R. "Hospital Expenditures in the United States and Canada." *New England Journal of Medicine* 328, no. 11 (1993): 772–78.

134. Himmelstein, D. U., Lewontin, J. P., and Woolhandler, S. "Who Administers? Who Cares? Administrative and Clinical Employed in the United States and Canada." *American Journal of Public Health* 86, no. 2 (1996): 172–78.

135. Poisal, J. A., Murray, L. A., Chulis, G. S., and Cooper, B. S. "Prescription Drug Coverage and Spending for Medicare Beneficiaries." *Health Care Financing Review* 20, no. 3 (1999): 15–27.

136. Weiner, J. P., Lyles, A., Steinwachs, D. M., and Hall, K. C. "Impact of Managed Care on Prescription Drug Use." *Health Affairs* 10, no. 1 (1991): 140–54.

137. Hillman, A. L., Pauly, M. V., Escarece, J. J., Ripley, K., Gaynor, M., Clouse, J., and Ross, R. "Financial Incentives and Drug Spending in Managed Care." *Health Affairs* 18, no. 2 (1999): 189–200.

138. Lyles, A., and Palumbo, F. B. "The Effect of Managed Care on Prescription Drug Costs and Benefits." *Pharmacoeconomics* 15, no. 2 (1999): 129–40.

139. Harris, B. L., Stergachis, A., and Ried, L. D. "The Effect of Drug Co-Payments on Utilization and Cost of Pharmaceuticals in a Health Maintenance Organization." *Medical Care* 28, no. 10 (1990): 907–17.

140. Gondek, K. "Prescription Drug Payment Policy: Past, Present, and Future." *Health Care Financing Review* 15, no. 3 (1994): 1–7.

141. Gross, D. J., Ratner, J., Perez, B., and Glavin, S. L. "International Pharmaceutical Spending Controls: France, Germany, Sweden, and the United Kingdom." *Health Care Financing Review* 15, no. 3 (1994): 127–40.

142. Weil, T. P. "A Cost Comparison of Canadian and U.S. Hospital Pharmacy Departments." *Hospital Pharmacy* 29, no. 1 (1994): 15–23.

143. Shikles, J. L. "Prescription Drug Prices: Analysis of Canada's Patent Medicine Review Board." HED-93-51. Washington, D.C.: Government Accounting Office, 1993.

144. Huttin, C. "Drug Price Divergence in Europe: Regulatory Aspects." *Health Affairs* 18, no. 3 (1999): 245–49.

145. Abernethy, D. S., and Pearson, D. A. *Regulating Hospital Costs: The Development of Public Policy.* Ann Arbor: AUPHA Press, 1979.

146. Coulam, R. F., Irvin, C. V., Calore, K. A., Kidder, D. E., and Rosenbach, M. L. "Managing Access: Expending Medicaid to Children through School-Based HMO Coverage." *Health Care Financing Review* 18, no. 3 (1997): 149–75.

147. Weil, T. P. "The Blending of Competitive and Regulatory Strategies: A Second Opinion." *Journal of Health Care Finance* 23, no. 2 (1996): 45–46.

148. Stigler, G. E. "The Theory of Economic Regulation." *Bell Journal of Economic Management* 2, no. 1 (1971): 20–21.

149. Bernstein, M. H. *Regulation of Business by Independent Commission.* Princeton: Princeton University Press, 1995.

150. Weil, T. P. "Competition versus Regulation: Constraining Hospital Discharge Costs." *Journal of Health Care Finance* 22, no. 3 (1996): 62–72.

151. Emery, D. W. "Value Based Formulas for Purchasing: PENP's Designated Service Provider Program: Valued Based Purchasing through Global Fees." *Managed Care Quarterly* 5, no. 1 (1997): 64–72.

152. Holahan, J., Blumberg, L. J., and Zuckerman, S. "Strategies for Implementing Global Budgets." *Milbank Quarterly* 73, no. 3 (1994): 399–429.

153. Bishop, C. E., and Wallack, S. S. "National Health Expenditure Limits: The Case for a Global Budget Process." *Milbank Quarterly* 74, no. 3 (1996): 361–76.

154. Weil, T. P. "Managed Care Merged with the German Model." *American Journal of Medical Quality* 12, no. 1 (1997): 19–24.

155. Glaser, W. A. "How Expenditure Caps and Expenditure Target Really Work." *Milbank Quarterly* 71, no. 1 (1993): 97–127.

156. McCall, N., Wrightson, C. W., Paringer, L., and Trapnell, G. "Managed Medicaid Cost Savings: The Arizona Experience." *Health Affairs* 13, no. 2 (1994): 234–45.

157. Paringer, L., and McCall, N. "How Competitive Is Competitive Bidding?" *Health Affairs* 10, no. 4 (1991): 220–30.

158. Barth, S. M. "Integrating Payer and Provider Risks through Capitation." *Managed Care Quarterly* 5, no. 1 (1997): 19–24.

159. Eastaugh, S. R. "Managing Risk in a Risky World." *Journal of Health Care Finance* 25, no. 3 (1999): 10–16.

160. Shortell, S. M., Waters, T. M., Clarke, K. W. B., and Budetti, P. P. "Physicians as Double Agents: Maintain Trust in an Era of Multiple Accountabilities." *Journal of the American Medical Association* 280, no. 12 (1998): 1102–8.

161. Melnick, G., Keeler, K., and Zwanziger, J. "Market Power and Hospital Pricing: Are Nonprofits Different?" *Health Affairs* 18, no. 3 (1999): 167–73.

162. Gifford, B. D. "New Factors in the Antitrust Regulation of Hospital Mergers." *Journal of Healthcare Management* 44, no. 5 (1999): 367–80.

10

America's Jewish-Sponsored Hospitals: An Endangered Species?—A Case Study

ABSTRACT. Immigration, "taking care of one's own," discrimination, and the special place that the medical profession occupies in Jewish culture encouraged by 1975 the establishment of 33 Jewish-sponsored, acute care, general hospitals in the United States. This case study first summarizes what occurred when some of these institutions' original supporters moved to the suburbs and lost interest in their continued existence; it then predicts the future outcome of the Jewish facilities they "left behind." Eight of the original 33 Jewish-sponsored hospitals already have been shuttered as inpatient facilities. Thirteen have "networked" with a Catholic or nonsectarian partner, often the city's dominant and most prestigious health network, either through a corporate merger (3 were acquired by investor-owned groups) or a more loosely designed alliance. The leadership of the remaining 12 freestanding Jewish hospitals, when assessing their future mission, are keenly aware that during the last quarter-century those of the Jewish faith have been assimilated into the mainstream of American society. Therefore, an increasing percentage of them can be identified in key nonsectarian private and public leadership roles. The future of most Jewish hospitals is murky, since many of the original purposes for their early existence may no longer be relevant, and often these facilities are located in areas where they experience intense competition for operating revenues and no existing health network is particularly interested in acquiring and then recapitalizing their physical plant and clinical services.

Jewish hospitals during the century from 1850 to 1950 offered a preferred environment for Jewish immigrants, particularly among those who desired a facility that served Kosher food and followed strict ritual practices. These institutions also afforded a haven for Jewish medical school graduates who sought internship and residency training and later hospital privileges and who often experienced anti-Semitic prejudices elsewhere.[1] During the past quarter-century these facilities have been forced to reassess the reasons for maintaining their original sponsorship, particularly as many people of the Jewish faith have moved to the suburbs and have became more culturally and politically assimilated into the mainstream of American society.

Often isolated from a contentious general public, the Jews of Talmudic times through the nineteenth century built a separate community structure. This isolation is now offering historians interested in Jewish communal healthcare the opportunity to trace its origins as far back as biblical times.[2] The first known Jewish institutions were, as they say in Hebrew, "hekdesh," meaning a small hospice or almshouse for the homeless or indigent sick. Scientific breakthroughs by Pasteur, Koch, Lister, and others in the middle and latter part of the nineteenth century played a critical role in gradually transforming these medieval hospices into modern hospitals, where both poor and wealthy patients were admitted with the expectation of regaining their health and well-being.

Immigration and discrimination are often cited as the principal reasons for the early formation of separate religious and ethnic hospitals in the United States.[3] Initially, these institutions primarily served the poor, as Americans of means received medical care from private physicians in their homes.

Jewish culture and values in the last 150 years have continued to serve as guiding principles when establishing policies for any Jewish-sponsored hospital. These tenets include: "taking care of one's own"; satisfying the fears among Jews of burdening the general public; "giving something back to the community"; emphasizing teaching and research; and serving total community health and social needs whenever possible.[4]

The Formation of Jewish Hospitals

With the primary objective being the care of their ailing indigent poor, Jewish hospitals were established in three waves that roughly correspond to the major influxes of Jewish immigrants into the United States. The first wave occurred in the 1850s, when hospitals were built to accommodate the newly arrived masses of western European Jews. With access to health services restricted by barriers of culture, language, and ability to pay for care, New York City's Mount Sinai Hospital (1855), Philadelphia's Jewish Hospital (1865), Chicago's Michael Reese Hospital (endowed by a German-born real estate tycoon) (1881), and the Jewish Hospital of Cincinnati (1850) were established. The latter facility was North America's first Jewish hospital and was founded before antiseptic or aseptic surgery was known. A majority of U.S. reformed rabbis continue to receive their rabbinical training in Cincinnati.

The second wave of Jewish hospitals occurred near the turn of the twentieth century, when additional facilities were organized to serve the needs of an influx of eastern European Jewish immigrants, who more frequently than those who came earlier adhered to strict Orthodox practices.

Among the hospitals built during this period were New York City's Montefiore (1884) and Beth Israel (1890) Hospitals and Boston's Beth Israel Hospital (1902). These facilities emerged over the next 100 years as among the most innovative in terms of developing meaningful teaching affiliations with medical schools and initiating creative programs and services to meet the health and social needs of the underserved, irrespective of religion or race.

The third wave occurred after World War II and saw the construction of such facilities as Denver's General Maurice Rose Memorial Hospital (1949), Detroit's Sinai Hospital (1953), and Long Island Jewish Hospital (1954), examples of three communities initiating their own Jewish acute care facilities. Somewhat later (1964) a new Jewish medical school was organized that was closely integrated with New York City's Mt. Sinai Medical Center. The creation of the State of Israel, reasonable prosperity, less concern about anti-Semitism, now being in the position of being able to give something back to the community, and solid support for its philanthropic causes gave U.S. Jewish-sponsored hospitals in the 1950s and 1960s a feeling of added vitality.

In 1975 there were 33 Jewish-sponsored acute care, general (including obstetrics) hospitals in the United States (see table 18). By using this definition, a significant number of Jewish specialty hospitals, rehabilitation centers, chronic disease facilities, long-term care, and related institutions are excluded from the analysis.*

---

*A partial listing of Jewish specialty hospitals, rehabilitation centers, chronic disease, long-term care, and related facilities that were excluded from this analysis.

Beth Abraham Health Services, Bronx
Beth Israel Hospital and Geriatric Center, Denver
Bickur Cholim Convalescent and Nursing Home, Pittsburgh
Blythedale Children's Hospital, Valhalla, New York City
Cedars Medical Center, Miami
City of Hope, Durate, Calif.
Deborah Heart and Lung Center, Brown Mills, N.J.
Hebrew Rehabilitation Center for the Aged, Boston
Jewish Chronic Disease Hospital, New York City
Jewish Convalescent Hospital, Cleveland
Jewish Home and Hospital for the Aged, New York City
Jewish Hospital and Rehabilitation Center, Jersey City
Jewish Memorial Hospital, Boston
Kingsbrook Jewish Medical Center, Brooklyn
Moss Rehabilitation Hospital, Philadelphia
National Jewish Hospital and Research Center, Denver
Schwab Rehabilitation Hospital, Chicago
Willow Crest–Banberger Home, Philadelphia
(D. E. Bridges, *The Rise and Development of the Jewish Hospital in America* [Rabbinic thesis, Hebrew Union College–Jewish Institute for Religion, Cincinnati, 1985].)

Options for Jewish-Sponsored Hospitals

By 1979 the chief executive officers of Jewish hospitals recognized a need
to undertake more joint planning, and 16 of them embarked on the formation of the Consortium of Jewish Hospitals. Their primary objectives
were to negotiate national purchasing contracts and to hire an insurance
broker to study the feasibility of group insurance contracts.[5] This group
grew rapidly into a 26-hospital consortium that was structured as a
member-owned cooperative. Early in 1986 it was renamed the Premier
Hospitals Alliance to attract a wider constituency and to expand into
additional endeavors.[6] New programs that were added included studying
the feasibility of developing local HMOs, obtaining reduced fees for
market research studies, upgrading information systems capabilities,
and possibly creating a captive insurance company for member hospitals
and their physicians.

In the 1980s and 1990s these 33 Jewish-sponsored hospitals, like
many other acute care facilities in the United States, had to make a decision whether to "tough it out" as a freestanding hospital; to form a new
integrated delivery system with other providers having relatively similar
culture and values; to merge into an existing health network and possibly face being shuttered later; to be sold to a not-for-profit or an
investor-owned chain and use the lump sum proceeds for the formation
of a Jewish charitable health and welfare foundation; or simply to go
out of existence.

By late 1999 fewer than half (12) of the 33 Jewish-sponsored hospitals
were being managed with their earlier ownership-governance structure
being reasonably intact. Given that 8 facilities had already been shuttered
and 13 were merging with a Catholic or nonsectarian organization,
thereby losing much of their earlier Jewish identity, freestanding Jewish
hospitals were becoming an endangered species. Here I will identify the
reasons why a number of these hospitals decided to modify their ownership or governance pattern and what might be the future prospects of the
remaining 13 freestanding Jewish-sponsored facilities. In every metropolitan area there are nonsectarian, religious, and government hospitals that
are now facing similar financial difficulties and are analyzing what form of
networking agreement, if any, to consummate with another organization.
The discussion is relevant to health managers, who can borrow the lessons
from the outcome of this "Jewish experience" that are directly applicable
to an environment where health networking is a prevalent organizational
option and where corporate consolidations are being consummated with
decreasing frequency.

An Overview of the 33 Jewish Hospitals
in the United States

Table 18 provides: (1) a short historical brief of each of these 33 Jewish-sponsored facilities; and, (2) the average daily (inpatient) census in 1975 and 1998 (when reported) to offer some measure of the volume of care provided previously by some of these hospitals now shuttered. These synopses illustrate that each organization tended to follow a slightly different course of action, frequently contingent on its operational and fiscal position and on available local options. Forming a not-for-profit national Jewish hospital network or a Jewish investor-owned hospital chain similar to HCA—The Healthcare Co. or Tenet today neither made much practical sense, nor was the concept considered to be politically acceptable.

In the last quarter-century many of these facilities continually reviewed their long-range plans and operational alternatives for two reasons in particular. First, following World War II many Jewish community leaders, patients, and physicians moved to middle- and upper-middle class suburbs; and, second, Jewish hospitals, many times because of their inner-city locations, experienced a weakening financial position, most often the result of a declining average daily (inpatient) census and an increasing number of patients living nearby being eligible for Medicaid or uninsured.

As a result of these demographic and financial trends, 13 of the original 33 Jewish-sponsored hospitals formed or joined an existing partnership made up of a nonsectarian facility(s) (a major exception being Hartford's Mt. Sinai Hospital with a Catholic facility), sometimes as an "equal" and at other times being dominated by a larger and fiscally more viable organization. By changing the institution's governance through this networking process, the facilities lost at least some, if not most, of their Jewish identity.

In almost every case when consummating a merger, the partner sought was known for its strong teaching programs and the quality of its patient care and often was considered the region's most prestigious health system. Examples of merging with equals were Boston's Beth Israel Hospital and the Deaconess Medical Center, New York City's Mt. Sinai and New York University Hospitals, and Long Island Jewish and the North Shore Hospitals; and of forming an alliance was New York City's Beth Israel Hospital with St. Luke's–Roosevelt Hospital Center and Long Island College Hospital. Somewhat surprisingly because of traditional Jewish social consciousness, three Jewish-sponsored hospitals were sold to an investor-owned group: Chicago's Michael Reese, Denver's General Rose, and Cleveland's Mt. Sinai Hospitals.

Whether these health networks will actually achieve their earlier pro-jected objectives depends on such factors as whether they can: obtain addi-tional referrals (or will the partners simply compete among themselves?); implement increased operating efficiencies that often require consolidating smaller clinical services; enhance their negotiations with HMOs on reim-bursement rates; and form a common culture during a period of "resiz-ing," when the viability of some key management and middle-manage-ment positions may well still be in jeopardy.

When a Jewish hospital decides to merge but is in fact acquired, for all practical purposes, by the region's dominant provider (as in the case of Providence's Miriam Hospital, Cincinnati's Jewish Hospital, Pittsburgh's Montefiore Hospital,[7] Detroit's Sinai Hospital, St. Louis's Jewish Hospi-tal, and San Francisco's Mt. Zion Hospital), there is a reasonable likeli-hood that the previously Jewish-sponsored institution eventually will be shuttered for acute inpatient services, if it is one of the smaller institutions within the network. With a precipitous decrease in total patient days dur-ing the past decade and a continuing surplus supply of acute care beds in almost every metropolitan area, a health network that acquires a Jewish hospital will only keep admitting inpatients to that facility as long as it maintains its own financial viability.

Eight of the original 33 hospitals have been shuttered for various rea-sons: having a marginal average daily census (fewer than 200 patients), which was even apparent in 1975; being unable to compete as a freestand-ing facility; being incapable of consummating a meaningful and acceptable merger (e.g., no other Jewish hospital in the community); having key lead-ers and physicians who were either too old to provide the needed policy or clinical direction or had moved to the suburbs, therefore slowly losing interest in their hospital; and, in a few cases, having trustees who where unwilling to take heed of the declining trends that were evident over the previous decade(s). The Hospital of Joint Diseases relocating from Harlem to become the orthopedic center for New York City's Beth Israel Hospital is an example of shuttering one institution and its clinical program being integrated into another Jewish hospital, a strategic effort that could have been replicated by other smaller New York City–based facilities.

Twelve Jewish-sponsored hospitals are still freestanding because they have been unable to consummate a suitable partnership, wish to maintain sole control over their own destiny, have developed a workable "niche," or a combination of these reasons. Some notable examples include: Montefiore Medical Center with the Albert Einstein College of Medicine; New York City's Maimonides Medical Center serving Brooklyn's Ortho-dox Jews; Louisville's Jewish Hospital, which has acquired small suburban hospitals that can provide the hub facility with tertiary referrals; and Los

Angeles' Cedars-Sinai Medical Center, which has been very attractive to the west coast entertainment industry.

Financial Data—Declining Performance

Based on the Medicare cost reports of the "remaining" Jewish-sponsored hospitals, each facility's net revenues, operating margin, net margin, and debt-to-equity ratio are provided in table 19. This fiscal overview suggests that the vast majority of these facilities now experience weak operating margins, and almost all of them have assumed far too much debt compared to their equity (0.50 national "standard" for hospitals). Almost all of these institutions are now or can be expected in the long term to be financially vulnerable. Those experiencing the most serious shortfalls were already shuttered, and those that are considered still "repairable" have often chosen to become part of an integrated delivery system or health network.

Of particular fiscal concern currently should be the Jewish-sponsored hospitals in New York City, Passaic, N.J., Paterson, N.J, Miami, Chicago, Detroit, and San Francisco (the latter two having been shuttered as acute care facilities in late 1999) (see table 18). The leaders of these and other teaching hospitals often claim that their fiscal woes are related to under-reimbursement, while public officials and insurers frequently believe that their operating deficits are the direct result of less than totally efficient management. In an attempt to shed light on this traditional dispute, the financials of New York City's Mount Sinai Medical Center and Columbia-Presbyterian Hospital were compared to four major teaching hospitals on the west coast (Stanford, ULCA, UCSD, UCSF), all heavily influenced by managed care (table 10).[8]

Each teaching facility's full-time equivalent employee man-hours were divided by the number of discharges adjusted by case-mix intensity; the result was that the two New York City hospitals had fewer man-hours than three of the four west coast facilities. When a comparison was made of net patient revenues divided by the number of full-time employees adjusted by case-mix intensity and the Medicare wage index, the west coast facilities reported twice the net revenues of the two New York City academic health centers. The weak financial position of New York City's Jewish-sponsored hospitals, therefore, could well be related more to the state's inadequate reimbursement system than to their institutions' sloppy management.

The most fiscally healthy is Louisville's Jewish Hospital, aspiring to be the region's dominant acute care facility. Those of the Jewish faith make up only 0.3 percent of Kentucky's population (11,000 persons),[9] so the question arises whether in fact this is a Jewish-sponsored facility. In any case, having acquired or signed management contracts with six small Kentucky or southern Indiana hospitals, Louisville's Jewish Hospital has thereby developed a referral base to help support its sophisticated services.

Whether any of these 12 Jewish hospitals that have merged or joined an alliance has enhanced its fiscal position by becoming a partner in a

TABLE 19. Selected Financial Data of Jewish Hospitals, 1996–97

Hospital and Location	Latest Year's Net Patient Revenues (in millions of dollars)	Percentage Change from Earlier Year	Percentage Operating Margin	Percentage Net Margin	Debt-to-Equity Ratio
Beth Israel, Boston	$374.2	NA	–23.6	+6.8	0.23
Miriam, Providence	111.7	–3.5	–13.6	–8.0	0.45
Mt. Sinai, New York City	735.2	+3.6	–10.2	+2.7	1.09
Beth Israel, New York City	659.0	+8.7	–13.0	+1.8	1.58
Montefiore, New York City	720.9	+1.5	–44.8	+0.6	4.05
Maimonides, New York City	394.4	+19.7	–4.0	+0.6	1.56
Bronx-Lebanon, New York City	303.6	–0.1	–7.0	+0.1	15.80
Long Island Jewish, New York City	434.4	+2.7	–20.2	+1.7	0.56
Barnert Memorial, N.J.	64.6	–17.2	–23.3	–18.0	1.90
Newark Beth Israel, N.J.	338.9 (1995)	NA	–6.9	+15.5	1.20
Beth Israel, Passaic, N.J.	51.6	–0.1	–0.8	+2.8	0.60
Albert Einstein, Philadelphia	217.7	–23.1	–3.5	+5.1	0.92
Sinai, Baltimore	227.0	+10.5	–5.7	+3.1	1.59
Mt. Sinai, Miami Beach	230.2	+1.3	–5.4	–1.6	$204 million debt No equity
Jewish, Louisville	274.2	+14.6	+4.2	+6.7	0.22
Jewish, Cincinnati	150.5	+11.5	–5.1	–2.7	0.49
Mt. Sinai, Cleveland	164.1	–0.1	–10.4	–3.7	0.52
Sinai, Detroit*	269.7	+5.0	–14.7	–11.0	0.90
Michael Reese, Chicago	171.4	–1.0	–9.6	–13.2	8.49
Mt. Sinai, Chicago	153.3	–2.3	–15.2	–0.6	3.62
Menorah, Overland Park, Kans.	23.5	+97.5	–26.6	–16.8	8.2
Rose Memorial, Denver	138.6	NA	+17.4	+17.4	NA
Touro, New Orleans	100.0	+1.0	–2.2	+10.1	0.49
Cedars–Sinai, Los Angeles	562.7	NA	–10.2	+3.3	0.44
Mt. Zion, San Francisco*	76.3	–17.5	–56.9	–51.6	10.84

NA = Not available

Source: G. M. Pearl, *Financial Statement for U.S. Hospitals, 1999 Edition* (compiled from 1996–97 Medicare Cost Reports) (Phoenix: Rate Control Publication, 1999).

*Now closed as an acute care facility

larger health network (most with annual revenues exceeding $1 billion) is explored in table 20. Overall, these systems' performance to date is disappointing, since their leadership is unable or unwilling to shutter some facilities (could be a previously Jewish-sponsored facility) or to consolidate clinical services that would generate significant operating savings. It is expected that it will take several more years, probably as a result of some inevitable future economic downturns, for these alliances to realize their earlier projected operational savings.

Most noteworthy to date among the health networks with one of the 33 Jewish-sponsored hospitals are Louisville's Jewish Hospital Healthcare Services system (+4.5 percent net operating margin) and Milwaukee's Aurora Health Care (+3.2 percent), a key partner being the Sinai-Samaritan Hospital. Somewhat disappointing is the 1.6 percent operating margin of the Barnes Jewish Christian (BJC) system, which includes St. Louis' Jewish Hospital, 14 other institutions, and is closely tied to Barnes Hospital and the Washington University School of Medicine.

Societal Shifts Affecting Jewish Hospitals

Over the past quarter-century a number of significant societal shifts have occurred that affect Jewish hospitals, such as the assimilation of Jews in the mainstream of American society, changes in philanthropic giving by those of the Jewish faith, and qualified Jewish doctors now obtaining privileges virtually on all hospital medical staffs.

Jews Being Assimilated

Those of the Jewish faith (6 million persons, or 2.3 percent of the U.S. population)[9] have become during the last quarter-century far more assimilated in the cultural, social, and political life of the mainstream in this country.

In European countries in which cultural and religious divisions run deeper than in the United States, various groups have created separate institutions to meet a broad range of social needs. Possibly the best example in the United States is among the Catholics, who have organized elaborate networks of primary schools through universities, hospitals, and various civic organizations. Blacks, particularly in the South, more because of race discrimination but also because of sociocultural differences with the majority population, have also created separate institutions.

Historically, Jews in the United States and even in Germany before World War II[10] were more anxious to be assimilated than to establish their

TABLE 20. Selected Data of Jewish Hospitals Participating in Health Systems, 1998

Name of System	Hospital and Location	Revenues of System (in millions of dollars)	Number of Acute Hospitals in System	Number of Acute Beds in System	Net Operating Margin of System (in percentage)
Lifespan Corp., Boston	Miriam, Providence	911.6	4	1,125	–8.6
Continuum Partners, New York City	Beth Israel, New York City	1,536.5	3	2,513	NR
North Shore–Long Island Jewish, New York City	Long Island Jewish Hospital	2,164.9	13	4,331	+0.2
St. Barnabus Health System, West Orange, N.J.	Newark Beth Israel Hospital	NR	NR	NR	NR
Jewish Hospital Health Care Services, Louisville	Jewish, Louisville	383.4	7	1,146	+4.5
Detroit Medical Center**	Sinai, Detroit	1,512.6	7	2,121	–5.1 (1997)
Aurora Health Care	Mt. Sinai, Milwaukee	1,124.8	12	1,699	+3.2
Allina Health System	Mt. Sinai, Minneapolis	1,255.0	20	1,935	+2.5 (1997)
Columbia–HCA	Michael Reese, Chicago, and Rose Memorial, Denver	18,681.0	282	50,860	+1.3
Barnes-Jewish-Christian, St. Louis	Jewish, St. Louis	1,560.6	15	3,275	+1.6
Health Midwest, Kansas City	Menorah, Overland Park, Kans.	652.7	12	1,710	NR
UCSF–Stanford Health Care*	Mt. Zion, San Francisco**	1,241.0	4	1,350	1.3

Source: D. Bellandi and B. Kirchheimer, "For-Profits Report Decline in Acute-Care Hospitals," *Modern Healthcare* 29, no. 21 (1999): 23–42.

Note: NR = Not reported.

* Health system now undergoing divestiture.

** Now closed as an acute care facility.

own separate resources. In education American Jews sought admission to the nation's most elite colleges and universities. Brandeis, the first Jewish institution of higher learning, interestingly, was only founded after World War II.

Jewish Americans made an exception when it came to their hospitals, often building larger facilities than they actually needed for their own purposes. Perhaps they felt that they should provide another sign of the Jews' acceptance of and by the United States' better-educated, upper-income social structure, or they had a desire "to give something back to the community," or perhaps this had to do with the special place that the medical profession occupies in Jewish culture. Careers in medicine, dentistry, and the law or being self-employed as a certified public accountant are attractive to Jews, not only for reasons of prestige and income, but because these roles allow for the professional autonomy of private practice, which has made it possible for these individuals to escape most organizational anti-Semitism.

The assimilationist pattern started after World War II as the economy in the United States improved, and by 1975 most Jews felt they fit relatively well into the mainstream in American society. By this time many Jewish-sponsored hospitals had become major teaching and research centers affiliated with some of the nation's most prestigious medical schools (Harvard, Columbia, and the University of California at San Francisco). In the sense of assimilation into U.S. society, the upward clinical and social mobility of the Jewish hospitals paralleled the larger experience of the total Jewish community.

The most prominent and wealthy Jewish leaders started to become more frequently recruited by the high-profile nonsectarian organizations. At the turn of this century those of the Jewish faith are the chairman and certainly a senior trustee of many of the nation's most prestigious cultural, social, medical, and educational institutions. Jewish leaders actively participating in the governance of nonsectarian universities, hospitals, performing arts, and museums has resulted, however, in Jewish hospitals experiencing more difficulty in recruiting young, highly qualified talent with extensive S&P 500-type experience for their own governing boards.

Jews Giving to Nonsectarian Causes

American Jewish philanthropy has been long hailed for its blockbuster successes in raising money in times of emergency or crisis, such as supporting immigration from Europe to Israel after World War II and underwriting many State of Israel endeavors. Now a major issue is how to strengthen Jewish identity, institutions, and philanthropy in the face of rising rates of intermarriage and indifference among younger Jews.[11]

Through the 1970s large gifts from wealthy Jews were of the magnitude that they could eliminate the annual operating deficit of a hospital or could fund a major capital project. In comparison, today's philanthropy is a far more modest income stream for Jewish hospitals, so they are forced to generate almost all of their income from operations and to assume long-term debt for major capital projects.

The percentage of Jews who give to charity is roughly the same as all Americans, but it is a relatively small group of wealthy contributors who donate most of the money that goes to Jewish causes. Now family foundations are the major vehicles for philanthropic giving by major Jewish donors, and an increasing number are channeling the majority of their wealth into non-Jewish causes. This trend is further complicated by major donors insisting on the right to designate how their money is spent. Furthermore, donors being more often interested in specific causes results in far more competition for Jewish hospitals in acquiring large philanthropic gifts.

More and more Jews are giving to nonsectarian causes because either the original donors of the foundation's assets or their heirs are disconnected from the Jewish community. With spiraling rates of intermarriage spurring disaffiliation from the Jewish community, some heirs to major donors to Jewish causes have severed their ties to Jewish philanthropy. In addition, wealthy Jews are earmarking ever larger percentages of their giving to non-Jewish causes because they are no longer excluded from the inner circles of those philanthropies or from high-visibility public offices (e.g., Secretary of State Albright, former Secretary of Treasury Rubin, and Secretary of Defense Cohen have at least a partial Jewish heritage). As major U.S. corporations and universities have opened their once-closed doors to Jews and hired them in senior executive positions (in 1998 the presidents of Dartmouth, Harvard, University of Pennsylvania, Princeton, and Yale were Jewish), wealthy Jews have begun to give generously to the causes favored by their non-Jewish counterparts.

The Recruitment of Jewish Physicians

As hospitals by the early 1990s experienced decreasing average daily censuses, admitting privileges were extended to Jewish physicians in some of the nation's most prestigious suburban facilities, particularly among those doctors with highly sought after subspecialty training. In fact, it is not unusual today that Jewish board members and physicians are assuming key hospital leadership roles in institutions that just decades earlier were "restricted" (i.e., had a small Jewish quota or had no Jews at all).

Those of the Jewish faith have become better assimilated into the mainstream of American society. As a result, Jewish-sponsored hospitals have lost some of their earlier glamour for their trustees and physicians, particularly as it has become more difficult for these institutions to avoid incurring significant operating losses as so many of them are in poor inner-city locations.

The Reason for Changes in Governance

There are many reasons why 21 of the 33 original Jewish-sponsored hospitals from 1975 to 1999 were either closed or merged with a nonsectarian organization. Some specific reasons are summarized as follows: Jewish patients, leaders, and physicians had moved to the suburbs; Jews were assimilated into the mainstream of American society; most Jewish-sponsored hospitals were in highly competitive, overbedded, poor, inner-city locations; and many Jewish philanthropists shifted their interest and gifts to high-prestige nonsectarian organizations.

What appears unfortunate is that two, three, or even four of the larger New York City Jewish hospitals (Beth Israel, Long Island Jewish, Montefiore, and Mt. Sinai) in 1995, based on a common religion but not always a common culture and values (continuing differences between western [Reformed] and eastern European [Orthodox] Jews), could have developed some form of alliance or merger, a pattern used in forming today's Catholic health systems. Instead, three of the four major medical centers decided to position themselves with "equally high-profile" nonsectarian organizations. It is far too early and perhaps impossible to assess whether the Montefiore Hospital freestanding model or a New York City–wide Jewish network might have been a more appropriate choice.

A number of these Jewish-sponsored hospitals are located in metropolitan areas where no other Jewish facility is available as a possible partner. As their "best" option, most often they decided to merge with the metropolitan area's dominant provider as a means to maintain their teaching programs, gain prestige, and insure the quality of patient care. As a practical matter, almost in each case the merger resulted in the nonsectarian organization acquiring the Jewish hospital. In five cities (Detroit, Hartford, Pittsburgh, Minneapolis, and San Francisco) Jewish hospitals have already been shuttered as an acute inpatient facility by a major health network.

This case study illustrates that when a hospital with a declining patient census and financial position decides to merge with the region's major provider, closure of that facility for acute inpatient care is a reasonable likelihood anytime after the smaller facility is no longer able to remain fiscally viable. Simply merging with a system "with deep pockets" does not insure that any partner will be cross-subsidized for any extended period. In fact, additional Jewish hospitals merging and then being shuttered is expected to be a more frequent occurrence as virtually all of the key Jewish leadership, philanthropy, and physicians are assimilated into nonsectarian organizations.

Future Prospects for Jewish-Sponsored Hospitals

The option of remaining as a freestanding Jewish hospital, when everyone else is networking, is not exactly without its perils. Whether in the long run these 12 Jewish hospitals can remain under primarily Jewish auspices is questionable, since most lack the critical patient care volumes to "stand alone" in their markets and already are experiencing serious fiscal difficulties.

Possibly an even more fundamental question is whether these remaining 12 Jewish-sponsored hospitals should continue to survive as "Jewish" hospitals. One could easily argue that they are no longer needed to serve their earliest intended purposes (of 100 to 150 years ago), such as: providing appropriate care for first generation Jews coming from Europe, offering training opportunities for Jewish medical school graduates, and extending admitting privileges to Jewish physicians. In addition, many of these facilities are in poor, inner-city locations where Jewish suburban patients have for decades been reluctant to seek care.

What has happened in reality is that a majority of the remaining Jewish-sponsored facilities now serve as the neighborhood community hospital for the local Medicaid eligible and uninsured, who are not Jewish. Whereas the older, more tradition-bound Jewish philanthropist may have supported such efforts, the next generation, who have never lived in the area and are now assimilated into the nonsectarian community, provide their large gifts to high-prestige non-Jewish organizations.

When the alternative of merging with an existing health network is more attractive than closing, it is predicted that over the next decade the following Jewish-sponsored hospitals will be forced, primarily because of fiscal difficulties, to become part of some existing alliance or integrated health system: New York City's Montefiore, Maimonides, and Bronx-Lebanon Hospitals (because of their poor operating margins and debt-to-equity ratios), New Jersey–based Beth Israel Hospital in Passaic and Barnert Memorial Hospital in Paterson, Philadelphia's Albert Einstein Hospital, Sinai Hospital of Baltimore, Miami's Mt. Sinai Hospital, Mt. Sinai Hospital in Chicago, and Touro Infirmary in New Orleans. The two New Jersey hospitals, if they were to consummate a merger with a major network because of their current low average daily patient census, could within a few years be tallied as the ninth and tenth Jewish-sponsored hospitals to be shuttered.

In spite of Jewish assimilation in the United States and the more fundamental question of why perpetuate Jewish-sponsored hospitals, because of their average daily census and their sound financial condition, Los Angeles' Cedars-Sinai Medical Center and Louisville's Jewish Hospital might well be the 2 organizations, based on information currently available, that demonstrate the best chance of the original 33 facilities to still be identified as Jewish-sponsored hospitals a quarter-century hence. The Jewish Hospital in Louisville may be more Jewish in name than in its Jewish sponsorship. But both facilities have been successful in finding an appropriate "niche" and building relationships with loyal patients, highly qualified physicians, and nearby institutions to obtain tertiary referrals, and they have established a track record of carefully and prudently focusing on their core operations.

Jews coming from Europe at the turn of this century would be gratified to see their grandchildren and great-grandchildren now serving in leadership roles among the United States' most prestigious nonsectarian institutions. Also, Jewish physicians can obtain residencies and fellowships and then admitting privileges at a broad spectrum of hospitals throughout the United States. Except in a few instances, the American Jew is so well assimilated that Jewish-sponsored hospitals, compared to their early historical role and religiously oriented mission, may today be an outdated institution or at least be considered as a seriously endangered species. In view of these current trends some might even ask why it might not be advisable for the remaining 12 freestanding Jewish-sponsored hospitals simply to be assimilated into the mainstream of U.S. nonsectarian institutions.

REFERENCES

1. Bridges, D. E. *The Rise and Development of the Jewish Hospital in America.* Rabbinic thesis. Cincinnati: Hebrew Union College–Jewish Institute for Religion, 1985.

2. Marcus, J. R. *Communal Sick Care in the German Ghetto.* Cincinnati: Hebrew Union College Press, 1978.

3. Starr, P. *The Social Transformation of American Medicine.* New York: Basic Books, 1982.

4. Wagner, M. "Jewish Hospitals Yesterday and Today." *Modern Healthcare* 21, no. 5 (1991): 32–38.

5. DiPaolo, V. "16 Large Jewish Hospitals Form a Group Purchasing Consortium." *Modern Healthcare* 9, no. 11 (1979): 12–13.

6. Graham, J. "Consortium of Jewish Hospitals Plans National Hospital Alliance." *Modern Healthcare* 15, no. 24 (1985): 40.

7. Otten, A. L. "Jewish Healthcare Foundation." In *New Foundations in Health: Six Stories.* New York: Milbank Memorial Fund, 1999.

8. Weil, T. P., and Pearl, G. M. "America's Best Hospitals: Heading toward Fiscal Distress?" *Managed Care Interface* 14, no. 4 (2001): in press.

9. U.S.-Israel Organization. "Jewish Population of the United States." MS. Washington, D.C., 1999.

10. Wyman, D. S. *Abandonment of the Jews.* New York: Pantheon Books, 1982.

11. Wertheimer, J. "Current Trends in American Jewish Philanthropy." In Singer, D., ed. *American Jewish Year Book.* New York: American Jewish Committee, 1997.

Epilogue

In strictly fiscal terms the new millennium was ushered in with an almost perfect previous decade—one with a record of remarkable economic expansion that was unprecedented in the last half-century. The health field in the year 2000 exhibits signs of managed care plans requiring a 10 to 11 percent annual increase in premiums and of providers focusing their efforts on securing rollbacks in reimbursement reductions that are contained in the Balanced Budget Act of 1997 (BBA). In addition, the number of mergers and acquisitions now under way in the health field compared to those consummated just three years earlier has started to slow down to slightly more than a trickle. The more modest corporate restructuring among health networks, often referred to as integrated delivery systems, is currently related to a number of factors including the deteriorating bottom lines, general downgrading of bond ratings and an unanticipated surge in varying types of divestitures and in the voluntary filings for bankruptcy protection.

Coming under more frequent public scrutiny today is the efficacy of the managed care concept, irrespective of whether the delivery of health services is actually being enhanced by all this merger mania, or whether these politically and fiscally powerful health networks, functioning as oligopolies in almost every metropolitan area, are always acting in the public interest.[1] As a result, the current political rhetoric, irrespective of party affiliation, often includes various incremental steps to shore up access to health services, to protect patients' rights under the HMOs, and to provide some fiscal relief to low-income senior citizens who are struggling with significant out-of-pocket pharmaceutical expenditures.

While the share of the U.S. gross domestic product (GDP) committed to health continues to hover around 13.5 percent, in 1998 the annual growth of health spending was 4.5 percent, inflation adjusted, far below the double-digit increases experienced in the 1970s and 1980s.[2] Because of the decelerating reimbursement for Medicare and Medicaid benefits, the total public expenditures continue to slow down. As a result, the share of private health spending paid for by health insurance and out-of-pocket sources has risen. While hospitals continue to experience a slow decline in their share of the total available medical care dollar, prescription drugs account for the most significant percent increase. Meanwhile, the expanded enrollment in managed care plans and the cutbacks in Medicare and Medicaid reimbursement have curtailed increases in the average annual spending inflation-adjusted for physician services from 11.6 percent during the 1960–91 period to only 4.5 percent in 1992 through 1998.

With these relatively constraining fiscal trends, it is readily predictable in this new millennium that the health field, one of the major growth industries since the end of World War II, might well witness some significant resizing or downsizing. Possibly the most noticeable example to the public of the corporate restructuring that is now under way, potentially to conserve resources, has been an area's hospitals and other related providers forming these large regional health networks or integrated delivery systems that are suppose to improve access and operating efficiencies, and to enhance their ability to negotiate contracts with third-party payers.

Physicians have consolidated their practices and in some cases have sold them to health networks or physician practice management corporations. Neither of these options has turned out to be particularly rewarding either professionally or fiscally.[3] A few drug manufacturers first bought pharmaceutical benefit management firms and then quickly sold them, since such vertically diversified acquisitions failed to produce the expected sales increases. Another strategy often used by these drug companies has included consummating numerous mergers among themselves to consolidate access to capital for research and to improve the marketing of new products.

Meanwhile, the overall U.S. economy, the pharmaceutical industry, and the biotech firms in early 2000 continued to be vibrant. There were several major sectors within the health industry, however, that in a comparative sense were already demonstrating significant operational and fiscal difficulties. Among the most obvious examples are: nursing homes / assisted living chains, physician practice management corporations, health maintenance organizations (HMOs), investor-owned and some not-for-profit hospitals, and specialty physical medicine and rehabilitation services.

An obvious concern was whether these sectors or sub-sectors of the health field, that were currently demonstrating relatively weak operational and fiscal performance, could cause in this decade significant peril to how health networks are now organized, managed, and financed. Health executives may now need to give more heed in the new millennium to how to deal with a increasing number of providers, insurers, and other related entities within the health industry that are now experiencing negative or marginally positive bottom lines. By somewhat expanding this argument, in this epilogue we weigh the risk of several sectors or subsectors within the health field experiencing such poor operating and financial outcomes, and being so far overextended in outstanding debt, that U.S. health networks and, therefore, the total U.S. health delivery system approach possible fiscal jeopardy.

Long-Term Care Facilities

Like other Western industrialized nations, the United States is witnessing an increase in the number of aged persons, who require a disproportionate share of health services. Yet the annual growth in spending for nursing home care, a sector historically dominated by the for-profits, decreased steadily from an inflation-adjusted 13.3 percent in 1990 to 3.7 percent in 1998. Much of the deceleration over the last decade represented a combination of the slowing down in the inflationary trend of medical prices generally along with the expanded use of alternative treatment settings such as home health care, assisted living facilities, and community-based day care.

The high rate of growth in Medicare spending for nursing home care (that averaged 34 percent annually in 1991–96) was the reason to include within the BBA of 1997 a significant cutback in their reimbursement. A change in how nursing homes were paid adversely affected Medicare payments to skilled nursing facilities. In 1997 Congress mandated a prospectively determined per diem Medicare reimbursement rate based on resource utilization groups (RUGs) rather than on the reasonable-cost basis that was previously in effect. The revised approach required that all services furnished by the nursing home be bundled into a single per diem payment amount.

Already experiencing excess capacity for the private (non-Medicaid) patient, the nursing home industry found these changes in reimbursement to be the principal reason for the Sun Healthcare Group, Vencor, Integrated Health Services, and Mariner Post-Acute Network filing for bankruptcy protection in late 1999 or early 2000. Financial statements in early 2000 for these four investor-owned nursing home corporations (table 21) might be summarized as follows:

1. Low current ratios ranging from 0.20 to 0.56.
2. Operating losses for the last four quarters reported (1998–99) for the four nursing home corporations totaled $3.9 billion. As of December 31, 1999, Mariner Post-Acute Care Network reported

an operating loss of $1.3 billion on $2.3 billion of revenues among its 400 nursing homes and 37 pharmacies, thereby increasing the earlier estimated $3.9 million operating shortfall.

3. Their total short- and long-term debt totaled $8.1 billion.
4. Their total equity was a minus $307.8 million.

Somewhat predictable based on these data is that over 10 percent of the nation's 17,000 nursing homes were managed by companies that have sought Chapter 11 protection. Investor-owned corporations providing nursing home care that was profitable in an operating environment where they were able to take advantage of a reasonable-cost basis reimbursement methodology, found themselves starting in 1997 completely out of sync when government officials changed the prepayment rules.

Other nursing home chains that have not yet filed for Chapter 11 may be in fiscal jeopardy too. Beverly Enterprises (table 21) is the second largest provider of nursing home services (behind Sun Healthcare) and has some 560 facilities in about 30 states. It also owns assisted living facilities, outpatient rehabilitation centers, and home health services. In February 2000 a record-breaking $175 million criminal fraud settlement was reached between Beverly Enterprises and the federal government raising eyebrows in the total provider community because of the size of the

TABLE 21. Selected Financial Statistics for Major Long-Term Care Corporations, 1998–99 (in millions except Current Ratio)

Name of Company	Revenues (for Year Ending)	Current Ratio (for Quarter Ending)	Total Net Income (for Year Ending)	Total Debt (for Quarter Ending)	Total Equity (for Quarter Ending)
Sun Healthcare Group	$3,088.5	0.56	$(753.7)	$1,625.6	$33.8
	(12/98)	(12/98)	(12/98)	(12/98)	(12/98)
Vencor	2,999.7	0.48	(650.8)	776.6	314.9
	(12/98)	(12/98)	(12/98)	(12/98)	(12/98)
Integrated Health	2,972.2	0.20	(1,819.4)	3,535.6	(528.3)
Services	(12/98)	(9/99)	(9/99)	(9/99)	(9/99)
Beverly	2,551.0	1.43	(134.6)	800.1	673.9
	(12/99)	(9/99)	(12/99)	(9/99)	(9/99)
Manor	2,135.3	1.13	(43.7)	901.6	1,157.1
	(12/99)	(9/99)	(12/99)	(9/99)	(9/99)
Mariner Post-Acute	2,035.5	0.40	(678.0)	2,206.7	(128.2)
Network	(9/98)	(6/99)	(6/99)	(6/99)	(6/99)

Source: www.hoovers.com, March 18, 2000.

penalty and the fact that the agreement required that the company divest itself of 10 facilities. With an operating loss for calendar year 1999 totaling $134.6 million and a total debt-to-equity ratio of 1.41, Beverly Enterprises could conceivably be the fifth large nursing home group in one calendar year to file for bankruptcy protection.

Providing the nation's aged with effective and efficient long-term care services is complicated because of a number of political, social (e.g., the nursing home is perceived as a place to die rather than to get well), clinical (e.g., senior citizens require vastly more services), and financial factors. In addition, often overlooked are several interrelated influences such as: elected officials historically being supersensitive to the large and active voting bloc dominated by senior citizens; the children and grandchildren of those requiring admission to a nursing home vigorously searching for a facility that provides high-quality services for their loved ones while equally anxious to keep the price (the cost to the family or their personal tax burden) at a minimum; and the inability of the senior citizens, the health system, and the public generally to sort out all of these conflicting pressures successfully.

A combination of a greater demand for long-term care beds, because of an increasing number of persons 75 years of age and older and a reduction in the supply of such facilities due to poor reimbursement could conceivably force hospitals to more frequently provide sub-acute nursing units. These areas would be for patients no longer requiring acute care services, but who are too sick or disabled to be discharged to their home and are awaiting transfer to a long-term care facility. Hospitals might well find themselves experiencing increased average lengths of stay without significant revenue enhancement. The health networks can be expected to avoid the strategy of purchasing long-term care facilities in order to reduce their backlog of patients requiring such care, simply because of the poor financial viability of such acquisitions. In fact, those health networks owning long-term care facilities might well be interested in divesting themselves of such subsidiaries because of the danger of incurring operating losses.

As more baby boomers start to phase out of the active labor force and many of their parents consider relocating to three-level retirement communities (senior citizen apartments, assisted living facilities, and skilled nursing homes), a critical societal issue will be whether Americans should spend more resources on education, health care, correctional facilities, and improving our general infrastructure rather than on programs for the aged and the indigent (e.g., social security, Medicare and Medicaid). In that process long-term care services provided in nursing homes, in assisted living facilities, and by home health care agencies are expected to continue receiving short shrift, as the "safety net" for the poor and infirm aged in this country remains lethargic. The six largest investor-owned nursing home corporations reporting within one year an operating loss of over $3.9 billion (table 21) should clearly illustrate that, from strictly a fiscal point of view, providing long-term care services is one strategy that an investor or a health network should probably avoid.

Physician Practice Management Corporations

In the early 1990s many solo physician practices, single-specialty groups, multispecialty groups, and independent practice associations (IPA) realized that they lacked the expertise to negotiate effectively with third-party payers, to underwrite the financial risk of capitation and other types of prepayment, to manage the full spectrum of clinical and business services, and to appropriately document the quality of their care. Increasingly, they affiliated in various ways with larger organizations to attain the overall business sophistication and the financial backing that was needed to compete effectively in this new market-driven, managed care environment.

An increasing number of physician practice management (PPM) firms were organized in the 1990s to offer capital financing, to provide expertise in managing various resources, and to assist in structuring workable contracts between physicians and various third-party payers. These PPMs have provided physicians with an alternative to being acquired by a local health network or for a medical group practice to remain as a freestanding provider.

These PPMs for a number of years were favorites on Wall Street as illustrated by their 38.2 percent gain in stock prices during calendar 1995. Suddenly, in early 1998, the collapse of the proposed MedPartners-PhyCor merger led to the rapid fall of most PPM stock prices, thereby increasing the wariness of physicians to sell to or invest in PPMs. In many ways the PPMs are having experiences similar to those of the health networks who acquired physician practices.[4–5]

Medpartners, the one-time largest U.S. physician practice management corporation, divested itself from 240 physician practices in 40 states to focus on Caremark, its prescription benefits and disease management subsidiary. Even after selling off its medical group practices, Caremark at the end of calendar 1999 had a negative net income of $143.4 million with an outstanding short- and long-term debt of $1.38 billion.

PhyCor is now the largest of the ailing breed of PPMs and operates multi-specialty groups, manages independent practice associations (IPAs), and provides healthcare decision-support services to consumers. The company operates over 50 medical groups with approximately 3,000 physicians in 24 states, manages IPAs with approximately 26,000 physicians in 36 markets, and through CareWise, Inc., provides healthcare decision support services to over four million consumers worldwide. This PPM is also experiencing fiscal distress with a $111.4 million operating loss and a debt-to-equity ratio of 1.63 as of December 31, 1998.

Some of the smaller physician practice management companies (e.g., ProMedCo Management and Sheridan Healthcare, Inc.) and those that limit their activities to a specific clinical specialty have tended to produce somewhat better operating margins. In an overall bullish economy, the fiscal difficulties faced by these PPMs are vividly illustrated by their stock prices declining 35.8 percent through the third quarter of 1999, after a decrease of 38.1 percent in 1998, and only a 1.8 percent increase in 1997.

Members of the medical professional are now often nervous about their professional future, particularly concerning the outlook for increased personal income. They must work longer hours to maintain their previous year's income for a number of reasons: only an annual 4.5 percent increase inflation-adjusted spending on physician services, an additional supply of physicians and patients, overhead costs for all practitioners rising significantly, and the difficulties being experienced by the PPMs and the health networks to successfully manage physician practices. Although the average income stream of U.S. physicians will continue to exceed that of practitioners in other Western industrialized nations,[6] their annual increases in net income inflation-adjusted are expected to be relatively modest, if any. Acquiring physician practices is another strategy that most health networks will want to avoid, except under some unusual circumstances.

Health Maintenance Organizations (HMOs)

The managed care plans, Medicare, and other forms of third-party prepayment for health services are the major structural components of the economic bridge which links the providers of health services with the population that uses these insurers' benefits. The United States already spends one-quarter more of its gross domestic product for health than most other Western industrialized nations.[6] Yet its health system still experiences significant fiscal pressures as there continues to be a sizable demand, particularly among the under- or uninsured, for additional medical services.

Hospital officials, on the other hand, were currently concerned that if the additional Medicare reductions proposed by President Clinton in his 2000 State of the Union address were to be implemented, a probable outcome would be 60 percent of all acute care facilities by 2004 experiencing operating losses on Medicare services.[7] Meanwhile, the strategy advanced in the early 1990s of health networks starting their own managed care plans (as a means to control the "premium dollar") is now being phased out by providers because it has resulted in significant operating losses. Reducing inpatient utilization so that the HMO owned by the health network is more fiscally viable is at odds with their hospitals securing more admissions to enhance their bottom line.

Many of the smaller provider-owned HMOs found it difficult to be competitive because of a lack of experience with underwriting and a shortage of working capital. Often they were then acquired by the region's dominant managed care plan, which was reluctant to pass on the potential economies of scale to its subscribers.[8] In 1996, 46 HMOs made deals valued at $21 billion; a few examples of these transactions follow: Aetna acquired U.S. Healthcare, thereby becoming the largest managed care plan. Number two Kaiser Foundation Health Plans purchased part of the assets of Humana as well as initiated a major alliance with Seattle's Group Health Cooperative and with Community Health Plan of Albany. And there was the acquisition of MetraHealth by number three United Health-Care.

In 1997 both the Aetna and Oxford health plans experienced a major computer snafu arising in part from an acquisition that presented an incompatible information system. This caused both companies to lose track of medical care costs, underestimate claims, and overestimate profits. During the same year, Kaiser, PacifiCare Health Systems, Cigna, and Foundation Health Systems were also battered by unexpectedly high claims and poor earnings.

The more recent history of HMOs is not particularly rosy either, as evidenced by the fiscal data of nine of the nation's large managed care plans (table 22). This is in spite of their offering a variety of healthcare plans and services including: managing HMOs, point-of-service, and preferred provider plans; developing distinct Medicare and Medicaid options; making available specialized insurance vehicles to offer vision care, dental care, transplant services, and other niche coverage; and sometimes providing such vertically integrated services as life insurance.

Even after these managed care plans consummated all their corporate restructuring, their percentage of increased revenues compared to the prior year and their net profit margin were far below those of the accident and health insurance sector generally and those of the enormously powerful financial industry (table 22). In this bullish economy with "full" employment, the HMOs' revenues increased by an average of only 5 percent inflation adjusted; and the bottom line of these nine plans ranged from a 2.7 percent net profit for Aetna to a 3.8 percent net loss for Humana. The HMOs, based on these data, cannot be portrayed as a major growth industry with strong underlying financials.

To enhance their financial position the managed care plans   must raise their premiums. As long as the United States experiences low unemployment and employers to be competitive are forced to provide, if at all affordable, their employees with relatively comprehensive health insurance coverage as a fringe benefit, the managed care plans can continue to pass along premium increases. The HMOs during the past decade have been relatively successful in controlling health costs by reducing inpatient utilization and by forcing physicians to more critically evaluate the use of sophisticated services. But for these HMOs to remain fiscally viable, in the

TABLE 22. Selected Fiscal Data for Major Managed Care Plans, 1998–99 (dollars in millions)

Name of Company	Revenues (for Year Ending)	Increased Revenues from Prior Year (%)	Net Income (for Year Ending)	Net Profit Margin (%) (for Year Ending)	Debt-to-Equity Ratio (for Quarter Ending)
Aetna	$26,453.01	+28.4	$716.9	2.7	0.43
	(2/99)	(12/99)	(12/99)	(12/99)	(12/99)
United-Health Group	19,562	+14.4	568.0	2.9	0.16
	(12/99)	(12/99)	(12/99)	(12/99)	(9/99)
Humana	10,113.0	+5.4	(382.0)	(3.8)	0.52
	(12/99)	(12/99)	(12/99)	(12/99)	(9/99)
PacifiCare Health	9,989	+4.9	278.5	2.8	0.28
Systems	(12/99)	(12/99)	(12/99)	(12/99)	(9/99)
Foundation Health	8,706.0	−1.0	142.0	1.2	1.33
Systems	(12/99)	(12/99)	(12/99)	(12/99)	(12/99)
Kaiser Foundation	15,500.0	+6.9	(288.0)	(1.8)	0.23
Health Plan	(12/98)	(12/98)	(12/98)	(12/98)	(12/96)
Empire Blue Cross	3,276.5	−1.6	42.0	1.3	0.14
and Blue Shield	(12/98)	(12/98)	(12/98)	(12/98)	(12/98)
Harvard Pilgrim	2,670.0	+13.7	(197.0)	—	—
	(12/98)	(12/98)	(12/99)		
HIP (N.Y.C.)	1,567.6	−9.6	1.4	0.1	(200.7 million in debt No equity)
	(12/97)	(12/97)	(12/97)	(12/97)	
Accident and Health Industry	—	+15.1	—	+3.9	—
Financial Sector	—	+15.7	—	+16.0	—
S and P 500	—	+20.5	—	+11.7	—

Source: www.hoovers.com, March 19, 2000.

long term and particularly in an economic downturn, they will need to be far more effective in managing their subscribers' medical care. Historically, insurers and providers have experienced major difficulties in managing patient care to achieve greater economies and improved clinical outcomes (e.g., establishing clinical protocols), since such approaches can interfere with a physician's usual and customary prerogatives of treating his or her patient.

The not-for-profit Harvard Pilgrim Health Care HMO, with 1.1 million subscribers, requested that the Commonwealth of Massachusetts appoint a receiver, and incurred a $197 million operating loss in calendar year 1999. When such a large and prestigious HMO needs legal protection from its creditors, one immediately wonders how fragile the financial position might be of the managed care plans generally and, particularly, how they would fare in a less than solid economy. An obvious concern is how many other HMOs are there nationwide that might be on the verge of seeking some protection from the courts in reducing their operating losses and indebtedness. The passage of federal legislation requiring the not-for-profit managed care plans to disclose the same financial information as the publicly owned corporations (i.e., the Securities and Exchange Commission filings) might be a major step so that providers can better gauge the fiscal risk of contracting with a specific HMO, whose financial statements were historically not in the public domain.[9]

If the stock prices are a valid predictor of an industry's future outlook, the managed care plans in the next few years will face a severe fiscal crisis. In this bullish market managed care stock prices through the third quarter of 1999 declined 25 percent, after having experienced a 6.7 percent decline in calendar year 1998. As long as the U.S. economy continues to be relatively robust, as evidenced by low unemployment, a strong record of housing starts, and the purchase of new cars, employers will reluctantly pay the HMO premiums in order to maintain a stable labor force. Some employers, who are unable to afford making the coverage available as a fringe benefit, are providing their employees with a cash payment in lieu of health insurance, so that with an additional out-of-pocket expense they can purchase their own coverage.

The 44.6 million uninsured Americans,[10] with this number until recently increasing at the rate of one million annually, the current financial position (table 22), and the stock market outlook for the HMOs all imply that the managed care plans could be expected to face some increasing fiscal and operational upheaval, particularly if a slight recessionary period occurs. The HMOs should not be considered to be a mature, stable industry. In fact, the opposite might be closer to the truth, and hard economic times would directly affect health networks.

Investor-Owned Hospital Industry

The average net profit or the median debt-to-equity ratio is rather mean-
ingless in the hospital field today, since there is a huge disparity between
those networks and facilities that have accumulated huge surpluses in the
past decade and those that are currently facing grave financial difficulties
(see chap. 6). Fiscal shortfalls are mounting among an increasing number
of the most outstanding hospitals in the United States (table 9), and, if
they are unable to take corrective action, they may be forced to implement
significant personnel cuts or, even worse, to file for Chapter 11 protection.
An obvious example of the latter was the Allegheny Health, Education,
and Research Foundation (AHERF), a major health network with a medical school, 15 hospitals, and over 600 physicians (whose practices were
previously acquired), located primarily in the Philadelphia and Pittsburgh
metropolitan areas. In the summer of 1998 AHERF filed for bankruptcy
protection, with $1.2 billion in debt. Adding complexity to this example is
that subsequently Tenet (the second largest investor-owned hospital
chain) purchased most of Allegheny's Philadelphia-based facilities. In
early 2000 Tenet announced that it was closing one or more of these facilities and laying off hundreds of its employees.

    Probably equally noticeable in the public media were the number of
integrated delivery systems, including the UCSF-Stanford Health Care
and Penn State Geisinger Health System, that divested themselves of their
major stakeholders. In both cases the divestiture occurred because projected operational savings remained "on paper," as reality set in that the
proposed cost reductions were more difficult to achieve than had earlier
been projected.

    During February 2000 Charter Behavioral Health Systems, the
nation's largest operator of psychiatric hospital and treatment centers,
which had gone into a financial freefall, filed for Chapter 11 bankruptcy
protection from its creditors. Charter listed less than $50 million in assets
and more than $100 million in debts. This psychiatric company's difficul-
ties, aside from some well-publicized clinical and management irregulari-
ties, can be traced to managed care plans limiting admissions and lengths
of stay among their subscribers requiring mental health services.

    In an attempt to identify super-effective and -efficient hospitals, a
number of studies have selected the "top," or "best," U.S. hospitals in
terms of their fiscal, operational, and clinical acumen.[11-12] Possibly the
most frequently quoted report in the hospital trade journals is the HCIA,
Inc., and William M. Mercer, Inc., study, "One Hundred Top Hospitals:
Benchmarks for Success," produced annually since 1993.[13] Using their cri-

teria (e.g., low mortality and complications, the effective use of personnel, and the shorter average length of hospital stay) and assuming that all U.S. acute hospitals were managed like these 100 facilities, total hospital expenses would have theoretically declined by an aggregate of $26.3 billion (roughly 8.9 percent of U.S. hospital expenditures in 1997).

Among the 100 reportedly most efficient facilities in the United States, 15 cited were major teaching hospitals, all with 400 or more beds. Somewhat unexpected was that 8 of these 15 supposedly superefficient facilities had negative operating margins, suggesting they must be placing considerable reliance on their nonoperating revenues (e.g., income from endowments) to achieve a positive net margin. Three of these 15 large hospitals had a debt-to-equity ratio above 1.0. Even among those hospitals considered by these experts to be among the nation's most efficient, an unexpectedly high number were experiencing operating and debt-to-equity difficulties.

Since these HCIA-Mercer hospital findings appeared to be equivocal, additional investigation was made of the financial position of the nation's best teaching hospitals as listed in the 1998 *U.S. News and World Report* survey.[14] Based on the latest Medicare cost reports available to the public, there is a huge divergence in the fiscal position of the most highly regarded academic health centers in the United States (tables 9–10). The University of Iowa Hospitals and Clinics for the year ending June 30, 1997, experienced a 6.4 percent increase in net patient revenues from the previous year, a comfortable net margin of 12.4 percent, a current ratio of 10.3, and virtually no long-term debt. At the other end of the spectrum, New York City's Columbia-Presbyterian Hospital for the year ending December 31, 1996, had a meager 1 percent increase in net patient revenues from the previous year, a slim 0.3 percent net margin, a current ratio of 1.7, and a disturbing long-term debt-to-equity ratio of 21.36. These data so clearly illustrate a huge and unhealthy disparity in the current financial position among the country's best hospitals.

Reducing costs by eliminating the duplication of services, enhancing managed care negotiations, and attracting additional referrals for its sophisticated tertiary services are among the prime reasons that major hospitals expend considerable resources in major corporate restructuring (e.g., mergers), forming integrated delivery networks, acquiring primary care physician practices, signing affiliation agreements, and engaging in other similar strategic endeavors. What is so disturbing is that healthcare organizations are spending considerable resources in centralizing their governance and operations by forming these huge networks and alliances, but this strategy according to a number of studies has not added financial value to the region's delivery of health services, at least at this point in their development.[15-17]

The disappointing fiscal and operational results from these health networking efforts might be related to experiencing difficulty in achieving a strategic fit, in finding a middle-ground when differences in culture and values surface, in implementing operational efficiencies, in countering the inflexibility inherent in these large bureaucratic structures, and in adapting to the strategies that are necessary to ensure their long-term survival. Some believe that it may be simply too early to judge whether all this corporate restructuring will pay off in reduced costs, improved bottom lines, and better clinical outcomes.

Although during the past decade there has been a "graying" in how the not-for-profit integrated delivery systems and the investor-owned chains are organized, managed and financed, the latter have historically focused more on selecting patients with comprehensive health insurance benefits, charging more than the not-for-profits, and reducing operating costs to enhance their stockholders' return on investment.[18-19] Disappointment in the performance of the for-profit hospitals is evidenced by the nation's five largest investor-owned hospital chains in 1999, squeezing out a bottom line of 2.9 percent (table 23).

Major factors in Tenet, Quorum, and HCA—The Healthcare Co. struggling for the past two years in the stock market are not only their low net margins and the legal issues promulgated by the Health Care Financing Administration, but their high debt-to-equity ratios, which in 1999 were 1.66, 1.33, and 1.23, respectively. Of no surprise, therefore, is that currently credit ratings of for-profit and not-for-profit hospitals look quite different from the median for-profit rating of Ba1 and the median not-for-profit rating of A3.[20] To improve their performance the current strategy of these investor-owned hospital chains is to divest themselves of unprofitable facilities rather than to consummate additional acquisitions, reflecting an attempt to consolidate their resources in regions where they already enjoy reasonable market penetration and more profitable operations.

Overall the fiscal position of, and therefore the degree of risk facing, U.S. hospitals and health networks is bimodal: those experiencing a higher payer classification are still able to achieve reasonable operating margins (although somewhat lower than in the past) and to replace their outdated facilities and equipment and acquire new technologies; and there are probably an equal number of other facilities that serve a high percentage of Medicaid and uninsured patients and are therefore experiencing a severe financial crisis and are unable to recapitalize their outdated physical plant, equipment, and information systems.

In either case health executives will need to spend more time on tough day-to-day operational issues in order to achieve the cost reductions and improvements in quality of care inherent in becoming the region's dominant healthcare provider. This is in spite of the fact that the strategy of a health network becoming an oligopoly to better control market penetration and to enhance negotiations with managed care plans will appear to its leadership to be at least as compelling.

Physical Medicine and Rehabilitation Services

Changes in reimbursement for physical medicine and rehabilitation (PM&R) services contained in the BBA of 1997 drastically modified the financial viability of providing physical, occupational, and speech therapy to those requiring restorative services. The investor-owned rehabilitation services stock prices in 1995, 1996, and 1997 increased by 43.3 percent, 32.3 percent, and 43.1 percent, respectively. By 1998, with the passage of the BBA, these PM&R stocks declined by 37.4 percent and decreased another 25.7 percent during the first three quarters of 1999.

HealthSouth, the nation's largest provider of rehabilitative healthcare and outpatient surgery services, has more than 1,900 locations in the

TABLE 23. Selected Financial Statistics for Major Investor-Owned Hospital Corporations, 1998–99 (dollars in millions except Current Ratio)

Name of Company	Revenues (for Year Ending)	Current Ratio (for Quarter Ending)	Total Net Income (for Year Ending)	Total Debt (for Quarter Ending)	Total Equity (for Quarter Ending)
HCA—	$16,657.0	1.16	$657.0	6,532.0	$5,309.0
The Healthcare Co.	(12/99)	(9/99)	(12/99)	(9/99)	(9/99)
Tenet Healthcare	10,880.0	1.83	249.0	5,816.0	4,089.0
	(5/99)	(11/99)	(5/99)	(11/99)	(11/99)
Universal Health	2,042.4	1.97	77.8	404.2	638.6
Services	(12/99)	(9/99)	(12/99)	(9/99)	(9/99)
Quorum Health	1,652.6	2.21	38.9	893.2	630.7
Group	(6/99)	(12/99)	(6/99)	(12/99)	(12/99)
Health Management	1,355.7	2.45	149.8	438.1	882.5
Associates	(9/99)	(12/99)	(9/99)	(12/99)	(12/99)
Total	40,540.7	—	1,172.5	14,083.5	11,549.8

Source: www.hoovers.com, March 20, 2000.

United States, the United Kingdom, and Australia. With a debt-to-equity ratio of 0.89 and a 0.8 percent net income for the year ending September 30, 1999 (see table 24), and a loss of $143.1 million for the quarter ending December 31, 1999, HealthSouth in a year or two could potentially follow the path of NovaCare. This second largest provider of rehabilitation services reported as of September 30, 1999, a 12.8 percent net operating loss and has a debt-to-equity ratio of 2.39. NovaCare is now busy liquidating those business interests that provide contract physical, occupational, and speech therapy to 2,700 nursing homes and hospitals in 44 states.

Physical medicine and rehabilitation services are no longer readily available to those patients discharged from an acute facility, but who would profit from restorative services before going home or into a long-term care facility. In fact, this situation lessens the probability that patients who need PM&R and are admitted to a nursing home will eventually return to their prior residence.

Are Health Networks in Fiscal Jeopardy?

As long as the U.S. expenditure for health hovers around 13.5 percent of the GDP and we continue to experience low inflation, capturing significant additional dollars for the delivery of health services is relatively remote, although it is possible to change the size of the pie for a specific sector(s). For example, physicians place far greater pressure than ever before on health networks and their hospitals to find ways to enhance the physicians'

TABLE 24.   Selected Financial Statistics for Major Investor-Owned Physical Medicine and Rehabilitation Corporations, 1998–99 (dollars in millions except Current Ratio)

Name of Company	Revenues (for Year Ending)	Current Ratio (for Quarter Ending)	Total Net Income (for Year Ending)	Total Debt (for Quarter Ending)	Total Equity (for Quarter Ending)
HealthSouth	$4,072.1 (12/99)	3.32 (9/99)	$76.5 (12/99)	$3,060.6 (9/99)	$3,406.7 (9/99)
NovaCare	1,477.9 (6/99)	1.13 (12/99)	(189.5) (6/99)	84.7 (12/99)	57.6 (9/99)
RehabCare Group	309.4 (12/99)	1.43 (9/99)	15.1 (12/99)	59.7 (9/99)	73.2 (9/99)

Source: www.hoovers.com, March 20, 2000.

personal income. In fact, if the United States for all practical purposes has set a ceiling on its total health expenditures, then those involved in health policy and management will need to focus more specifically on how to spend these available dollars more wisely.

In the potential redistribution of U.S. health dollars, it is unlikely that long-term care services will ever experience a sizable increase. The wealthy are able to pay out-of-pocket and will most frequently be admitted to upscale, three-level retirement communities offering a pleasant ambiance and quality of care. The vast majority of aged who require nursing home care are unable for any length of time to pay out-of-pocket and, therefore, are supported by Medicaid. They will receive care in a broad spectrum of facilities, some quite good and others that should be shuttered because of patient care and physical plant deficiencies.

Public officials are not reelected on the basis of providing high quality nursing home care to the medically indigent; instead, they are judged on how well they maintain reimbursement rates at a level just adequate for a majority of the nation's nursing homes to be barely acceptable to the tax paying public. For the majority of aged Americans the long-term care sector (nursing home, assisted living, and home health care) is already in serious fiscal jeopardy and it is unlikely that public officials will modify these reimbursement rates beyond providing an occasional band aid to keep these facilities from foreclosing. Interestingly, an increasing number of aged persons and a decrease in supply of long-term care beds and related resources could eventually create serious problems for hospitals as well as for those in the active labor force (e.g., the daughter-in-law staying home to care for her husband's and her elderly parents).

The PPMs and the integrated delivery systems who acquired physician practices frequently underestimated the skill required to manage the clinical and fiscal risk, to properly align financial incentives, and to implement total continuous quality management practices. The struggle for power, control, and monies that has been often reflected in the tension between the PPMs or health networks and the physicians has manifested itself in such issues as agreeing on vision, mission, leadership, control over decision-making, and managing conflict. It is no wonder with these inherent barriers that PPMs for the most part have been fiscal disasters for their stockholders, with limited possibility of their being bailed out in the future.

The divestiture by PPMs and by health networks of unprofitable physician practices and the firing of many employed physicians will become a relatively frequent occurrence in the next decade. The process of ridding themselves of these practices may be as complex as originally acquiring them was because of the terms of the initial acquisition agreement and "safe harbors"–type constraints. The leadership of PPMs and health networks might eventually publicly admit that the private practice of medicine is too complicated to be managed by outside business interests, while at the same time these divestitures cause considerable wrath among physicians who are adversely affected.

Although the managed care plans during the past decade have been relatively successful in holding down the earlier inflationary trend in healthcare costs, they have been less successful in enhancing access, social equity, or quality of care. Unless the HMOs become more effective in actually managing individual patient care, which is considered to be unlikely, their principal role will continue to be serving as conduits, receiving premiums and paying out to providers for services rendered.

It is highly unlikely, even with a deteriorating economic outlook, that the United States will implement a Canadian or German-style national health insurance plan. More likely is that the HMOs will be under intense pressure in the short term to implement a patients' bill of rights, expand on the points-of-service concept, and offer broader drug benefits. These "add-ons" have been avoided by the HMOs primarily because of their cost and because they lessen the plan's control over its providers and subscribers. In the final analysis, however, the viability of the managed care industry may well be more dependent on the nation's economic condition than on any other factor and particularly on the ability of employers to pay for a continuing increase in premiums. Whenever significant unemployment in the United States occurs and the Fortune 500 companies are in a position to reduce their fringe benefit costs, the HMOs will find it increasingly difficult to collect the premiums to sustain existing benefits. Such economic hard times will come, but it is impossible to predict when, why, how seriously, and for how long.

What has become somewhat alarming is the huge disparity in the financial position between the "carriage trade" hospitals with huge resources and their "poor cousins," who are facing Chapter 11 bankruptcy. A limited number of additional acute facilities will be closing, since hospitals have a great ability to shape their programs and services based on their revenue stream, and it can take a number of years for them to deplete their fund balance (equity). Before a facility is to close due to insolvency, the option of being acquired by the area's dominant network becomes far more plausible (i.e., selling out rather than closing). What usually happens then is that the network over time downsizes the new acquisition, along the same lines that should have been pursued by the facility when it was freestanding.

What is so noticeable among the investor-owned hospitals' corporations is that in order to become more profitable they are implementing a strategy to align their existing facilities as regional networks, divesting themselves of providers that are not generating net income and that are geographically isolated. Whether these changes will be sufficient to make them as attractive to Wall Street investors as they were in the early 1990s is questionable.

Although there will continue to be investor-owned hospitals in the United States, their number is expected to shrink further in the next decade, since privatization of the U.S. healthcare system no longer has the exalted appeal it once had. The major reasons are reportedly fraud and abuse and the hospitals' inability to make much headway in actually redesigning the delivery of healthcare. This is not to suggest that more government regulation should now be looked upon with any greater enthusiasm.

In addition, among the investor-owned as well as the not-for-profits, the fiscal outcome of forming these huge politically powerful health networks or alliances on an overall basis has been disappointing.[15-17] Primarily because of political constraints, the leadership has been unable or unwilling to make the programmatic, service, and facility cutbacks that are necessary to implement the many earlier projected savings and improvements in patient care. In fact, divestitures among health providers in 1999–2000 would suggest that at least some of the earlier corporate restructuring is not working well.

Getting rid of earlier acquired physician practices or selling provider-sponsored managed care plans might have been expected because of vertical diversification strategies being more far complex to implement and generally providing fewer rewards than horizontal mergers.[21] Two hospitals or hospital systems serving the same population base have historically constituted the most successful corporate consolidations.[22] Yet Optima Health in Manchester, N.H. (made up of Elliott Hospital and Catholic Medical Center), and Baptist St. Vincent's (made up of Baptist Health System and St. Vincent's Health System) in Jacksonville, Fla., in the spring of 2000 were proceeding with a corporate divestiture. At first glance it might appear that this move was the result of cultural issues (i.e., problems blending Catholic and non-Catholic institutions), but the real difficulties may be that the various vested interests made it impossible to implement the earlier projected savings.

U.S. managed care plans and hospitals as a whole are not in the fiscal jeopardy now experienced by nursing homes, physician practice management corporations, and physical medicine and rehabilitation services. What is to be expected is that the fiscally and politically powerful providers and insurers will continue to gain strength in the marketplace, while the weaker will be either acquired by the politically and fiscally strong ones or be shuttered. The obvious outcome is that there will be fewer freestanding providers and insurers. To avoid antitrust concerns, networks could eventually swing in the direction of expanding access to care and ceasing the corporate monopolization of care.

When we assess today which sectors of the health marketplace are in fiscal jeopardy, we often forget that the United States has been experiencing an economic boom for roughly a decade. The current economic viability of some of the sectors in the health field is now so fragile that the real test, in my opinion, will come when we experience our first recessionary period. I do not expect the downsizing of integrated delivery systems at that time to be "pretty." I do not visualize a national health insurance plan emerging, since Americans generally are so wedded to a pluralistic approach that relies on both a private and public sector.[23] What I do see at the end of the tunnel is much of what I see today: an emphasis on reducing healthcare costs in the United States, with limited improvement in enhancing access, social equity, or quality.

REFERENCES

1. McCue, M. J., Clement, J., and Luke, R. D. "Strategic Hospital Alliances: Do the Type and Market Structure of Strategic Hospital Alliances Matter?" *Medical Care* 37, no. 10 (1999): 1013–22.

2. Levit, K., Cowan, C., Lazenby, H. C., Sensenig, A., McDonnell, P., Stiller, J., Martin, A., and the Health Accounts Team. "Health Spending in 1998: Signal of Change." *Health Affairs* 19, no. 1 (2000): 124–33.

3. Robinson, J. C. "Consolidation of Medical Groups into Physician Practice Management Organizations." *Journal of the American Medical Association* 279, no. 2 (1998): 144–49.

4. Hill, J., and Wild, J. "Survey Profiles Data on Practice Acquisition Activity." *Healthcare Financial Management* 49, no. 9 (1995): 54–60.

5. Zismer, D. K., and Lund, D. E. "Health System–Sponsored Primary Care Networks: Achieving Best Practice Financial Performance." Chicago: Towers Perrin, September 1998.

6. Anderson, G. F., and Poullier, J.-P. "Health Spending, Access, and Outcomes: Trends in Industrialized Nations." *Health Affairs* 18, no. 3 (1999): 178–92.

7. Hansen, D. "Clinton May Have Tough Time Getting His Medicare Cuts through Congress." *AHA News* 36, no. 6 (2000): 1.

8. Feldman, R., Wholey, D. R., and Christianson, J. B. "Effects of Mergers on Health Maintenance Organization Premiums." *Health Care Financing Review* 17, no. 3 (1996): 171–89.

9. Weil, T. P. "Public Disclosure in the Health Field: Why Not the SEC Commission?" *American Journal of Medical Quality* 16, no. 1 (2001): 23–33.

10. Vistnes, J. P., and Zuvekas, S. H. "Health Insurance Status of the Civilian Noninstitutional Population: 1997." Rockville, Md.: Agency for Health Care Policy and Research, 1999.

11. Chen, J., Radford, M. J., Wang, Y., Marciniak, T. A., and Krumholz, H. M. "Do America's Best Hospitals Perform Better for Acute Myocardial Infarction?" *New England Journal of Medicine* 304, no. 4 (1999): 286–92.

12. Chen, J., Radford, M. J., Wang, Y., Marciniak, T. A., and Krumholz, H. M. "Performance of the 100 Top Hospitals: What Does the Report Card Report?" *Health Affairs* 18, no. 4 (1999): 53–68.

13. HCIA, Inc., and William W. Mercer, Inc. "One Hundred Top Hospitals: Benchmarks for Success, 1998." Baltimore: HCIA, 1999.

14. *U.S. News and World Report.* "America's Best Hospitals." 124, no. 4 (June 27, 1998): 65–91.

15. McCue, M. J., Clement, J. P., and Luke, R. D. "Strategic Hospital Alliances: Do the Type and Market Structure of Strategic Hospital Alliances Matter?" *Medical Care* 37, no. 10 (1999): 1013–22.

16. Clement, J. P., McCue, M. J., Luke, R. D., Bramble, J. D., Rossiter, L. F., Ozcan, Y. A., and Pai, C.-W. "Strategic Hospital Alliances: Impact on Financial Performance." *Health Affairs* 16, no. 6 (1997): 193–203.

17. Connor, R. A., Feldman, R., Dowd, B. E., and Radcliff, T. A. "Which Types of Hospital Mergers Save Consumers Money?" *Health Affairs* 16, no. 6 (1997): 62–74.

18. Gray, B. H. *For Profit Enterprises in Health Care,* 182–208. Washington, D.C.: National Academic Press, 1986.

19. Woolhandler, S., and Himmelstein, D. U. "When Money Is the Mission— The High Costs of Investor-Owned Care." *New England Journal of Medicine* 141, no. 6 (1999): 444–46.

20. Lee, D. "For-Profit Hospitals versus Not-for-Profit Hospitals." New York: Moody's Investors Service, June 3, 1999.

21. Walston, S. L., Kimberly, J. R., and Burns, L. R. "Owned Vertical Integration and Health Care: Promise and Performance." *Health Care Management Review* 21, no. 1 (1996): 83–92.

22. Alexander, J. A., Halpern, M. T., and Lee, S.-T.-D. "The Short-Term Effect of Merger on Hospital Operations." *Health Services Research* 30, no. 6 (1996): 827–47.

23. Weil, T. P. "Management of Integrated Delivery Systems in the Next Decade." *Health Care Management Review* 25, no. 3 (2000): 9–23.

Author Index

The numbers in parentheses are reference note numbers and indicate that the author's work is referred to in a reference number on the page number preceding the parentheses. Numbers not followed by parentheses show the pages on which the author's complete work is listed.

Gaskin, D., 139 (52), 178
Gaynor, M., 290 (137), 308
Gehlbach, S., 133 (9), 176
Geroski, P. A., 73 (50), 84
Gibbs, D. A., 196 (39), 218
Gifford, B. D., 298 (162), 309
Gild, L. S., 110 (32), 126
Giles, R. R., 43 (13), 60, 64 (7), 82, 273 (99), 306
Ginsburg, P. B., 152 (100), 181
Ginzberg, E., 110 (23), 125
Glaser, W. A., 297 (155), 309
Glavin, S. L., 290 (141), 308
Glied, S. A., 80 (69), 85, 207 (79), 220
Goertz, C., 195 (32), 217, 266 (82), 305
Goes, J. B., 287 (124), 307
Goldsmith, J., 72 (47), 84, 122 (58), 127, 195 (29), 217, 265 (79), 305
Goldsmith, M., 224 (7), 239
Goldwater, S. S., 16 (5), 39
Gondek, K., 290 (140), 308
Goodman, D. C., 110 (27), 125
Gorman, S. A., 207 (79), 220
Gottlieb, S., 20 (23), 39
Graham, J., 279 (117), 307, 313 (6), 325
Gray, B. H., 139 (58), 178, 258 (51), 303, 338 (18), 345
Greenberg, G., 139 (53), 168 (122), 178, 182
Greene, J., 67 (14), 82
Greenfield, S., 133 (10), 167 (119), 167 (121), 176, 182
Greenwald, L. M., 221, 221 (92), 289 (131), 308
Griffin, M. R., 136 (33), 177
Gross, D. J., 290 (141), 308
Grumbach, K., 104 (6), 124, 148 (85), 180
Gunn, E. P., 72 (42), 84, 251 (16), 301

Hackney, R. B., 205 (68), 220
Hadley, J. P., 136 (25), 177, 211, 211 (95)

Hahn, J. S., 148 (87), 180, 289 (130), 308
Hall, K. C., 290 (136), 308
Halpern, M. T., 52 (25), 60, 67 (18), 83, 249 (10), 301, 343 (22), 345
Hann, P., 173 (131), 183
Hannan, E. L., 197 (42), 218
Hansen, D., 333 (7), 344
Harrigan, K., 95 (14), 98
Harris, B. L., 290 (139), 308
Harris, R. S., 71 (40), 84
Hart, L. G., 104 (7), 124, 255 (29), 302
Harvey, L. K., 148 (83), 180, 260 (65), 304
Hassinger, E. W., 110 (32), 126
Haynes, M. M., 207 (79), 220
Hays, R. D., 208 (84), 221
Hazelwood, E. C., 105 (9), 125
HCIA, Inc. and Wm. W. Mercer, Inc., 139 (48), 178, 258 (48), 303, 336 (13), 345
Health Care Advisory Board, 92 (8), 98, 253 (22), 302
Health Care Merger and Acquisition Monthly, 63 (4), 82
Heffler, S., 119 (52), 127, 137 (36), 177
Hegeman, R. L., 110 (32), 126
Hellander, I., 134 (18), 176, 199 (50), 219
Hellinger, F. J., 134 (17), 167 (116), 176, 182, 257 (44), 303
Henderson, T. M., 121 (57), 127
Henke, K. D., 75 (60), 85
Hesselbein, F., 224 (7), 239
Hibbard, J. H., 196 (38), 200 (51), 218, 219
Hilberman, D. W., 276 (110), 306
Hiles, D. R. H., 170 (124), 182
Hill, J., 92 (9), 98, 136 (28), 148 (75), 167 (120), 177, 179, 182, 207 (77), 220, 253 (23), 260 (57), 302, 303, 327 (4), 344
Hillman, A. L., 133 (11), 133 (12), 176, 290 (137), 308

Subject Index

Managed care (*continued*)
  and hospital utilization, reduction in, 133
  and merger mania, 241
  performance of, 132–34
  and physician visits, increase in, 133
  satisfaction with, 134
Market-driven forces, and quality and utilization, 129–47
Medicaid benefits, decelerating reimbursement for, 326
Medicaid enrollment, 102
Medicaid expenditures
  cost projections for, 119
  and service, type of, 115
Medical resources, geographic maldistribution of
  and supply, factors affecting, 102–3, 118
  and physicians, 102, 115–16
Medical schools, additional, 103–4
Medical schools, foreign, graduates of, 107
Medicare, and support of medical education, 109
Medicare benefits, decelerating reimbursement for, 326
Merger mania, implications of
  and health networks, 28–30, 44–53
  and hospitals, 74–75
  and insurers, 78–79
  and medical group practices, 77
  and medical technology, 75–76
  and network's, 79–80
  and physicians, 77–78
  public response to, 79–82
Mergers
  decisions leading to, 41–59
  failure of, explained, 274–77
  of HMOs, 333–35
  practicality of, 65
  reasons for, 64
  slowdown in number of, 326
  types of, 28–29

Mergers, non–health field
  among equals, 251
  limited improvement in outcomes of, 251

National Health Planning and Resources Development Act of 1975, 24–26
National Health Services Corps (NHSC), 104–5
Networking
  in 1990s, 244–46
  and community health centers, 112–13
  and costs, inability to reduce, 66–71
  and HMOs, 273
  and integrated primary, secondary, and tertiary centers, 18
  and market penetration, increasing, 273
  and political process, 256–67
  process of, 50–53
  as reaction to surplus, 5–7
  and status quo, 340–44
Network-sponsored HMOs, 253–54
  and ambulatory services, 253
  failure of, reasons for, 254–55
  theoretical advantages of, 253
  and unrelated non-acute care services, 253
Nixon administration, 26–28
Nursing home beds, excess of non-Medicaid, 328–31
Nursing home chains, and Chapter 11 protection, 329–30

Outside directors, use of, 237

Pew Health Profession Commission, 108
Pharmaceutical expenditures, controlling, 164
Physical medicine and rehabilitation services, 339–40